Caste in Indian Politics

Caste in Indian Politics

Editor
Rajni Kothari

Sangam Books

SANGAM BOOKS LIMITED
57 London Fruit Exchange
Brushfield Street
London E1 6EP

By arrangement with
Orient Longman Limited
3-6-272 Himayatnagar
Hyderabad 500 029

© Orient Longman Limited 1970

Published by
Sangam Books Limited 1995
ISBN 0 86125 720 0

Typeset by
S.S. Graphics, Hyderabad 500 029

Printed in India by
Vinayaka Sai Offset Printers, Hyderabad 500 004

To
The late Professor R. Bhaskaran,
a pioneer in the Sociology of Indian Politics

Contents

Preface

This volume is the first in a series of empirical studies in modernisation to be brought out by the Centre for the Study of Developing Societies. The aim of the series is to examine the phenomenon of modernisation in varying contexts and different national and sub-national settings, and through different methods of empirical investigation. Individual monographs, comparative case studies, survey analyses and data books based on aggregate analysis have been planned under this series. The main emphasis in each of them is comparison across territorial and cultural units, both contemporaneously and historically, with a view to generate a body of theory on modernisation.

The confrontation in India between the age-old caste system and the parliamentary form of government based on universal suffrage vividly illustrates the manner in which old and historical societies get involved in, and provide content to, the modernising process. *Caste in Indian Politics* is a collection of studies dealing with this theme. Rejecting the prevailing dichotomy between traditional society and modern polity, these studies examine the interaction between the two in given community and territorial settings. An analytical essay in the beginning lays out a perspective on the subject. Out of the nine studies that follow, four are based on detailed investigation of individual caste movements and structures and their induction into the political process; the other five deal with certain important macro dimensions of the political involvement of caste. Each of the studies tries to bring out the substantial change that has taken place in the interrelationship between the antecedent social structure of India and democratic politics and underlines the emerging idiom of socio-political behaviour.

So far the relation between caste and politics has been treated at a very general plane. Some sociologists and political scientists have been struck by the increase in caste consciousness and bellicosity as a result of the operation of adult franchise; others see a gradual erosion of caste solidarities and symbols, and a growing secularisation of the social structure. The debate has raised basic issues on the nature of social change but has become sterile in the absence of concrete data on the behaviour and idioms of caste, and the forms through which it is responding to the political process.

The present collection of exploratory studies is an attempt to begin to fill this gap. Undertaken by young scholars from India and abroad who do not feel constrained by conventional phenomenological assumptions regarding the caste system, these studies hope to contribute to a growing trend in political sociology, not only in terms of the new data they bring forth, but also in terms of the theoretical insights and generalisations they advance.

It should, of course, be mentioned that political involvement is not the only major force that is changing the caste system; very many other processes — economic, occupational, religious, educational — are at the same time at work. Similarly, although the individual studies presented here provide a good cross-section of both regions and major caste movements, it is necessary to supplement this intensive work by aggregative and quantitative analyses.

A few of the studies in this volume were completed before the 1967 elections. The electoral data used in them therefore does not take into account the post-1967 developments. However, the electoral statistics are there only to illustrate how caste support influences the electoral performance of parties. These studies concentrate on relationships between political forms and social processes which are more enduring than the changing electoral fortunes of political parties.

Special thanks are due to Mrs. Ava Khullar, the Secretary of the Centre, for doing a careful job at various stages of production of this book, including proof reading, checking of facts and syntax, and negotiating editorial minutiae with the publisher.

Centre for the Study of Developing Societies
Delhi – 6.   Rajni Kothari

Part One

Part One

CHAPTER ONE

Introduction

RAJNI KOTHARI

The prevailing dichotomy between tradition and modernity has created a curious cognitive hiatus — in ideological thinking as well as in much of social science theorising — between society on the one hand and polity on the other. The former is conceived, as if by definition, as 'traditional', the latter as 'modern' and 'developmental'. In reality, however, this is a false approach to the phenomenon of modernisation; it is especially misleading when the phenomenon takes place in the context of democratic politics. Political and developmental institutions do not anywhere function in a vacuum. They tend, of necessity, to find bases in society either through existing organisational forms or by invoking new structures that cut across these forms. Moreover, a society that cares for legitimacy on a wide basis — and a democratic society is preminently such a society — can proceed only by a conversation between the old and the new, a fusion of elements, and a readiness on the part of both the moderns and the ancients to be flexible and accommodative. In the process, no doubt, elements that prove dysfunctional to the realisation of social purpose and the growth of a national consensus may need to be subdued; and this is the function of a determined leadership. The grounds for these, however, are not a priori but pragmatic and developmental.

The overall point of departure of the authors in this volume is that not until the institutional changes introduced in a particular society become part of the working relationships of that society, can they hope to gain stability and legitimacy. A 'modernising' society is neither modern nor traditional. It simply moves from one threshold of integration and performance to another, in the process transforming both the indigenous structures and attitudes and the newly intro- duced institutions and ideas. This is a point that needs to be emphasised. The doctrinaire orientation of much recent thinking on development in India and in the West has produced an unhelpful dichotomy in conceptualisation that stands in the way of a realistic appraisal of the development process. Fortunately, however, the processes of social change transcend the inhibitions of intellectuals and social scientists. This is especially true in an open and competitive polity. India was perhaps particularly fortunate in starting with a social system that had traditionally been flexible and capable of absorbing large shifts in the balance of social and political arrangements. It was further fortunate in having adopted a political framework which, among other things, involved a free expression of interests, made competition the great medium of change through adaptation and integration, and thus avoided sharp discontinuities and disruption in the process of politi- cal modernisation.

Everyone recognises that the traditional social system in India was organised around caste structures and caste identities. In dealing with the relationship between caste and politics, however, the doctrinaire moderniser suffers from a serious xenophobia. He begins with the question: is caste disappearing? Now, surely, no social system disap- pears like that. A more useful point of departure would be: what form is caste taking under the impact of modern politics, and what form is politics taking in a caste-oriented society? Those in India who com- plain of 'casteism in politics' are really looking for a sort of politics which has no basis in society. They also probably lack any clear conception of either the nature of politics or the nature of the caste system. (Many of them would want to throw out both politics and the caste system.) Politics is a competitive enterprise, its purpose is the acquisition of power for the realisation of certain goals, and its process is one of identifying and manipulating existing and emerging alle- giances in order to mobilise and consolidate positions. The important thing is organisation and articulation of support, and where politics is mass-based the point is to articulate support through the organisations in which the masses are to be found. It follows that where the caste structure provides one of the principal organisational clusters along which the bulk of the population is found to live, politics must strive to organise through such a structure. The alleged 'casteism in politics' is thus no more and no less than *politicisation* of caste. It is something in which both the forms of caste and the forms of politics are brought nearer each other, in the process changing both. By drawing the caste system into its web of organisation, politics finds material for its articulation and moulds it into its own design. In making politics their sphere of activity, caste and kin groups on the other hand, get a chance to assert their identity and to strive for positions. Drawing upon both the interacting structures are the real actors, the new contestants for power. Politicians mobilise caste groupings and identities in order to organise their power. They find in it an extremely well articulated and flexible basis for organisation, something that may have been structured in terms of a status hierarchy, but something that is also available for political manipulation — and one that has a basis in consciousness. Where there are other types of groups and other bases of association, politicians approach them as well. And as they everywhere change the form of such organisations, they change the form of caste as well.

The few who are free from the ideological compulsions of the doctrinaire modernists and are prepared to look into precise empirical relations suffer from another preconception and often a contrary theoretical construct. Reflecting the style of much social science theorising, these writers display an instrumental view of political activity. According to them, political relationships are no more than projections of social relationships — of systems of social and economic dominance — and have no independent capacity to influence the latter. Politics, in this view, is an instrument wielded by a particular stratum in society to consolidate or raise its position: it simply reproduces patterns of social dominance without itself affecting the prevailing or changing structure of society. Such an approach blurs understanding of the developmental reality which consists not in any approximation to a pre-conceived framework of antecedent society but in the changing interactions of the constituent elements in a dynamic situation. But in the particular case of caste and politics, even this is only partly relevant. Where caste itself becomes a political category it is futile to argue as to whether caste uses politics or politics uses caste. Such a controversy may help in strengthening individual or professional prejudices, but they do not contribute towards understanding. In many ways it is a sterile controversy.

There are still others who, while they do not suffer from such a reductionist compulsion and on the whole show a realistic understanding of the changes taking place in contemporary Indian society, have not been fully able to get rid of their professional rigidities into which their training seems to have pushed them. Essentially definitionist in their approaches, they feel compelled by an urge to simplify developmental realities into a neat model. As should be expected, there are great variations among them; what unites them is a compulsion to proclaim the autonomy of either caste or politics or both. There are among these the 'progressive' economists who seem committed to brand anything to do with caste as reactionary, and conceive change as essentially change *from caste to class relationships*. There are, on the other extreme, those 'experts' on caste who consider it their duty to protect caste from any pollution of politics. In order to do this they resort to neat logical arguments regarding the 'essence' of the caste system and then proceed to define away all other aspects as not properly belonging to the operation of the caste system. Most of the latter are Indologists and cultural anthropologists. Other social anthropologists, who are more sophisticated in their tools of analysis, and who clearly realise the importance of political forms, still feel compelled to protect the pedagogy of the caste system by proclaiming the autonomy of both caste and politics. When castes behave 'segmentally' and according to a system of hierarchy and 'closed stratification', they belong to the caste system; when they operate as political entities or as parts of a political entity, however, they belong to the political system and are not really part of the caste system.[1] There are, finally, slowly coming into the picture, the political scientists who, fascinated as they are by the importance of the caste system in politics, cannot, however, escape the compulsion to reduce the interactions between caste and politics to a neat model. Although they have given up the traditional political scientist's aversion to caste, and have also mercifully given up the erstwhile dichotomy between voluntary and political forms as belonging to the 'modern' secular order and caste forms as belonging to the 'traditional' order, they fall in the same trap again by imagining a total transformation of the caste system through their involvement in politics, 'the democratic incarnation of caste' as an American author calls it.[2] In the process such analysts tend to go over to the other extreme and to rarefy caste as *the* political force in contemporary India. Their approach once again is essentially one of explaining empirical phenomena in terms of a unified conceptual model that enables neat generalisations to be imposed on a complex reality.

All these approaches are basically dichotomous, oriented towards an ideal type 'contradiction' between caste and politics, and representing different variants of professional rigidity. What they all fail to see is that there never was a complete polarisation between the caste system and the political system, and that what is involved in the contemporary processes of change is neither a game of vested interests nor a total shift from one system to another but really a change in the context and level of political operation, a shift in social priorities, and a somewhat different picking and choosing between the variety of elements that in any case, at all times, have entered into the functioning of the social and political system in India. Thus a relative decline in the importance of pollution as a factor in determining caste hierarchy, and the diminishing emphasis on the summation of roles as involved in the *Jajmani* system, do not by themselves involve any basic destruction of the caste system, but only a shift in the critical criteria of social awareness and the structural differentiations through which such an awareness is mobilised and organised. It is the virtue of a sophisticated social system such as that found in India that a reorientation of this kind is possible without damaging the overall stability of the system and without giving rise to a widespread feeling of alienation and dissonance. The caste-politics problem in India is not a problem of definition but clearly one of empirical understanding of a competitive and mobile system which could give us a reasonable model of social dynamics.

In what follows, we examine the relationship between caste and politics as basically a relationship *for the specific purpose of organising public activity*. We shall do this by first examining the nature of this interaction and secondly its product, that is, the type of changes that have taken place in the political system as a result of differential involvement of caste organisations at different points in time and at different levels of the polity. Our focus is not so much on what happens to the caste system as a whole as a result of its involvement in the political process but rather what structures and networks of relationships enter into the political process and how. We cannot wholly avoid the question of what politics does to the caste system — for certain forms adopted by the caste system in the wake of a wider secular ordering of relationships such as the caste association or the caste federation, or even the more traditional inter-caste networks of patron-client ties, become very much the stuff of politics. But it still needs to be stressed that it is as political sociologists interested in studying the pursuit of collective interests and purposes that the authors in this volume have approached their subject. Thus, for instance, a number of authors were interested in how different parties or movements, or even different groups within a single party, mobilise different social strata as resources for their political objectives. It is from this perspective that social reform movements, caste associations and federations, and other networks and relationships in the social and economic sub-systems become relevant data for analysis. Or again the authors are interested in how a sense of discontent or exploitation prevailing within the caste order provide a viable basis for the mobilisation of masses; for their own reform in the first instance and ultimately for assertion of their rights vis-a-vis others. Once again the organisational and psychological conditions of caste organisation are turned into a resource for politics and hence relevant material for political analysis.

Keeping in mind the focus of our inquiry, namely the organisation of public activity and politics in a society articulated along caste lines, three aspects of the caste system call for special attention. The first is what may be called the *secular aspect*. In emphasising caste as a stratification system in which distances are rigidly maintained through endogamy, pollution and the legitimacy of rituals, caste as a system of conflict and interaction has received sparse attention. Yet the fact is that factionalism and caste cleavages, patterns of alignment and realignment among the various strata, and a continuous striving for social mobility have always been prominent features of the caste system. At any rate, they are highly relevant from the point of view of secular development.

Traditionally there were two aspects to the secular organisation of caste — the *governmental* aspect (caste councils, village arbitration procedures, and so on) and the *political* aspect (within caste and inter-caste authority and status alignments and cleavages). These were buttressed or dissipated by the authority relationships of local elites with the central political system or systems. Religion, occupation and territory provided the bases for secular mobility. These are still relevant for the generalised process of secularisation that characterises the major changes coming over caste society; only the emphases and proportions have changed. Instead of allegiance to a monarch or the justification of a new monarchy through the rise of a new sect or the elevation of certain caste or territorial groupings, and instead of management of the civil aspects of society at a variety of levels, we now have more participatory and aggregative modes of mobility and a greater coordination between *levels* through the agency of electoral and party politics. What has changed is the context because of the rise of the nation-state and political democracy and the organisational structure inherent in these. But the change is not as radical as it appears at first sight; it is incremental and continuous as found in the gradual involvement and co-optation of more and more strata in the political decision-making processes. Thus in many regions it was the Brahminic section that first responded to English education and was the first to benefit from political and administrative power, and with the slow expansion of the franchise and the party system, others came in. In some other regions, especially where the Brahmins were never so dominant and certain agricultural upper castes wielded social power, vertical inter-caste ties provided an ongoing structure of political recruitment in which by initiating these upper castes into politics almost the whole social structure got mobilised and precluded any strong formation of horizontal solidarities.

In still other regions the spread of new religious sects and the financial power wielded by the communities that responded to these (such as Jains and Vaishnavas in Gujarat and Marwar) made for a different model of sequence in regard to accession to political power. New solidarities in the middle castes were evident in many regions even before the advent of British influence and the phenomenon of hypergamy was an outcome of the influx of the new and 'lower' sections of society from pastoral and tribal elements into the agricultural mainstream of the social economy. This is an instance of occupational mobility transrorming itself in terms of both a modification of kinship patterns and an expansion of the secular-associational aspects of traditional society. Thus the process of secularisation so dominant in recent decades also owes considerably to the multi-caste society, its *varna* hierarchy and politheic religions which preceded the onslaught of more contemporary modernising forces. Yet another process was the breaking through the territorial restraints and thus widening the base of occupational mobilisation. The pastoral caste of Rabaris in Saurashtra turned into the agricultural low caste of Kanbis in Gujarat which later rose in status through their hypergamous affiliation with the regional dominant caste of Patidars. Similarly the shoemaker caste (mochis) of Saurashtra turned into the tailor caste (darjis) of Gujarat. Or again, to take another pattern, a new sub-caste of Deshmukhs got differentiated from the Patil sub-caste of the Marathas on their accession to special land rights, out of which developed a new hypergamous relationship which continued until the further development of a non-Brahmin political movement and latter-day land legislation led to a re-identification between the two sub-castes. Thus the formation of new monogamous and hypergamous sub-castes led to both greater differentiation and a blurring of the sharp traditional disinctions. Even the concept of man-woman relationship in terms of a superior-subsidiary affair that was peculiar to Indian society played its role in developing distinctive hierarchical relationships in the caste system and enabled special types of mobility and differentiation which later proved instrumental in facilitating political identities and secular associational urges.

Second, there is the *integration aspect.* The caste system not only determines the individual's social station on the basis of the group to which he is born but also differentiates and assigns occupational and economic roles. It thus gives a place to every individual from the highest to the lowest and makes for a high degree of identification and integration. At the same time it is an integration structure of a specific type, namely one that is more intense in its small group orientation and particularistic loyalties, and where wider loyalties operate only when they are structured through the prevailing differentiations. This aspect is important in understanding the structural impact of democratic nation-building. For the competitive style of democratic politics involves not only distributive and conflictual aspects but also aspects of group action and cohesion: democratic politics is as much a process of fusion and aggregation as of fission and segmentation. Similarly, the traditional emphasis in studies of the caste system on differentiation and affirmed segmentation has neglected the 'agglomerative' dimension.[3] The political age, however, emphasises both, sharpens the aggregative aspect, and at the same time widens the conflict potential of aggregative processes on to a broader context. Differentiation has all along been an essential ingredient in the Indian approach to aggregation, and it has now become an important variable in the development of democratic politics.

It has been rightly pointed out that in actual operation caste affiliations take not the vertical homogeneous class and status form of *varna* but the horizontal heterogeneous and segmental form of *jati*. And yet a system that has survived for so long creates a powerful symbolism, rationale and mythology of its own. The *varna* referent represents a 'scale of values' which provides both a spur to integrative behavioural patterns and a symbol of competition that enables the aspiring and mobile groups to lay claim to high status still affirming widely prevalent values. It 'furnishes an all-India frame into which myriad *jatis* in any single linguistic area can be fitted'. Furthermore, certain *varnas* also provide symbols of high status and at the same time symbols of 'opposition', as for example, the Kshatriyas against the Brahmins; 'disputes as to relative status are an essential feature of the caste system'. It thus enables the low-placed castes to affirm widely prevalent values in Indian society at the same time as laying claim to high status. Thus *varna* and *jati* are intimately connected in the Indian system which has made for a high degree of integration and containment of structural and psychological strains inherent in the process of technological and political change.[4]

Third, there is the *aspect of consciousness*. Again, in their concern with stratification, sociologists have generally neglected the ideational underpinning that is inevitably associated with any social system. Thus the contest for positions between various *jatis* often follows some variation of *varna*, either by approximating to the reality as in the case of Brahmins or by invoking a label as in the case of the claim of certain castes to be Kshatriyas. Indeed the very fluidity and nebulousness of the concept of Kshatriya, and yet its historically compelling symbolism for social mobility, has been an important lever in the secular struggles that have from time to time ensued in the various regions, following real shifts in the social and economic positions of different groups. The same holds true though in a lesser degree for the Brahminic symbol as well as the symbol of certain middle range castes. While *varna* has all the appearance of a neat and logical structure, *jati* on the other hand is characteristically ambiguous. It has several meanings, refers to *varna* at one level and to other meanings of segmentation at other levels. By shifting from one referent to another, it demonstrates the basic continuity between the various referents — doctrinal, territorial, economic and occupational, ritual, and associational-federal (political). It also shows the difficulty of describing caste by any single set of attributes. Indeed by being different things at different points in social interactions, it provides for immense flexibility, continuity and tension management capabilities. It thus enables people to draw themselves and others at different orders of existence; and in different contexts as the situation demands. It follows that the system can also withstand the decline of certain features (considered 'essential' by some) such as the *Jajmani* system of role differentiation and summation; or the importance of pollution as a system of hierarchical determination. Both functions can now be performed by other elements in the secularised setting of interrelationships.

All of this also brings out the importance of the manner in which traditional status urges such as 'sanskritisation' get intertwined with modern urges like 'westernisation' and 'secularisation'.[5] Under the impact of universalised aspirations (economic well-being; rationality urge; political integration) the Brahminised urges may be simply repudiated by the advance guard of a caste which, ironically, re-establishes its original (non-Brahminic) identity to foster solidarities and legitimise its contemporary strivings in the modernist sectors, as in the case of the various new industrial classes. Alternatively, a caste may sometimes reinterpret its traditional status in society to buttress its contemporary aspirations and develop a mythology about the same. Examples are to be found in the case of Patidars of Gujarat, Mahisyas of Bengal and Jats of Rajasthan. Yet another approach is found in regions where the Brahmins did not dominate the modernising process which was led by powerful peasant castes who were in turn closely associated in vertical ties with other castes. This enabled a cutting short of both the sanskritisation and the caste solidarity phases and led straight to inter-caste factional politics as an avenue of social mobility. Andhra Pradesh and Bihar provide good examples of a rapid succession of various caste groups into factional networks of politics which provided the best channels of mobility.

By itself the 'sanskritisation' urge produces some very basic psychological strains in the group that is trying to acquire a new identity in its search for status, as in the process its status becomes *subjectively* ambivalent and thus insecure: as with Jews, Negroes and other minority groups, it is a 'negative assertion', a mood of 'submitting yet opposing' the emulated group. Hence the tension, especially for the more conscious sections. Also, so long as they do not succeed in raising the status of the group — and this is always a long period — their infirm status necessarily creates an insecure and unsettled position in society — leading either to compensatory devices for social recognition or real withdrawal into something else. As it is, the status urge in Hindu society is an intensely frustrating and painful process. To this is added a further edge by resorting to a mechanism of status rise which starts from negating the original existence and striving for something which may turn out to be a mirage and may indeed lead to reprisal (as in the case of the smiths of South India)

It is a tribute to the subtle dynamics of Hindu society that in spite of this psychological cost, the adjustments of *sanskritisation* go on all the time; and one of the many reasons is that the structural distance that is sought to be jumped can often be related to the achievement of other indices of power and position in the modernist segments of society (as perceived both by the striving group as well as by a majority of other groups), thus facilitating the transition to a consensus on the new status of the striving group. Important in this respect is the crucial role that the distribution of secular power has always played in status ranking in Hindu society; and the consequent capacity of the system to keep adjusting to its changing hierarchical balance.

Altogether, then, the secular, integrative and ideological aspects of caste have provided a sophisticated and differentiated cultural background for receiving the modernist impacts and responding to them without either great disruption or great withdrawal or hostility.

On such a society came the impact of 'westernisation' and democratic secularism. Of interest here is the slow pace with which these influences penetrated Indian society and the positive manner in which it has on the whole responded to these changes. There is no need here to go into the details of recent history. Liberal education, governmental patronage and a slowly expanding franchise have been the three influences that have penetrated the caste system and involved it by stages. The involvement came as a result of a mutual give and take. Economic opportunity, administrative patronage and positions of power offered by the new institutions and the new leadership drew the articulate sections of society into the modernist network. In return, the leadership was provided with a basis of support that kept expanding from urban centres into the interior, and from one caste to another.

Democratic politics of necessity led to such an involvement of the traditional structure and its leadership. Two results followed. The caste system made available to the leadership structural and ideological bases for political mobilisation, providing it with both a segmental organisation and an identification system on which support could be crystallised. Second, the leadership was forced to make concessions to local opinion, take its cue from the consensus that existed as regards claims to power, articulate political competition on traditional lines and, in turn, organise castes for economic and political purposes. With this came into being a new species of political organisation, articulated around particularistic divisions, yet giving to these a secular and associational orientation. Politics and society began moving nearer and a new infrastructure started coming into being.

The actual process of interaction between caste and modern institutions was necessarily selective: it impinged on certain aspects of caste more than on others. The first to be drawn into the modernisation stream was the power structure of the caste system. The second was the distribution of economic benefits. These two were closely related: the distribution of divisible benefits was interlinked with the nature of the power system that operated. A third factor that tied in with these was what may be called caste consciousness and perceptions. All of these were traditional components of the caste system that got drawn into the new processes of change.

Three stages can be noted in this process. The struggle for power and for benefits was at first limited to the entrenched castes in the social hierarchy.[6] Leadership and access to governmental patronage came from a limited group of individuals who were the first to respond to new educational opportunities and were also traditionally endowed with pedagogic and sophistic skills that mattered most in the days of limited politics. This group consisted of individuals from certain 'higher' castes, was not yet based on any militant caste consciousness, and was united more by a common social and intellectual endowment and idiom than through any organisational or political mobilisation. However, whenever this took place mainly on the basis of one higher caste (or sub-caste), it soon gave rise to a feeling of deprivation and antagonism in other high castes, especially among those that had earlier enjoyed social or economic power, and resulted in the emergence of another political group, still drawn largely from the higher castes. The domination of an *entrenched* caste (when it took a caste form) thus produced a new response in the form of an *ascendant* caste, one that was not satisfied to simply function in the context of inter-dependence and complementarity in the social sphere that characterised the social and economic system for so long. The caste structure thus got polarised in its first encounter with the new secularism and gave rise to a bilateral structure of caste politics, very often between two castes or sub-castes, one entrenched, the other ascendant, but sometimes the latter including more than one caste or sub-caste.[7] Such a polarisation was avoided either where the one entrenched caste was greatly separated in social power and ritual status from all others or where the different 'higher' castes were entrenched at different power points, either regional or institutional, thus involving them in a legitimised coalitional pattern.

This bilateralism was followed by a second stage in which power strivings and demands for benefits exceeded the availability of resources, competing groups had to develop more numerous bases of support, and there started a process of competition *within* the entrenched and more articulate sections of society. This may be termed as the stage of caste fragmentation or of 'factionalism'.[8] Inter-caste competition — between the entrenched caste and the ascendant caste — was now supplemented by *intra-caste* competition and the process of politicisation. Again the process first started within the entrenched caste (or castes) which got factionalised and there followed a new structuring of political organisation. Leadership cleavages were created, political attitudes began to condition symbols of solidarity and consensus, and there came into being multi-caste and multi-factional alignments. Mobilisation of further support for each of the contending factions gave rise to a process of 'co-optation' from other castes that were till now kept out of the power system. A similar process took place within the 'ascendant caste' which was now as good a part of the system as the 'entrenched caste' and got similarly factionalised. The power structure of the caste system now became more complex and entered into a more sophisticated network of relationships, involving such other bases of support as economic patronage, patron-client loyalties, bond groups, and new organisational forms such as caste associations and caste federations.

Once again the process took a slightly different form in regions where there already existed vertical inter-caste ties by reason of agricultural and other economic bonds, traditional hypergamic relationships, or regional variations in dominant-dependent relationships. In such cases what took place during this stage was a further articulation of vertical factional networks of mobilisation and competition. Wherever vertical chains of relationship already existed, politics found a ready-made ground and the need for evoking new solidarities and forging new alignments in the form of caste associations and caste federations was less pressing. The upper tiers of each of the rival chains simply got recruited in politics and in the process carried the whole network with them. The process of further co-optation of elites from other castes became easy as traditions for such co-optation already existed. In other words, the expanding mobilisation of politics either found an ongoing vertical network or created one through its factionalising tendencies, and in both cases made the social structure of caste an important vehicle of political organisation and extended it to include other forms of patronage and socio-economic relationships.

The vertical framework of political organisation also enabled different entrenched (or 'dominant') castes at one level to come face to face with each other at the higher levels (as for example the Kammas and Reddis in Andhra, the Patidars and Annavils in Gujarat, the Lingayats and Okkalingas in Mysore, the various district and regional 'dominant' castes of Madras and 'entrenched' castes of Bihar regrouped at the State level). And at each level within this hierarchy there took place a new mode of segmentation of the caste in which 'associational' and 'federal' forms on the one hand and 'factional' chains on the other hand played an increasing part and cut across segmentation based on ascriptive and lineage groups, although frequently also taking advantage of the latter. With this the importance of individuals and of personalised networks increased and leadership took on a more positive role.

All of this, however, was limited to the leading two or three castes —well-to-do, educated, and generally upper castes. The lower castes were still found to be in a dependent relationship with the entrenched and the dominant castes. However, during the second stage itself there started a process of mobilisation of lower castes into politics for the purpose of adding to the factionalised support base of rival leaders. Caste identities, which were still strong and articulate, provided the principal media of political participation. This was true even where vertical inter-caste ties existed for long, for even this was always based at the sub-unit level on the norms and structures of a caste society.

The process was one of expanding the support base of rival leaders from the entrenched sections either by the simple process of co-opting leaders from hitherto dormant sections of society by providing them with junior positions and a part of the divisible benefits in return for electoral support; or, where it was not possible to tackle the problem on the basis of simple co-optation, by entering into a more organised process of mobilisation through coalitions of sub-caste groups, alignment with a large number of leaders, bargaining with 'link men', appeal to wider identities and animosities, and on these bases, a secure basis of support. Where the simple co-optation device worked, the task was of inducing critical leaders into the power elite and not worrying about the backward 'masses'; where it did not work and the masses were more enlightened, they had to be themselves organised into the new schemes of mobilisation. In the latter case, it was also likely that in course of time the new entrants to politics may themselves be able to forge a coalition strong enough to pose a challenge to the leaders from the 'entrenched castes'. This would depend upon their numerical strength, degree of economic independence and the nature of leadership. It would also depend on the extent to which the consciousness of caste in these sections took on the form of a *political class*, self-assertive and indignant against 'exploitation' from the upper castes, and eager to taste political power themselves.

It is also important to stress here that different stages in the social organisation of politics call for somewhat different leadership and organisational skills and the movement from one stage to another may entail displacement of one kind of leadership by another; and consequently of one social group endowed with one type of skills by another endowed with another type of skills. Thus in the early stages of intellectual awakening and urban-style political organisation, the need was for people able to deal with western and westernised administrators, well versed in fine points of debate and ideological disputation, possessing legal acumen, and capable of founding and sustaining small associations of public-minded persons that would agitate for specific causes. Such men were mainly provided by Brahminic and traditional administrative classes who not only took to the new education but had also been endowed by a long tradition of scholastic knowledge and formal brilliance. With the movement into a more diversified and 'mass' oriented politics, however, not only was there need for a wider base of support articulation but also new types of managerial and organisational skills were needed. With this happening, the Brahminic and administrative castes began to be outnumbered by men from commercial and peasant-proprietor occupations that had always called for a high level of interpersonal skills, a pragmatic and bargaining approach to problems, and an ability to marshal a new type of solidarity among their own castes, often times based on a reinterpretation of their traditional status and a 'populist' and anti-elitist ideology.

These were the new entrepreneurs, the new innovators, of politics. However they are called, what is important to grasp is that they were not more but less 'modern' than the elites they replaced, they were often less educated and more rural-based, and operated through an idiom that was decidedly more populist and traditional. But even more important is the fact that the innovativeness with which they are credited — their ability to organise, to show a pragmatic evaluation of things, to take risks, and to utilise 'modern' means of technology and organisation — came more from inherited characteristics and early socialisation in prevailing life styles than from any conscious adoption of a new culture. This is most important in analysing the course of political modernisation in India which is far less explained by the tradition-modernity dichotomy than a conceptual framework that assigns due status to antecedent traditions and skills in the articulation of the emerging political culture. Once such political and organisational skills came to the fore, and the corresponding displacement in the social base of politics took place, Indian politics not only achieved a new dimension but also got markedly differentiated from other social activities, and took on a life and character of its own, and its own internal structure and process. Of course, the full articulation of this comes in the third stage (to be discussed presently), with the still greater diversification of the base of politics, and with factors other than caste entering into the picture.

The process of factionalism within the entrenched castes, a similar structuring of other ascendant castes, the system of co-optations and caste coalitions — all of these, though they brought about a fragmentation of the caste system, were in reality still very much caste-oriented and sought their bases in caste identities, in the process, of course, also generating politicised values and impulses for personal power. We enter a third stage of development when the weakening of older identities and the introduction of politicised values coincide with other changes taking place in society through the impact of education, technology, changing status symbols, and urbanisation. New and more expanded networks of relationship come into being, new criteria of self-fulfilment are created, the craving for material benefits becomes all-pervasive and family and migration systems undergo drastic changes. With these, the structure of particularistic loyalties gets overlaid by a more sophisticated system of social and political participation, with cross-cutting allegiances, a greater awareness of individual self-interest, and forms of involvement and alienation that are pre-eminently the products of modern education and the modern system of social communications. An essential feature of modernisation is the development of new and sharp differentiations. Political, economic, educational and communications functions, traditionally performed by the same social structure, are now differentiated and get established in terms of their own purposes, structures, and dynamics.

Politics, of course, is still a big enough influence but it is better understood as an active partner in the modernisation process, more as providing schemes of integration and division to the developing social system than as either destroying or replacing caste as a secular social entity. What does take place is a widening base of institutional organisation in which, on the one hand, caste identities themselves take to new forms of articulation thus changing the very ethics of the social system and diminishing the importance of its ritualistic and ascriptive bases; and, on the other hand, more diverse forms of organisation and interest identification enter the political system and give rise to a highly mobile and cross-cutting loyalty structure in politics. Caste on one side ceases to be an exclusive political support base and on the other side lends itself to increasing political articulation, both of which contribute to its participation in a broader network of relationships and a shift of its emphasis from a static system of stratification to a dynamic base of competition and integration. In its traditional form, the caste system integrated society through ordering primary identities along a legitimised hierarchy of status positions and occupational roles, including the 'political' roles of arbitration and adjudication. By participating in the modern political system, it is at first exposed to divisive influences and later to a new form of integration resulting from a new scheme of universalist-particularist relationships. This is, however, as already noted, no simple replacement of one system by another. In the transition, caste provides to politics on the one hand an ongoing structure of divisions and accommodations and on the other hand a cohesive element which absorbs tensions and frustrations through its intimate, particularistic, channels. Such an interactional scheme of change, while it does not suppress strata differences and individual interests, and gives rise to relatively abrupt shifts in power relations, also provides a system of containment of conflicts and angularities that facilitates the process of transition to a modern society.

Secular involvement in the modern period has not only fostered new attitudes and offered new rewards; it has also exposed caste and communal ties as by themselves patently inadequate and often prejudicial for the building of stable support. For one thing castes, where they are large, are not homogeneous and where they are small, not enough of a numerical force. Second, too close an identification with one caste alienates other castes. Third, political parties gain stability only by involving all major sections of the community. Finally, the politicisation of caste makes for outward-looking, upward-moving orientations and as this results in the phenomenon of multiple memberships and overlapping identities, the result is highly secular for the polity as well as the society at large.

This 'development in depth' of the system calls for closer analysis. Widespread confusion characterises the discussion of 'casteism' and 'communalism' in politics, including in the leadership who should know better. An impression prevails that whereas things like education, urbanisation and industrialisation were making inroads into traditional sectarian loyalties, electoral politics have resuscitated them and re-established their legitimacy, and that this has given rise to disintegrative tendencies that will disrupt the democratic and secular framework of the Indian polity. Evidence is cited from the behaviour of political parties all of whom invoke primordial sentiments and organise their support on the basis of pockets of caste influence. Now much of the evidence cited, though exaggerated, is often true; what is not true is the inference drawn from it. For in reality the consequences of caste-politics interactions are just the reverse of what is usually stated. It is not politics that gets caste-ridden; it is caste that gets politicised. Dialectical as it might sound, it is precisely because the operation of competitive politics has drawn caste out of its apolitical context and given it a new status that the 'caste system' as hitherto known has got eroded and has begun to disintegrate. And the same is happening, though more gradually, to communal and religious loyalties and even to minority group sentiments such as among the Muslims and the Scheduled Castes and Tribes.[9]

It is an extremely involved process of adjustment that we have tried to describe here. The process gets crystallised in three distinct but related forms. First, there emerges what can be called a *dominant elite,* which is drawn from different groups but shares a common outlook and a secular orientation, which is structured into a diffuse network of relationships that stretches across social boundaries but yet continues to induct leaders from each important segment, which is homogeneous in terms of some of the values and rules of the game but is at the same time divided into so many special groups and various elite and sub-elite positions. Such an elite structure articulates special interests and meaningfully represents the more organised segments of society, while at the same time allowing the mass of society to have its own pace of change and make its own adjustments with the modern world.

Second, castes take on an openly secular form for new organisational purposes. There are several such forms such as (a) 'associations' of caste members ranging from simple hostels and recreational bodies to reform clubs and pressure groups, (b) caste 'institutions' or 'conferences' that are more broad-based and cover districts or even States, and (c) caste 'federations' composed of not one but several castes which may sometimes be socially homogeneous but which may at other times simply have some specific interest or political objective in common. It is this specificity of purpose that distinguishes these new organisational forms — caste associations and caste federations — from the more inclusive and ascriptive bodies traditionally known as caste. Generally speaking they are oriented to the securing of economic benefits, jobs or special concessions, or for the more clearly political purpose of uniting to fight the hegemony of the 'upper castes' or the 'ruling castes', or for bargaining with a political party or the government, but in all cases for one or more specific purposes. The interesting thing about the caste federation is that, once formed on the basis of caste identities, it goes on to acquire non-caste functions, becomes more flexible in organisation as time passes, even begins to accept members and leaders from castes other than those with which it started, stretches out to new regions, and also makes common cause with other voluntary organisations, interest groups and political parties. In course of time, the federation becomes a distinctly political group, wielding considerable bargaining strength and numerical power, but still able to appeal to caste sentiments and consciousness, by adopting a common label (such as 'non-Brahmin' or 'Kshatriya'), claiming high status in the past and fostering a sense of deprivation in the present, and out of all this forging a strong and cohesive political group. It has gone far beyond the earlier caste associations in articulating group interests along political channels. The 'dominant elite' talked of above either includes leaders drawn from such organisations or is in close touch with them.

Third, alongside these new organisations, there has developed a vertical structure of factions along which the elite groups and their various support bases have got politically organised and through which channels of communication have been established between social and political forms. We have seen that such a factional structure is either fashioned along ongoing interrelationships that characterise areas dominated by peasant castes, or evolved through the operation of the political and electoral systems on the antecedent social structure thus resulting in a new polarisation of solidarities and alignments. The resulting system of factions is such that it divides not only political groups but also social groups, both the traditional caste forms and the newly formed caste associations and other interest group organisations. It thus facilitates the process of cross-cutting identifications and provides an expanding network of political support for a leadership that is engaged in a competitive structure of power relationships. Factions thus provide common media of participation for both the traditional and the modernist sectors and make for their mutual accommodation and ultimate fusion.

We have seen how a process of exposure on both sides leads to new forms of integration between society and politics. It is an integration which, while it involves traditional social forms into modern political associations, does not seek to destroy their bases of allegiance, though it undoubtedly changes them by making their identity part of a larger system of participation. Indeed, to repeat a point made earlier, the fusion that takes place here is a fusion of different *systems* of organisation and integration. Caste in its traditional form also provided a system of integration, but it did this by stabilising localistic and particularistic identities and fixing respective positions of groups, and of invididuals within groups. At the same time, the segmental and factional manifestations of the caste system and the consciousness and identifications to which it gave rise allowed scope for secular organisation and struggle from time to time.

Politics, on the other hand, is intrinsically a system of division and conflict and seeks material for the same. But at the same time it too is an integrative system based upon its own logic and mode of organisation. When these two systems interact, what develops through various stages is a new mode of integration as well as a new mode of division. The process can be described as secularisation of the social system and it is this process that holds the key to the tremendous shift that politics has brought about in Indian society. Whereas sanskritisation brought submerged caste groups out into the mainstream of society, and westernisation drew the sanskritised castes into the framework of modernisation, it is secularisation of both kinds of groups through their political involvement that is leading to a breakup of the old order and is gradually forging a *reintegration* on secular-associational grounds.[10] During the transition, such a reintegrative process inevitably highlights parochial symbolism as providing reference points of identity and cohesion.[11] But the same process also builds up new mixes of universalist-particularist orientations, renders the primordial basis of secular ties inefficient in itself and often prejudicial to individual and group interests, initiates the formally untutored masses into a slow awareness of the political community, and develops in them a stake in the latter.

On the other hand, for any political system to get stabilised it is necessary that its procedures and symbols are both internalised and *traditionalised*; they should not be accepted just for their utility but should be valued as such, as intrinsically meritorious and valuable, endowed with inherent goodness: in other words, the new procedures and values must themselves be turned into 'tradition', something that must be nurtured with care, developed further and made strong. No society lives without traditions and the essential challenge of modernity is not the destruction of tradition but the traditionalisation of modernity itself. In the context of caste and politics, this means two things. First, those elements in the caste system that have a secular and integrational potential should get strengthened at the expense of the more obscurantist and dysfunctional elements. This, we have seen, is

already happening. Second, the new dimensions that secular democratic politics has provided to the social system must themselves
become enduring parts of India's traditions. This has yet to take place.
The essential test of India's strategy of social change lies in this
criterion of traditionalisation of modernity. And the rest of the great
social system of India with its proverbial capabilities of absorption and
tolerance also lies in the same criterion: will it prove pliable enough
to imbibe the new system of values and institutions as vital traditions
of Hindu society? It is a criterion that replaces the old dichotomy in
which the old is sought to be wholly replaced by the new. The
rejection of such a dichotomy forms the point of departure of the
collection of papers presented in this volume.

NOTES

1. F.G. Bailey, 'Closed Social Stratification', *Archives Europeennes De Sociologie*, Vol. IV (1963).

2. Lloyd I. Rudolph, 'The Modernity of Tradition : The Democratic Incarnation of Caste in India', *The American Political Science Review*, Vol. LIX, No. 4, December 1965. The dichotomy between 'voluntary' and caste forms of organisation alluded to in the text was also drawn by Lloyd I. Rudolph and Susanne Hoeber Rudolph in their 'The Political Role of India's Caste Associations', *Pacific Affairs*, Vol. XXXIII, No. 1, March 1960.

3. See, however, the illuminating essay of Irawati Karve, *Hindu Society — An Interpretation* (Poona : Deccan College, 1961).

4. On the integrating role of *varna*, see M.N. Srinivas, *Religion and Society among the Coorgs of South India* (Bombay: Asia Publishing House, 1952).

5. The concepts of 'sanskritisation' and 'westernisation' have been made familiar by M.N. Srinivas. For his most recent statements on the subject see his *Social Change in Modern India* (Berkeley: California University Press, 1966) and 'The Cohesive Role of Sanskritisation' (mimeograph, University of Delhi, 1966).

6. The term 'entrenched caste' is to be distinguished from 'dominant caste' as used by M.N. Srinivas. According to Srinivas' criteria, a dominant caste not only exercises preponderant influence economically and politically but is also 'numerically the strongest in the village or local area'. ('The Dominant Caste in Rampura', *American Anthropologist*, February, 1959.) The entrenched caste, on the other hand, while it fulfils the chief criterion of economic and political power and is usually ritually 'high', may be numerically quite small, and usually is small. On the other hand, in regions where large peasant castes are found in 'entrenched' positions at different power points as indicated later in the same para, there may be considerable overlap between 'dominant' and 'entrenched' castes, though all of Srinivas' criteria may not yet be fulfilled.

7. Examples are Brahmin versus non-Brahmin in Madras and Maharashtra, Rajput versus Jat in Rajasthan, Baniya-Brahmin versus Patidar in Gujarat, Kayasthas versus Rajputs in Bihar, Kammas versus Reddis in Andhra, Nairs versus Ezhavas in Kerala, and so on. Often in the development of this process, as one polarisation is resolved in favour of one caste or caste category, new polarisations emerge such as between Patidars and Kshatriyas in Gujarat or Marathas and Mahars in Maharashtra. At other times, however, more complicated and fragmented constellations of power have emerged.

8. This factionalism must be distinguished from the traditional factionalism prevalent in caste society which is more on lines of kin-group and lineage. The factionalism discussed here is one that grows out of political

competition in which more than one personalised network of support contend for secular power.

9. For trend analysis on these points, see Gopal Krishna, 'Electoral Participation and Political Integration', *Economic and Political Weekly*, Annual Number, Vol. II, Nos. 3, 4 & 5, February 1967. For an earlier attempt towards a statistical measure of cross-communal voting behaviour, see Rajni Kothari and Tarun Sheth, 'Extent and Limits of Communal Voting: The Case of Baroda East' in Myron Weiner and Rajni Kothari (eds.), *Indian Voting Behaviour* (Calcutta : Firma K.L. Mukhopadhyaya, 1965).

10. For a development of the concept of 'reintegration' and a fuller description of the process of, and transition to, such a reintegration, see D.L. Sheth and Rajni Kothari, 'Social Change, Political Integration and the Value Process', paper presented to the *International Roundtable on Values in Politics*, Dubrovnik, Yugoslavia. The theme has also been developed, in the author's 'Tradition and Modernity Revisited', *Government and Opposition*, Vol. 3, No. 3, Summer 1968.

11. We have already noticed the contention that the electoral system has given a new lease of life to caste identifications. This is a correct observation but should lead to an opposite conclusion from what is usually made out: it is precisely because the *legitimacy* of caste as the only basis of political power has been eroded that caste *calculations* have increased. Such things as respective numerical strength of different castes, choice of candidate, factions within castes, and economic ties between castes are calculated as variable in the situation. This is natural in any political system and applies equally to other types of social organisation and ethnic groups. What is important to grasp is that caste calculations were *not* needed when only persons belonging to some castes had a right to office: caste was irrelevant because it was omnipotent. Today with the breakdown of these barriers and the pragmatic pursuit of power caste has turned into just another variable in politics along with many other variables. As Harold A. Gould has put it, it has come down from being a 'determinant' of politics to an 'ethnic variable'. See his 'Changing Political Behaviour in Rural Indian Society', *Economic and Political Weekly*, Vol. II, Nos. 33-35, Special Number, August 1967.

Part Two

Part Two

CHAPTER TWO

Learning the use of Political Means: The Mahars of Maharashtra

ELEANOR ZELLIOT

Among all the Scheduled Castes in India, the Mahars of Maharashtra have used political means most consistently and unitedly in their attempt to better their condition. The term 'political means' covers both, early efforts of scattered groups to secure governmental benefits and representation on legislative and political bodies, and later and more direct efforts in the form of political parties that secured representation of their special interests, agitated for constitutional guarantees, and created for themselves a firm electoral base. Our attempt in this paper is to describe the process by which the Mahars, operating under conditions of social degradation, perceive the potency of politics as a means of ameliorating their social condition.[1] Our concern however is not so much to evaluate the extent to which they achieved these ends but rather to identify and describe the manner in which a community like this participates in the political process for the improvement of their social conditions, in turn acquires political skills and capabilities and develops behaviours and responses favourable to their assimilation in the broader political culture of the nation.

Mahars account for about nine percent of the present-day population of Maharashtra. The two next largest Maharashtra Scheduled Castes are small groups in comparison: Mangs 1.8 per cent and Chambhars 1.3 per cent. The total Scheduled Caste population including those converted to Buddhism constitutes 12.68 per cent of the state population of Maharashtra, somewhat lower than the nearly 15 per cent average for India as a whole.[2]

Mahars are found in almost every village of Maharashtra, always in minority. Their quarters, called the *maharwada*, are set apart, usually east of the village proper. A Marathi proverb, *jethe gao tethe maharwada* (wherever there is a village, there is a *maharwada*), underlines their prevalence and also their low status, since it is used idiomatically to mean the equivalent of the English proverb, 'There's a black sheep in every flock.'[3] A contemporary anthropologist, Irawati Karve, found the Mahars, and not the dominant agricultural caste of Marathas, the most thoroughly widespread caste of Maharashtra and ended an essay on 'Mahars and Maharashtra' with the statement of a Mahar minor village official on the border between Marathi and Hindi-speaking peoples, *jethaparyant mahar pochle tithaparyant maharashtra* (as far as the Mahars have gone, there is Maharashtra).[4]

A theory held by some scholars and writers is that the Mahars are the original inhabitants of Maharashtra. One of the old names used for them, *dharniche put* (sons of the soil) as well as some of their traditional village duties—the arbitration of boundary disputes and the care of the village goddess Mariai—suggest that they may at one time have owned the land. At least one early Mahar leader, Kisan Faguji Bansode of Nagpur, spoke of pre-Aryan land ownership to try to build the pride and spirit of the Mahars, but the chief Mahar leader in this century, Dr.B.R.Ambedkar, did not exploit this belief.[5]

The traditional place of the Mahar in the village community was as a *balutedar* or *watandar*, a village servant whose duty was to the village and whose recompense (*baluta* or gifts in kind, and *watan* or land) came from the village. The Mahar's hereditary duty may, in former times, have involved membership of the village governing body when the village servants, including the *patil* (headman, usually a Maratha) and the *kulkarni* (accountant, usually a Brahmin), sat as a panchayat.[6] The Mahar *balutedar's* duties included arbitrating in boundary disputes, acting as village watchman, serving as guide and messenger to government servants, calling landowners to pay land revenue at the village *chaudi* (village hall), sweeping the village roads, escorting the government treasury, tracking thieves to the neighbouring village, carrying death notices and messages to other villages, bringing fuel to the burning ground, and removing the carcasses of dead cattle from the village. The Mahar also had fixed duties in religious matters, including the kindling of the first *Holi* festival fire from which other fires were lit and the guarding of the shrine of the goddess Mariai, which was in the *maharwada*. Recompense given by the village for these duties included not only grain and the skins of the dead cattle, but a small amount of land known as *watan* and a host of perquisites numbering, in legend, fifty-two. Mahars not required for *balutedar* work (in recent decades at least, they have worked in turn) did agricultural labour, their own *watan* lands being insufficient to support them. This set of duties holds for the Konkan (coastal) and Desh (plains) areas of Maharashtra; in the Vidarbha region to the east, where a looser social structure prevailed, some Mahars were also weavers, tradesmen, and *malguzars* (village revenue collectors).

The Mahar's duties were performed in the context of his untouchability; his touch was polluting and he did not come into direct contact with a caste Hindu or enter a caste Hindu home. The temple, the school, the village well were closed to him. Some restrictions in clothing, ornaments, metal household wares and the observance of ceremonies seem to have been enforced. The Mahar role in village festivals was clearly specified and generally, though not always, indicative of his inferior status. The Mahar practice of eating the carrion beef of the carcasses which were his charge, an early target of the Mahar reformers, was justification, in the mind of the caste Hindu, for his untouchability.

The Mahar *balutedar* duties gave him a widely held reputation for cleverness and curiosity and fairly close association with caste Hindus and government officials inspite of the polluting consequences of his touch and, in some areas, his shadow. Many of his duties are those of Untouchable Castes in other areas, but some appear to be unique to the Mahar. The curious position of the village Mahar, inferior and yet responsible in a way beyond that of servants, is seen in the 1845 description of R.N. Gooddine: " (The Mahar is) the watchman and guardian of the village and the living chronicler of its concerns," to which R.D. Choksey adds, "He, it appears, was acquainted with everybody's affairs, and his evidence was required in every dispute."[7] C.B. Agarwal, in *The Harijans in Rebellion,* writes, "In cases of (land) dispute, his decision was willingly accepted by both the parties. The Mahar, therefore, played the part of a witness and judge simultaneously."[8] But, interesting as it is, there are few factors in the Mahar village position which are indicative of caste-wise unity. The inter-village contact of Mahars in pursuit of their duties and the participation of Mahars in *tamasha* and *jalsa* (travelling village entertainment and singing groups) may have created channels for the communication of new ideas, but the ideas and the impulse for the organisation came from non-village factors.

With the coming of British rule, other opportunities for work were opened to the Mahar, his traditional role being such that he was both free and pressed to take whatever new vocation presented itself. While the other Untouchable Castes in Maharashtra had tasks which carried over into modern life, the Chambhar leather and shoe work quite successfully and the Mang basket and rope-making with less financial success, the Mahar position as an 'inferior village servant' (a British term) lost significance with new methods of communication, justice and government. The post office, the courts, and the police replaced the Mahar as messenger, arbitrator of land disputes, and watchman. The system of *balutedar* work itself could not expand to care for increasing numbers of Mahars. Work on the docks, the railways and the roads, in textile mills, and in government industries such as ammunition factories[9] became outlets for Mahar labour, from the 1860s on.[10] Although Mahars evidently did not flock to the cities in as great numbers as did other castes (even now the percentage of urban Mahars including Buddhists is lower than the urban percentage for Maharashtra as a whole[11]), the railway centres and the mill towns, as well as Bombay, Poona and Nagpur, became the loci for a new Mahar push for education and improved social status. Major consquences followed such an exposure. Stimulated through contact with city relatives or the travelling of Mahar propagandists and entertainers, those Mahars remaining in the village began to discard both duties and caste practices that were associated with their low status: the dragging out of carcasses and the subsequent eating of carrion, begging for food, wearing the clothes of the dead. Eventually, under Dr. Ambedkar's leadership, the *watan-balutedar* system itself was attacked.[12]

II

While the new economic opportunities presented to the Mahars undoubtedly encouraged a movement up from their inferior position, another factor that contributed both to their economic and social progress and to their caste spirit was the Mahar *elan* (military service). Even before the arrival of the British, the Mahar had an outlet from traditional work in the time of Shivaji as guards in the hill forts and soldiers in the artillery. It is fairly clear that they had their own units in the later armies of the Peshwas. But it is from the records of their service in the armies of the British that the Mahars draw the contention that they are a martial race. A military monument at Koregaon near Poona serves as a focal point in the legend of Mahar heroism, and a number of Mahar gatherings have been held at its foot. The Koregaon pillar commemorates the soldiers of the British Army who fell during an 1818 battle with Peshwa forces. Of the 49 names of the 2nd/1st regiment recorded there, twenty-two are Mahar, or *Parwari*, as Mahars were known then, (identifiable by the *nak* ending of the names, a designation used for Mahars into the early years of this century), sixteen are Maratha, eight Rajput and other Hindu, two Muslim and one probably Indian Jewish.[13]

Though their record of military service dates back to the pre-British period and may lend some plausibility to their claim to the status of a martial group, it was their entry into the British army which proved significant for the subsequent history of the Mahar movement. It is important to gauge this significance. It consists not in any automatic elevation in the social hierarchy through military service, which indeed is ruled out in hierarchical system governed by considerations of ascriptive status and ritual purity. It rather consists in the fact that military service at such an early date exposed them to British institutions much before the dissemination of western culture took place on a large scale. Such an exposure socialised them sufficiently early to the new political order so that when new opportunities and alternatives became available, they were found prepared to use them more effectively than those groups which did not have this opportunity.

Dr. Ambedkar, probably basing his belief on the army experience of his ancestors on both sides for several generations almost solely attributed the beginning of the untouchables' movement to their contacts with the British Army:

> Until the advent of the British, the untouchables were content to remain Untouchables. It was a destiny preordained by the Hindu God and enforced by the Hindu State . . . Fortunately or unfortunately, the East India Company needed soldiers for their army in India and it could find none but the Untouchables . . . In the army of the East India Company there prevailed the system of compulsory education for Indian soldiers and their children, both male and female. The education received by the Untouchables in the army . . . gave them a new vision and a new value. They became conscious that the low esteem in which they had been held was not an inescapable destiny but was a stigma imposed on their personality by the cunning contrivances of the priest. They felt the shame of it as they never did before and were determined to get rid of it.[14]

With the abolition of the old Presidency armies in 1893 and the establishment of units on a class basis, together with increased recruitment from the northern martial races, the Mahars were denied further recruitment in the army. Ambedkar's father was of the last generation to be able to use this channel of financial security and social prestige. Two documents, one from the late 19th century and the other from the early 20th, illustrate the importance of army service to the Mahars. This was clearly the beginning of their efforts to induce government to intervene on their behalf, and their questioning of their traditional inferior status.

In 1894, Gopal Baba Walangkar, a Konkani military man, drew up a petition in Marathi requesting reacceptance of untouchables into army ranks, but secured little support from his less audacious caste fellows.[15] The petition was never translated into English or presented to the British, but it serves as documentation for Mahar attitudes of the time. Sent from the *Anarya Doshpariharakham* at Dapoli (Non-Aryan Group for the Removal of Wrongs at Dapoli, an army pensioners' centre in Ratnagiri), the petition speaks for Parwari (Mahar), Moci (Chambhar) and Mang peoples who have served loyally in the past in both the army and domestic service. It makes the claim that the Untouchables were former Kshatriyas, demoted by the Peshwa at the time of the Mahadurgadevi famine in 1676 for eating whatever they could find to save their lives. Because of education in the army, they have begun to read the religious books of the Hindus and to question the behaviour, thoughts and the ancestry of the caste Hindus. A challenge was issued by the author of the petition several years before, asking what religious scriptures proved that these people were low and what remedies there were in Hinduism that would remove this lowness. The writer claims that 'none of the caste-proud or their priests' have proved the Untouchables' lowness. Examples of the bravery of both Untouchable soldiers and domestics are given, and a plea made that Untouchables should be recruited in the army, police and civil administration in accordance with the promise made by Queen Victoria after the Mutiny.[16]

The Mahars of Poona, a large army camp centre, found themselves better organised and with a spokesman, Shivram Janba Kamble, eloquent in English. Ten years later a memorandum was sent to the Governor of Bombay on behalf of fifteen hundred Mahars in the Deccan (the Desh area) and Konkan. The reply from the Poona Collector's office indicated that he could do nothing about their requests: admission to the lower grades of public service, removal of restrictions in public schools, permission to join the police and the Indian Army.[17] A longer and more sophisticated document was sent by the Conference of Deccan Mahars, with Subedar (Captain) Bahadur Gangaram Krishnajee as president and the same Shivram Janba Kamble as secretary, in 1910 to the Earl of Crewe, Secretary of State for India, asking for employment in the lowest grades of the public service, in the ranks of police sepoys and of soldiers in the

Indian Army. The petition appealed for consideration for Mahars on the grounds of former service, English justice and human worth. The authors claim "our people (have) been employed in the Indian Army from the very commencement of the British Raj in our country, and they have risen to the highest positions by their valour and good conduct," and list the names of 107 Mahar officers (Jamadars, Subedars and Subedar Majors) in the infantry, rifles and marines as proof. Several strong pleas on the grounds of British morality were made including this one:

> And it is most encouraging to know that the Honourable House of Commons, as constituted in these times, is composed, to some extent, of the representatives of the lower strata of English society, the workingmen, who, only a quarter of a century ago, were regarded as but Mahars and Paryas by the more educated and affluent classes of their nation. If the Brahmanical castes and the Muhammadans have been given the full rights of British citizenship, we must be given the same.

The petition held up to the British 'the noble part which Japan played in the elevation of its outcastes.'

There seems to be no record of an answer to the 1910 Petition. Mahars enlisted in labour units of the army in World War I and toward the end of the war the 111th Mahars was raised but shortly disbanded. During the Second World War the need for troops plus the presence of Dr. Ambedkar, in the Viceroy's Cabinet resulted in the raising of the Mahar Regiment, now known as the Mahar Machine Gun Regiment.[18] In spite of the lack of immediate response to the Petition, it was important in setting a pattern for future Mahar petitions and protests to Government. The appeal is in terms of the rights of citizens; there is no attempt to invoke Kshatriya status as proof of worth as there was in the 1894 petition, nor does any other major 20th century Mahar document attempt to manipulate the *varna* system in order to claim higher status.[19]

The 1910 petition made little mention of religion. The British were reminded that Mahars as Christian converts had attained high status in the professions and that 'the kindly touch of the Christian religion elevates the Mahar at once and for ever socially as well as politically.' But aside from expressing the view that 'the abomination of caste, which sins both against God and man, has no authority in the Vedas,' reinforced by a quotation from Max Muller, the petitioners dealt with the matter of their condition in political and social, not religious terms.

III

There is also considerable evidence, that Mahars freed from traditional village services saw a need to try to adopt a Hinduism more sophisticated than that offered by village gods. A poem, probably by a Mahar, attached to the handwritten copy of the 1894 petition depicts the hardships and the bad habits of Untouchables in rough and direct language, and includes the complaint:

> Our religious names are Satvi, Jarvai, Mesai, Vetal, Mhasa, Bahiri, Bhadvi, Mariai. We do not know Brahma, Vishnu, Mahesh, Krishnarai, Rukhamai, Ram, Sita, Lakshman.

Many of the military Mahars joined the Kabir and Ramadi *panths,* sects which stressed equality. The fact that many Mahars of the Bawani sub-sect in Vidarbha joined the Mahanubhav *panth* may be related to their high status in the Mahar caste itself and to the greater economic freedom in their area, which permitted Mahars to be weavers, traders and shopkeepers.

Were the Mahars to have continued an effort to relate to Hinduism on a higher level than village status allowed, they had a natural channel in the person of their own saint, Chokhamela, a 14th century poet-saint. Chokhamela's *abhangas* (songs) are still sung by pilgrims of the *warkari* cult on pilgrimage to Vithoba's temple at Pandharpur.[20] There seems to have been a beginning towards using the name Chokhamela as a caste name, building temples in his honour, naming groups and institutions after him, much in the same way that the Chamars of Uttar Pradesh have used the name of their saint, Ravidas, in an attempt to gain status.[21] The resolutions of the Chokhamela Reform Society meeting at Ramtek, a pilgrimage centre near Nagpur, in 1923, illustrate the methods of this approach: (1) a temple should be built where Untouchables as orthodox Hindus could have equal rights in weddings and thread ceremonies along with Brahmins, Kshatriyas and Vaishyas; (2) there should be religious education to bring about the unity of the Hindu people; (3) upper class people should help educate the so-called Untouchables, and Government should give concessions to the upper classes to encourage them.[22] But even such a document dealing primarily with religion includes a recognition of the importance of education and a hint at the necessity of governmental help if change is actually to come.

There are numerous scattered efforts to create specific Mahar institutions within Hinduism, to join a reforming caste Hindu organisation, or to adopt higher caste ritual practices (*sanskritisation* in M.N. Srinivas' useful term) throughout the first third of the 20th century. As examples: Gopal Baba Walangkar, author of the 1894 army petition, encouraged the replacement of Brahmin *joshis* who cast wedding horoscopes, one of the few duties performed by Brahmin priests for Mahars, with Mahar *joshis*. Kisan Fago Bansode of the Nagpur area and G.A. Gawai of Amravati, both important Mahar leaders of social reform and spokesmen for increased participation in a higher form of Hinduism, joined the Prarthana Samaj in 1910. Vithoba Raoji Sant Pande built a separate bathing place for Mahars at Ramtek near Nagpur around 1914 and 'placed the whole community under a deep obligation.'[23] In the late 1920s Mahars in the Bombay area attempted to participate in the public worship of Ganapati at Dadar, started performing weddings in accordance with 'vedic rites', and at least on one occasion donned the symbol of the high caste Hindu, the sacred thread.

The most vigorous efforts by Mahars and other Untouchables to claim religious rights as the equal of the caste Hindus were three temple-entry attempts: an abortive temple-entry satyagraha at Amravati in 1927; a lengthy, somewhat violent (several Untouchables ended up in the hospital) attempt of Untouchables together with several caste Hindu reformers in 1929-30 to climb Poona's holy hill, Parvati; and a five-year long satyagraha at Kalaram temple in Nasik, ending in 1935, which served to unify and organise the Mahars and won them sympathy in England during the negotiations of the Round Table Conference in 1930-32, but did not open the doors of the temple to Untouchables.

In 1935 Dr. Ambedkar, by then the recognised leader of the Mahars, announced his decision to leave Hinduism. A conference of Mahars called in Bombay the following year, took a similar decision for the caste as a whole. From that date onward, there is no record of any organised attempt by Mahars to participate in Hindu ritual activities. The energy and sense of unity stimulated by the temple entry attempts could be turned to political and educational matters without losing momentum.

The 19th century claim of a Mahar that he was of Kshatriya status was dropped in the 20th century, replaced by the claim that the Mahar was of worth simply as a human being. The fact that the Maratha was involved in a battle for Kshatriya status at the same time rather preempted that field of action. But more important than this is the fact that their goal — re-entry into the army, places in the police force and civil service — required dealing with the British on western terms. The Mahar military past was now no longer employed as a ground for higher *varna* claims, but as a source for the educated, of discontent with their economic and social status, and of a mystique of militancy used by Mahar reformers to break down the apathy and sense of inferiority of the traditional Mahar.

The claim to religious rights lost ground as the consciousness of the importance of education and political power, articulated by the western-educated Ambedkar increased. Further, the experience of failure of religion-centred activity prepared Mahars to reject Hinduism altogether. The figure of Chokhamela remained as a source of caste pride rather than a stimulant to claiming a place of worth in the Hindu hierarchy. They now increasingly came to rely on the opening of new avenues for rising in status in a new stratificatory system that was beginning to be established with the advent of formal education and change in traditional occupational system.

Ambedkar's letter to the leader of the Nasik Satyagraha in 1934 proposes the new way upward for the Mahar. He suggests that the satyagraha should be stopped:

> I would advice the Depressed Classes to insist upon a complete over-hauling of Hindu Society and Hindu Theology before they consent to become an integral part of Hindu Society. I started temple entry satyagraha only because I felt that that was the best way of energising the Depressed Classes and making them conscious of their position. As I believe I have achieved that therefore I have no more use for temple entry. I want the Depressed Classes to concentrate their energy and resources on politics and education.[24]

As against this Kisan Faguji Bansode, 1879-1946, a labour leader, newspaper editor, social worker and a poet of the Nagpur area persisted with the approach of the Mahar claim to religious worth. Bansode went almost all the way with Ambedkar in social and political matters, but retained the belief that progress could be made within Hinduism. A poem illustrates his attitude, as militant as Ambedkar's, but couched in religious terms:

> Why do you endure curses?
> Choka went into the temple resolutely,
> Why do you, ashamed, stay far off?
> You are the descendants of Choka.
> Why do you fear to enter the temple?
> Brace yourself like a wrestler, come,
> Together let us conquer pollution.[25]

Respected as Kisan Faguji Bansode was in the Vidarbha area, the Mahars there followed Ambedkar perhaps even more enthusiastically than their caste fellows elsewhere.

The factors that led to the Mahar social awakening — military service and other contacts with the British, employment opportunities outside the village patterns, the beginnings of education, provided at first by caste Hindu reformers and Christian missions and from the 1920s onward at least in part by their own efforts; a latent caste spirit stimulated by reminders of their military past and the religious worth of Chokhamela; and a highly educated leader, Dr. Ambedkar, capable of forming them into a political force — equipped them for the use of political means toward a modern goal of social equality.

IV

The petitions to government for reinstatement in the army represent the first Mahar attempt to use what I have broadly defined as political means to gain their goals — at that time a modest goal of economic opportunity. The increased democratisation of British rule in India after the First World War offered a chance to engage in political activity on a larger scale. Two Mahars, G.A. Gawai of Amravati, and B.R. Ambedkar of Bombay offered testimony to the Franchise Committee (Southborough) which was gathering material for the implementation of the Montagu-Chelmsford reforms. Gawai spoke on behalf of the Depressed India Association, requesting separate electorates and direct representation in the forthcoming provincial elections for an enlarged and more responsible provincial assembly.[26] Ambedkar's testimony, making the same basic point, filled ten closely printed pages and initiated what can only be called the Ambedkar Era among the Mahars.

B.R. Ambedkar, a Mahar from a Ratnagiri army family, appeared on the political scene for the first time in 1919, when he was called to testify to the Southborough Committee. The Mahar community had exhibited an early interest in political means, exemplified by the petitions and the Depressed India Association begun in 1916, which G.A. Gawai represented. Ambedkar, highly educated and with a dedication to western parliamentary democracy, was able to guide this political awareness into far more effective channels. His education both enabled him to speak in modern political terms and won him the respect and admiration of his caste. By the time the Southborough Committee hearings took place, Ambedkar was a graduate of Elphinstone College, had spent three years at Columbia University and one year at the London School of Economics. His higher education was made possible by the financial support of the Gaikwad of Baroda.[27] He returned to India in 1917 and was a professor at

Sydenham College at the time of the Southborough Committee meetings. Later he resumed his London studies with the help of the Maharajah of Kolhapur[28] as well as his own savings, secured a D.Sc. from London University and was called to the Bar in 1923. His degrees indicated an accomplishment rare for an Indian, almost incredible for an untouchable. The Mahar reaction is shown by a song about Ambedkar, part of an enormous Mahar-Buddhist-Ambedkar song literature, that begins by listing his degrees: B.A., M.A., Ph.D., D.Sc., Bar-at-Law, in a sort of incantation.

In response to a question, Ambedkar told the Southborough Committee that there was, among the Depressed Classes of Bombay State, one B.A. (himself), six or seven matriculates, and about twenty-five men who had passed the sixth or seventh standard and who consequently would be literate in English. Gawai's testimony to the Committee in the Central Provinces added three or four matriculates to this number from among the Untouchables in his area. Ambedkar did not see the lack of education among his people as a bar to political participation, but pleaded that the franchise for Depressed Classes should be 'so low as to educate into political life as many Untouchables as possible.'

Ambedkar's testimony informed the Committee, in words that reflected his Columbia courses with John Dewey and Franklin Giddings, that India's social divisions on the basis of 'lack of like-mindedness and endosmosis,' were not Hindu, Mohammedan, Christian, Parsi, Jew, etc., but Touchable Hindu, Untouchable Hindu; Mohammedan, etc. In a statement that ranged far beyond demands for the Depressed Classes, he urged joint electorates with reserved seats for Mohammedans, lest communal representation sharpen the angularity of the division between Hindu and Muslim, and a low-pitched franchise for the Marathas, which would serve that large community better than reserved seats or separate electorates in allowing them a voice free from Brahmin domination. But he argued that Untouchables, whom he characterised as 'slaves', 'dehumanised', and 'socialised as never to complain', must have communal representation since 'untouchability constitutes a definite set of interests which the Untouchable alone can speak for,' and representation 'in such numbers as will enable them to claim redress'.

Of the Legislative Council of Bombay Presidency's proposed 100 members, he suggested that the Untouchables be allowed nine representatives, eight for their percentage of the population and one from among the nine to be elected by them to the Imperial Legislative Council. He stigmatised Congress followers as 'political radicals and social Tories', and summarised his position in these words: "British rule in India was meant to provide equal opportunity for all, and ... in transferring a large share of the power to popular assemblies, arrangements should be made whereby the hardships and disabilities entailed by the social system should not be reproduced and perpetuated in political institutions."[29]

Ambedkar's first public political plea in 1919 resulted in failure. The Southborough Committee, ignoring Ambedkar, Gawai and a number of caste Hindus from Bombay, including Vithal Ramji Shinde, V.J. Patel, R.P. Paranjpye and M.M. Joshi, who urged direct representation of the Depressed Classes, gave them one *nominated* representative in the Bombay Legislative Assembly. The first man selected for representation was D.D. Gholap, a Mahar from Satara who had been in charge of Ambedkar's paper, *Mooknayak*. Following the Muddiman Committee report on the working of the Montagu-Chelmsford Reforms in 1925, which among many other matters contained an admonition on the need to correct Depressed Class status, another nominated Untouchable representative was added to the Bombay Legislative Council, and Ambedkar was named to this seat in 1926.

The presence of two Untouchables on the Bombay Legislative Council probably had litle effect on the nature of its laws. A resolution was passed in 1923 urging that all public places and institutions maintained by public funds be open to Untouchables, and an attempt to put teeth in the resolution was made in 1926 by advising the Government not to grant money to municipalities which did not observe the rule. But these resolutions were the work of S.K. Bole, a caste Hindu reformer from the Bhandari community. Early bills presented by the Depressed Class representatives, but not passed, pertained to education and economics; they asked for free and compulsory education for Untouchables, and that the Mahar *watan* land be made *ryotwari*, and hence eligible for sale, a strike at the bonds of the *balutedar* system.

In the decade between the sessions of the Southborough Committee and those of the Simon Commission in 1928, which provided the next opportunity for Untouchables to plead for direct representation, a great deal of organisational and educational work went on in the Mahar community. In the pre-Ambedkar era, Shivram Janba Kamble had organised conferences as early as 1903; the Depressed India Association was formed in Nagpur (and continued to function in the 1920s, but without Ambedkar's cooperation); and four conferences were held in Bombay in 1917-18, some under caste Hindu leadership, all concerned with the Untouchables and their increased political importance in the coming Reforms.[30] Ambedkar's first full-scale conference seems to have been in March, 1920, at Mangaon in Kolhapur, a princely state whose ruler, Shahu Maharaj had been active in the non-Brahmin movement of the Marathas and in education for backward classes, including Untouchables. Ambedkar also spoke at the first All-India Conference convened by Untouchables at Nagpur later in 1920, before his return to England. At Nagpur, he persuaded all Mahar sub-castes, at that time endogamous groups, to eat together, although not all Untouchable castes were prepared to inter-dine.[31] Ambedkar also propounded a theory at Nagpur that has held for the subsequent Mahar political movement, the idea that the caste Hindu could not know the mind of the Untouchable, and hence could not lead him. He criticised Vithal Ramji Shinde, the most active of the caste Hindu workers among Untouchables, for suggesting that the Untouchable representatives should be selected by members of the Legislative Council rather than by Government or institutions of the Untouchables themselves.[32] Direct representation was their goal; if that was not possible, then a neutral British government or their own organised groups should select members, not a largely caste-Hindu body.

Ambedkar presided over or spoke at a number of conferences in the Maharashtra area after his return from England in 1923, but the Mahars themselves date their political awakening from a conference held in 1927 at Mahad, a town in Kolaba district south of Bombay. As is true of most conferences and organisations of Untouchables in the 1920s and 1930s, caste Hindus played a part in this event. A C.K.P. (Chandraseniya Kayastha Prabhu)[33] supporter of Ambedkar, S.G. Tipnis, then head of the city council of Mahad, invited Ambedkar to hold a conference of the Depressed Classes there. The venue of the conference was a field belonging to a Muslim outside the town. At the meeting, evidently without previous planning, a decision was reached to test the 1923 resolution of the Bombay Legislative Council, which had been confirmed by the Mahad city council, that all public places should be open to Untouchables. The conference attenders marched to Chowdar tank, a large pond on the outskirts of the town in a caste Hindu area. Leaders of the procession then stopped and drank water, attempting a symbolic fulfilment of the law, but a rumour had spread through Mahad that the Untouchables were going on to the Vireswar Temple to attempt entry, and the procession and conference ended in rioting.

The caste Hindus purified the tank and the Untouchables planned another demonstration. At the second conference, held later in the year, a copy of *Manusmriti*, the ancient law book which symbolised Hindu injustice to the Untouchables, was ceremoniously burned, but a second satyagraha for water did not take place. The district magistrate appeared with an injunction, based on a suit initiated by caste Hindus on the grounds that the tank was private property. Ambedkar evidently preferred to fight in the courts rather than on the streets, and persuaded the conference members to disperse. The legal struggle ended ten years later, with the judgement in favour of Ambedkar.

The Mahad Satyagraha failed to achieve its specific purpose at the time, but it was successful as a rallying point for the internal reform of the Depressed Classes, the public expression of their grievances, and the stimulation of a sense of unity. The resolutions of the Mahad Conferences express the mood of the 1920s. The first conference 'appealed to the caste Hindus to help the Untouchables secure their civic rights, to employ them in services, offer food to Untouchable students, and bury their dead animals themselves.' The government was requested to pass laws prohibiting Untouchables from eating carrion, enforcing prohibition, providing free and compulsory education, and making the Bole Resolution of 1923 effective. Ambedkar addressed a meeting of Depressed Class women, urging them to dress well, not to observe caste restrictions in dress or ornaments, to be clean, not to feed husbands or sons if they were drunkards, and to send their children to school.[34]

The numbers of Untouchables at the Mahad Conferences (Dhananjay Keer gives figures of 10,000 and 15,000, which may be too high), the unsuccessful but dramatic satyagraha to Chowdar Tank, and the burning of *Manusmriti*, which is remembered today by Mahar and caste Hindu alike, gave the Mahad conferences a legendary place in Mahar history. Its anniversary was celebrated as 'Independence Day' thirteen years later.[35]

As the Mahar political movement gathered momentum, the non-Brahmin movement, with which it was partially identified, died away, or rather took a new form as its leaders were slowly absorbed into the Congress. The two movements had some things in common: both groups had grievances against the Brahmins; both looked back on the nineteenth century figure of Jotirao Phule as a prophet,[36] such non-Brahmin leaders as Shahu Maharaj and Keshavrao Jedhe knew Ambedkar and attended Untouchable conferences. But the caste difference between the two groups and their social situations — the Marathas were a land-owning dominant caste, the Mahars a nearly landless minority — worked against any real co-operative effort between them. Although the Mahar grievances were voiced chiefly against the Brahmin, as it was the Maratha who dominated at the village level, the village protests in the form of quitting *balutedar* duties or claiming some form of social equality in fact got directed against the latter. The inability of a leader like Ambedkar to accept a subordinate role in a caste Hindu organisation also mitigated against co-operation. Just as the Justice Party in Madras failed to include significant numbers of Untouchables, the non-Brahmin movement in Maharashtra could not make common cause with the Untouchables.

V

The reaction of the Depressed Classes to the Simon Commission's tour of India was far different from that of Congress or the moderates. Eighteen Depressed Classes asssociations testified willingly to the Commission, sixteen of them asking for separate electorates for Untouchables. While Ambedkar's students walked out of his class at Government Law College in protest, Ambedkar told the Commission that the Untouchables were relieved of anxiety because the Simon Commission did *not* include an Indian, since such a nominee could not be truly representative of all groups. However, he did not renew his 1919 request for separate electorates. Adult franchise and reserved seats, to the number of 22 in a Bombay assembly of 140 (15 according to their numbers plus seven as weightage to insure their rights), would satisfy him and the organisation he spoke for, the Bahishkrit Hitakarini Sabha (Depressed Class Association).[37] He also requested guarantees for the Depressed Classes, as did an appeal from the Central Provinces Depressed Class Association, signed by five Mahars (including Kisan Faguji Bansode), two Chamars, one Mang and one Bhangi, which expressed a similar view of rights and privileges in even stronger and more distrustful language. This group requested: (1) an increase in the government power of veto for protection of the minority, (2) separate representation not only in legislatures, but all public bodies including universities in proportion to numerical strength, (3) posts in government service for Depressed Class members, with minimum qualifications required, (4) representation in Cabinet dependent only upon Depressed Class votes, (5) special grant for education, (6) no application of a bill affecting Depressed Classes if three-fourths of the community opposes it.[38] Both the Vidarbha and the Bombay demands reflect the feeling of the need for education (2.9 per cent of the Mahars were literate, according to the 1931 census), need for government jobs (Ambedkar pointed out that there was not one Depressed Class clerk in government service), and a desire for the Depressed Class not only to participate in all public bodies but to be able to control any legislation affecting them.

Ambedkar's nomination to the Round Table Conference called in 1930 in London to discuss India's future constitution was an acknowledgement of the leadership he had gained, and the very fact of his participation extended his fame to every corner of Maharashtra and beyond. For Ambedkar, his and Dewan Bahadur R. Srinivasan's nomination meant "that the Untouchables were regarded not merely as a separate element from the Hindus but also of such importance as to have the right to be consulted in the framing of a constitution for India."[39] Subhas Chandra Bose voiced another interpretation of Ambedkar's political rise: "In 1930 and after, Dr. Ambedkar has had leadership thrust upon him by a benign British Government, because his services were necessary to embarrass the nationalist leaders."[40] However, Ambedkar, on his own terms, identified himself with nationalism, if not with the nationalists. Before the first Round Table Conference, at a meeting of the All India Depressed Class Conference held in August, 1930, at Nagpur, Ambedkar said:

> I agree with the Congressmen that no country is good enough to rule over another. But I must also take the liberty to tell them point-blank that the proposition does not end there and that it is equally true that no class is good enough to rule over another class.

He added, "It is only in a Swaraj constitution that you stand any chance of getting the political power into your own hands without which you cannot bring salvation to your people,"[41] but he found it necessary to continue to press for political safeguards for Depressed Classes while the British continued to rule India, distrusting that those who put independence above social reform would allow the Untouchables equality.

At this Nagpur Conference, shortly before he left for London, Ambedkar stated that he would be satisfied with joint electorates provided there was adult franchise and reserved seats. Earlier, in 1919, he had asked for separate electorates, as did Jains, Marathas, Lingayats, Marwadis and a number of other groups in a sort of separate electorate fever, but in 1928, before the Simon Commission, he reversed his position. There he used the argument against separate electorates which Gandhi was later to use against him — that increased disunity would result. This ambivalence seems to show that Ambedkar's goal was direct, effective representation; the method of achieving that goal varied with the circumstances. At the Round Table Conference,

however, he reversed himself on the matter of electorates again.
Perhaps under a sense of representing all Depressed Classes, most of
whom wanted separate electorates, perhaps because communal
electorates for Muslims seemed to be guaranteed, perhaps because
Gandhi would not even concede that reserved seats for Untouchables
were necessary, Ambedkar came out strongly for separate electorates
for the Depressed Classes and held to his position through the three
Round Table sessions. From this time on, 'separate electorates' was
the battle-cry of the Untouchables under Ambedkar's leadership until
Independence.

At the Second Round Table Conference, the only one Mahatma
Gandhi attended, Ambedkar's attitude toward Gandhi hardened. At
the time of the temple road satyagraha at Vaikam in Travancore, in
1924-25, Ambedkar had referred to Gandhi critically but not without
respect. He felt that Gandhi did not give as much importance to the
removal of Untouchability as he did to the propagation of khadi and
Hindu-Muslim unity. "If he did, he would insist on the removal of
untouchability as a precondition for entrance into Congress as he has
insisted on thread spinning as a precondition for voting in Congress."
But he concluded, "when no one else comes near us, even Mahatma
Gandhi's sympathy is of no little importance."[42] Later, at the 1930
Nagpur conference, Ambedkar referred to Gandhi's moral influence
in the struggle for Untouchables' rights. However, an unproductive
meeting between the two and the confrontation in London in 1931,
where Gandhi denied the recognition of the Depressed Class as a
minority and hence eligible for political safeguards, made Ambedkar
bitterly critical.

After the Third Round Table Conference, the General Secretary of
the Depressed Classes Institute, S.N. Shivtarkar, a Chambhar, wrote in
Ambedkar's paper, *Janata,* a criticism of Congress and Gandhi that
reflects the feeling on Ambedkar's side:

> In spite of the fact that the removal of untouchability has been included in
> the constructive programme of the Congress, practically nothing has been
> done so far by the body to achieve that object, and in our fights against
> untouchability at Mahad and Nasik most of the local Congress leaders have
> been our bitter opponents.
>
> Gandhiji was prepared to concede (at the Round Table Conference) on
> behalf of the Congress special claims of the Mohammedans and the Sikhs
> including their demand for separate representation on 'historic grounds',
> but he was not willing even to concede reserved seats in general elector-
> ates to the depressed classes, although he knew, at least he ought to have
> known, what sort of treatment they would get, should they be thrown at
> the mercies of the caste Hindus.

The greatest presumption on Gandhi's part at the Round Table Conference was that he claims that he represented the depressed classes and not Dr. Ambedkar .... Leadership cannot be imposed, it must be accepted by those on whose behalf it is claimed. Congress is now dissecting the community of untouchables by playing one section of that community against the other.[43]

The *Free Press Journal* reported in 1931 that a large section which embraces the vast majority of the Depressed Classes community, under the leadership of P. Balu, B. J. Deorukhakar and Mr. Patel, repudiated Ambedkar's position on separate electorates and special representation and declared their faith in the Congress and Mahatma Gandhi.[44] There are indications, however, that Ambedkar's active supporters were more numerous. When Ambedkar returned from the second Round Table Conference, 114 Depressed Class associations of Bombay city and the Presidency presented addresses of welcome. The Muslim leader Shaukat Ali and Ambedkar came back on the same boat and addressed crowds of Muslims and Depressed Class members from the same platform. When Gandhi had returned a month earlier, Shivtarkar had arranged for a black flag demonstration for him. A free-for-all ensued between Congress supporters and some 8,000 Depressed Class demonstrators upon Gandhi's arrival in Bombay.[45]

The Poona Pact of 1932 did not alleviate tension for more than a few months. Gandhi's fast against separate electorates, which had been granted to the Depressed Classes by the Communal Award of 1932, brought Ambedkar and a number of caste Hindus to Poona, where Gandhi was imprisoned in Yervada jail, to negotiate an agreement that would somehow satisfy the Depressed Classes and yet allow Gandhi to end the fast. The Poona Pact did result in giving the Depressed Classes a greater number of representatives, 148 seats in provincial legislatures in place of the 71 allowed by the Communal Award. But a system of primary elections in which only Depressed Classes were to vote, to be followed by the general election in which caste Hindus and Untouchables would vote together took the place of the double vote, one in a separate electorate and one in the joint constituency, which the Communal Award had already provided. Both sides were later unhappy with the Poona Pact, the caste Hindus because they felt their own representation lessened, and the Depressed Classes because the double elections for their candidates seemed expensive and cumbersome, and not a proper substitute for a separate electorate. Nor did the long arduous campaign against Untouchability which Gandhi undertook after his release from prison or the establishment of the Harijan Sevak Sangh win over Ambedkar.

Ambedkar was named to the Board of the Harijan Sevak Sangh, but resigned when he felt his views were not being considered.[46] One way of explaining the conflict between Ambedkar and Gandhi, perhaps an over-simplification, is to say that Ambedkar saw advancement for the Untouchable in terms of using political means to achieve social and economic equality with the highest classes in a modern society, while Gandhi held to a more traditional concept of a *varna* system, cleansed of Untouchability, in which Untouchables would be Shudras and their unclean work made honourable.

One outcome of the Poona Pact, however, was to spotlight Ambedkar again, adding to his fame and giving his leadership more of an all-India stature. An Englishman said of him in 1932, "I think we may accept Dr. Ambedkar as the most important leader and accredited spokesman of the depressed classes. None of the local leaders have either his education, forensic ability, or pugnacity, and his recent conduct during Mr. Gandhi's fast, the extraordinarily favourable agreement which he exacted from Hindu negotiators, reveal him as a political tactician of quality."[47] Ambedkar's chief rival for Depressed Class leadership, Rao Bahadur M.C. Rajah of Madras, was also involved in political action. Rajah, the first nominated member from the Depressed Classes on the Central Legislative Assembly, also instituted Depressed Class conferences, testified to the Simon Commission, and had some following among the Mahars of Vidarbha as well as in the south of India. He and Dr. B.S. Moonje of the Hindu Mahasabha brought forward a compromise plan allowing reserved seats in a general constituency for the Depressed Classes in 1932 before the Poona Pact was signed, but although M.C. Rajah was present at the Poona Pact negotiations, he was eclipsed in importance by Ambedkar.[48]

VI

As the 1937 elections for the provincial legislatures under the new Constitution approached, Ambedkar gave the political movement a specific focus by establishing the Independent Labour Party. According to a news release issued in August, 1936,[49] he had been persuaded by friends to form a party with a broader base than the Depressed Classes alone, and a party modelled on the English Labour Party came into being. The programme of the new party was 'mainly to advance the welfare of the labouring classes,' and contained little direct mention of what were by then called the Scheduled Castes. Socialist in flavour, the party accepted 'the principle of State management and

State ownership of industry whenever it may become necessary in the interest of the people'. Aid to agriculturists through land mortgage banks, cooperatives and marketing societies; technical education and the promotion of new industries; reform of the *khot, talukdari* and *watan* tenant systems; free and compulsory primary education; and a pledge to bring about a fair mixture of castes in the administration were planks in the platform. The executive committee of the party included many of the caste Hindus who had worked with Ambedkar in social affairs for the previous ten years. In the elections of 1937, the party won ten of the fifteen reserved seats for Scheduled Castes and three general seats in the Bombay Legislative Assembly, and three of Central Provinces and Berar's reserved seats.

The list of candidates reveals something of the nature of the Mahar political movement in the 1930s. The majority of tickets were given to Mahars, although there were at least two candidates from other Untouchable castes, a Mang and a Gujarati Scheduled Caste man. Two of the caste Hindus elected were C.K.P. — one was a Brahmin. Candidates such as R.R. Bhole (Poona) and D. G. Jadhav (Khandesh) represented the new college-trained generation of Mahars; others, such as B. K. Gaikwad (Nasik), had less formal education but a history of work in the various Mahar satyagrahas and conferences. The lack of Chambhars, the wealthiest, ritually highest group among the Scheduled Castes in Maharashtra, is striking. The secretary of Ambedkar's Depressed Classes Association had been a Chambhar and the secretary of the coming Scheduled Castes Federation was to be a Chambhar, P.N. Rajbhoj, yet the caste as a whole did not follow him. The strongest factor in the lack of cooperation is probably the caste division and the resultant rivalry within the Untouchable groups themselves. Chambhars had already achieved some degree of economic advancement with their leather work, Mangs were the most educationally and economically backward of the three groups, and neither Chambhars nor Mangs could see a Mahar leader as their salvation. Ambedkar seems to have attempted to win these castes over, frequently appearing at Chambhar or Mang meetings. He gave a detailed reply to criticism raised at a Chambhar conference in 1939 [50] and devoted space in *Janata* in 1941 to a long letter from a Mang accusing him of being only a Mahar leader,[51] but by this time the Mahar conversion announcement had further alienated other castes. Neither group was active to a large degree in the Independent Labour Party or its successor, the Scheduled Castes Federation. Nor was the attempt to make the Independent Labour Party a working class party successful. Caste Hindu labour was not ready for Untouchable leadership, nor could the identification of Congress with Independence be overcome.

During its short lifetime, from 1937 until 1939, when the Congress ministries resigned, the Independent Labour Party functioned with vigour but without much effect in the Congress-dominated Bombay legislature. Ambedkar protested the minimum salary proposed for ministers, which he felt was impractical idealism. I.L.P. members also protested the use of the word *Harijan,* which the Untouchables felt was patronising in a proposed Local Boards Act, the Wardha Scheme of Education, and increased powers of the city police in matters other than riots. The education of Scheduled Caste students, the problems of Scheduled Caste teachers, the lack of adequate water supplies for Untouchables, and the need to abolish the *watan* system were raised at various times. The Harijan Temple Entry Bill passed evidently without comment by I.L.P. members, although orthodox Hindus protested outside the Council House. In two matters the I.L.P. participated in extra-parliamentary ways to add strength to their parliamentary voice. There was a march of peasants in Bombay in 1938, to protest against *Khoti,* a land tenure system in Ratnagiri which Ambedkar had introduced a bill to abolish. Also in 1938, the I.L.P. joined the Communists in calling a one-day strike to protest against the Industrial Disputes Act, which Ambedkar declared ought to be called 'The Workers Civil Liberties Suspension Act'.[52] The Khoti Abolition Bill was not passed; the Industrial Disputes Act was.

With the conversion announcement in 1935, the establishment of a political party in 1936, and considerable success in the 1937 elections, the shift from attempting to gain status in matters of religion to organising for political activity was nearly complete. Ambedkar considered but rejected various possibilities of converting to a religion that offered political as well as social advantages — Sikhism or Islam. The announcement of intent to convert was followed by a twenty-year hiatus, culminating in conversion to Buddhism, a religion that offered release from Hindu concepts of caste and a high moral standard but had no political overtones. Lloyd and Susanne Rudolph's general statement that as the processes of democratic politics began to reach the mass electorate, the aims of caste associations changed, and "instead of demanding temple entry and prestigious caste names and histories in the census, the associations began to press for places in the new administrative and educational institutions and for political representation,"[53] can be applied to the Mahars. Their political movement overrode efforts to claim religious rights, failed in its attempts to represent class or labour, and took on much of the nature of a caste association functioning in the political arena.

A note by a Harijan Sevak Sangh research worker indicates the depth of the political awakening and some of its consequences on the local level:

> Harijan leaders, especially those belonging to Dr. Ambedkar's party, have become fully conscious of their civic rights and encourage their followers to assert them. But as this is done in a somewhat defiant manner and no attempt is made for persuading the caste-Hindus or to secure the co-operation of the Harijan Sevak Sangh, often there arise as a result severe conflicts, boycotts, and even belabouring of Harijans by Hindu villagers.[54]

The next step of the Scheduled Castes associated with Ambedkar was a move further in the direction of separation from caste Hindu society. In July of 1942, the All India Depressed Classes Conference was held at Nagpur. The meetings were attended, according to Dhananjay Keer, by 70,000 people,[55] with representatives from Bengal, Bombay, Punjab, the Central Provinces and Berar, the United Provinces and with N. Shivraj from Madras in the presidential chair, but Mahars undoubtedly predominated. The first resolution of this Conference condemned the proposals of His Majesty's Government regarding constitutional changes brought to India by Sir Stafford Cripps as a betrayal of the interests of the Scheduled Castes and a breach of the assurances given them that a constitution would not be imposed upon them without their consent. Further resolutions restated the demands that had been part of Scheduled Caste political activity in some form since the earliest days of the movement, sums for primary and advanced education for the Scheduled Castes, representation in the public services and all legislative bodies and separate electorates. The two final resolutions were of a new kind. "After long and mature deliberation," the conference came "to the conclusion that a radical change must be made in the village system, now prevalent in India and which is the parent of all the ills from which the Scheduled Castes are suffering for many centuries at the hands of the Hindus." The resolution continued to ask for a constitutional provision for transfer of Scheduled Castes to separate Scheduled Caste villages, "away from and independent of Hindu villages." The last resolution established a political party for the purpose of carrying on the political movement of the Scheduled Castes, to be called the Scheduled Castes Federation.[56]

It is difficult to say how much the separate village resolution reflected the mind of the village Mahar, and how much it indicated an attempt by Ambedkar[57] to establish the desperate seriousness of Scheduled Caste demands. It was made at a time when the Muslim League's demand for Pakistan was of great concern to both Congress and the British, and when the early Cripps proposals seemed to overlook the problems of the Scheduled Castes in their anxiety to heal the Hindu-Muslim rift and carry on with the war. The demand for separate villages was ignored by the British as was the demand for separate electorates, although at least in the case of the latter there was a long-standing and widespread opinion among the Scheduled Castes that separate electorates were necessary for them to be truly represented in the legislatures.

The 1945 elections for the Provincial Legislatures saw the newly established Scheduled Castes Federation utterly defeated. Ambedkar's official position as Labour Member in the Viceroy's Executive Council prevented him from taking an active part in party organisation which may have been a factor in the defeat. He himself produced official election figures for the Cabinet Mission which showed that in the primary elections, in which Scheduled Castes alone voted, the Scheduled Castes Federation had received more votes than the Congress in Madras, Bombay and the Central Provinces.[58] He also offered proof that, in each province, the majority of Scheduled Caste votes had gone to non-Congress candidates.[59] There had been some violence in Nagpur and Bombay at the time of the elections, and Ambedkar also charged terrorism and intimidation as well as open hostility on the part of returning and polling officials as reasons for the election failure.[60] But Sir Stafford Cripps felt that it was not possible, "even had we decided to do so, to arrange for Dr. Ambedkar's organisation to have any special right of election of the Constituent Assembly. It had failed in the elections and we could not artificially restore its position."[61]

Ambedkar resorted to extra-parliamentary action to press the demand for recognition, and the Scheduled Castes conducted large-scale satyagrahas for separate electorates before state legislatures at Poona, Nagpur, Lucknow and Kanpur in 1946. The satyagraha and demonstration methods of political activity had been sparingly used in the Mahar movement. The Mahar satyagraha for water; the full scale temple satyagrahas, one at Parvati in Poona without Ambedkar's aid and one at Nasik with his early approval and later disinterest; the peasant march against Khoti and the one-day strike protesting against the Industrial Disputes Bill are the chief examples, and Scheduled Castes together with caste Hindus participated in all of them. Petitions, attempts to secure favourable legislation and occasionally battles in the courts were preferred to satyagraha when the issue concerned British law and administration. The comparatively small numbers of the Scheduled Castes and their dependent position in the village made demonstrations vis-a-vis caste Hindus a dangerous and not very effective weapon. On the eve of Independence and after, the method of extra-parliamentary demonstration became more widely used, probably both because of the increasing political awareness of the Mahars and the change in the nature of the governmental adversary.

The 1946 satyagrahas were conducted solely by Scheduled Castes demonstrating for separate electorates and recognition of their demands by those planning for Indian independence. The failure of all other methods, including numerous memoranda to the concerned bodies for Scheduled Caste demands, a book by Ambedkar entitled *What Congress and Gandhi Have Done to the Untouchable*, which stressed the necessity for considering the Scheduled Castes as a separate element in Hindu society, and a trip to London by Ambedkar, evidently prompted the use of the demonstration method.The phenomenon of 'separatism' which marked the political movement under Ambedkar from 1939 until Independence was strong enough even before the formation of the Scheduled Castes Federation for M.R. Jayakar, Bombay political figure and judge, to write to his fellow-moderate, Tej Bahadur Sapru, in April, 1941: "The depressed classes, under Ambedkar's guidance, are becoming more conscious of their separateness and not of their unity with Hinduism and perhaps in a short time a cry will go up for Mahar-stan."[62] Undoubtedly separatism was stimulated by the demands of the Muslims for Pakistan. It may also have been a macrocosm of what has been noticed on the village scale when Scheduled Castes' attempts to gain status are defeated. F.G. Bailey writes of the Boad Outcastes of a village in Orissa, "They are moving out of the social structure of the village.... They cannot rise within the existing ritual and political structure of the village.... they are showing the first signs of becoming a separate village community."[63] But both on the village and national level, separatism requires an outside force to relate to, if any gains are to be made. For the Boad Outcastes, it was the Congress Government; for the Mahars, it was the British. With the advent of Independence, separatism as a political device lost its value.

VII

The situation changed for the Scheduled Castes with the coming of Independence. Replacing the British Raj was the Congress government, committed by its long association with Gandhi to the removal of untouchability. The triple prongs of a British government willing to engage in social reform when it did not endanger its position, an Indian elite which accepted the necessity of correcting ancient injustice, and a Scheduled Caste political movement which articulated specific needs had resulted in considerable legislation. The Congress Government continued to add legal prohibitions of Untouchability, ameliorative economic and educational benefits, and reservations in public bodies and governmental posts. Lelah Dushkin wrote in 1957, "Probably nowhere in the world is so large a lower-class minority granted so much favourable special treatment by the government as are the Depressed Classes of India today."[64] The actual function of the political party under Ambedkar's leadership from Independence until 1956 was to see that the special treatment provisions were properly used, that the discrimination and injustice still practised was brought to public attention, and that the seats reserved for Scheduled Castes in legislatures were filled by men under obligation to speak for Scheduled Caste interests, although its platform was far broader than this.

The early years of Independence found Ambedkar in a position from which he was able to operate constructively and cooperatively. He had won a seat in the Constituent Assembly from Bengal in 1946, and later, after partition, from Bombay. He was named Chairman of the drafting committee for the Constitution, which meant he was responsible for guiding it through the Assembly, and was included by Nehru as Law Minister in the first Cabinet, one that 'contained a strikingly careful selection of representatives of communities and regions—far more so than any later governments'.[65] And Ambedkar responded with words which indicated separatism was a thing of the past. In a public meeting at which he was presented a golden replica of the draft copy of the Indian Constitution by the Scheduled Castes Federation in Bombay, he told his audience to place the country above their community to avoid 'our independence being put into jeopardy.' The Scheduled Castes, he said, should forget the narrow outlook of the past and think of the wider interest as a whole; they should forget past differences with Congress and other political parties. Cooperation, although not federation with any other organisation, should be the goal.[66]

The era of cooperation ended in the fall of 1951, just before India's first general elections. Ambedkar resigned from the Cabinet primarily because of lack of Congress support for the Hindu Code Bill, for which he as Law Minister was responsible, but also because he felt he had little voice in the Cabinet, and because, he charged the old oppression of the Scheduled Castes still existed. Nehru's foreign policy had cost India its friends, and the official position on Kashmir caused an unnecessary impasse, he stated. Ambedkar participated in the 1952 elections not as a friend of the administration, but as a bitter opponent.

The Scheduled Castes Federation entered the elections as one of only a few parties with previous election experience. In its platform, the Federation pledged that it would insist on reservations subject to minimum qualifications, so long as the Backward Classes, Scheduled Castes and Scheduled Tribes 'are not able to find their place in the Civil and Military services of the country.' Otherwise, the party's statements dealt with larger issues. Expansion of production, birth control, cooperative or collective farming, the need to partition Kashmir, the abandonment of neutralist foreign policies in favour of cooperation with the parliamentary democracies, the abolition of prohibition, the nationalisation of insurance, the formation of linguistic provinces — all were approved by the party.[67]

In the elections of 1951-52, the Scheduled Castes Federation lost badly. In Bombay state, four candidates contested seats for the Lok Sabha; only one P.N. Rajbhoj, standing from Sholapur, was successful. Ambedkar was defeated by his long-time Chambhar opponent, N.S. Kajrolkar, in the Bombay (North) constituency.[68] The Federation had put up thirty-eight candidates for the Bombay Legislative Assembly, its ambition going beyond the twenty-seven seats reserved for Scheduled Castes. With the exception of B.C.Kamble, standing from the Chinchpokli-Lower Parel-Love Grove constituency in Bombay, all lost.

Before the election, "at one stage there was an attempt to invite Dr. Ambedkar to stand on the Congress ticket. According to S.K. Patil, the Congress had kept a seat vacant for Dr. Ambedkar until the last moment, till it came to be known that his party entered into an electoral alliance with the Socialist Party."[69] The Congress had not read Ambedkar rightly. Even in the halcyon days of the Constituent Assembly and the first Cabinet, Ambedkar had advised the Scheduled Castes Federation to preserve its independence, and his resignation from the Cabinet was not likely to change that position.

The alliance with the Socialist Party, which was the logical group for the Scheduled Castes Federation with its socialistic platform to cooperate with, was not a happy experience for either group. In a study of the elections, Venkatarangaiya reports that some Socialists felt the alliance with the Scheduled Castes Federation had been injurious. Middle class resentment was increased because of the alliance of the Federation with the Peasants and Workers Party in some parts of the state and also because of alleged attacks by Federational leaders on Gandhi.[70] In another report, Venkatarangaiya adds that Ambedkar's proposal to include Bombay in Maharashtra cost him and the Socialists the Gujarati vote.[71] Ambedkar himself said he was 'at a loss to understand the defeat'.[72] The fact that the proportion of votes per candidate was higher for the Federation than for any other party but Congress, that the Scheduled Castes Federation had tripled its 1946 vote, which Congress did not quite do, and broadened its area of influence, winning twelve seats in the Legislative Assemblies of six states (Hyderabad, Madras, Pepsu, Bombay, Himachal Pradesh), did not relieve the general gloom. Hugh Tinker writes, "The most disappointed candidates were those of the Scheduled Castes Federation ... The great majority of these 'reserved' seats went to the nominees of the Congress: non-entities for the most part, but returned by the magic name of Nehru."[73]

In 1954, Ambedkar and his 1952 running partner, Ashoka Mehta, contested the bye-election in Bhandara, a district near Nagpur. Mehta, running on the Socialist Party ticket for the general seat,won; Ambedkar, as a Scheduled Castes Federation candidate for the reserved seat, lost. The factors in the loss of the Bhandara bye-election seem to be the failure of those voting for Mehta to also support Ambedkar; the alienation of caste Hindus by Ambedkar's bitter denunciation of Nehru, the Congress, and Gandhian policies, the thorough coverage of the area by a high-powered group of Congress leaders; and possibly the deflection of Mahanubhav Mahar votes as a result of the earlier leadership of G.M. Thaware, a Mahar leader who had broken with Ambedkar and joined Congress before his death in 1952.

The chief reason, however, for the Scheduled Castes Federation's defeat was that they had nowhere to go with their political power. The Federation constituency was limited to a minority by the factors of caste. In the 1937 election, the reserved seats in Bombay had evidently been left to the Scheduled Castes at the time of voting; votes recorded for these seats were in most cases considerably fewer than votes recorded for general seats. In the following elections, this factor does not seem to have held. With the coming of Independence and the partition, separate electorates became a psychological impossibility both for Muslims and Scheduled Castes, and the occupant of the reserved seat was to be determined by the general vote. Ambedkar evidently realised the necessity of both winning the reserved seats and using the votes from that limited number of seats in a larger alliance. In 1948 he told an Uttar Pradesh Scheduled Caste conference, according to a newspaper report, that political power was the key to all social progress and that the Scheduled Castes could achieve salvation if they captured this power by organising themselves into a third party and holding the balance of power between Congress and Socialists.[74] The 1952 election alliance with the Socialist Party was evidently an attempt to use this strategy, but the overwhelming victory of Congress made it clear that there were no two fairly equal political groupings and hence no balance of power to be held.

VIII

In 1956 Ambedkar made an attempt to transform the Scheduled Castes Federation into a party which would speak for all the 'dispossessed', the Scheduled Castes, Scheduled Tribes and Backward Classes. The move to create the Republican Party came at about the same time as the conversion to Buddhism in Nagpur on October 14-15, 1956. Both were efforts to take the Scheduled Castes out of untouchability and into a larger group, one religious and the other political.[75] Both trace back in origin to decisions made twenty years earlier when the Mahar Conference in 1936 in Bombay opted out of Hinduism and the Independent Labour Party was founded. And inspite of Dr. Ambedkar's intentions, both movements have been largely confined to the Mahars and other groups which had been involved in political activities under his leadership. Dr. Ambedkar died on December 6, 1956, two months after setting the conversion movement and the idea of a new political party in action, and without making plans for the development of either.

The Republican Party was not formally organised until October, 1957, and the elections earlier in the year were fought by the Scheduled Castes Federation under its old name and with its old personnel. The factor which entered into the election was not the Buddhist conversion, but the battle-cry for a linguistic state of Maharashtra. The Scheduled Castes Federation campaigned in the elections under the banner of the Samyukta Maharashtra Samiti (United Maharashtra Committee).[76] In the spirit of unity engendered by linguistic state feeling, plus the careful allotment of tickets, the Federation won nineteen places in the state Legislative Asembly (counting those won in later bye-elections), and six in the Lok Sabha. The lesson learned by the party in the election was that no harm seemed to come from cooperating with other parties, even the Communists hitherto avoided because they did not come in Ambedkar's category of groups committed to parliamentary democracy, and that a state-wide issue helped the constituents to forget caste.

The next elections reinforced the need of the party both for issues that identified them with the larger electorate and for control of the number of candidates in each constituency. Without either, the party lost the 1962 elections to Congress, winning only three seats in the Maharashtra Legislative Assembly and none in the Lok Sabha from that state.[77]

The figures on winning candidates from the Republican Party in the 1962 elections conceal the Party's strength in Maharashtra. In actual number of votes, the party is second to Congress with 11.66 percent of the total, twice as much as the nearest opposition party.[78] At the local level, the Republican Party has a strong voice in a number of Maharashtrian urban centres, particularly in Vidarbha and in the railroad towns. In Zilla Parishad elections the Party gained at least one seat in twelve of twenty-five districts, a better record than the Communist Party or the Jan Sangh. In Amravati District, the Republican Party ran a number of caste Hindu candidates and won, defeating the Congress by twenty-three to twenty-one seats.[79] But even the victories make it clear that only when the solid Mahar strength behind the Republican Party can be combined with a larger issue or with other groups in election alliances can the party show that strength in the polling results.

In addition to the problem of alliances, the Republican Party faces the difficulty of splits in the party leadership. A group led by B.C. Kamble, a Bombay lawyer, and some other generally young and well educated men pulled away from the party dominated by B.K. Gaikwad, Ambedkar's long-time associate, in 1959 and contested the 1961-62 elections separately, adding to the disastrous results for the party as a whole. In Bombay city itself, the Kamble group put up 21 candidates for the municipal elections, the R.D. Bhandare group ran twenty candidates. A chart showing seats contested and won by the Scheduled Castes Federation over a period of four municipal elections suggests the effect of the split:[80]

1948		1952		1957		1961	
Seats contested	Won	Seats contested	Won	Seats contested	Won	Seats contested	Won
9	7	11	5	14	12	41	6

While the Kamble split now seems confined to Bombay city, a new rift has come with Bhandare's expulsion from the party. The factionalism that was kept more or less in order during Ambedkar's lifetime has now come to visible ruptures, and the ensuing competition for leadership may cut into the Mahar political unity severely. Still another problem affecting the political leadership is that most educated Mahars and Buddhists enter government service, one of the few ways up economically that are open to Scheduled Castes, which effectively places them beyond political activity.

Faced with inconsequential representation in the legislatures, the party seems to be turning more to extra-parliamentary methods, as perhaps are other opposition parties also, to press its demands. Two massive land satyagrahas have been held, one in 1954 in the Marathwada area of Maharashtra, the second in 1959 around Nasik, Jalgaon, Dhulia and Ahmednagar, evidently with some result in the distribution of wasteland to the landless. Silent marches in a number of cities in 1964 called attention to the harassment of Buddhists in a Maharashtrian village, where a personal quarrel had erupted on a caste basis, ending in public insult to Buddhist women. A large but scarcely publicised satyagraha was held in Uttar Pradesh and Maharashtra and a few areas in other states in December 1965 and January 1966 in which the party claims 300,000 satyagrahis participated. A conference between B.K Gaikwad, Barrister B.D. Khobragade and B.P. Maurya, leaders of the Republican Party, and Congress leaders, including the Prime Minister, ended the satyagraha, which had filled Maharashtrian jails. The Charter of Demands for which the demonstration took place details the present aims of the Republican Party: (1) a portrait of Dr. Ambedkar as 'Father of the Indian Constitution' in the central hall of Parliament,[81] (2) the nation's land given to the tiller, (3) idle and waste land given to landless labour, (4) adequate distribution of grain and control over rising prices, (5) improvement of the situation of slum dwellers, (6) full implementation of the Minimum Wages Act of 1948, (7) extension of Scheduled Caste privileges to the Scheduled Caste members who have embraced Buddhism,[82] (8) the ceasing of harassment of the Depressed Classes, (9) full justice under the Untouchability Offences Act, (10) reservation in services for Scheduled Castes and Scheduled Tribes completed by 1970.[83]

Since that large satyagraha, two smaller demonstrations have been organised. A *morcha* (protest procession) of 5,000 men and women marched to the Council House in Bombay on July 13, 1965, 'to protest against the single member constituency on behalf of the Republican

Party'.[84] Also in July, Republican Party members joined other opposition parties in an 'anti-starvation' protest, chiefly in Satara and Kolhapur,[85] calling off the agitation only when the Kashmir troubles erupted.

In the 1967 elections, the Republican Party again faced the problem of alliances. The Buddhist conversion lessened the number of Scheduled Caste voters, and hence the number of reserved seats in Maharashtra. The Republican Party repudiated the concept of reserved seats, however, as had the Scheduled Castes Federation in 1955, a pragmatic decision based on the inability of a minority group to determine the outcome of the vote. A way out of the dilemma is an agreement on the distribution of tickets at the top level. This fact, plus the liberal record of Congress under the leadership of Yeshwantrao Chavan in Maharashtra, seems to have led to an attempt at an entente with Congress in that state. A press interview with Republican Party President B.K. Gaikwad in the summer of 1966 indicated that the Republican Party might cooperate with the Congress in Maharashtra, trading its support for a suggested fifty Assembly and fifteen Lok Sabha seats, a number far above those previously reserved for the Scheduled Castes. The alliance would be minimal, and the Republican Party candidates would contest seats under their own banner: "The Republican Party would prefer annihilation to contesting the elections on the Congress ticket."[86] Whether Congress will agree to an alliance so favourable to the Republicans; whether Mahars and Buddhists will vote according to plan, forgetting the twenty years of belief that Congress is the arch enemy; whether Republicans yoked to Congress can retain independence in the legislatures — these are questions to be answered in time.

NOTES

1. The political movement which the Mahars have dominated has never been confined exclusively to their caste and since 1942 has included non-Marathi speaking groups. Since 1956, a majority of the Mahars have converted to Buddhism and no longer use the caste name. Nevertheless, in the interests of a workable title, and to bring into relief the substance of the movement we are about to consider, I have used the present title.

2. Scheduled Caste census figures are from *Census of India* 1961, Volume X, Maharashtra, Part V-A by B.A Kulkarni (Delhi: Government of India, 1964), p.29. Buddhist figures are from the same volume, p.31.

    The term, Scheduled Caste, came into use with the Government of India Act of 1935. Previous to that the terms Untouchable and Depressed Class were generally used. Mahatma Gandhi's term *Harijan* which gained currency about 1933 is unacceptable to the Mahars.

3. Alexander Robertson, *The Mahar Folk* (Calcutta: Y.M.C.A. Publishing House and Oxford University Press, 1938), p.1.

4. Irawati Karve, *Paripurti* (Fulfilment) (Poona: R.J. Deshmukh, 1951), p.81; *Marathi*. This and other translations have been made with the help at various times, of Rekha Damle, M.D. Panchbhai, Lalita Khambadkone, D.R. Maheshkar, S.D. Gaikwad, and Pramod Kale, but I am to be charged for any inaccuracies in the final version.

5. Dr. Ambedkar, asked during the question period after his report to the Simon Commission, "Are you pre-Aryan?" said, "Well, I do not know. That is a view." *Indian Statutory Commission*, Vol. XVI (London: His Majesty's Stationery Office, 1930), p. 54.

    In his book, *Who Were the Shudras?* (Bombay: Thacker & Co., 1946), Ambedkar claimed the Shudras of Indo-Aryan society were Kshatriyas, but that the Shudras of today are unrelated to the ancient Shudras. In the *Untouchables* (New Delhi: Amrit Book Co., 1948), he denied a racial origin for Untouchability and proposed the theory that the Untouchables were 'Broken Men' who, in contrast to 'Settled Tribesmen' did not give up Buddhism when Brahminism triumphed in India. Both books are too complex to serve as polemics for the masses.

6. A.S. Altekar, *History of Village Communities in Western India* (Madras: Oxford University Press, 1927), p. 43.

7. R.D. Choksey, *Economic History of the Bombay, Deccan and Karnatak — 1818-68* (Poona: R.D. Choksey, 1945), pp. 66-7.

8. C.B. Agarwal, *The Harijans in Rebellion* (Bombay: Taraporevala and Sons, 1934), p. 67.

9. The British seem to have employed large numbers of Mahars in their ammunition factories, and the towns in which these factories are situated today seem to have a disproportionately large number of Mahar residents. Harold Mann's *Land and Labour in a Deccan Village* (Bombay: Oxford University Press, 1917), offers some witnesses to this and also suggests that village Mahars within cycling distance of some plant were

factory employees. In the village he studied were ten Mahar *watandar* families, too many for the necessary *watan* duties. Of the 30 Mahar men in the village, 24 were employed at the Kirkee ammunition factory.

10. One of the few available dates for the beginning of Mahar urbanisation is found in Morris David Morris' *The Emergence of an Industrial Labour Force in India* (Berkeley and Los Angeles: University of California Press, 1965), p. 73n: "One would probably be safe to suggest as a first approximation from the census data that before 1864 untouchables were much less likely to move to Bombay than other groups and that afterwards they tended to move in at a slightly more rapid rate than all other groups combined, at least until 1921."

11. The 1961 census indicates that 13.81 per cent of Mahars and 20.8 per cent of Buddhists in contrast to 28.22 per cent of Maharashtra's general population is urban. Mahar and general percentages from *Census of India* 1961,Vol. X, Maharashtra, Part V-A, pp. 32-3. Buddhist percentage taken from figures in *Census of India* Paper No.1 of 1963, 1961 Census — Religion (Delhi: Government of India, 1963), p.24.

12. In a paper entitled 'Social Condition of the Mahar in Poona and Vicinity,' read at the Association for Asian Studies, New York, April 1966, Robert J. Miller said, "I ... emphasize the readiness of the Mahar ultimately to follow leaders who attacked the system *as a whole* .... The most renowned leader of them B.R. Ambedkar proposed a breaking of the link with the system at its only point of strong connection with the village Mahars — abolition of the status of hereditary servant."

13. Sir Patrick Cadell, *History of the Bombay Army* (London: Longmans, Green and Co., 1938), pp. 154-55.

14. B.R. Ambedkar, *What Congress and Gandhi Have Done to the Untouchables* 2nd edn. (Bombay: Thacker and Co. Ltd., 1946), p. 189.

15. Viththal Ramji Shinde, *Majhya Athvani va Anubhav* (My Memories and Experiences), (Poona: R.B. Andre, Shri Lekhan Wacan Bhandar, 1958), p. 214; *Marathi.*

16. A handwritten copy of the petition is in the C.B. Khairmode collection of materials on Ambedkar and the Mahars now in the Library of the University of Bombay.

17. The memorandum and the reply are reproduced in English in the Marathi biography of *Shivram Janba Kamble* by H.N. Navalkar (Poona: S.J. Kamble, 1930), pp. 157-64, 166-68.

18. A military history of the Mahars may be found in *The Regimental History of the Mahar MG* (Machine Gun) *Regiment* by Major General S.P.O. Thorat (Dehra Dun: The Army Press, 1954). Photographs show a replica of the Koregaon pillar and the word 'Koregaon' on the cap badge of the Mahar Regiment from 1942 until Independence.

19. The Somwanshi sub-caste of Mahars may have made some effort to identify themselves with the Rajputs, and G.M. Thaware, a Nagpur Mahar leader, made the claim, "The Scheduled Castes formerly belonged to a class of Warriors and from the Indian History these classes and specially the Mahar Community rose to a high position in Shivaji's Raj" in a letter

to Gandhi. *Gandhiji's Letters Re: Untouchables* by G.M. Thaware (Nagpur: L.P. Meshram and M.G. Dongre, ca. 1941), p. 52. Nevertheless the emphasis on Kshatriya status has been a minor part of the Mahar movement. For contrast, see the history of the Jatava caste of Chamars in Agra in Owen M. Lynch's 'The Politics of Untouchability', a paper read at the Conference on Social Structure and Social Change in India, June 3-5, 1965.

20. For a historical and contemporary account of the Bhakti religion centred at Pandharpur, see G.A. Deleurey, S.J. *The Cult of Vithoba* (Poona: Deccan College, 1960).

21. See Bernard S. Cohn, 'The Changing Status of a Depressed Caste,' in *Village India,* McKim Marriott, ed., 4th impression, (Chicago: University of Chicago Press, 1960), pp. 53-77. Ravidas is also honoured by the Chambhars of Maharashtra.

22. A copy of the resolutions of the Chokhamela Sudharak Mandal in Marathi is in the possession of V.W. Moon of Nagpur.

23. From the minutes of the Loyal Mahar Sabha, in English, in the possession of V.W. Moon of Nagpur. A separate ghat was also built for Mahars at Nasik on the Godavari River, but I have no information on its date.

24. Kisan Faguji Bansode, *Pradip,* edited by Shamrao Bansode, (Nagpur: Jagruit Prakashan, ca. 1958), p. 48, *Marathi.* Choka is an abbreviation of the name of the Mahar poet-saint Chokhamela.

25. Letter to B.K. Gaikwad, March 3, 1934.

26. (*Franchise*) *Evidence Taken Before the Reforms Committee,* Vol. I (Calcutta: Government of India, 1919), pp. 723-25.

27. The support of Ambedkar's education was one of many gestures toward reform made by Maharaja Sayajirao, Gaekwad of Baroda, who had encouraged the education of Untouchables in his own state. In return for the financial aid, Ambedkar was to give ten years service in Baroda State. He actually gave only a few months service at two different times, claiming that the treatment he received in the Baroda offices and the lack of suitable housing available for an Untouchable made it impossible to stay.

28. Shahu Maharaj of Kolhapur was an important figure in the non-Brahmin movement. He established a hostel for Untouchables in Kolhapur around 1908 and was in close contact with Ambedkar until his death in 1922.

29. *The Reform Committee,* Vol. II; pp. 729-39.

30. One conference was held under caste Hindu leadership to rally Untouchable support for the Congress-League scheme; the conference in turn asked for a Congress resolution for the removal of the disabilities of the Depressed Classes. The second conference was held later in 1917 under non-Brahmin Party leadership to counteract the pledged support of the first conference to the Congress-League scheme. A third conference was held in 1918 under the leadership of Subedar Ganpatrao Govind Rokde, probably a Mahar, demanding separate electorates. A fourth conference was held by V.R. Shinde's Depressed Classes Mission and produced an All-India Anti-Untouchability Manifesto.

31. Dhananjay Keer, *Dr. Ambedkar, Life and Mission,* 2nd ed. (Bombay: Popular Prakashan, 1962), p. 43.

32. Cangdev Bhavanrav Khairmode, *Dr. Bhimrav Ramji Ambedkar,* Vol. I (Bombay: Yeshvant Bhimrao Ambedkar, 1952), p. 267; *Marathi.*

33. The C.K.P.s are among the 'advanced castes' of Maharashtra. In Ambedkar's circle of caste Hindu supporters and friends, the majority were from this community. A possible reason is that they were, in certain situations, in competition with the Brahmins.

34. Dhananjay Keer, pp. 70-71, 104-105.

35. *Times of India,* Bombay; March 21, 1940.

36. Jotiba Govindrao Phule, 1827-90, began the Satyashodhak Samaj (Truth-seeking Society) in 1873. Its objects were "to redeem the Shudras and Atishudras (Untouchables) from the influence of Brahminical Scriptures ... to teach them their human rights, and to liberate them from mental and religious slavery." Dhananjay Keer, *Mahatma Jotirao Phooley — Father of Our Social Revolution* (Bombay: Popular Prakashan, 1964), p. 126. Phule belonged to the Mali caste, an agricultural community ranked with the Marathas. He was the first Hindu to conduct schools for the Untouchables. Ambedkar considered him one of his three *gurus,* along with Buddha and Kabir, and Phule's picture is often found in Mahar Institutions.

37. *Indian Statutory Commission,* Vol. XVI, pp. 27-37. Dr. Ambedkar was also a member of the Provincial Committee in Bombay. His report in that capacity appears in Vol. III of the Indian Statutory Commission. The Bahishkrit Hitakarini Sabha was an organisation founded by Ambedkar in 1924 to work for the social and economic betterment of the Depressed Classes.

38. Petition to the Indian Statutory Commission from the Central Provinces Depressed Classes Association, Nagpur, February 24, 1929, privately printed.

39. B.R. Ambedkar, *What Congress and Gandhi...,* pp. 40-41. Srinivasan was a member of the Depressed Classes from Madras who seems to have faded out of the political picture after the Round Table Conferences.

40. Subhas Chandra Bose, *The Indian Struggle,* part II — Netaji's Life and Writings, 1920-34 (Calcutta: Thacker, Spink and Co., 1948), p. 40.

41. 'All India Depressed Classes Conference', *The Indian Annual Register,* Nripendra Nath Mitra, editor, 1930, Vol. II, (Calcutta: Annual Register Office), pp. 367-74.

42. C.B. Khairmode, *Dr. Bhimrav Ramji Ambedkar,* Vol. II; pp. 117-18.

43. *Janata,* Bombay; January 9, 1932.

44. *Free Press Journal,* Bombay; October 11, 1931.

45. Dhananjay Keer, *Dr. Ambedkar...,* pp. 191-93.

46. B.R. Ambedkar, *What Congress and Gandhi...,* pp. 134-40.

47. John Coatman, in a speech before the East India Association, published in *Asiatic Review* Vol. XXIX, No. 97, London, January 1933, pp. 46-7.

48. M.C. Rajah and Dr. Ambedkar joined forces only in 1942, when they

protested together against the lack of provision for separate electorates for Scheduled Castes in the Cripps Proposals. *Times of India*, Bombay, April 1, 1942.

49. *Times of India*, Bombay, August 15, 1936.

50. *Bombay Chronicle*, July 4, 1939. The Chambhar criticism is not available. Ambedkar replied that "he had no ambition for the Mahars, in fact would do everything in his power to liquidate it as a community though he would want them to progress as human beings." He accused Congress of playing a political game, giving as an example: "Although it was the Mahars who fought for right of entrance in the Police Training School at Nasik it was all non-Mahars who were admitted."

51. *Janata*, Bombay, June 14, 1941; *Marathi*. The letter from 'the first educated Mang in the Nizam's state', D.N. Kamble, makes the following requests: (1) Mahars must consider Mangs as equals, (2) promising Mang young men should have a chance to go forward, (3) Mahars must not obstruct Mang processions, (4) Mahars must not take *watandari* rights from Mangs, (5) Ambedkar must give as much concern to the improvement of Mangs as to Mahars. Ambedkar replied that he had successfully encouraged inter-caste dining, that the Mahar hostels were open to all, that the Independent Labour Party considered quality, not caste, and warned the Mangs against taking the way of Congress.

52. Ambedkar's lengthy testimony is in the *Bombay Legislative Assembly Debates*, Vol. IV, Part I, pp. 1330-59.

53. Lloyd and Susanne H. Rudolph, 'The Political Role of India's Caste Associations', *Pacific Affairs*, XXXIII, No. 1, University of British Columbia, Vancouver, March 1960, p. 7.

54. Vamanrao A. Bhatt, *The Harijans of Maharashtra* (Delhi: All India Harijan Sevak Sangh, 1941), pp. 16-17.

55. Dhananjay Keer, *Dr. Ambedkar . . .* , p. 348.

56. *Report of Depressed Class Conference* (Nagpur; G.T. Meshram, 1942).

57. As early as 1926, Ambedkar had suggested at a meeting in Jejuri that Untouchables seek land for colonisation. Keer, p. 63: "In 1929 at a conference in Ratnagiri District at Chiplun, Ambedkar said he would try to secure land for cultivation in Sind and in Indore State for Untouchables." Keer, p. 127. A recommendation of the Starte Committee, of which Ambedkar was a member, stated: "We also consider it possible that some of the Depressed Classes would take up land in Sind if a suitable scheme could be worked out by the Barrage Revenue authorities in consultation with the Backward Classes offer." *Report of the Depressed Classes and Aboriginal Tribes Committee*, Bombay Presidency (Bombay: Governmental Central Press, 1930), p. 42.

58. A copy of his chart is in C.B. Khairmode's collection of Ambedkar materials in the Bombay University Library.

59. B.R. Ambedkar, *What Congress and Gandhi . . .* , pp. 378-86. The charts are not entirely convincing.

60. B.R. Ambedkar, *The Cabinet Mission and the Untouchables* (Bombay: privately printed, no date).

61. Anil Chandra Banerjee and Dakshina Ranjan Bose, *The Cabinet Mission in India* (Calcutta: A. Mukherjee, 1946), p. 108.

62. Jayakar to Sapru, April 7, 1941, Letter J 65 in the Sapru Collection, National Library, Calcutta.

63. F. G. Bailey, *Caste and the Economic Frontier* (Manchester: Manchester University Press, 1957), pp. 224-26.

64. Lelah Dushkin, *The Policy of the Indian National Congress Toward the Depressed Classes — An Historical Study*, (unpublished M.A. thesis, University of Pennsylvania, 1957). Miss Dushkin has also discussed Scheduled Caste policy in a series of three articles in *The Economic Weekly*, Bombay, October 28, November 4 and 18, 1961.

65. W. H. Morris-Jones, *The Government and Politics of India* (London: Hutchinson University Library, 1964), p. 87.

66. *Times of India*, Bombay, January 12, 1950.

67. *Asian Guide to the First Elections* (Bombay: Asia Publishing House, 1951), pp. 191-93.

68. It is probable that Ambedkar was defeated by caste Hindu votes. The Scheduled Castes Federation with 16.92 per cent of the electorate in the Bombay North constituency got 17.27 per cent of the valid votes. M. Venkatarangaiya, *The General Election in the City of Bombay* (Bombay: Vora and Co., 1953), p. 146.

69. *Ibid.*, p. 40.

70. M. Venkatarangaiya, 'Bombay City', In *Reports on the Indian General Elections*, 1951-1952, by S.K. Kogekar and Richard L. Park (Bombay: Popular Book Depot, 1956), pp. 66-7.

71. M. Venkatarangaiya, *The General Election . . .* , p. 146.

72. M. Venkatarangaiya, in Kogekar and Park, p. 65.

73. Hugh Tinker, *India and Pakistan — A Political Analysis* (New York: Frederick A. Praeger, 1962), p.55.

74. A.P.I. news release, April 27, 1948.

75. For a fuller discussion, see 'Buddhism and Politics in Maharashtra' by Eleanor Zelliot, in *Religion and Politics in South Asia*, Donald Eugene Smith, ed. (Princeton: Princeton University Press, 1966).

76. Ambedkar had reluctantly given the party permission to align with the Samyukta Maharashtra Samiti in the fall of 1956. He had been an earlier supporter of the idea, publishing a defense of *Maharashtra as a Linguistic Province* (Bombay: Thacker and Co.), in 1948. Later he feared the possible 'nationalism' of large, linguistic states, and the rule of the numerically dominant caste (in Maharashtra, Marathas, not Brahmins), and recommended that Maharashtra be divided into four states. *Thoughts on Linguistic States*, privately printed, 1955.

77. The number was later reduced to two. D.P. Meshram was declared unqualified, as a Buddhist, to hold a reserved seat after a legal battle that reached the Supreme Court. The Republican Party in Uttar Pradesh, allied with the Muslims in some areas in 1962, had more success, winning three Lok Sabha and nine Legislative Assembly seats in that election.

78. *Report on the 3rd General Elections in India*, Vol. II, Statistical (New Delhi: Indian Election Commission, n.d.), pp. 12-13.

79. A discussion of the Zilla Parishad elections in Maharashtra is available in Barbara J. Ravenell's *The Scheduled Castes and Panchayati Raj*, (unpublished M.A. thesis, University of Chicago, 1965;) pp. 102-104. The Amravati figures are from the *Times of India*, Bombay, June 6, 1962.

80. B.A.V. Sharma and R.T. Jangam, *The Bombay Municipal Corporation-An Election Study* (Bombay: Popular Book Depot, 1962), p. 54.

81. This demand indicates the need of Untouchables for recognition of their place in Indian history, represented by the contributions of Dr. Ambedkar. Allied to it are attempts to enhance the prestige of Buddhism, such as the proposal of Maharashtrian Republicans that the Buddha's birth-date be a public holiday. *Maharashtra Legislative Assembly Debates*, Vol. I, No. 30, August 18, 1960.

82. In Maharashtra, "The State Government has from 1st May 1960 extended all concessions and facilities available to Scheduled Castes also to the Scheduled Caste converts to Buddhism except the statutory concessions under the Constitution and certain special schemes for the removal of untouchability, etc. which cannot by their very nature apply to non-Hindus." Government Resolution, Education and Social Welfare Department, SCW 2260, 6 July 1960. *Census of India* 1961, Vol. X, Part IV-A, p. 31. In other states and in matters pertaining to the Central Government, converts to Buddhism lose their privileges.

83. *The Charter of Demands* (New Delhi, Dada Sahib B.K. Gaikwad, B.P. Maurya and B.D. Khobragade for the Republican Party of India), 1964:

84. *Dainik Maratha*, Bombay, July 13, 1965; *Marathi*.

85. *Maharashtra Times*, Bombay, August 21, 22, 1965; *Marathi*.

86. *Maharashtra Times*, Bombay, May 28, 1966; *Marathi*.

CHAPTER THREE

Federating for Political Interests: The Kshatriyas of Gujarat*

RAJNI KOTHARI AND RUSHIKESH MARU

The impact of modernisation processes on indigenous social structures has been a subject of much recent discussion on the new nations. The crucial question in this respect relates to the extent to which violent upheavals can be avoided in the processes of adjusting time-honoured institutions to the exigencies of modern times. In so far as such an adjustment is to take a permanent and legitimised form, it would depend upon two things. It would depend upon the ability of the indigenous system to absorb new changes and adapt its own structures and values accordingly. It would also depend upon the ability of the new institutions and leadership to take into confidence the inherited authority structures and media of communication and identification. Evidence suggests that such a process of mutual exposure and functional interaction will succeed better in a country where neither existing pluralities nor newly emerging differentiations are suppressed for the exclusive preservation of either the traditional or the modern sectors of society. It follows that where this happens what emerges out of this interaction is neither mainly traditional nor mainly modern.

A study of the interactions between the caste system and political democracy in India rejects the familiar dichotomy between a traditional society and a modern polity. On the contrary, it underlines the functional relevance of indigenous patterns of communication and

* An earlier and shorter version of this paper was published as 'Caste and Secularism in India: Case Study of a Caste Federation', in *The Journal of Asian Studies*, Volume XXV, No. 1, November, 1965.

differentiation in modernising a new nation. Much, of course, depends on the developmental potentiality of a particular social system. Where a relatively open society, by an act of conscious preference, resolves to undertake the task of building a modern nation through a democratic polity, the result is a purposive fusion of various elements. In India, under the impacts of western education, the nationalist movement, and adult franchise, the traditional community structure has undergone continuous change and adaptation. What is important is the mutual exposure and adaptation of traditional and modern authority structures, communication media, and identification symbols. The new institutions have established their hegemony precisely by taking into confidence the pluralities of the antecedent culture. Caste has been politicised but in the process it has provided to Indian politics processes and symbols of political articulation.

The process of articulation has taken one of may forms. (1) In places where a large and homogeneous 'dominant caste' prevails, rival factions within the dominant caste led by individual leaders tend to draw their additional political support from adjacent and non-adjacent caste groups. This makes for competing alignments in which personal networks of influence and power both run along and cut across caste networks, thus giving rise to cross-cutting loyalties within the broad framework of a dominant caste.[1] (2) In a multi-caste situation made up of three or four castes, each fairly large but none in a position to acquire a place of dominance, the alignments take the form of coalitions of castes and sub-castes struggling for power. There are many variations of both these types. In all cases other solidarities besides caste enter in the process. And in all cases it is the secular potential of caste that is brought out by its adopting an associational form of organisation and then functioning in an interactional framework. Reinforcing as well as cutting across changes in the status system brought about by other factors both internal to the system (such as emulation of 'sanskritised' practices) and external to the system (such as land legislation), is this changing orientation of caste organisation for participating in the secular political process.

A clear instance of the secular orientation of caste organisation is provided by the political articulation of the 'lower castes' in India. These are found to federate together into a common organisation and then press for their demands. Instances of such an upsurge are to be found all over the country. In what follows we provide an illustrative case study of such a movement in the State of Gujarat. It is a movement that has gained in importance over the years in the mobilisation of mass political support in the State. The study shows how once a caste organisation (in this case a caste federation) acquires a position of strength through numerical power and organisational cohesion, it can not only devise strategies with reference to political parties, but also feel confident enough to bargain with a more powerful caste group which has been its age-old rival and of which it had for a long time felt apprehensive. It also shows how such a process of secularisation brings about great shifts in the structure, policy priorities and leadership to the several castes and, in consequence, allows both the caste system and the political system to gain in sophistication and adaptability. The study is based on published and unpublished records and on interviews, and has been brought up to the third general elections in 1962.

The concept of caste federation refers to a grouping together of a number of distinct endogamous groups into a single organisation for common objectives, the realisation of which calls for a pooling together of resources or numbers, or both. By and large, the objectives pursued are secular and associational, although the employment of traditional symbols for evoking a sense of solidarity and loyalty towards the new form is not uncommon. The traditional distinctions between the federating groups are on the whole retained, but the search for a new organisational identity and the pursuit of political objectives gradually lead to a shift in group orientations. A caste federation is, therefore, to be distinguished from a caste association both because of the range of social reality that it covers, and because of its search for an inclusive rather than a 'functional' identity. The former often takes a class or *varna* form and cuts across the ascriptive identity of caste in its *jati* form.[2] The caste federation is thus no mere agency of an endogamous group or groups set up for undertaking a specific task. Rather, it represents a new notion of caste organisation, is based on real or supposed sharing of interests and status attributes, and gives rise to its own symbolism.

Gujarat Kshatriya Sabha is a caste federation, representing many castes and lineage groups, most of them drawn from the economically depressed communities of cultivators. The Sabha is largely responsible for spreading the 'Kshatriya' label, and the consciousness that goes with it, to many caste groups ranging all the way from Rajputs who are highest in the Kshatriya hierarchy, to Bhils who are semi-tribal, with Bariyas (a Koli caste) middle of the way. Socially, there is great distance among the various caste and lineage groups in the Kshatriya hierarchy, although Rajput hypergamy does permit the daughters of Bariya chiefs to be married into some Rajput families. Economically, barring the well-placed Rajput nobles, most of these castes are poor and landless, some of the Rajput families as destitute as the Bariyas, if not worse. It is common economic interest and a growing secular identity born partly out of folk-lore but more out of common resentment against the well-to-do castes that have brought these different castes together in a broader organisation. On the other hand, barring a few exceptions, the more aristocratic Kshatriyas from the former ruling families, have in the past generally kept away from the Sabha.

In this process of assimilation, still going on, the economic factor was supplemented by the Kshatriya Sabha's constant efforts to upgrade the position of the lower castes in the social hierarchy of Gujarat. This was in fact a strong uniting force in the Kshatriya organisation. The process was one of group enfranchisement whereby entire castes and caste-groups were 'accepted back' into the Kshatriya fold.[3] There was a conscious and deliberate attempt on the part of the leaders of the movement to break the shackles of tradition. Symbols of caste pollution were deliberately done away with. One of the first to go was the eating restriction: high and low were made to sit together in common feasts. More gestures followed. Thus an incident when progressive rulers, including the Maharaja of Baroda, were made to sit on the floor with other Kshatriyas in one of the annual conventions of the Sabha has been proudly chronicled. The Kshatriya Sabha has proved to be the great levelling force for its various constituents.

Alongside emulation of higher castes (sanskritisation) and social and educational reform (westernisation),[4] such an urge to come together in a larger association (secularisation) is an important factor in social mobility, one that is likely to gain in importance under universal franchise and democratic politics. While it partly derives from 'sanskritised' attitudes in the lower castes, it also derives from the 'westernised' egalitarian attitudes of the upper castes. Cutting across both these orientations, however, is the associational-federal urge motivated by the need to mobilise adequate support in order to function in a competitive polity. The search for status takes on a more complex character, composed of both conflicting and emulative components. Social emulation, a continuous process in any society, will now relate to the politicised attitudes and ideas of the upper castes. The stage of Brahminic adaptation is likely to be skipped or will take on a totally different connotation. Secularisation, while thus narrowing wide social distances between castes, is also narrowing the gulf between the reformist and the orthodox sections within the upper castes created by 'westernisation'. It is a mechanism of caste integration that is more powerful than any of the other influences discussed in the literature on caste. See, however, in this connection,

F. G. Bailey, *Tribe, Caste and Nation* (Manchester: Manchester University Press 1960), pp. 186-93. The critical point about such a process of secularisation is that it is based on an identification that is known and understood and one that raises rather than dampens consciousness of social being. At the same time, such a consciousness also becomes a basis for change and serves as an adaptive mechanism in a changing society.

In the case of the Kshatriyas in Gujarat, the initiative for such a process of secularisation came from upper caste, well-to-do Rajputs. In December 1946, Narendrasinh Mahida, a western-educated noble of high standing, launched the publication of *Rajput Bandhu*, a community mouthpiece with the object of propagating social reforms and liberal-democratic ideas among the Kshatriya community. He was inspired by his elder brother Motisinh's career as a writer and social reformer. Motisinh died young and Narendrasinh carried on his work. At the same time, Natvarsinh Solanki, another educated Rajput, a Talukdar[5] of Kaira district, a skilful organiser and one with bitter experience of the politically dominant Patidars, was running an association called the Charotar Kshatriya Samaj.[6] He joined Mahida as co-editor of *Rajput Bandhu*. Mahida and Solanki were to be the two major influences in the course that the Kshatriya movement took in the next fifteen years, Mahida providing the movement with an ideological sweep and a dominating personality, and Solanki skilfully building up organisational support and the allegiance of locally influential community leaders. There were also other prominent Rajput leaders who especially felt the need of promoting educational activities among the Kshatriyas. With a donation from Mahida, they started an educational society called the Gujarat Rajput Kelavani Mandal,[7] with Mahida as President and Solanki as Secretary respectively. The Mandal, which was started in December 1946, was at first conceived as an educational institution. Gradually, however, it developed into a broader social organisation.

It was soon discovered by the leaders of the Mandal that it was not enough to collect a few thousand rupees and distribute scholarships. The need was to create a social consciousness among the fragmented and disorganised mass of Kshatriyas. In order to do this, Mahida suggested that the leaders and workers should tour villages on foot, an idea he got from Gandhi's *padyatra* in riot-stricken Bengal. A meeting of Kshatriya workers was held on 24 April 1947 to chalk out the details of a programme. The meeting was presided over by Ravishankar Maharaj, a saintly and devout Gandhian and the foremost 'constructive' worker of Gujarat, whose influence on the Kshatriya movement has been remarkable.[8]

At this meeting of April 1947 it was decided that the Mandal should send batches of workers into the villages, each batch to be composed of twenty-two Kshatriya youths in traditional Kshatriya uniform.[9] The main purpose of the *padyatra* was four-fold: the enlistment of members, propagation of abstinence from drink, emphasis on education, and mobilisation of support for the removal of restriction on arms, especially the wearing of the sword.[10] The mixture of reformist and traditionalist appeals should again be noted. The burden of the effort, however, was directed to the removal of drinking habits and the conscious promotion of a civilised way of the life that would bring the community out of its lowly existence and enable its members to stand as equals with others. Attempts were also made to change traditional customs and introduce reforms such as abolition of marriage dowries. The enthusiasm was kept up by organising in each village that was covered a non-official militia which emphasised the martial tradition of the Kshatriya and sought to instil a sense of organisation and discipline in the Kshatriyas, an otherwise inchoate and apathetic mass. Seemingly revivalist, the idea was to unite these various caste groups by making them conscious of their common 'Kshatriya' heritage. The *Rajput Bandhu* was refashioned to become the mouth-piece of the Mandal from July 1947.

The *padyatra* was a great success. The Kshatriya leaders, some of them from highly placed families, toured from village to village, covering entire districts.[11] The impact of this was considerable. Several drinking houses were closed down and vows of abstinence taken. People were persuaded to send their children to school, a general fund was collected and reform activities were launched. For the village masses, this was a new experience altogether.

In 1948, after Gandhi's assassination, the government introduced measures to curb 'communal' movements. The Kshatriya militia was banned. The District magistrate of Kaira ordered suspension of the programme of *padyatras*. After a time, they were allowed to be revived, but without the uniform and the sword.

Thus what had started as an educational fund soon developed into a social movement based on a subtle combination of the Gandhian technique and Kshatriya symbols. The technique of *padyatra* which had a mass appeal made the Kshatriya castes conscious of their corporate strength. It is this consciousness which led them at a later date to assert themselves in the political sphere in the form of a populous and powerful caste federation.[12]

The extent of response evoked by the *padyatras* was realised when a convention of the Mandal was held in Nadiad on 11 January 1948. About 50,000 people turned up from all parts of Gujarat. There were also some from the adjoining territory of Saurashtra who were attracted by the movement launched in Gujarat. It was proposed at this meeting to enlarge the area of operation so as to include Saurashtra and Kutch where too there was a large Kshatriya population.[13] There were already Rajput organisations in these areas; what was proposed was an integration of these into a larger organisation. It is interesting to look at this attempt at integration of a region whose economic and social structure differed widely from that of Gujarat, as it brings out the sort of conditions that promote or retard the growth of a caste federation.

In Gujarat, the *ryotwari* system of land rights, direct revenue administration under the British, and increasing fragmentation of the few jagirdari estates were factors that militated against concentration of landownership. Under these conditions, it was the peasant proprietor caste of Patidars, who treated land as a basis of prosperity and power rather than as a hereditary title, that came to own the bulk of the land. A majority of the Kshatriyas, including high-caste Rajputs, were gradully turned into tenants and labourers. In Saurashtra and Kutch, on the other hand, ownership rights were vested in the princely and *girasdari* families. Here the Rajputs were the land-owning class and the Patidars and other lower castes their tillers.[14] This difference in the economic structure led to a different composition of the Kshatriya community in the two regions. Common economic interests helped to narrow down the social distance between different layers of the Kshatriyas in Gujarat. One of the main purposes of the Kshatriya movement in Gujarat was to reform and upgrade the Bariyas, Thakardars and Bhils, the lower castes in the Kshatriya hierarchy.[15] In this the Rajputs themselves took the lead. Such a process of assimilation led to two important results. Firstly, the lower castes felt upgraded and readily accepted Rajput leadership of the movement. Secondly, a common lack of economic and political power forced upon these various caste-groups the need to depend upon numerical strength as the only effective weapon in pressing their demands. In contrast to this, the Rajputs of Saurashtra and Kutch did not recognise the claims of the lower castes such as Kolis, Kathis and Mers, to be accepted into the Kshatriya fold. And this was the direct result of the wide gap that existed between the economic conditions and political status of the Rajputs as compared to the other caste groups.

Gujarat and Saurashtra differed also in the response evoked by land reforms from the various Kshatriya communities. While the Saurashtra Rajputs opposed these measures as they impinged upon their economic power, the Rajputs in Gujarat, being cultivators, welcomed them. These divergences in the approach to social and economic reform introduced from the very beginning a discordant note in the attempt at bringing the Kshatriyas of these regions into a common organisation under Rajput leadership.

In spite of these differences, however, the effort to integrate Kshatriyas of the different regions was undertaken, motivated partly by zeal for reform and partly by discontent with the administration. In Saurashtra, a Girasdar Association composed of land owning and high-caste Rajputs was already functioning. In Kutch also, there was an organisation of high-caste Rajputs known as the Kutch Rajput Sabha. The leaders of these organisations were contacted and an informal meeting of the concerned leaders was held at Dhrol on 15 November 1947. At this meeting it was decided to make necessary changes in the constitution of the Gujarat organisation and to rename it as the Kutch-Kathiawar*-Gujarat Kshatriya Sabha. The decision was ratified at the Nadiad convention referred to above. Narendrasinh Mahida continued to be the President and three Joint Secretaries, one from each of the three regions, were elected. It was decided that the *Rajput Bandhu* would now be published as the mouthpiece of the new organisation.

The new organisation was beset with difficulties inherent in the situation. The divergence in social composition and economic interests discussed above got articulated in the form of conflicting attitudes to land rights and the reforms introduced by the Congress government. While the Girasdars of Saurashtra and Kutch fought bitterly against the legislation which impinged upon their economic rights, the Kshatriyas in Gujarat, being tenant cultivators, readily took to the legislation which, among other things, bestowed ownership rights on the tenants and threatened the absentee landowners among the Patidars.

The differences on land reforms also led to divergent attitudes to the Congress. At the time of the elections to the Interim Legislative Assembly in Saurashtra held in 1948, some of the Girasdar leaders pressed the Congress to give a balanced representation to different 'interests' in the State. When the demand was rejected, a concerted move was made by the Girasdar Association to put up candidates against the Congress. Nothing much came out of the move. The rift

---

* 'Kathiawar' is another name for Saurashtra.

with the Congress widened further when the demand for retention of a portion of the land by the landlords was also rejected. The situation in Gujarat was totally different and the Kshatriyas there did not share the anti-Congress attitude of Saurashtra leaders. Foremost among the believers in the Congress was Mahida.

Mahida as President of the Kshatriya Sabha, and having access to well-placed Congress leaders, made efforts to bring about a rapprochement between the Kshatriyas and the Congress in Saurashtra. Himself a staunch supporter of the Congress, Mahida emphasised that the Congress was the only party capable of representing all sections of society. "The structure of Congress will be broadened day by day and all different interests in society will have to be merged in it." Moreover, being the party in power, the Congress alone could help the Kshatriyas in meeting their economic and political demands. "We should not forget that Congress is an unparalleled institution of our nation. We also should not forget that Congress has brought us independence through great struggle. We must strengthen the Congress by accepting her ideals. This is the only way in which we can convince the people that we are not reactionaries in our thinking, but are as progressive and democratic as any Congressman."[16]

Amidst the storm of conflict in Saurashtra, Mahida and his lieutenants in Gujarat openly advocated an alliance with the Congress. "In the present age, even social and educational activities cannot strengthen themselves without gaining some political colour. This becomes more emphatic in times of elections. All our fellow Kshatriyas shall have to use their right of vote in the next elections. This has necessitated a rapid solution of the problem."[17] Such an awareness of the role of political activity in strengthening social organisation was, in a sense, the result of the experience in Saurashtra where the Kshatriyas were found alienated. Mahida put forward his alliance plan in a letter addressed to all the important Congress leaders of Gujarat, the leaders of the Kshatriya movement and prominent social workers. Many welcomed the plan. The Saurashtra leaders, on the other hand, strongly opposed it. An unofficial meeting of Kshatriya leaders and workers was held at Ahmedabad in November 1949 to decide on the issue. It was resolved at this meeting that the Kshatriya Sabha should adopt the 'Sarvodaya' policy of the Congress in the political field and advise the Kshatriya population to follow the same.[18] Upon this the Saurashtra Kshatriyas demanded withdrawal from the organisation. The demand was finally conceded at the Ahmedabad convention of the Kshatriya Sabha held on 28 May 1950 and inaugurated by Mr. Morarji Desai. It was decided at the convention to split the Kutch-

Kathiawar-Gujarat Kshatriya Sabha and to make the *Rajput Bandhu* the exclusive mouthpiece of the Gujarat Kshatriya Sabha.[19] Thus came to an end the short-lived experiment of a State-wide association. Lacking a basic identity of interests, the ideological appeal of Mahida to support the Congress created a crisis in the organisation, and led finally to a split. In the process, of course the Gujarat Kshatriyas moved closer to the Congress.

During this same period the work of the Kshatriya Sabha in Gujarat gained further momentum. The same convention at Ahmedabad also discussed the problem of 'forced labour' in Banaskantha, a backward district in the north of Gujarat. In this district, nearly eight to nine thousand Rajputs had been subjected to forced labour since the beginning of the rule of the Muslim state of Palanpur. They were allowed to till some land without payment in exchange for which they were obliged to give their free services in guarding the border areas. With the passage of time this was exploited and they were virtually turned into forced labour. Now with the new consciousness of social justice that came with the Kshatriya movement, the Rajputs opposed such a system of forced labour. Upon this, the government — now the Congress government — threatened to take away the land from them. This gave rise to a protracted struggle and finally resulted in the Rajputs resorting to non-violent resistance under the banner of the Kshatriya Sabha and the leadership of Ravishankar Maharaj. They claimed that the land had been in their possession for the last seven hundred years. The Government, on the other hand, took the position that the Nawab of Palanpur had given this land to Rajputs in the past in exchange for their free service and that accordingly they must either resume their duty or surrender the land. Mr. Morarji Desai, in his inaugural speech to the Sabha's convention, referred to this problem. He reiterated the stand of the government. The convention, in the presence of Morarji Desai, resolved that "the views expressed by Shri Morarjibhai are devoid of real facts. These units of landholding are in the possession of Rajputs since last 700 years. Their claim must be viewed with the right attitude."[20] This resolution reflects an important priority of motives. Inspite of their acceptance of the Congress ideology, the Kshatriyas were not ready to compromise in a matter which affected their vital interests. The incident also highlights the importance of conflict with the government machinery in raising the level of political awakening. Finally, it throws interesting light on the developing relationships between caste and politics. The Kshatriya community had in the past enjoyed certain privileges as a caste. With changes taking place in the social and economic organisation, these privileges were infringed at some stage. And this, in turn, led to a rallying together for the preservation of privileges and interests in a deliberate and organised manner. Ascriptive status is here turned into a symbol of mobilisation for building up an interest organisation. With this takes place a marked shift in both the nature of the caste organisation and its idiom of communication.

The short-lived attempt at building up a larger organisation for the Kshatriyas covering divergent interests not only underlined the important fact that a viable caste federation could be created only on the basis of an identity of social and economic interests but also brought to the surface pertinent problems of political articulation that the Gujarat Kshatriya Sabha was to face in the coming years. The problems were also of immediate relevance. To what extent should the Sabha take an active interest in politics? And to the extent it did, how far should it identify itself with the Congress? As we shall see, both these issues were to crop up again and again giving rise to a controversy between those who emphasised political action and those who urged staying away from politics and concentrating on education and reform activities. The controversy will be highlighted in the pages that follow.

During the first general elections in 1952, specific directives were given to the Kshatriyas of Gujarat by their leaders to vote for the Congress. A few of these leaders were themselves elected on Congress nomination. Social and educational activities suffered during this period of involvement in politics. After the elections, an annual convention of the Kshatriya Sabha was held on 13 April 1952, where it was demanded that the government should classify the Kshatriyas under the category of 'backward classes', and make them eligible for the benefits that went with such a classification. The reasons urged were poverty and backwardness of the majority of the Kshatriyas.[21] The demand was rejected by the government.

In November 1952, Mahida resigned as President because of bad health and was replaced by Bhagvansinh Chhasatia, an active leader of the movement but not as highly placed as Mahida.[22] With this change, and with greater freedom from political activities, many leaders felt the necessity of reviewing the social programme of the Kshatriya Sabha initiated during the *padyatras*. The unit of operation was decentralised and each unit allotted to one batch of workers. Training camps were also organised for these workers, and Congress leaders were invited to lecture at these camps on important problems of social policy and implementation. These trained workers were to be responsible for the execution of social reform measures and educational activities initiated by the Sabha.

While the Sabha was engaged in defining a social programme for the Kshatriyas, the Congress party resolved at its Avadi Session in 1955 that no active member of the Congress could hold simultaneous membership of any caste or communal organisation. While this created a stir among the politically-inclined Kshatriyas, it confirmed those that emphasised the social programme of the Sabha. In December 1955, the Executive Committee of the Sabha considered the implications of the Congress resolution and decided that the organisation should confine itself to its social activities. In the annual convention held in May 1956, no politicians were invited, and a deliberate attempt was made to emphasis the Sabha's 'non-political' character. Although prompted by the Avadi resolution, the convention also underlined the Sabha's growing disillusionment with politics and especially with the Congress.

Events, however, were soon to overshadow such a mood of the Kshatriyas. The aspiration for a separate linguistic State had not materialised in Gujarat which continued to be part of bilingual Bombay State even after most of the States were reorganised on the basis of language. A powerful agitation for a separate State of Gujarat was launched in 1956, in which all the opposition parties and a number of independent and non-political groups joined together under the banner of the 'Mahagujarat Janata Parishad'. The Congress opposed the move. For the Kshatriya Sabha, the agitation is important in that its leadership was faced with divided loyalties, one towards the Congress and the other towards their own people within the Sabha who had spontaneously joined the 'Mahagujarat' upsurge. The upsurge took on the character of a mass movement based on solidarities that cut across both party and caste. As so many of the workers of the Sabha joined the movement, the leadership found itself in a great dilemma.

As always happened with this extremely active organisation, a general meeting of all Kshatriya leaders was called in December 1956 to take a decision on the Sabha's stand in the 1957 Elections, especially in the context of the Mahagujarat issue. Most of the speakers advocated support for the demand of linguistic autonomy. This made the leaders uneasy as the Congress, whom they had considered their natural ally, stood against such a demand. It found a way out by leaving the decision to 'individual discretion'. No specific directions were given. A resolution was adopted which reflected this indecision. Apart from its indecisive character, the resolution is important in voicing the Sabha's disillusionment with the Congress for not taking any interest in the development of the community. The resolution took note of "the painful fact that the different political parties of Gujarat have taken practically no interest in the overall development of the backward Kshatriya population." Though it refers generally to the indifference of all political parties, it is clear that it was to the Congress that the criticism was directed. Moreover, it was in this convention that Mahida for the first time openly confessed his failure to get any cooperation from the Congress. "I cannot ask you", he said; "to support the Congress because they have neglected you throughout these years. You are all free to decide according to your own discretion."

On the other hand, Mahida's lasting contribution to the ideology of the Kshatriya Sabha was made in these circumstances of great strain, when he exerted himself desperately in finding some way of reconciling his great failure in serving the Kshatriya cause with his still unshaken faith in the Congress. The second general elections in 1957, fought on the issue of Mahagujarat, divided the Kshatriyas politically. Mahida attributed these divisions to the lack of a common political ideology for the whole community. He based his thesis on the premise that to have an integrated approach towards social problems, unanimity on political matters was essential.[23] With great eloquence and incessant logic, he pressed his viewpoint on other Kshatriya leaders who, though they were reluctant to agree that it should be the Congress ideology that they should adopt, had no alternative to offer, and owing to the great veneration in which they held their leader, a resolution was passed at the convention held in April 1958 at Dakor which pledged the Sabha's support for the Congress. The Sabha's constitution was amended to incorporate this change.[24] Mr. K.K. Shah, a prominent Congress leader, attended the convention as its Chief Guest and assured the gathering that their interests would be safeguarded by the Congress. With this the Sabha entered a new phase in its development, the phase of direct participation in politics.

The Kshatriya leaders made earnest efforts to implement the Dakor resolution. Taluka and village tours were undertaken and attempts were made to enroll Congress members from the community. Training camps for workers were held, and lectures on social and economic development and the ideology of the Congress were organised. Congress policies were popularised through the *Kshatriya Bandhu*. But the response of the Congress was poor. It took no step whatsoever towards accommodating and recognising the Sabha as it did for other backward, tribal and Harijan organisations, nor did it even take important Kshatriya leaders into positions in the Congress. The end, however, came abruptly when Mahida took up the matter personally with Mr. Morarji Desai and was told that the Sabha, being a communal organisation, could not be recognised by the Congress.

Such an outcome deeply humiliated the Kshatriya leaders and aggravated the already growing trend of anti-Congress feeling. After this, through a rapid succession of events, the political complexion of the Sabha underwent a complete reversal. A powerful group of Kshatriyas led by Natvarsinh Solanki, the Sabha's Secretary and the organisational brain behind the Kshatriya movement, called for a reversal of the Dakor decision. This was done at the 13th convention of Kshatriya Sabha held at Bayad on 25 March, 1961. Mahida did not attend the meeting. The convention re-amended the Sabha's constitution, deleting the portion relating to the strengthening of the Congress and allegiance to it.

The Bayad resolution of 1961 should not be thought of as a sudden reversal of the Kshatriya Sabha's political positions. In fact, a careful scrutiny of the Sabha's deliberations brings out the gradual development after 1953 of a trend towards increasing unwillingness of the Kshatriyas to involve the Sabha too closely in the politics of the Congress party. The Avadi resolution against communal bodies, and the indifference of Congress leaders at district and State levels to the Kshatriya leadership, contributed to this. The trend away from the Congress was accentuated during the Mahagujarat movement, and the 1957 general elections. The resolution at the Dakor convention of April 1958 to affiliate the Sabha to the Congress comes against the run of this developing trend and can only be explained by reference to Mahida's tremendous power over the Kshatriyas. The reversal of this decision that came at the Bayad convention, though it made explicit the alienation of the Sabha from the Congress, was something to be expected. To fully grasp the change from the Sabha's close association with the Congress to its final departure, one must turn to the personality factor in the development of the Kshatriya Sabha, and the shift in leadership that took place in it.

From the very inception of the Kshatriya movement, two persons, Narendrasinh Mahida and Natvarsinh Solanki, provided its leadership. Though widely differing in their approach towards practical problems of politics, a common social purpose kept these two men united in the Sabha. Mahida, a Rajput of high standing, was moved by high idealism which was the product of the simultaneous impact of western higher education and Gandhian ideology. Solanki, on the other hand, a graduate of an Indian University, had as a small talukdar to contend for status and power with the powerful Patidars of Kaira district, and had thus learnt his first lessons of politics in the field. Mahida's appeal to the masses flowed from his liberal idealism and urban orientation. His ideological flair, high social status, and his sacrifice of prosperous landlordism and a budding career in Bombay, made him an idol of the Kshatriya masses. He was deified by his followers, and his power in the Kshatriya organisation derived from his mass appeal. Solanki, on the other hand, was a hard-headed organiser and wielded power in the Sabha through his command over the organisation. Mahida's link with his followers was direct and he did not need an elaborate organisation to perpetuate his following. Solanki depended almost wholly on the organisation for his strength. When the two worked in the same institution, it was natural that Mahida occupied the president's chair, a position which associated him with the masses and yet enabled him to keep above the mundane routine of the party organisation, while Solanki was the Secretary, attending to every detail, being in constant touch with the field, and closely controlling the organisation and the men. In reality, Solanki knew the Kshatriya masses better, perfectly followed their idiom of communication, and knew what motivated them to action. But he was not their idol, which Mahida was beyond any doubt.[25]

Natvarsinh Solanki did not share the devout enthusiasm of Mahida for the Congress, still less for its ideology. If he went with the Congress upto a point, it was no more than a strategy to countercheck the power of the Patidar group. To belong to Congress gave him no sense of fulfilment as it did to Mahida. It was not an end, only a means to the strengthening of Kshatriya power. Mahida, on the contrary, was so overwhelmed by the Congress posture of righteousness that he did not hesitate to use the Kshatriya Sabha as a means of strengthening the Congress. Solanki, as soon as he discovered that there was no longer any elbow room left within the Congress, turned hostile to it. Mahida, on the other hand, strained hard to make virtue of his disappointments, still hoping that the Congress would come to his rescue. His was a tragic plight in politics.

The root of Solanki's attitude to the Congress can be traced back to the Patidar-Kshatriya cleavage in Kaira district. Both the land-owning Rajputs, and the evicted Bariya tenants suffered from the tenancy legislation, which benefited the peasant proprietor class of Patidars. On the other hand, the Patidar leaders of the Kaira Congress organisation early realised the potentialities of a 'Kshatriya' alliance between the Rajputs and the Bariyas under the leadership of the former. They tried to curb the power of men like Solanki and gave them no place in the Congress.

In 1952, however, the Congress faced a challenge from the

'Khedut Sangh' movement, an anti-Congress peasant organisation born out of resistance to the Land Tenancy Act. The movement was led by Bhailalbhai Patel, a dynamic and powerful person who was himself a Patidar. Architect of the rural University of Vallabh Vidyanagar, in Kaira, a man of tremendous drive and power, an outstanding Patidar and a known protagonist of the late Sardar Patel, 'Bhaikaka' posed the first major threat to the congress in Kaira. He himself stood against the Congress in the first general election. Such a powerful Patidar candidate could only be countered by putting up someone like Solanki who commanded the votes of the numerous Kshatriya population. Though the Patidars of Kaira were reluctant, Mr. Morarji Desai invited him and gave him the responsibility of defeating Patel. At the same time, as if being given a bargain, he was also given the responsibility of winning another seat in a neighboring constituency which had a large Kshatriya vote for a Muslim candidate of the Congress. The task appeared difficult. Solanki, however, took up the challenge and won both the seats for the Congress.

On joining the Congress, Solanki found the Patidar leadership of the party cold-shouldering the question of sharing power with the Kshatriyas. He decided not to suffer this. Thus in 1957, when he was not consulted in the nomination of the Congress candidates in Kshatriya-dominated constituencies, he protested strongly, and in public. His position was that if the Kshatriyas were not given the recognition of a special interest within the party, there was no sense in continuing with the Congress. Other leaders of the Sabha agreed with him.[26] The calculated indifference shown to the Kshatriyas by the leaders of the Congress organisation gave an edge to the unpopularity of the party caused by the Mahagujarat issue. Even when Mahida's appeal for affiliation to the Congress was accepted, it was done in the teeth of severe opposition and was considered by many as an imposition from above. In one of our interviews with him, Mahida admitted that he had to exert his personal influence in getting the resolution passed.

The resolution stands as a testimony to the respect and affection in which the Kshatriya masses held Mahida. Soon afterwards, however, his failure to get recognition for the Sabha from the Congress shook their faith in him. It was the defeat of a leader who had failed to lead the masses towards the promised goal. It was exactly at this moment that Solanki took the initiative in leading the Kshatriyas out of the Congress, in the process also weaning them away from the influence of Mahida. The prevailing anti-Congress feeling created an atmosphere in which Solanki's action found the approval of the rank and file. It facilitated the shift in leadership.

The fact was that Mahida's indifference to problems of organisation left him a mass leader without a base. At a time when the Congress let him down so completely, his sudden dissociation from the Sabha rendered him powerless. It was now his turn to follow the masses. For a time he stood away but was soon forced to return to the Kshatriya fold. The lesson is important. Mahida realised that his importance in the political field derived from his command over the Kshatriya masses. His return was not dictated by any caste considerations but followed inevitably from the nature of his position in politics. At the same time, it is important to realise the personality dimension of this relationship. Mahida's influence on the masses was out of the ordinary. He had been the unifying symbol of the Sabha for such a long time that his departure created a void in its organisation. His self-imposed isolation from the Sabha appeared unnatural to the Kshatriyas who had made him their idol for so long: the concern to bring him back into their fold was expressed again and again. Solanki and other leaders sensed this feeling; they also realised that for mass appeal there was no substitute for Mahida. He was subjected to intense pressure, including pressure from very close kinsmen of his, before which he at last gave way. He contested against the Congress during 1962 General Elections and was elected with great public backing. For Mahida, however, it was both a victory and a defeat. The event broke his confidence in politics and in himself, and he found solace only by returning to the Congress shortly after the election.

With all their differences, both Mahida and Solanki shared one basic approach. They were both proponents of a political solution of the Kshatriya problem, of course with the vital difference that whereas for Mahida ideology constituted the core of politics, for Solanki politics was a serious and sustained struggle for power. There were others in the Kshatriya fold who wanted the Sabha to keep aloof from politics. These have, however, been largely ineffective. Although lip-service was paid to their sentiments, and although Solanki sought their support in his conflict against Mahida, for all practical purposes the Kshatriya Sabha, at first under Mahida and later under Solanki, established itself as a political organisation of a larger and hitherto submerged section of Gujarat society.

The rapprochement with Mahida was followed by another remarkable rapprochement in the politics of Gujarat (and of Kaira in particular). Old Bhailalbhai Patel, doyen among the anti-Congress forces in Gujarat and one-time rival of Natvarsinh Solanki, was the key figure in the newly formed Gujarat Swatantra Party. He tried to persuade Solanki to put up a common front against the Congress. His argument was based on the numerical strength that could be mobilised if the Kshatriya and Patidar communities in Gujarat joined hands. A Patidar-Kshatriya alliance would indeed provide a formidable opposition to the Congress. Such a prospect attracted the Kshatriyas whose dominant motive at the time was to demonstrate their strength to the Congress. Under the impact of politics, the traditional Kshatriya hostility to Patidars turned into hostility to Congress Patidars only. As evidently the Congress was losing its grip on sections of the Patidar community, it was natural for the Kshatriyas to join hands with the latter. It was this alliance that became the basis of the Swatantra Party in Gujarat. In turn, the alliance was also to create problems for the new party, as we shall presently see.

The choice of the Swatantra Party as compared to any other opposition party or group in Gujarat — with many of whom the Kshatriya leaders were in negotiation — was conditioned by two other considerations. Firstly, being in its formative period, the Swatantra Party provided an opportunity for the Kshatriyas to capture important positions in the party organisation. The Sabha's bitter experience with the Congress had made this a prime consideration for its leaders. Secondly, the new party provided financial and other resources necessary to build the organisation and to mobilise the large mass of Kshatriyas spread over a large area. The antagonism to the Congress had made the Kshatriyas more conscious than ever before of the need to build an organised mass base through politics. The Swatantra offer provided them with the wherewithal to launch such an offensive.

There followed a period of intense negotiations with the Swatantra Party. The Kshatriyas squarely put forward their demands. These demands were accepted, although not without opposition from the orthodox Patidar elements in the party. Accordingly, a reshuffle of the party executive was made to accommodate the Kshatriya leaders in the organisation. A similar accommodation was made in the allocation of party nominations for the 1962 elections. Natvarsinh Solanki was given the charge of organising elections on behalf of the Swatantra Party in the whole of Gujarat. Kshatriya candidates were also financed and given vehicles to organise their election campaigns.

Such a sudden reshuffle of power created a sense of dissatisfaction amongst the established group in the party. Most of them were Patidars. The feeling of newcomers taking away power from old workers revived the historical Patidar-Kshatriya antagonism. Although the top leadership fought hard to counter this, there is no doubt that the Swatantra Party started its career in Gujarat divided into two factions based on caste. It was a case of politics bringing together traditionally rival castes into an alliance based on a new identity of interest, and then once the alliance took the form of a single organisation, the traditional groups reasserting themselves. These factions substantially influenced the outcome of the elections. Kshatriyas being the most numerous caste and Kshatriya workers aspiring for power everywhere, they demanded seats in each district, which it was not possible to give without alienating substantial local leaders from the Patidar community.[27] Thus the formula of a Kshatriya-Patidar alliance against the Congress could not work at all places. Where it worked, it brought handsome rewards to the Swatantra Party whose impressive success in some parts of the State (e.g. Kaira) in its very first and hurriedly organised attempt owed much to this alliance. Elsewhere, however, the very attempt at forcing an alliance between the two castes turned the party into a divided house (e.g. Ahmedabad and Mehsana districts).

The Congress too had not completely lost its hold over the Kshatriya voters. In quite a few places it also managed to put up Kshatriya candidates, some of them with a good standing in the locality. The outstanding example, of course, was the Prince of Baroda who not only bagged practically all the seats in Baroda district for the Congress but also obliged the Kshatriya Sabha, to whose activities he had generously donated in the past, to lie low as far as Baroda was concerned. Thus political divisions within the Kshatriyas helped the Congress. So did political divisions within the Patidars. Thus to cite again an example from Baroda district, the Congress there has been controlled for a long time by a Patidar group. But there also emerged in 1962 in the city of Baroda a powerful group of Patidar industrialists against the Congress. This group was with the Swatantra Party. The Patidar leaders of the District Congress, however, used the influence of the Prince of Baroda on the Kshatriya Sabha which did not allow the rival Patidar group to gain control of the District Swatantra Party and secure nominations from it. In this the Patidar leaders at the State level were also made to concur through the persuasion of Solanki and Mahida. Here is a truly subtle case of the interaction between different levels and forms of political power. Both caste groups and political groups were divided, resulting in caste factions within parties and party factions within castes,[28] providing the cross-cutting nature of loyalties which politicisation brings in its wake. The Swatantra Party in Gujarat, even before it had consolidated its power, became a base for such a process of factional interactions which characterises Indian politics everywhere.

We have examined the impact of the Kshatriya Sabha's alliance on the internal structure of the Swatantra Party. What was the effect of the Sabha's alliance with the Swatantra Party on its own organisational structure and leadership?

The new relationship with the Swatantra Party crystallised the already increasing politicisation of the Sabha's activities. As we have seen, even before 1962 there had taken place in this respect a noticeable shift in the character of the Sabha. Although the social programme of the Sabha and the political involvement of its leaders always exerted competing pulls on its organisation, the emphasis on the political side kept increasing, with Mahida driving the organisation towards the Congress. Even when frustration with the Congress began to mount, Mahida's remedy was not less but more involvement in politics: he advocated complete identification with the Congress. Indeed to some extent Mahida was able to drive the Kshatriyas along his way precisely because of the absence of a political alternative to the course proposed by him. As for those of his critics who emphasised the Sabha's social functions at the expense of politics, he silenced them by demonstrating that an apolitical Sabha would only become the scene of factionalism as happened under the Mahagujarat movement.

Despite Mahida's naive faith in the unifying role of politics, there is also no doubt that a compartmentalisation of the Sabha's work into the social and political was also misleading. The two were closely interrelated. It was the awareness of strength that came out of the movement for social integration and reform that had made the leadership conscious of its power. In turn, political power opened up new vistas for the Kshatriya masses and gave them a sense of unity and strength that they had never before possessed. With this there also took place a shift from voluntary effort to demands for State protection and political placements as a means to the welfare of the community. Finally, with the departure from the Congress, the alliance with the Swatantra Party, and the acceptance by the leading Kshatriya leaders of formal positions in the Swatantra organisation have crystallised the Sabha's political identity more clearly than at any time in the past. To that extent, the alliance has hastened the process of politicisation.

With the direct entry of the Kshatriyas into politics, the Sabha has also begun to extend its area of operation. In Gujarat itself the mobilisation of Kshatriyas under a common leadership has been spreading to districts which could not hitherto be properly attended to. In the process, new leaders with considerable regional hold have been brought into the organisation in formal positions. Of more interest is the change that is coming in Saurashtra where earlier the

Sabha had completely failed, first on account of different social conditions and the land issue, and secondly because of the pro-Congress leanings of the leadership in Gujarat. Here two developments are important. In Saurashtra during the 1962 elections, Rajput leaders from former princely families contested against the Congress and won in a few places.[29] In order to win, however, they had to mobilise support from the lower strata of the population. The princes and girasdars in Saurashtra have since realised the advantage of bringing together the lower castes such as Kathis, Kolis and Mers into single organisation of 'Kshatriyas'. They have seen that the basis of power has shifted from hereditary rights in land to organisation of political support. A gradual integration may thus follow on the lines of Gujarat, although it will take time and will perhaps come through a more directly political process of mobilisation.

With these developments in Saurashtra, efforts at a State-wide integration of the Kshatriyas have been revived. A committee consisting of Kshatriya representatives from Gujarat, Saurashtra and Kutch has been formed. It is important to note that the prince of Jasdan, a representative of the Kathis, a low-placed Kshatriya caste in Saurashtra, is a prominent member of this committee: politics has again worked as a cementing force. The result has been rewarding. For it was the Jasdan prince who was one of the important factors in defeating the Congress in the 1963 parliamentary bye-election in Rajkot where the Swatantra leader, M.R. Masani, was elected. Rajkot has been a stronghold of the Congress for the last thirty years and had returned U.N. Dhebar, former Congress President, with a large majority in the 1962 election only a year earlier.[30]

The other development has been on the side of the Gujarat Kshatriya leadership which has also turned hostile to the Congress. This has narrowed the differences amongst Kshatriya leaders and has opened the way to expansion of the Kshatriya base of the Swatantra Party in the State as a whole. During the 1962 general election, the Swatantra Party could not gain substantially in Saurashtra. There was general lack of organisation and mobilisation of significant leaders from relevant social strata — strata that have been neglected or taken for granted by the Congress. This is precisely what the Swatantra accomplished in Gujarat and failed to accomplish in Saurashtra in 1962. But the Rajkot bye-election has shown the way to such mobilisation in Saurashtra too. The Swatantra Party has made overtures to the Rajputs, Kathis, Mers and other Kshatriyas in Saurashtra, and the latter have responded favourably.[31] All these trends point to the possibility of some form of integration of the Kshatriya organisation in the three regions that could be effected by a political party. What could not be achieved socially may be achieved politically.

It has been argued that "the appeal of India's relatively weakly articulated voluntary associations is confined to the urban educated who are more or less attuned to the modern political culture. Caste, however, provides channels of communication and bases of leadership and organisation which enable those still submerged in the traditional society and culture to transcend the technical political illiteracy which would otherwise handicap their ability to participate in democratic politics."[32] An examination of the history of the Kshatriya Sabha bears out this general contention but leads to a different emphasis. It is found that caste provides not only channels of communication and leadership support for 'submerged' sections of society but also an important basis for joint and 'voluntary' action in the organisation of which the urban-educated take the initiative. The urban-rural dichotomy is in fact misleading. Caste federations, for instance, are conscious creations of the urban-educated political elite seeking institutional bases and numerical strength for their support. The absence of highly developed interest organisations of the Western form is being filled in India by the federal form that caste is taking, thus abridging hierarchical rigidities and adapting the indigenous social structure to the exigencies of democratic political institutions.

Caste is thus found not only performing *functions* performed by voluntary organisations elsewhere, but also assuming *forms* that are comparable to the latter.

The difference in India between Western-type voluntary organisations and castes underlines the crucial role of the latter. Here voluntary organisations as commonly understood have to a considerable extent been fed on external stimuli, either sponsored or triggered by the government. They haven't the character of self-governing associations found in some other countries. In India, the castes display an autonomy of their own with a distinctive way of life and corporate strength found in voluntary associations in the early development of Western societies.[33] They play an important role in absorbing substantial changes in the balance of social power and adapting a traditional culture to modern impacts and are a vital factor in avoiding the traumas of an uprooted 'mass' society.

On the other hand, caste besides being a system of segmental differentiations *jathis*, is also a system defining status, possesses a secular character, and is endowed with a class symbolism in the form of *varnas*. With these latter aspects gaining in function and importance, caste is shedding some of its old-time character and is acquiring a new emphasis and orientation. While still retaining a good part of the traditional modes of integration, it has entered a phase of competitive adjustment in the allocation and re-allocation of functions and power among various social groups. The institution of caste association and caste federation are the media through which such an adaptation in roles is taking place.

The important thing is the motivation that lies behind such a process of group assertion. Here caste consciousness no doubt plays an important part in mobilising and consolidating group positions. But the motivation behind it indicates an important shift in emphasis from the preservation of caste traditions and customs to their transformation through political power. It is essentially a secular motivation in which mobilisation of group support follows rather than precedes individual competition for power. Caste always had a political aspect to it but now the political aspect is gaining in emphasis more than ever before, especially in regard to individualised rather than group orientations to power. The network of kin and caste relationships is by stages drawn into personal networks of influence and power, and in the process greatly politicised. To this extent, caste identification and caste consciousness become means in the power struggle, the latter also influencing the normative orientation of such consciousness. Even social motivations such as the anxiety of the groups higher-up to preserve their positions, and of the lower groups to rise in status through identification with some higher groups become fused with political considerations. With individuals in the upper castes keen on building numerical strength and those in lower castes agreeing to give such support provided the former comply with the new rules of the game, the status overtones in the original motivations become blurred. In the process, inter-group orientations undergo a radical change. Although the lower castes still grant the privilege of one or more upper castes to govern and rule, such deference is increasingly conditioned by norms of accountability and notions of interest and right.

Leadership struggles within either the same caste or caste federation, or between castes, tend to follow from political differences and the competition for power. The new divisions very often take the line of horizontal and regional divisions and cut across vertical divisions. The disparities (social and economic) of the latter are now countered by disparities (political) of the former in which the low-placed caste groups gain an advantage.[34] The change involved is towards cross-cutting interactions and identities in the communication between society and politics. It is the essence of secularisation in a caste society.

It is impossible to say whether politics divides or unites castes, for it appears to do both. The political technique consists of articulating existing and potential divisions, fostering new alignments and loyalties, and giving rise to a structure of interests and identifications based on its own standards. If it appears to bring certain proximate strata together, it is only part of a more organised process of division and confrontation in the context of a new awareness of interests and loyalties. In this process some of the traditional loyalties and identities may be allowed to persist, be reinforced, or simply disintegrate, depending upon how functional or functionless they have become to the political society.

On the whole, however, the following can be said. A strong caste solidarity is conducive to political strength and power, but the possession of power tends to weaken the solidarity by creating internal competition. Such competition may be mitigated in an organisation with a strong authoritarian structure and orientation (such as was the case with the Kshatriya Sabha until 1958), but participation in democratic processes and spread of egalitarian values undermines such authoritarianism, gives rise to competition, and leads to new alignments that cut across solidarities and commitments which initially brought power.

The usual dichotomy between caste and politics is misleading and what is called for is a more systematic examination of the changing form that a caste society assumes under the impact of new and dynamic forces of change. One such force comes from the diffusion of new cultural values as expressed in the sanskritisation-westernisation syndrome. Another comes from technological impact and takes the form of economic individualism and territorial expansion.[35] Both these impacts are further conditioned by the operation of a new scheme of allocating influence and power in society. Politicisation of power relationships has thus brought about a striking shift in the preoccupation of a caste society already under the impact of social and economic transformation. The shift consists in activising the secular and mobilisation aspects of caste at the expense of other aspects, and making secularisation the dominant theme in the ordering of caste-relationships. The phenomenon of caste federation discussed in this paper is one form that such a shift in orientation takes.[36] A highly diffuse and plural society is here found to come to terms with the centralising tendencies of a modern polity. By inducing diverse social strata to enter into larger identifications and by providing to political leaders significant communications channels and a relatively stable loyalty structure, such a reorientation of the caste system fills an important place in the emerging infrastructure of modern India.

NOTES

1. For an authoritative statement on the concept of dominant caste, see M.N. Srinivas, 'The Social System of a Mysore Village' in McKim Marriot (ed.), *Village India* (Chicago: Chicago University Press 1955) and 'The Dominant Caste in Rampura', *American Anthropologist,* February 1959. The concept and the analysis underlying it have also attracted adverse criticism. See, for instance, Louis Dumont and D. Pocook, 'Village Studies' in *Contributions to Indian Sociology,* April 1957. Although the empirical viability of the concept of dominant caste has been a matter of continuous debate, it seems to us that the political significance of a dominant caste situation has not been adequately stressed so far. Where splits and factions occur within the general framework of a dominant caste sharing a common heritage and a common idiom of communication, politics serve as a medium of integration through adaptation and change. Factions within the same dominant caste also make it easy to bring in other castes to strengthen the support base of rival factional leaders. The task is much more difficult where rival groups are made up of whole castes that between them have little in common. A dominant-caste model of politics makes cross-cutting loyalties more easy to develop than in the case of a confrontation of exclusive caste groups (e.g. the Nairs and Ezhavas in Kerala, or Kammas and Harijans in Andhra, or Rajputs and Bhumihars in Bihar until very recently). In cases like the latter, although the development of political attitudes ultimately leads to some flexibility in caste relations, the process is far more strenuous and often destroys the forces of cohesion in the antecedent social structure.

2. It has been emphasised, and quite rightly, that the operating caste system in India functions not along the *varna* typology found in the texts but along the *Jati* lines of primary marriage groups. (Thus see Iravati Karve, *Hindu Society: A New Interpretation*; David G. Mandelbaum, 'Concepts and Methods in the Study of Caste', *The Economic Weekly,* Special Number, January 1959.) This ignores and thus puts in proper perspective, the *varna* symbolism employed by some castes for social and political mobility. The symbol of *Kshatriya* is both sufficiently indigenous and hallowed by tradition and sufficiently loose and nebulous to be invoked for claims to status and power. Because of the traditional claims of the Kshatriya to be the class of warriors and rulers, the label is particularly handy for political purposes. It has been invoked by ritually differently placed groups for functionally the same purpose, namely, a claim to high status and power. (Examples: Coorgs in Mysore, Jats in Rajasthan and Punjab, Marathas in Maharashtra, Kammas and Reddis in Andhra, Ahirs, Kurmis and Koeris in Bihar and U.P., Kathis in Saurashtra and Bariyas in Gujarat, alongside Rajputs everywhere.)

3. This included acceptance back into the Hindu fold. Thus the *Moresalam Rajputs* who had been converted into Muslims in the Moghul period were 'purified' through a religious ceremony in March 1953 by which

they re-entered the Hindu Kshatriya community. The Kshatriya Sabha took the initiative in this move.

4. 'Sanskritisation' is an influence that leads lower castes to emulate the Brahminic castes in their search for status and prestige while the latter are exposed to another influence, namely, 'westernisation'. M.N. Srinivas, *Religion and Society among the Coorgs of South India* (Oxford: Clarendon Press, 1952). See also his *Caste in Modern India and Other Essays* (Bombay: Asia Publishing House, 1962), Chapter II, and 'A Note on Sanskritisation and Westernisation', in *Far Eastern Quarterly*, Vol. XV, No. 4. A feature of the simultaneous operation of the two influences is that while 'sanskritisation' leads to a narrowing of the gap between castes, 'westernisation' may narrow the gap, widen it, or leave it as before, depending upon the differential impacts on upper and lower castes.

5. The term 'talukdar' refers to a class of small estate holders most of whom were Rajputs with a background of political rule. The British under the Gujarat Talukdar Act of 1889 gave protection to this class and appointed a special officer called the Talukdar Settlement Officer for this purpose. There were also attempts to redeem their debts and help them by establishing schools and hostels for raising their educational levels. Natvarsinh Solanki was the first Talukdar to pass the matriculation examination.

6. Charotar is the name of a prosperous part in the Kaira district of Gujarat, well known for its agricultural yield and for the powerful caste of peasant proprieters known as *Patidars* who emerged from this area to be one of the most influential communities in Gujarat. The Kshatriya movement, having its roots in this area, was directed against Patidar dominance from its inception. Solanki inherited the Charotar Rajput Samaj from his father and, true to his reformist ideas, changed the Charotar name to Kshatriya Samaj.

7. It is interesting to note that the other leaders agreed to most of what Solanki proposed when setting up the organisation — except its name. They insisted that the term 'Rajput' should be retained. Apparently, they were still afraid of being polluted by the lower castes who were presumably to be included in the 'Kshatriya' ideology. They agreed to give scholarships to members of the lower castes but were not prepared to give up their own identity as Rajputs.

8. Because of his Brahmin origin, the *Maharaj* enjoys the status of a revered priest in the Kshatriya community. At the same time, his association with reformist activities and with Gandhi and the Congress during the independence movement has been an influencing factor in the Sabha's approach to politics. His non-political posture in politics has been a convenient device for linking the Kshatriyas to politics while at the same time asserting that they were a non-political organisation. He has also influenced the techniques adopted by them in the programme of mass-awakening. He has been to them both a prophet and a man of their own. He has provided the spiritual symbol for attracting the Kshatriya masses

who may not have been amenable to the usual reformist jargons. The weapons of *Satyagraha* and non-violence, usually anathema to the Rajputs and the Kshatriyas, became acceptable when taught by the *Maharaj*.

9. The figure 22 provided an emotional symbol. It represented the twenty-two thousand courageous soldiers of Rana Pratap, who fought against the Moghul Empire at Haldighat. It was a symbol of Kshatriya prowess. The uniform consisted of a sword, a saffron coloured turban and the traditional Kshatriya apparel, the 'surval' and the 'bhet'. Thus the appeal for unity and discipline was made by invoking tradition. It was the caste-spirit that would make for unity and discipline.

10. For the last of these, a hundred thousand signatures were collected.

11. The first tour lasted thirty-seven days, the next, twenty-six days in four batches, after which there were two tours every year.

12. Their conflict with the administration made the Kshatriyas realise the importance of political power. And as they knew too well, they could get their demands accepted by the administration through their association with the Congress. There are several instances in which redress against grievances was sought through influential men in the Congress. Quite often this led to further disappointment, with Congressmen refusing to favour, which only made men like Natvarsinh Solanki more determined to build up the Kshatriya organisation as a power in itself. Indeed, as will be seen from what follows, the Sabha's policy kept fluctuating between the 'political line' of wooing the Congress and the 'organisation line' of building its own power. In the outcome, the latter approach succeeded but only by expressing itself politically against the Congress Party.

13. Saurashtra and Kutch are unions entirely consisting of former princely States. Each had a separate existence for some time until they were merged with the bilingual State of Bombay. They are now part of Gujarat State.

14. It should be noted here that the social status of the Patidar community differs between different regions of Gujarat. Thus in central Gujarat, in Ahmedabad, Kaira and Baroda districts, the Patidars are very prosperous and have achieved high status. In north Gujarat and Saurashtra, on the other hand, especially in princely regions, the Patidars, still under the domination of the mercantile community, have until recently enjoyed a low status. It is only lately, largely owing to land legislation, the operation of adult franchise, and the fraternal support of the Patidars of central Gujarat, that their condition is beginning to improve. See Rajni Kothari and Ghanshyam Shah, 'Caste Orientation of Political Factions — Modasa Constituency: A Case Study', *The Economic Weekly*, Special Number, July 1963.

15. It has been observed since Independence that special privileges granted to backward class communities, especially Bhils, weakened the appeal of such a process of assimilation. Bhils found it convenient to remain classified as 'backward' and to be placed lower than the Kshatriyas in order to take advantage of economic privileges. Here, economic interests

cut across social aspirations.

16. The two quotations are from Mahida's appeals to Kshatriya leaders of Saurashtra, one before and one after the election, as reported in the issues of *Rajput Bandhu* of 11 Nov.1948 and 16 Dec. 1948 respectively. The last few words represent an anxiety to obtain recognition from the Congress through an identification with democratic institutions and values.

17. From the leading article in *Rajput Bandhu* dated 29 Sept.1949. During the same period the Kutch Rajput Sabha also resolved to join the Congress. The Resolution justified the decision by saying that "the economic problems of Kshatriyas are decided in accordance with policy decisions at the national level. This requires us to make our demand felt at the national level. This can only be done through a national organisation like the Congress." *Rajput Bandhu*, dated 13 Oct. 1949.

18. Again note that affiliation with the Congress is justified in terms of the Sarvodaya ideology, which is esssentially the non-political and 'Gandhian' aspect of the Congress programme.

19. Partly, this was the result of the direct impact of Mahida. Partly, however, it arose from their experience of conflict with the district administration, and the failures of the Sabha to press their demands with the State government. Its failures as a pressure group led it, under Mahida, to adopt the 'political line

20. Ultimately a compromise was arrived at through the efforts of Ravishankar Maharaj.

21. The demand shows the levelling effect of this caste federation's attempt to expand its numerical base by bringing in more and more caste groups. Only two years ago the Sabha was fighting for the restoration of land rights to the Rajputs of Banaskantha, a northern district of Gujarat. It now demanded the benefits due to backward communities. Clearly both its strategy and its social composition had undergone a substantial change.

22. It is noteworthy that Mahida introduced Chhasatia as 'a representative of the lower sections of the Kshatriya community'. Although a pure Rajput, Chhasatia came from very poor conditions, and worked his way up. He thus represented a large section of 'lowly' Rajputs, indistinguishable from other Kshatriyas.

23. "We have seen during the last General Elections that the organisational strength for social work that we had built through the Gujarat Kshatriya Sabha was shattered owing to internal political differences ... In times like this, organisations which lack unity of thought cannot survive. This is clear. Hence for the sake of the organisation it is imperative that all Kshatriyas should adopt a single political ideology." *Kshatriya Bandhu*, dated 16 Nov.1957.

24. The amended article under the head Purposes, now reads as follows: "This institution will work for strengthening the Indian National Congress to achieve a classless social order and to strengthen the basis of democracy."

25. This difference in temperament and approach of the two leaders is reflected even today in the respective roles they play in the Swatantra Party. While Solanki (bored by his term in the Bombay Legislature) has refrained from contesting elections and has preferred to work as the organisational secretary of the State Swatantra Party, Mahida has chosen to be a colourful addition to the Lok Sabha (his lustrous turban being second only to the glamour and beauty of Maharani Gayatri Devi of Jaipur). On the other hand, Solanki's son, a polished young man who received his education abroad, perfectly at home with the tenor of upper level politics in India, has gone to the Lok Sabha as an M.P. on a Swatantra Party ticket.

26. The Patidar leaders of the Congress regarded the Kshatriya approach as an attempt on their part to capture the Congress. They were apprehensive of such a prospect. Mr. Tribhuvandas Patel, President of the Kaira District Congress Committee in 1962, and later, President of the Gujarat Pradesh Congress Committee, in interviews with us, explained that he could not allow the Sabha to nominate Kshatriya candidates, as that would have compromised the integrity of the Congress.

27. It may be noted that the Congress was put in the same dilemma when faced by the Kshatriya demands in allocating seats. It could have given more seats to them only by denying the same to its Patidar activists. The Congress, of course, chose not to do so as it had miscalculated the power of the Sabha's leaders on the Kshatriya masses.

28. To complete our account, we must also add that political divisions within the Patidars also helped the Swatantra Party, as for instance in Kaira.

29. Similarly the prince of Kutch went against the Congress and helped the Swatantra bag all the five seats from Kutch.

30. For a study of this bye-election and the role of the Kshatriya movement in its outcome, see Rushikesh Maru, 'Fall of a Traditional Congress Stronghold', *The Economic Weekly*, XVII, No. 25, June 19, 1965.

31. As a result of this mobilisation in the last four years, the Swatantra Party made handsome gains in the 1967 general election. In Saurashtra, it won 19 out of 46 Assembly seats and 4 out of 6 Parliamentary seats. As against this, in the 1962 general election, the Swatantra Party had failed to gain a single seat from Saurashtra in both the Assembly and Parliament.

32. Lloyd I. Rudolph and Susanne Hoeber Rudolph, *op. cit.*

33. Even in the West it has been noticed that voluntary organisations have been losing their autonomy and are increasingly turning to the government for concessions. See Reinhard Bendix, "Social Stratification and the Political Community", *European Journal of Sociology*, Vol. I, No. 1. At any rate, there is need to distinguish between voluntary associations that are self-sufficient and those that are politicised. The classic presentation of the role of voluntary associations in a democracy as principally being one of minimising governmental interference is to be found in Alexis de Tocqueville's account of American democracy. The caste groups in India have traditionally performed a somewhat similar role and have managed to keep the government at arm's length. Both in America and in India,

however, the current trends are against de Tocqueville's ideal type and towards greater politicisation.

34. Robert Dahl, in *Who Governs?* (New Haven: Yale University Press, 1962), uses the concept of 'dispersed inequalities' to describe the phenomenon discussed here.

35. F.G. Bailey, *Caste and the Economic Frontier* (Manchester: Manchester University Press, 1957).

36. Other forms include caste association, regional conference of one or more castes, specialised agencies of a caste to promote employment, educational and other interests of caste members, and the systematic use of caste and ascriptive symbols to mobilise pressure, resources, or votes. Sometimes caste symbols are substituted by occupational and class symbols for the same purpose.

CHAPTER FOUR

Political Participation and Primordial Solidarity: The Nadars of Tamilnad

ROBERT L. HARDGRAVE, Jr.

India has been traditionally characterised by a system of vertical economic and ritual relationships between hierarchically ranked and functionally integrated castes of a localised community. The economic system of the village was a symbiotic relationship of occupational castes functioning according to rigidly prescribed patterns of behaviour, providing at once economic security and a clearly defined status and role. With little economic differentiation within a single caste, there was a high correlation between the economic position of a caste and its position in the Hindu hierarchy of ritual purity. The vertical relationships of dependence, however, fragmented the cohesiveness of the caste, dividing its members into factional client groups. The solidarity within a caste was further weakened by the minimal access to communications which precluded the horizontal extension of caste ties and forging of unity over a wide geographic area. Thus, in the traditional Hindu society, each caste was geographically fragmented into village units, and within each village, development of caste unity was prevented by vertical patron-client relationships crossing caste lines.

Historically, the caste system has, in contradiction to its normative rigidity, been comparatively elastic. With modifications and changes economically, a tendency towards commensurate readjustment of ritual ranking often came into operation. Thus, the equilibrium between economic status and ritual rank was often maintained. The impact of economic change and social mobilisation beginning in the nineteenth century under British rule, however, fundamentally affected the structural equilibrium of the traditional society. With the loosening of the vertical ties of economic dependence and the extension of horizontal ties, a new caste solidarity emerged where before there had been only the divisiveness of village factionalism. The new polarisation of caste against caste soon projected itself from the village to the wider social and political arena.

The role and effectiveness of a caste in politics, however, is necessarily dependent on the solidarity of the group and the degree to which it shares a common political culture. The degree to which any group may be said to possess a common political culture will be a function of (1) the elaboration of differentiation with regard to other groups, and (2) the elaboration of differentiation within the group itself. With regard to the analysis of a single caste, we might then hypothesise that the degree to which a caste may be said to possess a political culture common to the community as a whole will be a function of (1) the elaboration of caste ranking, and (2) internal differentiation within the caste itself.

McKim Marriott has suggested four structural conditions for maximal elaboration of caste ranking.

> ... (1) The concrete structural units of a community — in this case its hereditary, generally endogamous groups — must themselves be numerous. (2) Secondly, their members as corporate groups must interact with members of other groups in a clearly stratified order. (3) Furthermore, so that members of such castes in a community may agree with each other on an elaborate ranking of castes, their interactions as individuals must not deviate widely from the stratified order of interaction among their respective castes taken as wholes. (4) Finally, the totality of such a community structure must be separated from any possible confusion which it may suffer by connection with inconsistent structures outside.[1]

Following our hypothesis, the continuum from the more 'traditional' to the more 'modern' may be represented diachronically in three stages, the parochial, the integrated, and the differentiated political cultures. What we here call the parochial political culture of a caste is essentially that of tradition. While sharing a common economic position, with little internal differentiation, the caste is nevertheless fragmented by the relationships of dependence which divide its members into opposing factions. In the multi-caste village, the relationship between each caste is prescribed in a high elaboration of caste ranking. A single caste village, while lacking the elaborate distinction of ritual usages, may be taken as functionally equivalent, insofar as the economic groups, often themselves endogamous sub-castes, are hierarchically ranked and the structure of the village is characterised by a factionalism of economically dependent client groups.

The integrated political culture represents a high degree of cohesion and solidarity within the caste. The breakdown of economic dependence on other castes and the extension of horizontal caste ties over a wide geographic area gives the caste a new solidarity. In the first stages of the integrated culture, there continues to be a relatively high elaboration of caste ranking and a minimal differentiation within the single caste itself. While the elaboration of caste ranking continues to act as an agent to enforce solidarity within the caste, under the impact of economic change, there gradually emerges internal differentiation. While a multiplicity of factors affects the differentiation which arises within a caste in the process of change, such as education, communication exposure, generational conflict, the most salient factor in differentiation is the economic. The integrated political culture often gives rise to the emergence of associations for the social, economic and political uplift of the community. Ironically, the association itself inevitably contributes to the disintegration of community solidarity insofar as its goals are attained.

Differentiation within the caste community fundamentally affects the elaboration of caste ranking. The traditional correspondence between economic position and ritual status loses all meaning, for within each community there becomes available an increasingly wide range of occupations and economic positions. The demands of deference to new economic status erodes the hierarchy of ritual purity. With the decline in the elaboration of caste ranking and the increasing differentiation within each caste, the political culture of the community is affected accordingly, rendering a breakdown in the caste solidarity in favour of new inter-caste associations. As economic interests within the community are differentiated and as the political culture becomes increasingly secular, so the political identity of the individual will reflect cross-cutting vertical and horizontal ties and a plurality of commitments, associations, and interests. The loosened moorings of caste and tradition, while freeing the individual for the possibility of association along class lines, also renders him available to the flux of ambivalence, apathy and anomie. The differentiated political culture represents, perhaps most accurately, simply a decline in the former homogeneity of the community, but it provides the foundation for the emergence of a political culture reflecting identities based on economic interests and growing political awareness.

In exploring these propositions, this paper examines the case of the Nadars of Tamilnad.[2] Considered by high caste Hindus in the early 19th century to be among the most defiling and degraded of all castes, the Nadars suffered severe social disabilities and were one of the most economically depressed communities in South India. In their response to the social and economic changes during the last century, however, the Nadars have today become one of the most economically and politically successful communities in the South. In the fields of trade and education, they are unexcelled, and in politics, the power of K. Kamaraj Nadar extends across the whole of India.

The Nadars, or the Shanars as they were formerly known, were traditionally toddy-tappers by occupation. Defiled by their ritually-impure calling, the Nadars were forbidden entry into Hindu temples. Wells were strictly forbidden to their use; they were denied the right to carry an umbrella, to wear shoes, golden ornaments, to milk cows, to walk in certain streets; and their women were forbidden to cover their breasts. Indeed, a Nadar could not even *approach* a Brahmin within twenty-four paces.[3]

The Nadars lived in a social limbo somewhere between the Sudras and the outcaste Untouchables. Writing in 1850, Bishop Caldwell of Tinnevelly described the Nadars as belonging to the highest division of the lowest classes or the lowest of the middle classes; poor, but not paupers; rude and unlettered, but by many degrees removed from a savage state.[4]

At that time, as even today, the Nadars were concentrated predominantly south of the Tambraparni River, which crosses Tirunelveli district roughly from Ambasamudram to just south of Tuticorin on the coast. Although the origins of the Nadars are in doubt, the family deities of most Nadars throughout Tamilnad are to be found for the most part in the teris, the sandy palmyra topes, of Tiruchendur and western Nanguneri taluks. Although some traditions among the Nadars cite Ceylon or the southern portions of Travancore, now Kanyakumari district, as the homeland of the community, it appears more likely that they migrated at an early date from the Tiruchendur region to these more hospitable areas.

In the sandy stretches of Tiruchendur, often the only vegetation is the brambled *udai*, used for firewood, and the palmyra palm with which the Nadars have as a community been traditionally associated. In the palmyra forests, where the trees often number several thousand per square mile, the Nadars secured a meagre living from the fabled one thousand and one uses of the tree. The tapper, climbing as many as forty trees twice in each day during the six-month season, extracted the juice which would then be boiled into jaggery sugar or else be prepared as sweet or hard toddy.

In the areas of northern Tirunelveli and Ramnad districts, and throughout Tamilnad wherever the palmyra was to be found, the Nadar climbed the trees, retaining sole monopoly over the palm. To the north of the Tambraparni, however, the palmyras were few, often growing only along the edges of the fields. With insufficient trees for jaggery production, the few palmyras did at least provide the juice for fermented toddy, and the scattered minorities of the Nadar community in the northern districts largely depended on this trade. In these areas where the Nadars numbered usually not more than a few families in a single village, they suffered the full brunt of their community's social disabilities. Forced to reside outside the village itself in a separate *cheri*, the Nadars were refused even the service of the barbers and washermen used by the caste Hindus of the village. Economically dependent on the owners of the trees, the Nadars climbed the palmyras during the tapping season and worked as agricultural labourers during the rest of the year.

To the south of the River Tambraparni, the Nadars constituted the vast majority of the population, and if the greater proportions of the people were no better off economically than their caste fellows to the north, they were subservient to landed families of their own caste. The *Nadans*, lords of the land, were of aristocratic Nadar families invested as petty lords over the *nads*, or countries, of Tiruchendur by the Nayaks who held sway over the southern districts after the fall of the Pandyas. With the disintegration of the Nayak rule into a multitude of warring feudatories, many of the *Nadans* retained control over their lands. One, the lord over Nattatti, was given zamindari rights under British rule. These landed families, such as the Adityans of Kayamoli, formed an endogamous sub-caste within the community, and by their economic power demanded deference from those of other communities to be found in the area. They too, however, shared many of the disabilities of their caste fellows, for though given special rights in the Tiruchendur temple, for example, they were in fact refused admittance into the temple itself.

With the end of the Poligar Wars in 1801, British rule at last brought peace to the seventy-two *nads* of the southern districts of Tirunelveli and Ramnad. Many of the Poligars, most of whom were of the warrior Maravar community, were given zamindari rights over what had been their feudal states. With peace and at least relative security of travel, Nadar traders, who had formerly travelled with their wares among the weekly *shandy* markets in Tiruchendur, now loaded the side packs of their bullocks and pushed northward into the Maravar country with jaggery, dried fish, and salt. With the improvement of roads, many acquired carts for more extensive trade. Travel in the Maravar country, however, was by no means wholly safe, and along their trade routes, these Nadars established *pettais*, fortified enclosures in which they might safely keep their cart and bullocks and in which they might market their goods.

Around these *pettais*, small shops were established, and increasing numbers of the Nadar traders migrated with their families to build their houses and business around the new trade centres. These Nadars settled in six centres primarily, Aruppukottai, Palayampatti, Virudhunagar, Tirumanagalam, Sattankudi, and Sivakasi – the famous 'Six Towns of Ramnad'.

The vast majority of the Nadar community continued to live as before in the lands from the Tiruchendur *teris* down to Cape Comorin. Their lot, however, was not unchanged, for it was here that the European missionaries made their most intensive efforts and reaped their greatest successes. Soon after the first Nadar conversions were made in the early 19th century, a 'mass movement' brought whole Nadar villages and as much as fifty per cent of the Nadar population in these southern regions into the Christian fold. Even today, one of the heaviest concentrations of Christians in India is in the Tirunelveli and Kanyakumari districts, and of their numbers as many as eighty to ninety per cent are Nadars. Suffering severe social disabilities as a defiled caste, the Nadars sought escape from the hierarchy of ritual purity in Christianity. They saw the European missionaries as protectors, and in them they saw the possibility for economic change and advancement. Education rose rapidly among the community of new converts and many sought to abandon the arduous occupation which had degraded them in the eyes of those of high caste. Increasingly, with the aid of the missionaries, Nadars secured small landholdings and intensively cultivated garden crops. In southern Travancore, if their economic position had not greatly improved, education and Christianity had given the Nadars hope of a release from their sufferings under the dominance of the Nair landlords. No longer isolated by their economic subservience, the Nadars now found a new unity through the organisation of the Church.

The movement for social uplift among the Nadars of Kanyakumari soon grew into the famous 'breast cloth controversy'. By tradition in Travancore, the women of the lower castes did not cover their breasts, but in response to the pressures of the Christian Nadars and European missionaries, the Government issued a Proclamation in 1829, permitting native Christian women to cover their breasts in the manner of the

Syrian Christians and the Mopla Muslims – but they were denied the privilege of covering their breasts in the fashion of the high caste Hindus.

Disturbance over the Proclamation culminated in widespread rioting in the largely Christian areas of southern Travancore as Nadar women appeared in the streets wearing the upper cloth after the manner of the Nair women. During the riots, villages were attacked and churches and houses were burned throughout the district before police and military action put down hostilities. There was, however, no loss of life. Keeping a watchful eye on events in Travancore, the Governor of Madras observed that the Dewan's Report was 'temperate', but,

> The degree of interference which for many years past has been exercised by the representative of the British Government in the affairs of Travancore is so large, and his intervention so general, that the credit or discredit of the administration greatly rests with the British Government and it has thereby become their duty to insist upon the observance of a system of toleration, in a more decided manner, than they would be at liberty to adopt, if they had merely to bring their influence to bear on an independent State.[5]

Having consulted the Maharajah, the Dewan wrote to the British Resident that

> His Highness now proposes to abolish all rules prohibiting the covering of the upper parts of the persons of Shanar women and to grant them perfect liberty to meet the requirements of decency any way they may deem proper, with the simple restriction that they do not imitate the same mode of dress that appertains to the higher caste.[6]

A Royal Proclamation was issued accordingly on July 26, 1859. With only a partial victory, the agitation for the breast cloth, nevertheless, marked the first major movement among the depressed classes of the south for a release from the disabilities under which they suffered.

While the women of the Nadar merchant communities in Ramnad had to suffer no such indignities, the Six Town Nadars, though of increasing wealth, retained their formerly low status in the ritual hierarchy. Further, overwhelmingly dominated by the more populous Thevars (Maravars), Reddiars, and Naickers in the countryside around the towns, the Nadars were in a precarious position.

The traders using the facilities of the *pettais* were taxed a certain amount on all goods bought and sold. These 'common good funds', *mahimai*, were then used for the *pettai's* maintenance and expansion.

As the towns themselves grew around these *pettais*, each of the resident merchants and businessmen were required to contribute *mahimai*, the amount of the levy to be decided by the common decision of all the Nadar family elders. This council, which included the head of each household in the community, became known as the *uravinmurai*, and it drew to itself the corporate power of the community. A smaller body of leaders, informally selected, controlled the *uravinmurai*, and the formal leadership within the council was rotated monthly among these men. Their power was absolute within the community. Violations of moral conduct might result in beatings, or, if severe, in ostracism. A failure to pay *mahimai* would only double the levy, and from the *uravinmurai*, there was no appeal. In order to maximise unity within the community, any contact with governmental authorities would be in terms of the community as a whole. Litigation within the community was forbidden: the *uravinmurai* was the final court of authority for the Nadars.

As the wealth of the community grew, the common funds of *mahimai* were used for the welfare of the community as a whole. The poor among the caste were fed and clothed, and jobs were secured for those of able body. Business failures were prevented by the considered use of *mahimai* funds. Wells and public buildings for the use of the community were constructed, and in each of the towns, a Mariaman temple was constructed to the community deity, Kali, the goddess of destruction. Perhaps the most important use of *mahimai* was in the establishment of schools by the Nadar *uravinmurais*. The Virudhunagar *uravinmurai* in 1890, for example, founded the Kshatriya High School, one of the first free schools in Tamilnad open to the children of all caste communities.

The incongruity between the economic position of the Six Town Nadars and their low social status led these Nadars to increasingly attempt to disassociate themselves from the community's traditional occupation. The palmyra became a curse to the Ramnad Nadars, to whom it was an unwelcome reminder of their defiled ritual status. Having abandoned the cultivation and climbing of the despised palm, these Nadars now began to adopt the Brahminical customs of the higher castes. During the latter part of the 19th century, the Nadar community began slowly to sanskritise their manner of life. Among the men, many cropped their hair in the fashion of the Brahmin tuft. They adopted the sacred thread of the 'twice born' and vegetarianism came into vogue. Fathers named their children after the 'new' sanskritic gods which had come into favour among the community, and Brahmin priests were found who were quite willing to provide the

services to the wealthy Nadar temples and to officiate over the ceremonies of the caste.

Behind these pretensions lay the newly-advanced Nadar claim to
high Kshatriya status. Often conflicting and more often without base,
these claims, advanced by the Nadars of both Ramnad and Tirunelveli
in more than fifty books, pamphlets, and periodicals between 1860
and the early 1920s, sought to create a historical myth as to the origins
and greatness of the Nadar community. It sought, however, to do so
in the context of the ritual hierarchy. In the Census of Madras Presidency, 1871, it was reported that:

> A whole literature of ponderous tomes is springing up in Southern India
> with no other object than the exaltation of caste. 'The Shanars of
> Tinnevelly', writes a reverend missionary, 'have just now had their heads
> turned by an absurd tract written to prove that the Shanars are descendants
> of the great warrior caste. They do not merely mean that they were the
> original kings of the soil, but that they are descended from the Aryan
> Kshatriyas.'[7]

From this growing literature, what might be taken as an 'official'
history of the community began to take shape, one that has gained
wide acceptance among the Nadars. This history asserts that the
Nadars are the descendents of the Pandyan kings who ruled over the
southern districts of Tamilnad until they were defeated by successive
Muslim invasions and the final victory of the Vijayanagar Nayaks in the
16th century. With their defeat, the Pandyas were allegedly stripped
of their lands and properties and dispersed over the country. Bur-
dened with all manner of social disabilities imposed upon them by
their Nayak overlords and without other means of livelihood, the
Nadars were forced to accept the demeaning labour of tapping the
palmyra. Others of their number, without lands or home, became
wandering nomads, and from their travels, fathered the trading routes
which were later to succour the rising merchant community of
Ramnad.

Although surely not Aryan Kshatriyas, the identity of the Pandyans
still remains a question. It may well be that the dynasty represented a
number of different groups which rose and fell during the long
centuries of Pandyan rule in Tamilnad. Archaeological and early
textual evidence points to Korkai as one of the origins of Pandyan rule.
Korkai, lying in the region of Tiruchendur, is today predominantly
Nadar in population, and it is conceivable that one of the early
Pandyan houses was in fact Nadar. Certain customs within the
community would also suggest a higher status than the one in which

they have more recently been held by caste Hindus, but there is little evidence to suggest that the Nadars were the Pandyan rulers of later times, as their caste historians claim.

Determined to raise their social and ritual status to a level comparable with their new economic position, the Nadars sought to challenge the ban on temple entry. In 1874, in Madurai, where many of the Six Town Nadars had found new business opportunities, the Nadars filed a criminal complaint in assertion of their right to enter the great Meenakshi Temple. The case failed, and two years later again without success, the Nadars sought entry into the temple at Tirutangal in eastern Ramnad.[8]

Conflict between the Nadars and other communities soon arose in a village near Sattur in 1883, when the Nadars attempted to take a procession through the village streets. Ten years later in a similar dispute at Kalugumalai, the Zamindar of Ettaiyapuram, a trustee of the local temple, obtained an injunction to restrain the Nadars from conducting a procession through the car streets reserved for caste Hindu festivals. The Nadars converted as a body to Roman Catholicism, and the converts set up their place of worship in a converted shop on the very street in question. On the day of the Hindu festival in which the temple car would be dragged by the devotees through the streets, the Nadars set up a *pandal* across the road in front of the new chapel. With the car unable to pass, the Nadars then set upon the crowd with stones. In the ensuing riots, the Brahmin manager of the Ettaiyapuram estate was stabbed to death, together with two of his followers. Seven Nadars were killed, and the chapel was burned and Nadar houses were looted.[9] The dispute, however, was only a preface to what was to follow.

In that same year, 1895, the Nadars of Sivakasi, one of the wealthiest of the famous Six Towns of Ramnad, petitioned the Temple Committee for the appointment of a Nadar Trustee to the managing body of the local Siva temple. When the request was rejected, some Nadars tried to force their way into the temple, and in the disturbance which followed some temple property was burned. The Nadars were tried and acquitted, and when they re-attempted the entry, they were acquitted again. The Sivakasi temple was then closed altogether. Mutual hostility soon erupted in open conflict, and in April 1899, the Nadars of Sivakasi attacked their Maravar antagonists, burning fifty-five of their houses.[10]

Jealous of the rise of the Nadars to great wealth and outraged at their pretensions to high status, the high caste Hindus nursed a bitterness only heightened by the events in Sivakasi. Supported by the

Brahmins, Vellalas, and the Maravar zamindars, roving bands of Maravars and Pallars, drawn from the regions of eastern Ramnad and northern Tirunelveli, soon began to attack and pillage Nadar villages in the area of Sivakasi. As the marauding insurgents moved closer to Sivakasi itself, the Vellalas and people of other communities, together with their properties and goods, evacuated the town, throwing the Nadars into a panic. Unable to secure the protection of local authorities, who were believed to be either in league with the attackers or at least intimidated by them, the Sivakasi Nadars pleaded with the Government to protect them from the forthcoming doom.

The attack on Sivakasi itself was set for June 6, and the residents of the town were forewarned of their impending disaster. Unable to secure protection, the Nadars evacuated many women and children, but most of them stayed behind to protect their town and properties.

On June 6, at the appointed hour of 10.00 a.m., 5000 Maravars attacked the town of Sivakasi, and, although the Maravars were finally repulsed, 16 Nadars were left dead. The following day, military troops arrived from Tiruchinopoly, but in the next few weeks, roving bands of Maravars attacked nearly 150 villages, looting and burning some 4,000 houses.[11]

Of the 1,958 people arrested, 552 were convicted, and 7 were sentenced to death.[12] While the details of the riot's origins never became clearly known, the concurrent disturbances in Kamudi, forty miles west of Sivakasi, undoubtedly contributed to the intensity of the situation, and it was charged that the Raja of Ramnad, the Nadar's antagonist in the Kamudi matter, had in fact himself incited his Maravar caste fellows to attack Sivakasi.

On the 14th of May, 1897, a group of 15 Nadars in the town of Kamudi entered the Hindu temple of Meenakshi Sundareswara. As the facts of the case were established in the Subordinate Court at Madurai, these Nadars, carrying torches and accompanied by drums, forcibly entered the temple in spite of remonstrance by the temple servants. Entering into the inner shrine, they garlanded the idol, offering it coconuts and swung lighted camphor before it. They further went into the sanctum sanctorum of the principal deity, relighted their extinguished torches from a lamp burning near the festival idol, and touched the sacred image.[13]

Alleging that the temple had been defiled and that the Nadars, being of low caste, were denied by tradition the right of admission into the temple, the Zamindar of Ramnad, Rajah M. Bhaskara Sethupathi, as the hereditary trustee of the temple of Kamudi, filed a suit against the Nadars. With 75 witnesses of all castes and a mass of evidence from the caste histories to which we have referred, the Nadars sought to establish their right as a high caste to enter the temple and "to participate in the puja and worship therein performed in the same manner and to the same extent as other classes in the village except Brahmins ..."[14]

The judgement went against the Nadars. The Nadars appealed to the High Court of Judicature at Madras and then to the Privy Council. Sitting in 1908, the Privy Council affirmed the decree of the Subordinate Judge of Madurai, citing the decision of the High Court.

> In the process of time many of the Shanars took to cultivation, trade, and money-lending, and today there is a numerous and prosperous body of Shanars who have no immediate concern with the immemorial calling of their caste. In many villages they own much of the land and monopolise the bulk of the trade and wealth. With the increase of wealth they have, not unnaturally, sought for social recognition and to be treated on a footing of equality in religious matters.
>
> ... According to the Agama shastras, which are received as authoritative by worshippers of Siva in Madura district, entry into a temple where the ritual prescribed by these shastras is observed is prohibited to all those whose profession is the manufacture of intoxicating liquor and the climbing of palmyra and coconut trees ... No doubt many of the Shanars have abandoned that occupation and have won for themselves, by education, industry, and frugality, respectable positions as traders and merchants, and even as vakils and clerks, and it is natural to feel sympathy for their efforts to obtain social recognition and to rise to what is regarded as a higher form of religious worship; but such sympathy will not be increased by unreasonable and unfounded pretensions, and in the effort to rise, the Shanars must not invade the established rights of other castes.[15]

If the Nadars had suffered a defeat at the hands of the Court, they had gained widespread sympathy and, even more important, through the litigations and the concurrent rioting, community consciousness was aroused. While the vast majority of the Nadar community remained miserably depressed economically and socially as well, the increasingly important role of education and the rise of the Nadar business classes had given the community a new sense of self-respect. The development of roads and communications facilities broke down the barriers of spatial distance which had divided the community, and increasing interactions within the caste over a wide geographic area eroded the distinctions between endogamous sub-castes into which the community had been divided.

With the new impetus for unity and uplift, a number of prominent Nadars assembled in 1895 at Madurai, but 'The Kshatriya Mahajana

Sangam', the name given to their association, never really developed.[16] It was not until 15 years later that Rao Bahadur T. Rattinasami Nadar of Porayar, Tanjore, sought to revive the association. Of a distinguished and wealthy family of *Akbari* contractors, Rattinasami invited a number of leaders within the community to Porayar for a plenary session in February 1910. His son, V. Ponnusami Nadar, was elected President of the new association, the Nadar Mahajana Sangam. In December of that same year, the second conference of the Sangam was held at Madras, with more than 750 delegates attending. Soon after this, however, the death of the Sangam's founder and that of the chairman of the second conference dealt the association an almost fatal blow. Thus greatly weakened it was not until 1917 that another conference was convened.

The objectives of the Nadar Mahajana Sangam were:

(a) To promote the social, material, and general welfare of the Nadars;

(b) To protect and promote the interest and rights of the community;

(c) To take practical measures for the social, moral, and intellectual advancement of the Nadars;

(d) To start schools and colleges for imparting western education to Nadar children and to help poor but deserving pupils belonging to the community with scholarships, books, fees, etc.;

(e) To encourage and promote commercial and industrial enterprise among the members of the community;

(f) To foster and promote the spirit of union and solidarity among the members of the community;

(g) The raising of funds by subscription, donation or other means for the above objects, and the doing of all such other things as are incidental and conducive to the attainment of the above objects or any of them.[17]

Among the first immediate concerns of the Sangam was to disassociate itself from the word *Shanar* and to seek official recognition of the community's Kshatriya status. The hierarchy of caste status was recorded dutifully in the Government Census. Each caste was listed, citing its traditional occupation, in an order which reflected the ranking in the Hindu hierarchy of ritual purity. The 'Shanars', as traditional toddy drawers, came very near the bottom.

In January 1921 the Executive Council of the Nadar Mahajana Sangam passed a resolution calling upon all Nadars to return their caste as 'Kshatriya' in the forthcoming 1921 census, and the circular was distributed throughout the community urging compliance with the resolution. In explaining their position in a letter to the Chief Secretary to the Government, Madras, the Sangam stated that "The

term Shanar had acquired an offensive and contemptuous significance in common parlance, [and] there is no reason why the Government should continue to retain an offensive expression in describing
a community which is among the most loyal of His Majesty's subjects."[18]

In deference to the objections that 'Kshatriya' was, as a caste name,
'too general and too vague', the Council of the Nadar Mahajana Sangam
agreed that the members of the community should return their caste
as 'Nadar-Kshatriya' rather than as 'Kshatriya' alone. G.T. Boag,
Superintendent of Census Operations, Madras, received a delegation
from the Sangam and agreed to instruct all census enumerators to
accept 'Nadar-Kshatriya' as the community's name if so returned.[19]
Seeking legal recognition of Boag's assurance the Sangam reiterated
its plea in a memorandum to the Governor of Madras.[20]

On April 8, 1921, a Government Order was issued, informing the
petitioners "that the procedure followed at the recent census was to
leave everyone to return his caste name as he chose, adapting for use
in the report that name which the majority of the caste actually return."
The Order further indicated the government's decision "to discon-
tinue the tabulation of the traditional occupation of particular castes
and to record only the actual occupation by which each person
lives."[21]

In compliance with the order, Boag, in the Madras Census Report,
states :

The 1921 Census records the caste as *Nadar* rather than as in 1911 ...
In deference to the wishes of the representatives of the Nadar community,
the Madras Government have decided on this occasion not to show
traditional occupation of the Nadars as has hitherto been shown as toddy-
drawing; but they now claim that they are by tradition and inheritance
lords of the soil and that toddy-drawing was the occupation only of a
comparatively few degenerate members of the caste.[22]

Following the Government's order with regard to the Census, the
Council of the Sangam resolved "to request the Government to adopt
the term 'Nadar-Kshatriya' in place of 'Shanars' for use in all Government records."[23] While responding to the Sangam's petition, the
Government chose to recognize the term *Nadar* simply rather than
Nadar-Kshatriya. In July, a Government Order was issued to the
effect that :

"the term 'Nadar' shall in future be adopted in place of 'Shanar' in all
official documents".[24]

During this same period, the Sangam began to campaign against toddy-tapping within the community. As it was described in a letter to the Government :

> In view of the fact that toddy-drawing is held in low estimation by the people, the Council of the Nadar Mahajana Sangam, which stands for the social and moral advancement of the Nadars, resolved ... to appeal to such members of the community as live by toddy-drawing to abandon the occupation .... This resolution, we need hardly state, has nothing whatsoever to do with politics and is not to be confounded with the Non-co-operation propaganda now so much talked about.[25]

While the greater number of Nadars in Tiruchendur taluk and throughout the palmyra forests of south-eastern Tirunelveli district were engaged primarily in the manufacture of jaggery, many Nadars in the other regions of Tirunelveli and to the north in Tamilnad were engaged in the tapping, distribution, and sale of hard toddy. Touring agents from the Sangam were dispatched throughout these areas for anti-toddy propaganda.

The Nadar Mahajana Sangam continued to support prohibition, but as the community became more secure in its advancing position, the Sangam worked increasingly for the welfare of the palmyra climbers, who still formed a large proportion of the community. The Sangam fought to abolish the tax levied on palmyra trees in Tirunelveli and Ramnad districts and with the introduction of prohibition in October 1948, the Sangam together with the Dakshina Mara Nadar Sangam of Tirunelveli,[26] sought government benefits for the displaced tappers. By this time, however, only a relatively small number of Nadars were exclusively engaged in toddy manufacture. Although the far greater number were engaged in the production of 'sweet toddy' and jaggery, the stipulations of the Prohibition Act endangered the entire palmyra industry and threatened to economically displace the climbers altogether. The licensing procedures and the requirements governing the tapping of the trees brought the industry to a virtual standstill in the months immediately following the enactment of the law. Only with the pressure of the two Sangams and a number of *ad hoc* committees was the enforcement of the regulations eased.

As the community continued to rise and to increasingly gain the respect of traditionally higher castes, a new confidence was revealed in the Sangam's efforts to have the Nadar community listed among the 'Backward Classes' when thirty years before, they had fought to remove the caste from such Government schedules. As early as 1935, and again in 1940, the Nadar Mahajana Sangam had requested that the Government include the Nadar community among the educationally backward communities so that fee concessions might be given to Nadar students. It was not, however, until after Independence, with the establishment of the Backward Classes Commission, that the Nadars made a concerted effort to have themselves listed as a Depressed Class. In December 1952, at Sivakasi, the 22nd Nadar Conference "resolved to request the Government of India, the Government of Madras and the Government of Travancore-Cochin to include the Nadar community in the list of Backward Classes in education as, with the exception of few towns inhabited by Nadars, 90 per cent of the Nadars living in other areas are backward in education, economic conditions and industries."[27]

The Nadars were placed in a peculiar position. Having for so long tried to build the image of an advanced community, they now had to depict its depressed state for the benefit of the Commission. The fact was, of course, that while sections of the Hindu Nadar community in Ramnad and Madurai had advanced so significantly as to become one of the most important business communities in Tamilnad, the far greater proportion continued to scratch out only the barest existence in the village — and the Christian Nadars fared little better when taken as a whole, although many of their number had taken prominent positions as educators, lawyers, physicians, and government servants.

The Backward Classes Commission was confronted by a situation in which vast numbers of the caste surely met the Commissioner's criteria for a Depressed Class, yet a sizable portion of the community was among the most advanced communities educationally and economically in Tamilnad. Their solution was to designate 'Shanars' as among the 'Most Backward Classes' on the list to receive educational concessions. Although their use of the word *Shanar* was designed to restrict benefits to those families actually engaged in tree climbing, it soon gave rise to confusion. First it was extended to include Christians of the community so designated.[28] The difficulty regarding the word *Shanar* was finally resolved in recognising *Nadar* as synonymous with *Shanar*. Children were then required to produce a certificate attesting to their parents' occupation in order to receive the educational benefits.[29]

The Nadar Community, however, was by no means solely reliant upon the Government for educational advancement. Perhaps more than any other community in Tamilnad, the Nadars have recognised the importance of education for social uplift. Education was greatly stressed by the missionaries among the Nadar converts in Tirunelveli district, and during the 19th and 20th centuries, the Church Missionary Society and other missionary efforts established elementary schools and high schools throughout the district, together with several important colleges. The Hindus were at first less responsive to education, but in Ramnad, as the Six Town Nadars began to advance in the fields of business, schools were established through *mahimai* funds by the *uravinmurai*. Among the first of these schools was the Kshatriya Vidhyasala High School at Virudhunagar. Established in 1889, the School provided free education to the children of all caste communities. A complex of lower schools has grown up around the High School, now serving some 4,000 students with the modern facilities of what is one of the finest school systems in India.

The most important advance in education among the Hindu Nadars came with the founding of the Nadar Mahajana Sangam in 1910. From its inception, education became one of its primary concerns. Among the early objects of the Sangam was that of providing financial aid to needy students. In 1921, the first scholarship-loans were awarded, and from that date to 1964, 3,024 students received scholarships amounting to more than 400,000 rupees.[30] The Sangam has also assisted villages and towns in establishing their own schools, and each year as many as 40 or 50 schools receive direct financial assistance from the Sangam. The Sangam, too, has played an important role in the founding of new colleges. Rao Bahadur M.S.P. Senthikumara Nadar, at the 1947 Nadar Conference, announced that he was prepared to contribute two lakhs of rupees towards the founding of a Nadar college. In response to his offer, the leaders of the Nadar community in Virudhunagar agreed to accept the responsibility, and in August of that same year, the Senthikumara Nadar College was inaugurated.[31] A women's college and a polytechnic at Virudhunagar and the Ayya Nadar Janakiamal College at Sivakasi soon followed. The newest of the Nadar colleges, now under construction at Madurai, is endowed by the Sangam itself, which will accept the responsibility of management. The college is, in the words of Sangam General Secretary, P.R. Muthusami Nadar, 'a turning point in the history of the Nadar Mahajana Sangam.'

The Sangam has also founded libraries, reading rooms, a co-operative bank, and it has given financial assistance to Nadars to start new industries and small factories. But, beyond education, the primary concern of the Nadar Mahajana Sangam has been community solidarity. Nine travelling agents, kept constantly in the field by the Sangam, visit villages and towns throughout the southern districts in an attempt to organise the Nadar community in each place as an *uravinmurai* or as a sangam, which are in turn established as autonomous branches of the Nadar Mahajana Sangam. The *uravinmurai* is then encouraged to collect *mahimai* for the establishment of schools and public buildings for general community welfare. Disputes over the management of these *mahimai* funds and properties, however, have often posed a threat to the unity of the caste. At the 10th Nadar Conference in 1925, a prominent Nadar leader warned that :

> Communal riots or commotions are . . . of far less moment and fraught with much less danger than evils caused to our community by factions and feuds among ourselves. I pray therefore our leaders to continue to keep the same watchful eye upon all members of our community as before and at the first symptom of any intensive trouble to hasten with all speed to the locality affected and suppress all such factious outbreaks at their very inception.[32]

Recognising the *uravinmurai* as the foundation of the community's strength, the Sangam accordingly established a panchayat system whereby any internal dispute within the community could be placed before a body of uninvolved Nadar leaders for mediation. Upon request to intervene in a dispute, the Sangam will appoint an *ad hoc* panchayat committee under the direction of one of the Sangam officers. An initial investigation of the facts is made, and all parties to the dispute are required to sign their names in agreement to accept as binding any decision made by the panchayat. This agreement is rarely broken, although the number of internal disputes may now be on the rise.

If there has been an increase in the number of internal disputes, there has been a concomitant decline in the number of disputes between the Nadars as a community and other castes. Each year the Sangam has received fewer complaints by Nadars describing their sufferings and ill-treatment at the hand of other community people. The Nadars are, however, by no means yet free of caste oppression. In many areas where the Sangam has not effectively organised the Nadar community, they remain weak, divided, and at the mercy of the dominant caste. In many villages where the Nadars number only a minority, as in western Ramnad, they continue to suffer various social disabilities, and in scattered villages they still face harassment on refusing to pay protection money to self-appointed Maravar watchmen.

In organising the Nadars of any village, the Nadar Mahajana Sangam backs them with the strength of the larger community. In any dispute arising between Nadars and the members of other communities, the Nadars may petition the Sangam to intervene. The Sangam will take action, however, only after an investigation to establish the truth of the situation as described by the 'plaintiffs'. If a settlement of the dispute is possible only through police investigation and subsequent court action, the Sangam will make a full report to the proper authorities, presenting the situation as accurately as they have been able to ascertain. While the Sangam will neither contest the case for the Nadar claimants nor provide financial support for litigations, the Sangam will give all assistance in securing legal counsel and in seeing that the Nadars' case is properly heard. If however, the dispute does not involve deep caste antagonism and if police intervention can be avoided, the Sangam will approach the leaders of the other community to discuss the possibilities of a settlement. In many cases, a panchayat will be formed for compulsory arbitration, as in the case of internal disputes.

Where once the Nadars sought the high Kshatriya status in the ritual hierarchy, increasingly the Nadar Mahajana Sangam has sought the relations of equality among all castes. The Sangam, while seeking the unity and uplift of the Nadar community, has sought to create the image of itself as a *community* but not a *communal* organisation. Indeed, the Sangam has recently changed the name of the Nadar Bank to 'The Tamilnad Mercantile Bank', and in the establishment of a new lodge, it was by general consensus agreed that the word Nadar should not appear in the name, as its facilities would be available to all communities. In reviewing '42 years of service' in 1952, the Sangam said that it sought not to create 'Caste feeling', but rather it aimed at "bringing up the Nadar community and the country along with it." [33] And among their resolutions for the uplift of the Nadar community drafted by the Sangam's annual meeting in 1964 was the desire "to have cordial relationship with other communities. The Nadar community must allow other communities to use the schools, tanks, temples and wells started or established by Nadars." [34] Although the Nadars still retain a high degree of antagonism towards certain castes and are themselves one of the most 'clannish' communities in Tamilnad, their response to the image of the casteless society reflects fundamentally the role of the Nadar community in the contemporary political history of Tamilnad.

At Porayar in 1910, the first conference of the Nadar Mahajana Sangam expressed its "genuine and sincere loyalty and devotion to the throne of his Imperial Majesty King Edward VII, Emperor of India, and his august representatives in India, the excellencies the

Viceroy of India and the Governor of Madras for the manifold blessings enjoyed by their community under the benign British rule."[35] This loyalty was reaffirmed in each of the subsequent Nadar Conferences held before independence. The Sangam sought to assure the Government "that our community is loyal to the core and keenly alive to the benefits of the British rule. The Nadars are law-abiding people and have no sympathy whatsoever with any movement which tends to weaken the forces of law and order."[36]

Three factors contributed to the Nadars' support for the Government. Among the Nadar converts in Tirunelveli, association with the missionaries favourably disposed the Nadars to European rule. They were seen also as protectors, not by the Christians alone, but by the Hindu Nadars as well. European rule was seen as a blessing which militated against the oppressive tyranny of the high caste communities. Further, the Nadars as a mercantile community found it in their interests to support whatever government might be in power. Thus, from its founding, the Nadar Mahajana Sangam pledged its loyalty to the Government, and in its early years, sought to associate itself with the Government by inviting ranking Government officers to preside over the yearly Nadar conferences. These early conference presidents were largely Brahmins, who by their presence endowed the Conference not only with the aura of the official but the sanctified as well. As the non-Brahmin Justice Party[37] came to power in Madras after the Montagu-Chelmsford Reforms of 1919, the Nadars gave the new party its wholehearted support, and in the conferences of the 1920s and 1930s, the presiding officers were the luminaries of the non-Brahmin movement.

With the new reforms, the Nadar Mahajana Sangam urged the Government to consider the nomination of Nadars to the Council as 'indispensable for the protection of its interests'.[38] A few days later, the Governor, on the recommendation of P. T. Rajan, leader of the Justice Party, announced the nomination of W.P.A. Soundarapandian Nadar to the Legislative Council. Soundarapandian, the 27 year-old son of a wealthy planter family of Pattiveeranpatti estates near Kodaikanal, became the first Nadar to enter the Madras Legislature. He rapidly rose in the echelons of Justice Party leadership, and, in his later career, served as a General Secretary of the Sangam for 4 years and as its Vice-President for 17 years. In his efforts for the community' s uplift, Soundarapandian came to be known as 'the uncrowned king' of the Nadar community.

W.P.A. Soundarapandian soon fell under the spell of E.V. Rama-sami Naicker, the non-Brahmin militant and leader of social reform.

Seeking to draw in the mass support of the Nadar community for his new movement, E.V.R. selected Soundarapandian as the president of the first Self-Respect Conference, held at Chingleput in 1928. The third Self-Respect Conference was held in the predominantly Nadar town of Virudhunagar. The Nadars' response to the Self-Respect movement was tremendous. Increasingly within the community, the Nadars began to de-sanskritise their manner of life, in abandoning the pretensions to high caste adopted in the last years of the 19th century. The sacred thread was thrown away and the use of Brahmin *purohits* was discouraged. The self-respect marriage became widespread, as the people sought to release themselves from the priestly authority which had held them in at least psychological subservience to the high castes.

Although there was within the Nadar community some degree of support for the Congress and for Swaraj, the Nadar community remained almost wholly united in its support of the Justice Party and in its loyalty to British Rule. In 1937, following the new Reform Act by which suffrage was widely extended, the first Congress ministry came to power in Madras. As Chief Minister, C. Rajagopalachari introduced legislation for the removal of the civil and social disabilities under which the lower castes had suffered. This legislation included the Temple Entry Authorisation and Indemnity Act of 1939, which paved the way for the opening of the temples to the people of all communities, and in that same year, the great Meenakshi temple at Madurai threw open its gates to the Harijans and to the Nadars. The Temple Entry Act was the watershed in the political history of the Nadar community. The tide began to turn away from the dying Justice Party, which had in its years of power done nothing to remove the ban on temple entry. The image of Gandhi and the growing momentum of the movement for Swaraj soon brought growing numbers of Nadars into the Congress fold. Further, although Kamaraj had had little influence within the Nadar community, his ascendency in the Congress and his election as President of the Tamilnad Congress Committee in 1940 acted as a catalyst to draw the support of the Nadar community.

Although the Nadar community as a whole, including the Sangam's leadership as individuals, had given support to the Justice Party, the Nadar Mahajana Sangam itself had never officially supported any party or candidate — though, in its loyalty to the Raj, it had pointedly denounced the non-cooperation movement. As the forces of the Congress grew within the Nadar community, however, the leadership of the Sangam remained in the hands of the old Justice Party men, and at the Nadar Conference of 1940, the Nadars' loyalty to the British was again proclaimed. The sentiments within the community, however, were rapidly shifting, and in 1941 the Sangam was confronted by political schism within the community. The Sangam officers had extended an invitation to G. T. Boag, who with the resignation of the Congress Ministry took control of the Government as Adviser, to preside over the forthcoming Conference. The invitation brought cries of outrage from the Congressmen within the Sangam. Boycotting the Sangam Conference, they convened in that same year their own conference under the name of 'The National Nadar Association' Demanding immediate Independence, the new association sought to bring the Nadar community into the ranks of the Congress. Urged by Rajagopalachari to change the name to the Nadars' National Association, they held their second conference under the presidentship of C. R.

The Nadars National Association was shortlived by its very success. In 1942, at the height of the Quit India Movement, the Congress Nadars gained ascendency within the Sangam, as P. R. Muthusami Nadar was elected as General Secretary. The next Nadar Conference was not held until June of 1947. With Independence, the overwhelming majority within the Nadar community supported the Congress Party. It had brought temple entry. It had brought Swaraj. And, most important for the business classes, it had brought a new Government to which their economic interests owed allegiance. For most Nadars, however, the Congress was the party of Kamaraj, their illustrious son who was to become the Chief Minister of Madras and the President of the All-India Congress Party. If Kamaraj brought them no special benefits, he did endow the Nadars with a new sense of pride. He was the symbol that the community had at last 'arrived'.

The very success of the Nadar community in its rise socially, economically, and politically has eroded the unity of the community which had in fact made the uplift possible. Differentiation within the Nadar community and the concomitant decline in the elaboration of caste ranking has increasingly undermined the community's political solidarity. The community continues to predominantly support the Congress, but an increasing multiplicity of interests and associations have fragmented its former unity.

In the villages, insofar as the Nadars remain essentially undifferentiated and insofar as the elaboration of caste ranking retains its significance, the Nadars are still characterised by a high degree of unity, and their political behaviour reflects a cohesive political culture. In villages and towns where the Nadars are in the overwhelming majority, as in Tiruchendur Taluk, the elaboration of caste ranking is necessarily minimal. The candidates of all parties tend to be Nadars, and the politics of the region is not so much between communities as *within* the Nadar community itself. As there is still little differentiation within the community and with economic dependence of the lower classes upon the landowners, the politics of the Nadar-dominated areas of south-east Tirunelveli has been essentially in terms of factional client groups. The aura of Kamaraj and his association with the Congress has, however, drawn the Nadars here primarily towards the Congress party. Caste thus continues to play a major role, and it is clearly evidenced in that the minority communities in these areas, primarily the Thevars and Muslims, tend to polarise around the non-Congress Nadar candidate.

The cities, the locus of economic change and social mobilisation, most clearly reflect the decline in the elaboration of caste ranking and the rise in differentiation within the single caste communities. Traditional occupations long abandoned, each community is represented by an increasingly diverse range of economic pursuits. In Madurai or in Madras, the range within the Nadar community would include coolie labourers, government clerks, small shopkeepers, physicians and teachers, and wealthy businessmen with trading interests all over the world. The differences *within* the caste have become increasingly more significant than the differences between the individuals of different castes sharing similar social and economic backgrounds. The decline in the barriers of ritual purity have in the cities released the individual for the possibility of forming new interests and associations, cutting across caste lines. The Nadar mill workers in Madurai are far more likely to vote Communist along with the Thevar workers than they are to vote Congress, despite the continuing charisma of Kamaraj, and the young Nadar students are drawn with their fellows of other communities to the image of Tamil nationalism in the Dravida Munetra Kazhagham. The increasing differentiation within the community and a concomitant decline in the elaboration of caste ranking has fundamentally affected the homogeneity of the caste community, and if, as we have said, these loosened moorings render the individual available to ambivalence, they too provide the foundation for the emergence of a political culture characterised by the interests of economic class.

NOTES

1. McKim Marriott, *Caste Ranking and Community Structure in Five Regions of India and Pakistan,* Deccan College Monograph Series No. 23, Poona: Deccan College, 1960, p. 27.
2. For a more extensive analysis of the Nadar community, see Robert L. Hardgrave, Jr., *The Nadars of Tamilnad: The Political Culture of a Community in Change,* Berkeley: University of California Press, 1968. Also see 'Varieties of Political Behaviour Among the Nadars of Tamilnad' *Asian Survey,* Vol. VI (November, 1966), pp. 614-21.
3.. J. N. Bhattacharya, *Hindu Castes and Sects,* Calcutta: Thacker, Spink & Co., 1896, p. 255.
4. Robert Caldwell, *The Tinnevelly Shanars,* London: Society for the Propagation of the Gospel, 1850, p. 5.
5. V. Nagam Aiya, *The Travancore State Manual,* Vol. 1, Trivandrum. Government Press, 1906, p. 530.
6. *Ibid.,* pp. 530-31.
7. Census of Madras Presidency, 1871, Vol. 1. Report, p. 118.
8. *Madras District Gazetteers,* Tinnevelly, Col. 1, p. 126.
9. *Ibid.*
10. *Ibid.,* pp. 126-27.
11. Madras Mail, July 19, 1899.
12. *Report of the Inspector-General of Police,* quoted in Edgar Thurston, *Castes and Tribes of Southern India,* Madras: Government Press, 1909, Vol. VI, p. 364.
13. *Ibid.*
14. *Irulappan Nadar et al v. Rajah M. Bhaskara Sethupathi, Rajah of Ramnad et al.* In the Subordinate Court of Madura, East. July 20, 1899. O.S. 33 of 1898.
15. *Sankaralinga Nadan et al v. Rajeswara Dorai et al.* On appeal from the High Court of judicature at Madras. Privy Council. Indian Law Reports 31 Madras 236 (1908). See also: 35 Indian Appeals 176 (1908).
16. *Rules and Regulations of the Nadar Mahajana Sangam, Madura* Madurai: Nadar Mahajana Sangam, 1919, p. 3.
17. *Ibid.,* pp. 12-13.
18. Letter to Chief Secretary to Government, Madras, from the Nadar Mahajana Sangam, January 1921.
19. Letter to Nadar Mahajana Sangam from G.T. Boag, Superintendent of Census Operations, Madras, February 2, 1921.
20. *To His Excellency the Governor of Fort St. George in Council, the Humble Memorial Presented by the Nadar Mahajana Sangam, Madura,* 1921 (printed).
21. Government of Madras. Law (General) Department, G.O. No. 56, dated 8th April 1921.
22. Madras Census Report, 1921, Part I, pp. 153-54. It should be noted here that Christian Nadars were classified under the term *Indian Christian*

rather than *Nadar*.

23. Letter to Chief Secretary to the Government, Madras, from Nadar Mahajana Sangam, May 16, 1921.

24. Government of Madras, Law (General) Department, G.O. No. 78, dated 7th July 1921.

25. Letter to the Deputy Commissioner, Salt, Akbari, and Customs Department, Tinnevelly, from Nadar Mahajana Sangam, May 23, 1921.

26. The Dakshina Mara Nadar Sangam was established in a court settlement in 1942, for the management of a number of *pettais* under dispute in the southern districts. While providing some scholarships and representing the Nadars in various disputes, the Sangam is primarily concerned with *pettai* management. Its range of activities is almost solely limited to Tirunelveli district.

27. Quoted in a letter to the Secretary of Education Department, Government of Madras, from the Nadar Mahajana Sangam, February 10, 1953.

28. G.O. Ms. No. 889. Department of Industries, Labour and Co-operation, Madras, July 3, 1958.

29. G.O. Ms. No. 561. Education, Madras, April 3, 1963.

30. *Report of the Nadar Mahajana Sangam 55th Annual Meeting,* Coimbatore, May 31, 1964. *Tamil.*

31. P. Thangarajan, Principal, 'History of the College', in *V.V. Ramasami E. Paaraatu Malar,* Virudhunagar : V. H. N. Senthikumara Nadar College Old Boys' Association, 1964, p. 289

32. Address by V. Balaguruswami Nadar, 10th Nadar Mahajana Sangam Conference, June 9, 1925.

33. *Nadar Mahajana Sangam: 42 Years of Service,* Madurai: NMS 1952.

34. Nadar Mahajana Sangam, 55th Annual Meeting, Coimbatore, March 31, 1964. *Tamil.*

35. Telegrams to Viceroy and the Governor of Madras from Nadar Mahajana Sangam, 1st Conference, Porayar, February 6-8, 1910. *Tamil.*

36. Letter to the Chief Secretary to the Government, Madras, from Nadar Mahajana Sangam, April 23, 1921.

37. See Eugene F. Irschick, *Politics and Social Conflicts in South India: A Study of the Non-Brahmin Movement and Tamil Separatism, 1916 to 1929.* Berkeley : University of California. For a study of the Development of the politics of Tamil nationalism through the Self-Respect Movement, the D. K. and the D.M.K., see Robert L. Hardgrave, *The Dravidian Movement,* Bombay: Popular Prakashan, 1965.

38. Letter to the Governor of Madras from Nadar Mahajana Sangam, December 14, 1920.

CHAPTER FIVE

Caste and Faction Among the Dominant Caste: The Reddis and Kammas of Andhra

CAROLYN M. ELLIOTT

Questions concerning the role of caste in politics raise crucial issues regarding the interaction between a traditional society and new institutions of political life. They focus on two particularly interesting issues: the transformation of a caste-based society as its members begin to participate in the new institutions, and the impact of such primordial loyalties on the electoral politics.[1] In so doing they tend to assume the existence of caste as significant groupings, selecting for study instances in which castes have mobilised politically and through this demonstrating how caste ties have enabled these groups to win the right to political participation.[2] By turning the question around, however, one might seek to identify conditions which favour the articulation of caste as a significant grouping in comparison with those which do not. One might ask how members of a traditional caste have won this right to participate, and look at the various forms in which they organised. From this perspective, caste is a significant category of persons in the traditional society who are organised into many small but interlocking groups. The question would focus on whether these groups articulated a broad caste loyalty in modern politics, or formed other kinds of associations with different ideologies and mixed caste membership.

The experience of similarly placed groups confronting similar political systems may help in suggesting variables which differentiate between conditions producing caste organisations and those producing other kinds of political organisations. For this purpose the

Reddis and Kammas of Andhra Pradesh may be compared. These castes are similar in status to the highest non-Brahmin landowning castes in the state. They also form roughly the same proportion of the population in the areas they occupy, each the largest group in its area except for Harijans.[3] Their experiences in modern electoral politics are also similar. Both have been accommodated into leadership of factions in the ruling Congress Party. These factions, however, are not caste factions. Both Reddis and Kammas participate in factions established before they entered politics, which have recruited members of many castes into an ongoing factional structure. Therefore a large part of the analysis of Reddy and Kamma political experiences must be concerned with this process of mobilisation into factions, a mobilisation which has undercut the organisation of solidarities along caste lines. Yet there are some differences in these experiences, both differences between the two castes and between high and low status members of the same caste. Examination of these differences in experience may thus provide countervailing examples of caste solidarities which help in formulating hypotheses about the conditions under which different types of political organisations are formed.

At the risk of oversimplification, the possibilities may be viewed along two dimensions, caste solidarity on a horizontal dimension and factional mobilisation on a vertical one. The important role of caste loyalties in forming horizontal solidarities has been demonstrated in many studies of Indian politics, including several in this volume. Formation of these solidarities necessitates the breaking of traditional patron-client and factional ties in the village. Such groups must also overcome traditional divisions within their own groups, notably differences of sub-caste rank and economic status. When access to sources of power in the state has been denied to them, however, many castes have found these solidarities necessary to make effective demands for recognition and participation. This self-conscious and formal articulation of caste-wide ties is a modern phenomenon, associated with the expansion of loyalties beyond the village and the secularisation of goals characteristic of modern societies.

Political life in Andhra Pradesh suggests, however, that the breaking of vertical ties to achieve a new horizontal integration may not always be a feasible or useful means to power in democratic politics. The traditional position of a caste, the degree of social distance between castes, and the feeling of external domination over the whole society may favour the perpetuation of vertical structures. Furthermore, political and economic change may augment the articulation of traditional differences within the caste, making horizontal integration more difficult while bringing about other types of solidarity. Finally, the state political system may accommodate individual members of the caste as they begin to ask for recognition, making the formation of new kinds of associations at the local level unnecessary. In these cases, the expansion of loyalties and the democratisation of power takes place within the pattern of continuing vertical ties between castes. In areas where there is a dominant caste, the process of vertical mobilisation often enhances its political power. Where this has occurred, vertical mobilisation under dominant caste leadership may be an alternate means to modernisation.

The basic structures for both horizontal and vertical mobilisation exist in the traditional village society. Every villager is a member of several groups in the village which may be ranged schematically along the same two dimensions of a smaller scale. As a member of a family and caste, he interacts with persons of similar social status, participating in relationships of ritual, kinship and group regulation. As a member of an occupational group in a village he interacts with persons of different caste and occupation, conducting relationships based on economic exchange, deference behaviours, and political status. These relationships between castes constitute vertical ties which connect persons of differing social status. Thus the village society is marked by cross-cutting alignments, providing different bases for conflict, integration and authority. Villagers look horizontally to leaders of their caste for authority in matters of ritual, domestic affairs, and caste prestige. But they look vertically to the economic and political leaders of the village for authority in matters of land, employment, and political representation to outside authority. Similarly, village leaders use their position in the hierarchies of both caste and class to maintain their dominance over village affairs.[4]

Current political groups, both factions and parties, build on both of these patterns of structures to win elections and to gain access to government benefits. If the vertically integrated structures from traditional village society are able to perform the new tasks, they may be endowed with new rewards and authority under democratic politics. On the other hand, if they deny status and rewards to less advantaged groups, these groups may form horizontal caste solidarities to challenge the established groups. Thus the process of inducting new caste groups into politics may be viewed as a tension between the articulation of new caste solidarities and factional recruitment into ongoing political structures.

Since the argument rests on the fact that vertical mobilisation has successfully brought the upper peasant castes into modern state politics, it is useful first to examine the extent of their participation. Representation of Reddis and Kammas in Andhra politics is higher than their proportion in the population and increases at higher levels of politics. As 25 per cent of the population in 1962 they occupied 39 per cent of the legislative assembly seats, 53 per cent of the ministerial posts and the presidencies of the Congress, Communist and Independent parties. The increasing predominance of these castes at higher levels is also evident in the Panchayati Raj institutions. Across the State Reddis held 39 per cent of the samiti presidencies and 55 per cent of the zilla parishad chairmanships. Within two districts sampled, Chittoor and Warangal, they held 46 per cent and 37 per cent of the sarpanch posts respectively, 56 per cent and 53 per cent of the samiti presidentships, and both of the zilla parishad chairmanships.[5] All parties have a predominance of peasant caste MLAs with few of the twice-born Brahmins and Vysyas. The twice-born continue to have a representation disproportionate to their strength in the population, but it is much less than previously.[6]

For the fourth general election, caste statistics are available only for the members of the Reddy caste who are identifiable by name. Reddis now appear to occupy 28 per cent of the assembly seats, exactly the percentage they had in 1962. The ministry formed after this election has fewer Reddis, who now form only 33 per cent of the Cabinet. It also has fewer representatives of other dominant castes, bringing down the total representation of dominant castes in the Andhra ministry from 66 per cent to 56 per cent in 1967. This is one indication of the greater middle class representation in the new ministry, which on a class basis contains fewer ministers from traditionally powerful families and more who have achieved their present high status through political activity.

Comparison of the representation of Redddis and Kammas in the organised parties reveals little variation. In 1962 Reddy MLAs occurred in exactly the same percentage in Congress and Communist parties, while in 1967 there appears to be a slightly higher percentage of Reddis among the Congress MLAs than among the Communist members, 24 per cent compared to 21 per cent. This contrasts with the situation in 1955 analysed by Selig Harrison who noted the predominance of Reddis in the Congress Party and their relative absence in the Communist Party.[7] Harrison's observation is comparatively more true in relation to Kammas. For a number of reasons, which shall be explored historically, there is a greater percentage of Kammas among Communist MLAs than among Congress members. Like the Congress, however, the Communist Party has a much larger Reddy than Kamma representation.

II

The Reddis and Kammas are excellent examples of those castes which M.N. Srinivas has called dominant castes in Indian society; they are "numerically the strongest in the village or local area, and economically and politically exercise a preponderating influence."[8] The most important source of their power is control over land. As the major landholders in the village they employ many villagers as farm servants, they have the most ready capital to loan, and they have the resources for moving outside the village to represent cases to the administration. This base of power is further augmented by the state's appointment of certain dominant caste persons as official headmen of the village, giving them the power of tax collection and the prestige of state recognition.

With these resources, Reddis and Kammas have become the political leaders of the village. In many respects political power is derived from positions of dominance in other arenas of village life. The competition for power takes place between groups first formed for purposes other than politics, while political leaders reach prominence initially through sources of power other than political authority. But political leadership of the dominant castes is not solely a reflection of other forces, for there are processes through which the resources for political competition may be augmented. Political power in the village depends not only on material ties of dominance and obligation, but also on qualities of persuasiveness, assertiveness, and leadership. These are individual qualities which add to economic power, differentiating the wealthy political leader from the wealthy individual in the village. In problems for arbitration, for example, resolution depends on the arbitrator's persuasiveness and reputation for fairmindedness as well as on his ability to apply sanctions to enforce his decision. Once accepted, the process of arbitration becomes a further independent source of authority in the village. The choosing of an arbitrator is a symbolic affirmation of the power of the arbitrator over the parties to the dispute. This creates a tie of obligation to the arbitrator which he may later invoke for political purposes. Similarly, the leadership of village factions depends on the skill and application of the faction leader. He must mobilise his supporters by activating his ties to them, exhibiting skill in managing groups of people, and at the same time being willing to spend money in hospitality, to increase obligations to him. Many of the traditional elites have continued to be powerful in the new setting of politics because these traditional skills in political calculation continue to be useful.

The political potential of the dominant castes is increased by their strength in the population. Political power depends much more directly on the numbers of followers that can be rallied for competition than the possession of resources or power in other arenas. Since kin and caste ties are two of the important means of rallying followers in the village, the leader from a large caste group in the village has more potential followers than one from a small caste group. And if a caste group has many powerful men within it who have their own client ties to lower caste persons in the village, then leaders from that caste have potential for gathering even more followers. In this way a rich Reddy family with many caste brethren in the village may become more powerful than a rich Brahmin family which is alone in the village. Therefore the large number of Reddis and Kammas assures their political power, even though they seldom form a majority in a village.

Where all or most of these leadership roles are centred in one dominant caste in a village, conflict in village politics is usually within the dominant caste. Factional disputes are between brothers, kinsmen, or lineage groups within the same caste over issues of land division or prestige in the village. Such disputes do occur frequently among members of low castes as well, but their disputes do not become political matters unless they are adopted by the dominant caste leaders as their own. Conflict among the low castes does not enter the public arena of the village and affect the relative statuses of those holding power in the village. Only quarrels with dominant caste leaders or quarrels represented by them can concern the distribution of authority in the village, for only such persons have authority. And only they have control over the public resources of the village. If the dominant persons in the village are united, they are able to settle disputes arising in other castes, or at least prevent them from disturbing other castes. Latent conflicts which may exist between dominant castes and labourers are not expressed because of differences in power. Only when the dominant castes divide among themselves, do such disputes find political expression in the village.

When political disputes occur between members of the dominant caste in the village, the opposing parties mobilise factions to support their cause. The factional organisations are built on the relationships between master and servant, patron and client. The intensity and depth of factional organisation varies with the history in the village, but in most cases the organisation is strikingly casual. During quiet periods the factions exist only as social circles which may gather for conversation in the evenings.[9] These circles involve only the factional leaders and their small group of followers, while the rest of the village remains relatively unconcerned. They may participate intermittently in the social groups, but without the commitment of the constant attendants. Only in times of conflict do the parties to the dispute activate all possible ties of kinship, dependence, and friendship within the village. Elections have now made it even more imperative to recruit all such potential members, providing the occasion for much bargaining and manoeuvering which reveals the essentially fluid nature of factions at the boundaries. This gives some currency to the common complaint of villagers that elections have brought about factions and disrupted village life. Elections have certainly increased the opportunities for disputes to be expressed in political terms dividing the entire village, and they have made mandatory the recruitment of all possible villagers into the framework of political support. This has increased the opportunities for subordinate groups to express their problems, but it has also sharpened the lines which were left somewhat more vague when all men were not to be counted. Modern politics have intensified the vertical processes of mobilisation in the village. Though still based on the traditional ties between patron and client, this intensity at election time gives factional alignments a modern face.

Politics outside the village have been carried on by the same dominant caste persons. The political relationships between villages are uneven in breadth and direction. Usually several villages are grouped as a cluster around a particularly dominant village.[10] The most formal ordering of these clusters is that based on the designation of revenue villages for administrative purposes. These villages are usually collections of hamlets which are grouped around a main village that gives the official name to the cluster. These clusters function more or less like single villages, depending on the nature of caste, economic and political relationships between the units. The most integrated units are those which consist of a main village with hamlets of only service caste persons living outside the village because of caste restrictions, but who are wholly dependent on the main village for employment and representation of cases to outside authorities. Such clusters may properly be considered to be one village. Among hamlets with more than one caste group, however, there are lesser degrees of integration. Particularly in the hamlets containing members of the dominant caste, social and political relationships may exist quite independent of the main village.

Informal clusters are formed by groups of villages connected to a particularly dominant village through a network of other ties. These clusters are less well-defined than market or revenue clusters and are usually smaller. They do, however, sustain a network of political relationships which are more intense within the network than with villages of other networks. The direction of politics is uneven because it is based on a pattern of dominance, in which the public events of the dominant village are more relevant to the whole cluster than are the events of any other single village. Factions within the dominant village provide opportunities for disputants within the other villages to find representation of their disputes, whereas unity in the dominant village prevents factional disputes in the other villages from being expressed outside the village. This is because the dominant village assumes the functions of arbitration and representation for the other villages in the same way that dominant castes do for lower castes in a single village.

The intensity of these political relationships varies considerably. In some cases the dominant village is merely a strategically located village, one through which villagers from other villages must pass on their way to markets, public transportation, etc. At the most informal level these relationships establish more intense networks of communication which may become useful in subsequent political activity. These relationships may assume political importance if the visitors accept hospitality, seek advice, or in other ways establish client relationships with leading members of the dominant village. At this low level of interaction, the idea of dominance may be too strong for describing the nature of the relationship between the villages. There are many clusters, however, in which the relationships of dominance are very similar to those within single villages. These are clusters gathered around a dominant village which is itself dominated by a single powerful elite. In these instances the dominance usually centres on one large family which had extended its influence throughout a region of villages through landholdings, money-lending, arbitration, and representation to the administration. Villagers living under these dominant families participate in politics in much the same manner as subordinate persons within the single village, except that in these clusters there is a higher level to which disputes may be taken for arbitration. The instances in which *zamindari* families have assumed such dominance are, of course, numerous. It is more interesting to note the many cases in which families achieve such political dominance within the *ryotwari* system of land tenure.[11]

There are many villages which are not clustered around such dominant villages, but sustain political interaction with surrounding villages through regional elites acting as local notables in concert. These are relationships between equally powerful families, each of which is head of a 'natural association' based on traditional dominance. Kinship ties are frequently the basis of such relationships, but there are others. Landholders may have occasion to meet other landholders in the course of their dealings with revenue and settlement officials of the administration. Some landholders become known as having good contacts with officials and may be called upon for help in cases. Others become known as particularly judicious men through arbitrations and are called in to settle other disputes. Many have simply been known to each other for years with no memory of their first acquaintance. As transportation, communication and monetisation of agriculture have increased mobility, larger and larger circles of notables have been formed. Mobility has enabled the expansion of kinship ties, which has brought about further interaction. More recently delineation of electoral constituencies has brought notables into the same political arena who had not previously interacted. As the notables attempted to win political support in unfamiliar arenas, they have turned to their local counterparts to build wider coalitions of village elites. The political purposes and methods of these new district elites vary greatly from those of the traditional society, but the basic structures emanate directly from the local notables acting in concert.

These informal networks are sustained by a common culture of dominance which makes persons at similar levels of rural society feel comfortable with each other. The culture is identified partially by life styles which demarcate notables from others of lesser status. Certainly no notables would do physical labour, and wealthier persons would not even go directly to their fields. They are reluctant to allow their women to go out in public, though the degree to which the Hindu castes observe *pardah* varies by region and by caste. More important is the deference which they demand from subordinates, from lower castes in their own villages, and from landlords of less important families in other villages. Notables know which families can be summoned to their verandah and which can summon them.

Caste ties are an important source of this common culture among the dominant peasant castes. It is generally accepted that in early times these castes were indistinct from each other, forming a class of feudal chiefs under various kings. There are several legends which trace the origins of the three major peasant castes in Andhra to an undivided group of Kapus living under the Kakatiya king Pratap Rudra who ruled in the thirteenth century.[12] The story of common ancestry is supported by the borrowing of names among the castes even now; many persons from the peasant caste of Kamma have surnames containing Reddy, while one sub-caste of the Reddy caste calls itself Chowdhary, a name often used by Kammas as a surname.[13] Caste legends thus provide legitimacy to their recognition of each other as equals. Therefore when the Kammas were trying to articulate a more conscious caste solidarity, their caste historian had to devote much effort to separating the origin of Kammas from that of Reddis before claiming higher ritual status for Kammas as Kshatriyas.[14] This equality of caste status is important in sustaining the culture of dominance, for in a culture in which authority has been associated with status, it means that Reddis and Kammas accept each other's right to rule. This becomes an important issue when persons of lower traditional status rise to positions of dominance. Such persons are accepted on the basis of their power, but only grudgingly, as *nouveau riche.*

Explicit caste organisation, however, has little to do with the sustenance of this culture. In contrast to many of the lower castes, dominant castes in Andhra have not maintained caste *panchayats* within the village or outside, within the memory of persons living today. Their organisation is primarily through the lines of kinship which may encompass several districts, particularly among the notables of the caste. These kinship ties are made stronger by the common South Indian practice of marrying within the family. Marriage ceremonies bring together persons who have met many times before, and provide occasions for continuing interaction. The culture is transmitted through informal ties arising from the transactions of a regional elite and maintains the common cultural expectations of rule.

The continuing role of kinship ties in the political organisation of dominant castes may be seen in the example of a very prominent Reddy family which has enjoyed great influence in the politics of one district. This family has been dominant in a large area of villages in a backward taluk of the district. It is known by its head, a particularly powerful man who was respected and feared throughout the region. Villagers came to him for advice and arbitrations, for money, and for some of them, "even a land transfer had to be done by him." He entered into State politics at an early period, first in the Justice Party and then in a Congress at the invitation of Congress Brahmins who saw the need for rural support in the 1937 elections. This man became the basis for non-Brahmin leadership of the district Congress, which was concentrated in the district boards while Brahmins continued to hold the post of district party president — an amicable sharing of power. His lateral entrance to Congress in a high position, as president of the district board, brought him into immediate contact with State Congress leaders and established channels which became increasingly useful as he began to build his own group within the Congress. Kinship provided the basic foundation of this group. Thus when the party was choosing tickets for the first general elections in 1952, he secured three for members of his family. As party organisation became enmeshed with the administrative apparatus of govern-ment, nephews of the family have used the same channels for influencing official decisions. Much of their current power is based on their reputation for 'knowing officials', which has helped them to do such things as remove a rival's village from eligibility to samiti elections, win coveted bus permits, and accomplish many errands for followers.

Alongside this access to patronage, the political standing of the family continues to draw upon traditional relationships. Kinship ties have provided a continuing source of trustworthy personnel to staff an increasingly complex family political organisation. The family's political founder died in 1946, just after becoming vice-president of the State Congress, leaving three nephews who have perpetuated his influence. They have staffed three important levels of politics, main-taining a strict division of labour. Until the 1962 election there was one nephew in Parliament, another in the State Assembly, and a third resident in the district to watch over business and local politics. With the 1967 election, there is no representative in Parliament, but his wife has taken the Assembly post while the local man has become chair-man of the district council.

A strategic expansion of kinship ties has helped to sustain their very influential position. On the advice of a Brahmin Congress leader who was looking for Reddy ties in the other half of the district, in 1937 the family leader married his daughter to a young man who had just become disaffected from his own Justice Party family through a series of land disputes. The youth was brought to the family village, and upon the death of the head of the family he was given a seat in the Madras Legislative Council. He later returned to his own village, became chairman of a district council, and with the support of his in-laws in the other half of the district was able to influence the selection of the District Congress President. A second marriage was concluded between another of the major family's daughters and a wealthy Congressman from a neighbouring district. When this man rose to become Chief Minister of Andhra, the family had powerful connec-tions with State leaders. The value of this marriage was enhanced when that Chief Minister was deposed and joined the opposing faction within the Congress, for it enabled the family to remain allied with both State groups. The family's nephew who was most closely related to the deposed Chief Minister's wife joined him in the opposition faction, while another nephew joined the incoming Chief Minister. This alliance has now been made stronger by a marriage of another nephew's son to the Chief Minister's daughter.

With this combination of elite status in their own locality and official patronage outside, members of the family have been extraordinarily powerful in the district, and have survived drastic changes in the State factional alignments. Were they less powerful themselves, the marriage alliances to opposing groups would have made them appear untrustworthy to both groups, as politicians 'playing sides'. But with their independent sources of strength in the district, they are in an advantageous bargaining position. From their traditional position they can secure the support of constituents with less expenditure of resources than new competitors. This makes control of the district less costly to the state leaders with whom they are allied. In the bargain their indiscretions committed against Congress candidates for the sake of local power are allowed by the State leadership. In 1952 they supported a Reddy representing a splinter peasant party against the official Congress candidate, because the Reddy had more chance of defeating an independent candidate who had long been a family rival. This was tolerated even though they were supposed to associate themselves with the State faction which had driven the peasant party out of Congress in a bitter fight over Congress leadership.

The story of this family has been documented in some detail here in order to show how factions unified at the top, by caste and kinship interactions, and sustained at the bottom by the vertical ties of village factions, have been successful in the district politics of Andhra. But such a strategy of coalition-making also limits the possibilities of mobilisation in areas where there is no dominant caste recognised as equal in stature to the Reddis and Kammas. In areas where political leaders have arisen among lower castes, there is little possibility for dominant caste leaders to organise coalitions for support. One Andhra district provides an example of the boundaries imposed by the geographical spread of dominant castes. The Reddis who are vying for power in the district have paid remarkably little attention to the hilly taluk of the district in which there are no Reddis. Even though these areas have representatives on the important district councils, Reddis have not included their representatives in district factions nor otherwise sought their support. There are no local networks of Reddy caste ties which they can draw into a larger caste solidarity, nor are there potential kin who can be drawn into a political group through marriage. And because there are no Kammas there either, the Reddis cannot even use their alliances with Kammas elsewhere in the district to build a following in the hills. Neither caste knows members of the hill castes from social occasions at which members of dominant families have traditionally met, they don't consider them their equal in status, and they are not interested in them except on grounds of pure political calculation.

A different source of discomfort arises when the leadership of contending factions or parties is drawn from different strata of the traditional society, as is seen in the conflict between Congress and Communist parties in another district. There the Communist Party arose out of a peasant revolution known as the Telengana Movement. As a movement against feudal landlords it mobilised large numbers of supporters including many lower class Reddis. Its leadership has been drawn, however, primarily from Brahmins and Backward Class persons, neither of which have been part of the dominant caste culture in the district. Although their techniques for mobilising support are very similar to those of the Reddy politicians, the Communists' work is not considered legitimate. Almost by definition, Communists are considered 'goondas' in Reddy vocabulary. This is in contrast to the attitude of Congressmen towards the Communists elsewhere, where the Communists are an accepted part of the political scene. The party's acceptance there seems to arise from the different nature of the leaders, who are dominant caste Kammas working through village factions in the same manner as the Congress. They have mobilised a large section of the agricultural labourers as well, but each village group has a dominant caste as leader, usually a Kamma of a slightly lower economic status than the village leaders. The culture of dominance is such that conflict among Reddis, or between Reddis and Kammas, is honourable and understandable within the system, but conflict between Reddis and Weavers, for example, upsets the system and is to be feared. Therefore political conflict in this district tends to be more divisive than in the other districts.

Caste also determines boundaries of interaction between the dominant castes. Ties between Reddy and Kamma notables can never be as close as ties within either caste, for they cannot share kinship. Sub-caste divisions have a similar effect. Both Reddy and Kamma castes have been divided into endogamous hierarchical groups which have only recently begun to mesh into a single caste group. These lines have remained important in the district which is divided by rivalry between prominent Reddy families of different sub-castes. The major family rival to the Congress Reddy family in the district is another Reddy family of equal traditional stature. Traditionally these families were neither rivals nor friends, for they did not frequently interact. Their areas of local power were thirty miles distant from each other, so their interests did not clash. Nor did they have marriage ties, for their sub-caste differences had prevented inter-marriage. It was only as each family began to reach out into larger arenas that their interests began to conflict. The Congress Reddy family moved both laterally and vertically, leaving their native village to settle in a town closer to the seat of the second family and moving up to the level of district elites which necessitated wider spheres of control. The second family has been much less interested in such mobility, for they have tended to modernise more along commercial lines, developing a very profitable business in agricultural exports. Though not expanding politically, they have been very jealous of their traditional area of control, both, for the commercial purpose of buying raw material cheaply, and for prestige reasons. As they sensed political encroachments by the Congress family on this area, they have reacted by always opposing the Congress family, choosing whichever party had greatest chance of defeating the Congress candidates. Motivated always by local disputes, they supported three different parties in the 1962 election: a Communist Vysya, a Swatantra Kamma and an Independent from their own family. The contest has become very bitter, for there have been no mediating structures of kinship to act as cross-pressures and mollify disputes. They had no traditional ties because of distance and caste, and they have no modern ties because of their differing paths of modernisation. It is a rivalry which is not based on intrinsic or historic sub-caste rivalry, but on differing political interests which have diverged because of lack of association.

The lower castes participate very little in this political structure. Their political interactions with the world outside the village are almost entirely mediated through the dominant elites of the village. Through them they secure representation of cases to officials, arbitration of disputes with landlords, and now electoral representation. These castes do, of course, have horizontal ties with their own caste members in other villages. They conduct elaborate and often far-reaching searches for marriage partners which extend kinship through an increasingly broad region. Many castes have also developed caste panchayats to deal with disputes among caste members in surrounding villages.[15] Inter-village ties among the lower castes have not, however, been politicised. The domains of their caste panchayat do not coincide with the political domains established by dominant caste interactions, and they have not begun to wield political influence during elections. The political and economic interactions within these castes have been largely confined to the face-to-face primary groups within the village. Politics between villages is conducted by the elite of the village, the local notables. As Bailey noted in his earlier study, "only the dominant castes enjoyed a corporate political existence."[16]

It is against this context of clusters of notables that the concept of dominant caste becomes salient.[17] Not all village leaders in a region are members of the same caste, for there are many individuals who have risen to positions of importance above their caste fellows through particular circumstances in single villages. Nor are all members of a dominant caste in positions of village leadership. Within the large Reddy and Kamma castes there are many poor members who cannot maintain the life style of a notable or wield political influence. Because a majority of the village leaders are of the dominant caste, however, political interactions between villages are maintained within the dominant caste structures.

III

As Reddis and Kammas sought to advance into modern society and politics, they drew upon these traditional caste and kinship ties, forming broader networks of interaction. Throughout the districts there were wealthy landlords known for their contacts with government who aided peasants to obtain services. Caste members who had moved into the towns provided accommodation and advice to villagers unfamiliar with the urban world. These persons became informal patrons of the caste. Their relationships within the caste were based on ever-widening circles of family ties through which work of their benefactions spread. Though broader than the face-to-face groups of village caste society, these were still 'natural' caste relationships in their comparative unselfconsciousness. That is, in terms of Kothari's introductory essay, these relationships did not articulate caste as an ideological basis for mobilisation. They were important structurally, however. In connecting wealthy caste members with poorer members of the caste, they increased the depth of interaction among persons of different levels in the society. And in easing the transition to urban life, they helped to form more widely-based elites, increasing the breadth of interaction among those from village society.

In a few instances, these relationships became even more public, as certain patrons became known as caste leaders throughout a large area. One notable example is a very wealthy Kamma landlord who is known as a modern *zamindar* because of his large holdings acquired through commercial agriculture. His public activities have done much for the Kammas in his district. As founder of the Andhra Bank he enabled the development of modern banking facilities for the peasants whose agriculture was becoming increasingly commercial with the introduction of irrigation. And as a leader of the Justice Party he also gave help to the peasant movement of N.G. Ranga which was working for middle peasant interests in the Congress context. Most important, he has been very generous to Kammas as individuals, giving much financial support to Kamma candidates in elections, paying little attention to party or factional divisions within the caste.

These patronage relationships became useful for conscious political purposes when the patrons started to use caste to support their own political ambitions. Because they had such extended ties, they could represent themselves to district politicians as spokesmen for their caste. Reddis in other districts followed this path. They entered Congress politics when the Brahmin-founded organisation turned to 'representative' Reddis to help widen and deepen support in the countryside. In this way traditional structures headed by Reddy notables became connected to new sources of power and benefits in the government.

Eventually both Reddis and Kammas formalised these patronage relationships into caste associations. A Telugu history entitled the *East Krishna District National Movement* tells of Kamma and Reddy conferences held in connection with the district social reform movement initiated in 1905.[18] One of the early activities of these associations was the foundation of hostels near educational institutions to accommodate village youths during their education in the towns. It is reported that the first hostel association for Kammas was actually begun by a Reddy school teacher living in a Kamma area of Krishna District. This association built four hostels in towns of the delta area in a period when agriculture was increasingly prosperous and many peasant youths sought education. The Reddis of the former Hyderabad State reached this stage of mobilisation somewhat later. At a marriage in 1930 a group of Reddy landlords residing in the city felt sorry at the lavish waste of funds and decided to contribute to a hostel. A Reddy who had risen in the Nizam's police service took up the project, and using his wealthy connections, gathered funds for a hostel with accommodation for 150 youths in Hyderabad city.

The activities of these associations were concerned primarily with the elites of the caste, those with sufficient land to contribute funds and those with aspirations for education to seek employment in the cities. But they were significant as an expression of solidarity between wealthy members of the caste and the poorer members who were benefited. And they were significant in making education available to youths whose families did not maintain city residences, enabling a new class of participants to enter State politics. For a time the Reddy hostel in Hyderabad even provided a meeting place for the incipient Communist Party which was led by one of these youths, a middle peasant Reddy from a village.

Explicit caste solidarity among Reddis and Kammas, however, has not extended into areas beyond the building of hostels. By comparison with caste associations elsewhere, those in Andhra have been less self-conscious in their conception. Their histories show an increasing embarrassment over identification with caste. The establishment of one Kamma hostel in Krishna brought much controversy over the use of Kamma in the hostel name, for the leaders were anxious to demonstrate that all castes could use the facility. They eventually used the name in order to appeal to traditional landlords for funds, but did not restrict the membership. Similarly the Reddy hostel in Hyderabad did not restrict the use of its facilities, though it did have special funds to aid youths of the Reddy caste.

In place of caste solidarity, the dominant pattern of party politics among Andhra's rural elites was the continuing association of notables. Traditional notables in many parts of Andhra were first recruited into party politics by the Justice Party which was founded in 1917 to demand greater representation of non-Brahmins in educational institutions and government jobs.[19] Though the party claimed to represent the interest of all non-Brahmins, its limited programme appealed primarily to elitist groups in the rural society. The party in the districts was essentially an informal association of friends and relatives, coordinated by informal contacts between old families. The elitist composition is evident in the leadership of one district branch of the party. Of the two state chief ministers from the district, one was a wealthy *zamindar* holding the title of 'Raja' who represented a landholder constituency in the legislature, while the other was a prominent Kamma lawyer from the district centre. A third important member was the son of a large landholder resident near the town who had studied in England and served as director of education in neighbouring Mysore State before joining active politics. Similarly in another district two of the important leaders were called Raja, both non-Brahmin *zamindars* who were prominent upholders of the landed interest in the district. Party membership was confined to elite members of elite non-Brahmin castes, and did not even attempt to encompass low caste groups.[20] It did attempt to work through the caste associations, but these also were built on traditional channels already existing among the elite castes. The Justice Party achieved its measure of success in Andhra by recruiting persons who held personal power as traditional notables in the locality. Thus a party which was founded to articulate caste interests was transformed in the Andhra setting to a party of landed elites.

Why have horizontal solidarities not played a more important role in the mobilisation of Reddis and Kammas into modern politics? Several factors arising out of their traditional village position may be adduced from the previous discussion. Furthermore, there are characteristics of the political system they entered which made articulation of caste solidarities less likely. The significance of these factors may then later be judged by comparison with the situation in which caste solidarities did become significant among the two peasant castes.

With the traditional prerequisites and organisation of a dominant caste, Reddis and Kammas had less need for caste organisation to facilitate their modernisation. The social mobility function of a caste association was less relevant, for they already enjoyed positions of high status. They also had less need for such an organisation to widen communication networks within the caste, for the elite members of the caste already knew each other across wide areas through marriage ties, land negotiations, and political dealings with the colonial power. And they clearly had less need for creating new political organisations to mobilise strength for democratic elections, for they already led traditional factional groups within the villages through which they could organise support from other castes. Thus many of the functions which caste associations have served for members of lower status castes elsewhere were already being fulfilled in Andhra by the traditional structures of interaction among elites.

Reddis probably also found it more difficult to organise a caste association than did members of lower caste groups. Reddy notables were already politicians in the traditional system. They had been socialised through their landed occupation into the art of managing men, and showed great skill in managing groups to maintain their positions of influence and power. In their relations with each other they were used to exercising reciprocal influence, for power was widely dispersed among many members of the caste. Mobilisation of such groups to form an effective caste association capable of pursuing group goals would have necessitated a centralised organisation of authority which they resisted. Thus one Reddy elder commented about a Reddy caste association meeting in 1924 in Chittoor, "We decided to keep the association out of politics for we were all already in politics and we would only fight and destroy the associations."

These notables thus limited the functions of the organisation to matters which were of less concern to them, the building of student hostels.

There were other factors at play. The wide differentials in political and economic power within the large Reddy and Kamma caste groups made organisation on the lines of a caste association more difficult. Some members of the caste are usually dominant in a village, but not all members of the caste have such power, nor are all accorded the same deference by other villagers. The degree to which the individually less powerful members share in the power of the dominant' members through caste ties depends on the degree of status differentials within the village. In the Hyderabad districts the differentials between village leaders and lower status caste members are particularly great because of the land tenure system before independence. This system recognised certain families with the honorific title of *deshmukh*. These were small local landlords whose families are said to have been the founders of many of the villages. During the permanent settlement in the nineteenth century their revenue powers were taken away, but they were compensated with the official title which gave status before state officials and an annual payment called *russom*. In addition they were granted hereditary rights to the village offices and the rights to appoint their own collection agents, by which they were able to continue personal control over large areas of territory. Through the unofficial powers which stemmed from this formal position they were able to retain effective power in their villages, lending a feudal character to traditional authority in Hyderabad villages. This degree of differentiation between members of the same Reddy caste was symbolised in the patterns of social interaction. Traditionally only upper status Reddis have used the caste name of Reddy, while others have been known by common names which do not connote any caste.

Under these conditions of extreme differentiation within a caste, and lacking any great challenge from other groups the formation of caste solidarity is unlikely. In the modern politics of former Hyderabad districts, lines of class have been more important than caste, though again not in the sense of any stable pattern of 'class cleavages'. Reddy *deshmukhs* have been closer aligned to the *deshmukhs* of other castes then with the middle class Reddis who have recently arisen to challenge their position. Economic divisions are thus more salient in the ideology of district politics. In one such district there are now two groups, both of which claim to represent the middle-class while attempting to label the other as feudal. In actual practice each group draws upon both elements. Both work through traditional notables in the areas in which they have no traditional strength while seeking to develop autonomous bases of support through more modern techniques directly appealing to the various groups in the society. Thus the segmental nature of traditional political interactions has made the articulation of class organisations as difficult as caste organisations. In the early stages of mobilisation, which this district represents, political leaders may gain the support of villagers more economically through their local elites than through other types of organisation, encouraging vertical mobilisation.[21]

Finally, one might consider the demographic distribution of the castes in Andhra Pradesh.[22] Reddis and Kammas are each the largest high status caste in their areas, forming about 10 per cent of the population. The next largest single caste is one of the two formerly untouchable castes of menials and leather workers, Malas and Madigas, who form 10 per cent and 5 per cent of the state population respectively. In between are a host of minor castes, none of which is present in numbers comparable to the four major groups. The comparative equality of the two castes at top and bottom levels suggests competition between castes at the same level, between Reddis and Kammas, and between Malas and Madigas. This is the configuration of conflict suggested by Selig Harrison in his analysis of the rise of the Communist Party.[23] This point can be pushed too far, however, because of the nature of political organisation necesary for electoral politics; it is regional distribution which is of greater importance. In Andhra this makes competition *within* the castes more likely. Reddis and Kammas are not equally distributed within regions, and in the few areas where they are in relatively equal numbers, one of the castes tends to be wealthier and more prestigious than the other. In one district studied where each caste forms 10 per cent of the population, Kammas have become much wealthier and more influential because they occupy the very rich eastern region where irrigation facilities are highly developed. And in the one taluk of another district where caste numbers are equal, Kammas have all occupied the same economic position as self-cultivating peasants, while a few Reddy families have enjoyed traditional positions of dominance over large areas. The existence of these few elite families among Reddis in that taluk has enabled the caste to take advantage of modern opportunities much more readily than the Kammas. Thus in any one area, the rural elites are usually of the same caste, and traditional village politics take place within the caste. Only when they move to much wider arenas of modern politics would they confront elites of the same status from other castes.

The argument so far has suggested why Reddis and Kammas might have found organising their caste on the lines of an association difficult. The quality of the caste society in which they lived also made such solidarity less important as ideological identifications for modernisation. The bases of political authority in this society are essentially secular. The dominance of Reddis and Kammas in economic and political affairs, is relatively dissociated from ritual status, for neither enjoys a high ritual status. Though their caste genealogies do claim descent from former ruling dynasties of South India, Reddis and Kammas have not traditionally shown appurtenances of twice-born status in their ceremonial or customary behaviour. They do nôt wear the sacred thread nor use the ritual Vedic fire in marriage. They are peasant castes of the Sudra *varna* with no strong claim to Kshatriya status. They enjoy secular dominance, however, in a society which has few upholders of sacred tradition. The proportion of Brahmins is very small and that of Vysyas not much greater.[24] Within the large Sudra *varna*, ritual is less sanskritised and less indicative of hierarchical differences among the constituent caste groups. The methods and symbols of dominance in Andhra are essentially secular, without claims to religious sanctions of rulership. Because these dominant castes do not symbolise their authority in sanskritic ritual, ritual distinctions have been less important throughout the society. Ultimately ritual distinctions among castes in Andhra appear to be less important than secular measures of prestige. The secular attitude seems to have affected even the Brahmins. "Telugu Brahmins are less particular about what castes they will officiate for than the Tamil Brahmins. Ideas about pollution are weaker among the Telugus than others in the South," reports the Madras Census of 1901.[25] With less importance accorded to sanskritic ritual, the Brahmin presence is less noticeable and less resented in Andhra society. This was reflected in the fortunes of the non-Brahmin Justice Party, which was less strong in Andhra than in Tamilnad because, as a member testified to the Statutory Commission in London, "Brahmins and non-Brahmins got along much better in Andhra than they did in Tamilnad."[26] The more secular basis of Andhra society has had an important influence on patterns of social mobility. Because Brahmins had less prestige, fewer people imitated them as they sought to raise themselves in the society. Instead they imitated the persons who did have importance, the Sudra dominant castes. Persons from many low castes have adopted the name of Reddy, but few castes have sanskritised caste rituals, for such ritual was not an overriding symbol of status.

Differences between Brahmins and non-Brahmins were tempered

also by the identification of an external enemy which threatened both groups. As Andhras became interested in modern education and government jobs, they constantly bumped into the Brahmins from Tamilnad who occupied these posts. Rising education brought about a new interest in modern Telugu literature and culture which Telugus felt was being suppresed by Tamilians. Therefore Andhra Brahmins and non-Brahmins together formed a sub-national movement to demand a separate State in which Andhra interests could be expressed. This movement was important in articulating an ideological basis for unity between the castes as they began to mobilise for political participation. It sought to demonstrate the common ancestry of all Andhras regardless of caste, arguing that caste distinctions had invaded the society only after its days of former glory. Furthermore, the movement provided an organisation which demanded the co-operation of all castes to achieve their common interest. The sub-nationalism of the Andhra movement provided an arena in which definition of elites could be formulated outside of caste, though undoubtedly still with traditional roots in Andhra culture.[27]

Had the incumbent leaders in party politics, the urban professional Brahmins, not responded as Reddis and Kammas sought to participate, however, they might have formed new organisations to demand entry. Because of the responsiveness of the nationalist leaders to peasant leaders, this was not necessary. Reddis and Kammas did not have to form caste associations to achieve political recognition, for they were 'coopted' individually by incumbents who sought their support. This confirms the Kothari thesis of the growth of a 'dominant elite' and the 'stages of politicisation' (including cooption) through which it is articulated though admittedly in the peculiar Andhra context of landed notables.

One of the major reasons for this cooption was the pressure of competition in the nationalist politics. The urban elites who initiated the nationalist movement needed to broaden their base of support to impress the British with the strength of their demand. Congress needed to recruit traditional notables to contest local government elections and defeat the Justice Party which was supporting the colonial regime. At the same time these urban leaders were engaged in competitions for leadership of the nationalist movement, and needed to recruit supporters for their own group within the movement. Therefore Brahmin leaders brought many dominant caste notables into the highest circles of the party, even at the eventual risk of their own displacement. One of these new men was Sanjiva Reddy, the very successful Reddy Chief Minister and later Congress President and Speaker of the Lok Sabha until July 1969.[28] The non-Brahmin notables did not have to demand this accommodation by Congress; rather they were courted by the organisation which needed them as much as they desired it. As the son of a landed village family, Sanjiva Reddy was brought into politics by a Brahmin lawyer seeking support in the rural areas to defeat a Brahmin rival within the Congress. He developed broad ties among Reddis throughout the state and won control of the party. It is characteristic of Andhra politics, however, that he won with the support of his Brahmin sponsors, in competition against a member of the Kamma caste.[29] The caste competition cut across caste boundaries and identities, a peculiar symptom of the process of 'secularisation'.

Such a strategy of accommodation has had important effects on the nature of political change in the Reddy districts. Change proceeded from the top down, led always by the traditional elites whose superior access to city and State-wide trends brought them into politics, ahead of other groups in the district. Since the Justice Party involved primarily landed elites who led the traditional structures of dominance in rural society, it did not need to alter these structures to search for support. And since the political parties were coopting and accommodating these elites, there was no need for a caste association which would have necessitated a new articulation of ties between high and low status Reddis. Thus the elite's reservoirs of political support in the village system were not significantly altered by the top persons joining a new organisation.

The success of this accommodation depended, however, on two complementary factors. On the one hand, the traditional elites had to accept the modern system — in this case the goals and rules of the Congress — and desire to participate in it. Thus in the case of the Reddy districts, many of the traditional notables had belonged to the Justice Party which upheld their interests in land. But when that party began to lose the support of the non-Brahmin population through deaths of eminent leaders and short-sighted policies, the notables saw the desirability of changing their loyalties to a more viable party. Thus throughout the 1930s many members of the traditional elites were recruited into Congress. Complementary to this acceptance of the 'Congress System' by these elites, however, was the need on behalf of the Congress leaders, also to realise the value of these leaders to the type of competition in which they were engaged. During the early nationalist period when India's national leaders were engaged in constitutional representations to British authorities, they did not consider it important to mobilise these rural leaders. Only when the nature of the struggle shifted to mass mobilisation did they turn to the rural elites, as well as to other groups in society. Once this happened, Congress leaders had also to accept the legitimacy of the goals which these rural leaders wished to pursue in politics, and command sufficient resources to win their support. The significance of these points will become more clear as we discuss below cases where caste solidarities did in fact arise.

IV

Recruitment of Reddis and Kammas into ongoing vertical factions in the party system did not always work. Where they operated in a different context of caste organisation, and where the party system was not able to accommodate them, horizontal solidarities of caste and class emerged. Consideration of these instances may enable us to bring into relief the variables which have been identified above as significant in determining more typical patterns of mobilisation among Reddis and Kammas.

The significance of traditional dominance is revealed by contrasting the political experiences of those with high and low traditional status. When peasant Reddis and Kammas entered politics, they organised themselves on terms quite different from those of the landed notables. Peasants were less interested in wielding political power and less capable of winning it. Instead of joining political parties or contesting for elections, they formed a movement based on the interests of the peasants and agitated for rural reform. Many became followers of the peasant movement led by N.G. Ranga.[30] He used Marxist terminology of class struggle and agrarian revolution to "uphold all those who live by the cultivation of the soil".[31] Though Ranga did in fact receive support from many notables, the major force of the movement came from the middle peasantry. Ranga encouraged them to action through a programme of summer schools, where he taught rural economics, Marxism, and political techniques to peasant youths. Though all were non-Brahmins, the peasant movement drew youths whose interests were distinct from the elites of the Justice Party. Those elites were interested primarily in change external to the village society, vis-a-vis the city Brahmins, while the kisans wished to alter the power balance within the traditional society. The populist attitudes implicit in their desires to learn economic and political procedures for themselves contained a challenge to elite leadership.

The peasant movement drew much more explicitly on caste ties for mobilising support than the Justice Party. Looking at the movement in the delta areas, Selig Harrison describes how Ranga "solidly built up his political career on a Kamma base."[32] This is undoubtedly an over-simplification; in the non-Kamma areas Ranga recruited many lieutenants from the dominant Reddy caste. These Reddis remained with him even after his Kamma lieutenants left. This was during the historic conflict between Ranga and Sanjiva Reddy over the Congress presidentship in 1951, when three of Ranga's major Kamma supporters deserted to the winning Reddy group. There are differences between leaders and followers, however. Among the followers of the peasant movement, caste ties were a more important means of mobilisation. It is probably for this reason that Ranga chose lieutenants whose caste matched those of the peasants they sought to organise. Kamma leaders worked primarily among Kammas while Reddis worked among members of their own caste.

A lively current example of caste politics is the conflict which has recently developed between Reddis and Kammas in one district. Previously not many Kammas had participated in district politics. They were followers of the caste patrons who acted as Kammas' representatives in the district Congress. Now, however, Kammas are no longer happy with receiving these welfare benefits through a patron, for they are desirous of achieving political recognition in the district. The extent of their caste consciousness in this move appears to be much greater than the Reddis have ever exhibited in the district, because their position in the traditional society has been different. Kammas there were traditionally less than dominant in their areas, for they lived under *zamindars* drawn from other castes. Therefore the Kammas did not have the corporate political existence which the notable Reddis had enjoyed elsewhere in the district. This had made the Kammas less useful to the Congress when it was expanding its organisation into rural areas, so fewer Kammas were recruited into the party. Later when the Kamma leaders desired a greater place in the politics of the district, they encountered an established organisation manned primarily by the Reddis who had been recruited earlier. Therefore they have had to develop a group based on caste solidarity to force the hand of the politicians, a tactic which the notable Reddis never had to employ.

The Kamma experience is, however, quite similar to that of the middle class Reddis who joined Ranga in the peasant movement.[33] Both groups enjoyed some economic independence in the traditional society as owners of land, but neither enjoyed political power. In one important respect the Kammas had even fewer political opportunities than the middle peasant Reddis. Since they were of a different caste from the ruling *zamindars* they could enjoy no caste identification with the political leaders of their area, nor could they hope to become part of the elite through kinship. In contrast with the notable Reddis, however, the middle class peasant Reddis and the Kammas just described, occupied a similar position in the traditional political system. Their less than dominant position has therefore been a factor in the articulation of horizontal caste solidarity in the political sphere.

Hyderabad district provides a third example of different modes of organisation, between notables and middle peasants of the Reddy caste. There, a traditionally wealthy landowning Reddy has built a self-consciously inter-caste faction, recruiting many followers from subordinate castes. In contrast a middle class Reddy lawyer seeking to establish himself has gathered an explicitly Reddy-based group. Throughout the State it is remarkable that the politicians with the strongest caste orientation are from middle-peasant rather than notable status. This does not mean that middle peasants are necessarily more caste-minded, but it does suggest the nature of the political resources available to groups of less-than-dominant status. Leaders among these peasants found that the evocation of loyalties to local caste networks enabled the mobilisation of peasants with whom they had no previous affiliation. Caste served the peasant movement as the first level of communication for reaching persons who had no established political ties outside of the village. These leaders do not have the advantage of traditional structures uniting notables through which they can reach members of subordinate castes as well. Therefore they have turned to a conscious articulation of caste solidarities to provide a basis for building a new organisation. It is interesting that notables have also used such caste ties in regions where they have no traditional access. In another district the notable family which has sought to rise into higher state politics has mobilised caste loyalties as an attempt to build a new district-wide organisation. In constrast, their rival family which is interested only in reconfirming its traditional power through participation in local politics has eschewed caste appeals.

It is not only the structural position of these castes in the traditional society, however, which affects these patterns of mobilisation. The discussion of the secular basis of dominance in Andhra has argued that the ideational basis of the society affects the kinds of ideologies which will be articulated in the mobilisation. Comparison of caste behaviours within Andhra reveals how horizontal cleavages and solidarities are strengthened under conditions of greater Brahmin domination. Kammas in the delta areas are a dominant caste according to the secular criteria, dominating the rural economic and political structure, as do the Reddis elsewhere.[34] But there are more Brahmins there, and ritual authority became a more important basis of status. Therefore Kammas did not hold the pre-eminent social position which the Reddis enjoyed in their areas. To assert a claim for higher status, the Kammas emulated the Brahmins by adopting the sacred thread, and followed this by replacing the Brahmins in setting up their own Kamma priests. Both moves show much more concern for ritual and caste status than the Reddis have ever exhibited. Sanskritisation became a more important mode of social mobility in Krishna, because the greater Brahmin presence made ritual position a greater issue.

This factor contributed to the greater development of horizontal solidarities in delta districts. The caste associations among Kammas built more hostels than those of Reddis in other districts. And the Justice Party showed greater concern for caste definitions in its demand for political participation. The Kamma leaders talked more of Brahmin exclusiveness than party leaders in Reddy districts. The caste associations did not participate directly in the Justice Party politics, but the party did its utmost to utilise the caste association, sending its speakers to the meetings organised by the association, to urge caste advancement. Finally, more Kamma *zamindars* and other landlords supported the peasant movement because of their identification with Kamma caste interests.

Whether these traditional factors alone would have brought about caste solidarities cannot be determined, for there were also features of the party system which gave impetus to formation of new solidarities, just as both the nature of traditional loyalties and the nature of the party system account for vertical patterns of mobilisation discussed earlier. In more politically active areas of the State the nationalist Congress was not able to accommodate the rising demands for participation. There came forward a generation of students from newly rich families of the Krishna delta area where irrigation had made agriculture very profitable. These students learned of Marxism as students in Madras and Banaras and returned to the district, eager for sweeping reforms. There they felt stifled by the slow-moving methods of their Gandhian elders who held all the leadership posts in the Congress Party. Therefore they turned to organising sectoral interests to demand the participation which they were not granted, working in the peasant movement, labour unions and Marxist student organisations in the district colleges.[35] These formed the basis for the Communist Party in Andhra which became particularly strong in the delta areas. Also at issue was the legitimacy of the students' substantive demands. Nationalist Congress leaders held independence as their primary goal, and sought to unite the entire country in this demand. They feared that the economic goals of the students would both divide the movement and deflect attention from the major goal. Therefore they were unwilling to grant the legitimacy of the students' demand for participation, for they disliked the direction in which the students would take the party.

Congress did try to win the support of other Kammas by bringing them into the organisation as it accommodated Reddy leaders. One of the Kamma peasants who later became President of the Pradesh Congress Committee was recruited by Brahmin elders who wished to build him up as a spokesman of Kammas in Congress. He came into the Congress, however, at a time when the Congress did not have much to offer to the Kammas. Congress was not big enough to accommodate the numbers of Kammas who wished to enter at the levels of leadership they demanded. Nor did it have enough else to offer for Kammas to consider it necessary to maintain connections with the organisation. Not being in power, it did not have the control over allocations of benefits and status positions which it enjoyed at a later date. Lacking sufficient resources, the Congress was unable to build up this particular Kamma as a leader in the face of the strong individual attractions of the competing Kamma leaders outside the Congress. The peasants found that the peasant movement articulated their demands as the Congress organisation was unwilling or unable to do.

It is extremely significant, however, that such horizontal solidarities were expressed more in terms of class than of caste. Because many of the Communist leaders were Kammas, the party has often been considered a Kamma party.[36] This analysis must be qualified, however. The Communist movement did not represent a continuation of the sentiments which first emerged in the caste hostel movement and continued in the Justice Party and self-respect movements. Its demand for greater participation of deprived groups was generalised beyond the specific experience of Kammas or non-Brahmins. With this demand it was able to mobilise persons from many castes, including many Brahmins among the founders of the party. There were also several Reddis, including the brother and brother-in-law of the then young Congress leader, N. Sanjiva Reddy. To these persons, youth and a desire for reform were more important than caste. The Kamma support given to the Communist Party does not represent a caste-wide solidarity which consciously opted for communism in order to oppose the Brahmin dominated Congress. It was more an explosion into politics by a group of persons who were doing the same things at the same time, and the first large generation of Kammas to be educated joined this trend.

For these persons to articulate their demands in the language of caste would have been inappropriate. Caste status alone did not have the compelling force as a requisite of social mobility because of the largely secular tradition of the society. Furthermore, external circumstances were rapidly changing, when the Reddy caste associations were being formed, Reddis were already thinking of ways to maximise their support for new kinds of competition. For this purpose their ties with many castes through traditional dominance were more useful than caste solidarity. Similarly, the Kammas in the Communist Party were concerned with mobilising persons to make new kinds of demands. In all of these cases, the caste groups saw that more was to be gained through direct political participation than through other avenues of mobility. The expansion of government activity into so many areas of life had politicised the allocation of social and economic resources. Decisions concerning the distribution of these resources which formerly were made according to social status or economic wealth were now made according to political influence. With this it appeared that social mobility had itself been politicised. Hence the voluntary caste association whose initial technique of mobility was adoption of higher caste customs, was found less useful than the political party. Groups wishing to rise chose to follow the rules of the new political system, which forced them to mobilise support beyond their caste limits in order to win elections. For this purpose, the traditional alliances of notables in a caste were useful, for through these ties the vertically integrated village factions could be mobilised. But articulation of caste solidarity among the notables might have alienated their supporters from other castes and made winning in multi-caste constituencies more difficult.

Even the groups which first articulated horizontal solidarities have developed into multi-caste factions for carrying on political activity. As they entered Congress they too have been divided by the ongoing factional divisions of the Congress.[37] With increasing experience in politics, the amorphous ties of caste are individuated by personal contacts and ambitions for leadership. Caste leaders circulate among political elites of other castes in the wider arenas of higher level politics. In this manner caste ties which may have been useful in the initial mobilisation of support are supplemented, if not replaced, by other types of communication. Political participation develops political loyalties which take on a life of their own apart from ties of caste and class. This is a process of political differentiation within the caste group which may or may not be related to simultaneous economic differentiation in the caste. Some observers have discerned this differentiation to be a result of economic and occupational change within a modernising caste group.[38] The experience of the rich peasant castes demonstrates, however, that such change is not necessary. Among the Kammas of the delta, factional differences are due to resurgence of traditional factional conflicts, rather than to articulation of class interests cross-cutting the caste groups.

V

What is the shape of politics now in Andhra ? Andhra parties, both Congress and Communist, are divided into factions which are linear developments from the traditional vertical structures of politics. The modern factions are broader in membership and more temporary in duration, but there is much similarity between them and the traditional animosities and ties of dependence on which village factions were founded. The dominant castes have successfully politicised these traditional factional structures by supplementing local and primordial obligation with bargaining for benefits and status in state politics. This process may be demonstrated by examining such factions at two levels of politics, a district group and the State Congress Party.

In one district the strongest faction is headed by a Reddy who was a minister in the state cabinet until the 1967 election. He initially entered politics at the insistence of a Reddy minister in the old Hyderabad cabinet who wanted to bring young members of the rural elite into the Congress to defeat the Communists after the Telangana Movement. Thus the young Reddy entered politics through the support of the dominant rural elite. His own local group was built on the ties available to him through his traditional position as a member of one of the leading families of the taluk. He formed an alliance of notables of which he rapidly became the acknowledged leader, but only because the others had little interest in state politics. His notable allies in the district, known as *deshmukhs*, proved too quarrelsome and unreliable, however.[39] There were many histories of family quarrels among them over land and inheritances, several of which were activated by modern politics, and there followed a series of contests among disaffected cousins. As the Reddy experienced difficulties with these allies, he saw that they would not stay with him in cases where their local interests diverged from his, and thus could not be expected to provide a stable political following. He therefore began to develop a group whose members did not have such an independent base of support, who could be trusted to observe his interests even when he was away in Hyderabad as a State Minister. For his most important personal representative in the area he chose a Kamma agriculturist of middle peasant status with whom he first became associated while settling a dispute between Kammas. This Kamma has since been acting as the most direct representative of the Reddy in village affairs, travelling constantly to investigate complaints, draft applications, secure official sanctions, and so on. Due to his connection with the minister, his status has become so enhanced that he has often been called in to arbitrate even in non-political disputes. Despite this importance, however, the Kamma has not demanded any official position. He is more interested in his business as a contractor which the Reddy leader has helped to prosper.

The formal posts in administration, State assembly and party have been divided among other supporters. The samiti president is the Kamma's cousin, an agriculturist with a reputation for hard work and good agriculture. He also cannot sustain higher political ambitions for there are very few Kammas in the constituency. The District Congress President is a middle-class Reddy from a neighbouring village who joined politics before the ex-minister, but has never gained prominence on his own because of his modest family means. As the MLA for the constituency neighbouring the ex-minister's, a wealthy Tapper resident in a small town, who was formerly a member of the Communist Party, was chosen and brought into the Congress. Finally there is a young advocate as president of the District Cooperative Credit Society, also a Reddy of a non-*deshmukh* family with no previous prominence outside his own village.

None of these persons have enjoyed status or power in the traditional political system, for none are *deshmukhs*, none are Brahmins, two are members of a minority agricultural caste, one is from a Backward class, one is from a town, and one is very young. In these followers the ex-minister has found a group which he can depend upon, for they are equally dependent on him. But the group is based on more than the interests which the members bring to it, for participation in the life of the group provides its own rewards to the members. Closely-knit groups like this one sustain a social life which accords meaningful recognition to the members and provides a basis for commitment to the organisation. They have developed loyalties based on friendship, dedication to the leader, and years of service. And through this they have significantly furthered the process of political integration in the district. Traditional ties existing in the villages between high and low status persons have been extended beyond the traditional limits of village factional ties to wider areas. This faction has repeated the traditional types of vertical dependence relationships, but for new purposes at higher levels of politics.

State level factions have been built in similar ways. During the 1962 election it appeared that Congress was divided between Reddy and non-Reddy groups in the contest between Sanjiva Reddy and Sanjivayya (a Scheduled Caste leader) for the chief ministership. This non-Reddy group had many Reddy members as well, however, because of individual enmities and friendships between leaders. Since 1962 both the Congress factions have been led by Reddis, one headed by Sanjiva Reddy from his position at the national level and the other by Brahmananda Reddy, the State Chief Minister, who formerly was Sanjiva Reddy's lieutenant. Each man has mobilised factional support in most of the state's twenty districts, cutting across caste and regional lines for political interests. Since the 1967 election each group has recruited members from the important castes in the State. The ministry contains several Reddis, two Kammas, two members of other minor landed castes, one member of a lesser status agricultural caste, two Brahmins, one Vysya, one Muslim, one Weaver, and two Scheduled Caste persons. The dissident group has almost exactly the same composition, for it has recruited the rival to each of these persons, usually some one of the same caste group. Similarly the two wings of the Communist Party have mobilised persons from both dominant castes, both under the leadership of Reddis. As in the villages, so in the State, political conflict in Andhra takes place within both of the dominant castes which have assumed state leadership. And as one goes higher, the term 'caste conflict' begins to lose its usual meaning.

Caste remains an important variable, however, as both of these instances reveal. In fact it acquires a new secular meaning. Factions are usually very careful to include members of all the important castes in the group. Caste is important less as a symbol of cohesion and more as a network of groups which the party's or party faction's representatives try to activate by contacting village caste groups and awarding benefits to prominent members. Faction leaders see caste ties to be useful channels of support in the absence of more individual or ideological attachments within the constituency.

Such a new patterning of caste ties proved especially useful in state level politics, when the three regions of Andhra Pradesh were joined to form the new state in 1957. The existence of caste ties across regions provided channels for political integration. Reddis from Telengana and Rayalaseema might not have already known each other, but the commonality of caste made the extension of kinship ties possible.

Reddis from different regions began to meet at marriages, providing more opportunities for extending political ties as well. This has not worked in every case, for there continue to be strong rivalries between caste leaders from different regions in several of the castes, particularly in the Backward Classes which usually have only one major leader in each region. Among Reddis, however, it is striking how seldom the State factions are articulated along regional lines.[40] Each state faction contains leaders from each region, providing very important integrative structures in state politics. It is true that politics add pliability to caste structures but nonetheless the availability of such structures in turn provide politics with ongoing channels of integration. The role of caste ties in facilitating this type of integration may be demonstrated by a counter example. Kamma leaders feel less accommodated and are less loyal to state level factions than Reddis. The lack of caste-like ties between Reddis and Kammas may be one reason for the fluidity of support for the Reddy State leaders in the non-Reddy regions of the delta.

   In these cases caste, although a traditional structure of relationships, is drawn upon for new purposes. Caste also continues to be important as a hierarchical structure which governs rates of modernisation and access to new opportunities. To the extent that caste determined occupation, caste and occupational interests were identical. To the extent that horizontal caste boundaries followed the outlines of ancient tribes, castes had regional distinctiveness which brought about an identity between caste and regional interests. The process of modernisation has moved selectively along three lines, as indicated by comparing educational and occupational attainment between Brahmins and non-Brahmins. This selective scale of opportunities brought about the Justice Party complaints against Brahmins. In the same way the village dominant castes were the largest landowners, and hence the most able to experiment with modern agriculture and the most qualified to receive many of the community development benefits. This is one of the reasons why Reddis have assumed such a prominent place in current politics. Looking over the number of Reddy MLAs, one Reddy remarked, "The reason there are so many Reddis in State politics is that there are so many Reddis in local politics, and that is where politicians come from." The statement sums up the patterns of recruitment in Andhra politics. These patterns represent a series of consistent cleavages between Brahmin and non-Brahmin, bureaucrat and peasant, urban dweller and town dweller. And as these interests find political expression, loyalties based on caste and kinship provide important means of defining an interest group.

VI

Political mobilisation presents very different problems to lower castes, however, than it did to either of the dominant caste groups. The distribution pattern of caste makes it very difficult to challenge the political leadership of the two peasant castes. For the hitherto untouchable castes to challenge the peasant castes, would demand a radical breaking of dependence ties between landholder and labourer which has seldom been achieved. The castes which are most free from traditional structure of dominance in the village are the artisan groups, which are divided into many different caste units. It would be very difficult for any of the small intermediate castes to muster enough members to challenge a larger and wealthier peasant caste. For them to unite against the Reddis or Kammas would require developing new kinds of ties not based on traditional caste relationships. This also has seldom been achieved in Andhra.

Thus the leadership of the peasant castes in State politics has not been seriously challenged. Not having been traditional leaders of village factions, the lower castes lack both the skill of leadership and the authority to claim leadership. Even aspiring individuals from these castes are not used to being political leaders and they have done it badly, frequently allowing personal considerations to outweigh group concerns. Nor are members of these castes used to following leaders from their own ranks, so they place undeserved mistrust and accusations of corruption against their incipient leaders. Their situation is made more difficult by lack of traditional structures of obligations which they can invoke to gather political support. Lower class leaders must develop new ties with other castes on new bases, a difficult matter when they have few economic resources and little access to positions of power. One base they have tried to use is the organisation of a united front of Backward Classes consisting of various castes, but this has not proved to be successful because of traditional divisions among the groups. The Backward Classes Federation of Andhra Pradesh has continually suffered from accusations of caste favouritism against the leaders, bringing about a debilitating disunity in the organistion. It has also suffered from political divisions among the Backward Classes; when the president joined the Swatantra Party, Congressmen felt they could no longer take an active role. Recently a rival Congress organisation, the Backward Classes Congress, has been formed, but it has encountered the same problem. Because of the affiliation of the president to one of the State factions, members of the other Congress faction have been hesitant to join.

It is not clear that subordinate caste groups in Andhra have yet demanded significant political power. They are groups which were not politicised in the village system, participating in politics only occasionally as subordinate members rallied by dominant caste faction leaders in moments of direct conflict. The traditional relationship of dominance and interdependence between the high and low castes was considered both inevitable and appropriate and this has survived into the modern age to be the major means of political mobilisation. There is no tradition of horizontal division between dominant and subordinate groups, only one of cleavages between equally powerful groups. Acceptance of this traditional view continues among many members of the subordinate groups in Andhra . Even in prosperous and advanced Krishna district, subordinate groups have not won important political recognition, despite the commercialisation of agriculture and the consequent mobility in traditional economic relationships.

The rise of new caste groups would pose an entirely fresh problem for the ongoing hierarchical structure of political parties and factions in Andhra, especially if they enter by forming themselves in horizontal solidarities, thus challenging the vertical integration of seniority and status. The traditional party factions have been anxious to recruit leaders from lower castes, not only as symbols of multi-caste appeal, but also as insurance against lower caste solidarity. So far this technique has succeeded in dividing low caste groups even before they have entered politics. The appeal of factional organisations with their connections to important benefits and positions is tempting to low caste leaders. They are divided before entering politics, but without the advantages of traditional dominance. But it is only so that they secure access to opportunities.

Some members of these caste groups have tried to rise within the vertically integrated organisations led by dominant caste leaders. Through this method they have reached intermediate positions of power in the organisation as caste representatives, further reinforcing the multi-caste support of the particular group. They have not been able to do much for their own caste, however, without endangering their own positions in the organisation. Thus Andhra's Harijan Chief Minister, D. Sanjivayya, lost his position when he began to use his power on behalf of special Harijan interests in government services. Politicians from these castes are often caught between two constituencies: they may be rejected by their own militants if they work within party organisations, but they are considered communalist if they articulate caste demands.

Whether low caste groups in Andhra will form caste solidarities to force political accommodation in the future depends to a large extent on whether existing factions are willing and able to devolve benefits and status as their low caste members make demands. These castes will be politicised, but not necessarily in the form of caste groups with the structure and ideology of a caste solidarity. The real issue is not whether dominant castes will continue to rule, but whether the vertically integrated structure of politics, the multi-caste factions, will be maintained. Ultimately this depends on whether low caste leaders can rise to positions of leadership in the multi-caste factions. This would necessitate the articulation of new criteria for leadership, for the caste criterion limits them to the subordinate status of 'caste representative' So far the vertically integrated structures from traditional society have been able to meet the new organisational challenges of democratic politics, essentially by further articulating inter-caste political groups within the parties. In the process new types of loyalties have emerged and political groups have attained a life of their own. The development of loyalties to political groups *per se* may continue to provide a process for definition of elite status, through seniority, personal loyalty and party identification; in other words, through induction in the 'dominant elite' of the region. So far, however, these new definitions have been extended only to peasant castes. If they deny participation in real power to less advantaged groups, these latter groups may form caste solidarities to challenge the established groups. It may still be that horizontal solidarities of caste will be necessary to force ultimate permeability of political elites in Andhra, but this must be kept an open question. Meanwhile political change in Andhra has demonstrated the viability of vertical mobilisation into multi-caste factions that have continued from the past, thus making the transition to modern politics take place without great dislocation in society. The traditional structures provide pliable and ready - made material to the politicans of a modern, democratic, Andhra.

NOTES

1. For use of this term see Clifford Geertz, 'The Integrative Revolution: Primordial Sentiments and Civil Politics in the New States', *Old Societies and New States* (New York: The Free Press, 1963), pp. 105-157. The term is in many respects an unfortunate one, for it appears to emphasize the primitiveness of sentiments which in fact are characteristically first expressed publicly in the process of modernisation. Geertz himself makes this clear in his essay.

2. For several such studies see the fine one by Hardgrave, Kothari and Maru, and others in this volume.

3. The study will draw on their experience in three districts, one from each of the three major regions of the state: Krishna district in the rich delta area where Kammas and Kapu-Reddis each form 10 per cent of the population, Chittoor district in dry Rayalaseema, where Reddis outnumber Kammas 14 per cent to 7 per cent and Warangal in the former Hyderabad State where Reddis form 10 per cent with almost no Kammas. In a few areas there are persons of a Kshatriya caste who held some of the *zamindari* positions before *zamindari* abolition in 1948.

   The percentage of Rajputs in each of the three districts was less than 1. As *zamindars*, individual Rajputs held considerable power in local areas, but without the strength of numbers their influence has been reduced to very little after the introduction of adult franchise. In contrast, many of the former *zamindars* of Reddy and Kamma castes have maintained their political positions in the new context.

   These figures are drawn from the last census in which these castes were counted: for the districts formerly in Madras Province this was the 1921 Census; for the former Hyderabad districts the 1931 Census. The figure for Reddis in Krishna is probably inflated, for no distinction was made in the census between Kapu-Reddis and another large caste known simply as Kapus. The figures for Kammas in Warangal was not listed in the Census, but field observations indicated that the percentage must be very small.

   Sources: *Census of India*, 1921, Volume XIII, 'Madras', p. 118.
   Census of India, 1931, Volume XXXIII, 'Hyderabad', p.245.

4. For an excellent analysis of the relationship between these hierarchies in a village of Madras, see Andre Beteille, *Caste, Class and Power* (Berkeley: University of California Press, 1965).

5. These statistics are based on an analysis by names of MLAs, and so are available only for Reddis. Not much importance should be given to the lower percentage of Reddis among the Communists because some of those MLAs, as their leader, P. Sundarayya, may have dropped Reddy from the name and thus it may have escaped the count.

6. With 3 per cent of the population, Brahmins have 8 per cent of the seats in the Assembly; Vysyas are 3 per cent in the population and 4 per cent

in the Assembly. The striking change in representation may be seen in the caste composition of the ministries: the first Andhra ministry in 1954 was 29 per cent Brahmin, the 1957 ministry was 18 per cent Brahmin, and the 1962 ministry 7 per cent Brahmin. The percentage of Reddis has remained the same in all three ministries, with the Brahmin representation replaced by members of other peasant castes.

The transfer of power was slower in Hyderabad State: before the amalgamation of Hyderabad Telugu districts with Andhra in 1957, the Brahmin representation was 46 percent in 1952, and 56 per cent in 1954.

7. Selig Harrison, *India, the Most Dangerous Decades* (Princeton: Princeton University Press, 1960), p. 218.

8. M.N. Srinivas, 'The Dominant Caste in Rampura', *American Anthropologist*, (February, 1959) pp. 1-11. In his introductory essay, Kothari has referred to castes which do not form a majority as 'entrenched castes.' It seems useful here, however, to continue to refer to Reddis and Kammas as dominant castes, since, though they do not form a numerical majority, their large numbers are a significant source of their power.

9. Oscar Lewis, *Village Life in Northern India* (New York: Vintage Books, 1965), emphasises this aspect of factions.

10. For a pioneering analysis of the nature of relationships between village units, emphasising particularly the relationship of the village to the centres of the civilisation, see McKim Marriott and Bernard S. Cohn, 'Networks and Centers in Indian Civilization', *Journal of Social Research* (September, 1960), pp. 1-9. See also Robert Eric Frykenberg, *Guntur 1788-1848* (Oxford: Clarendon Press, 1965) for an excellent study of the relationships between village leaders and the district administration in Guntur district of Andhra Pradesh.

11. For a discussion of *zamindari* and *ryotwari* systems of land tenure, see Henry Baden-Powell, *Land System of British India,* Vol. 3, 'Raiyatwari and Allied System' (Oxford: Clarendon Press, 1892).

12. Kotha Bhavaiah Chowdary, *History of Kammas* (Sangamijargarlamudi, 1939). (Translated from Telugu for the author.)

13. Edgar Thurston, *Castes and Tribes of Southern India* (Madras: Government Press, 1909), Vol. 3, pp. 94, 222; Vol. 6, p. 247.

14. Chowdary, *ibid.*

15. See Adrian C. Mayer, *Caste and Kinship in Central India* (London: Routledge and Kegan Paul, 1960), pp. 5-6, for an excellent discussion of caste regions. Bailey points out that traditional caste groups are small, and must be so in order to preserve the obligations of kinship and to maintain the ritual system of pollution, both of which depend on personal familiarity and geographic proximity. See Frederick G. Bailey, *Politics and Social Change, Orissa in 1959* (Berkeley: University of California Press, 1963), p. 126.

16. Frederick G. Bailey, *Tribe, Caste and Nation* (Manchester University Press, 1960), p. 190.

17. Adrian C. Mayer in 'The Dominant Caste in a Region of Central India',

Southwestern Journal of Anthropology (Winter, 1958), pp. 407-427, found in a region of Madhya Pradesh that it was not possible to speak of a single dominant caste in a region, but that it was meaningful to talk of Rajput-allied castes as dominant. These were castes with common values and friendly equality which shared political power in the region.

18. Manikonda Satyanarayana, *East Krishna District National Movement* (Vallabhaneni Rama) (Masulipatam: Vallabhaneni Ramabrahmam, 1937). (Translated from Telugu for the author.)

19. Eugene Irschick, 'Politics and Social Change in South India: The Non-Brahmin Movement and Tamil Separatism, 1916-1929', Ph.D. thesis, Department of History, The University of Chicago, 1964. Irschick demonstrates how the party catered primarily to elite interests in Madras as well, but sees a much stronger caste articulation in Madras than in Andhra.

20. Irschick states that the Justice Party did not seriously attempt to enlist the support of lower caste non-Brahmins by including their demands in the party platform. *Ibid.*

21. The Telengana Movement presents a striking contrast to this picture. Yet it is amazing how easily traditional notables were reinstated in their villages after the Movement, and are now winning election contests for village leadership. For further discussion of this history, and for other points in this paper, see Carolyn Elliott, 'Political Participation in an Expanding Polity: A Study of Andhra Pradesh'.

22. Lloyd I. Rudolph and Susanne Hoeber Rudolph in *The Modernity of Tradition: Political Development in India* (Chicago: University of Chicago Press, 1967), have considered this question in terms of the number of castes in the middle range which may be thought to mediate between high and low castes in matters of ritual and social deference. They argue that in societies where there are many such middle range castes, enmity between castes is less likely to develop than in those where there is a large gap.

23. Harrison, pp. 210-12.

24. The percentage of Brahmins in Krishna district is 5, Chittoor district 1.5 and Warangal 1.6. Krishna and Chittoor: *Census of India, 1921, ibid.* Warangal: *Census of India, 1931, ibid.*

25. *Census of India,* 1901, Vol. XV, 'Madras'.

26. Great Britain, Parliamentary Papers, Vol. IV (Reports of Committees, Vol. II), House of Commons Paper No. 203, 1919, 'Joint Select Committee on Government of India Bill', Vol. II, 'Minutes of Evidence', p. 218.

27. In a volume written during the Andhra Movement to extol Andhra culture, a writer says, "It is only we, the so-called cultured and English educated classes that have fallen away from our ancient and hereditary tradition signifying our unity of descent, and with this fall, lie caught up in 'Communalism' which has replaced the community spirit of our glorious days." Gurty Venkat Rao,'Andhra Social Life and Organization', *Krishna Pushkaram Souvenir* (Bezwada: Kalepeetham, 1945), pp. 389-390.

28. See Harrison, p. 237, for an account of Sanjiva Reddy's entry into politics.
29. It is this competition, which occurred in 1950 over presidentship of the Andhra Congress, which suggested to many observers that Andhra politics was divided between Reddis and Kammas at the state level. For this argument see Selig Harrison, p. 227.
30. Harrison, p. 218. Mr. Ranga is now a leader of the Swatantra Party.
31. N.G. Ranga in *Revolutionary Peasants* (New Delhi: Amrit Book Company, 1949), p. 73 ff. states his differences with the Communist Party with which he had worked previously. He accused them of taking over his organisation for their own purposes, neglecting the true interests of the peasants which he was defending.
32. Harrison, p. 209.
33. Among the Kammas differences appear less great, for Kammas of Krishna do not remember the sub-caste differentiations which were reported by early ethnographers of caste in Andhra. When pressed, older members of the caste refer to vague distinctions between Pedda Kamma and Chinna Kamma, meaning big and little Kammas. These are not endogamous units in the manner of the Reddy sub-castes, or even in the manner of the Reddy *deshmukhs,* for they had no formal status in either ritual or government. They are merely distinctions according to individual status, indicating the greater interaction between different status levels among Kammas.
34. The percentage of Brahmins in Krishna is about 5, compared to less than 2 in Warangal and Chittoor, *Census of India,* 1921.
35. The editor of a communist newspaper commented: "Most of the big Congress leaders were all Brahmins. We used to sit at their feet while they were big on the platform. We didn't like this so we went for the left Congress, mostly because we wanted to do more for people."
36. Harrison, p. 209.
37. Paul Brass in 'Meerut: Caste and the Congress', *Factional Politics in an Indian State* (Berkeley: University of California Press, 1965), pp. 137-66, concludes that factional politics reveals no consistent communal divisions because factional leaders must mobilise support from many castes to win power.
38. Hardgrave and the Rudolphs have emphasised the increasing economic and occupational differentiation within modernising caste groups as the major cause of political differentiation. This process may take place without major economic changes, however, as the experience of rich peasant castes indicates. Among the Kammas of Krishna, factional differences are due to the resurgence of traditional factional conflicts, rather than to articulation of class interests cross-cutting the caste groups. See Hardgrave in this volume, and Rudolph, *Modernity of Tradition* (Chicago: University of Chicago Press, 1967).
39. A *deshmukh* was a lord similar to the *zamindar* in British India, but with somewhat different perquisites.
40. The Telengana Movement begun in early 1969 has changed this optimistic assessment of regional integration, though the circumstances do

not invalidate this analysis. When the state was formed in 1957, Telengana people feared that personnel from the wealthier and more educated Andhra regions would take over Telengana administration and dominate its politics. A number of formal and informal safeguards were devised, including an agreement that posts in Telengana would be reserved for Telengana personnel whenever they were available and an understanding that a deputy Chief Minister would be chosen from Telengana when the Chief Minister was from Andhra. In addition, it was agreed that revenues from Telengana would be spent on Telengana development. There have been grumblings since the amalgamation that these have not been fully honoured but the careful balancing of factions in Telengana by the Andhra Chief Ministers seemed to manage the potential protest. Recently, however, one of the two major Telengana leaders who had been sent to the Centre as a Union Minister was dismissed because of strictures by the Election Commission. Without a place in state politics, he returned and took up the growing discontent in Telengana first articulated by the Telengana students. He has been joined by a Telengana Backward Classes leader who has never been able to work cohesively with the Andhra Backward Classes leadership. This failure of the Congress to manage factions and accommodate important political leaders may be seen as the condition which enabled the articulation of grievances growing out of the increasing regional disparities in development. For further analysis of this issue see my *Peasants Rise to Power*.

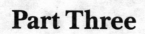

Part Three

Part Three

CHAPTER SIX

Caste and Political Factions in Rajasthan

RICHARD SISSON*

The Congress Party in Rajasthan, as in other Indian States, has been characterised by intra-party groupings or factions which have competed for positions of leadership and control within the party organisation as well as in the formal institutions of government. The nature of factions has tended to vary from level to level in the political system, those at the lowest levels of political organisation, such as Municipal Boards and Tehsil Congress Committees, being based largely on a caste (*jati*), while at successively higher levels these units have tended to coalesce around a dominant political figure and to form a new political group which involves a number of smaller units. These larger factional coalitions have always been socially heterogeneous and include in their fold political groups drawn from numerous castes.

The purpose of this paper is to analyse the development of the Congress Party in one part of Rajasthan in terms of its support base: to identify the manner and conditions under which elite groups at different levels and representing different social strata have been mobilised into the political process, to determine how diverse conditions of political grouping have been handled by those in the party organisation and how, in turn, groups have aligned within the party

* The author is Assistant Professor in the Department of Political Science, University of California, Los Angeles. The research, of which this study is a partial result, was made under a fellowship granted by the Foreign Area Fellowship Program. The statements and conclusions made herein, however are those of the author and are not necessarily those of the Fellowship Program. The author wishes to thank Mr. Indu Shekhar Sharma for assistance in the conduct of this research.

for the pursuit of particular political goals, and to establish those conditions which have tended toward permanence in certain factions and factional coalitions and change in others.

The focus of the study is on Nagaur District, a part of Jodhpur Division of Rajasthan which, prior to independence, constituted Jodhpur State.[1] This area is of particular interest and importance in the study of Rajasthan politics. First, it produced one of the most venerated leaders in the All-India States' Peoples' Movement, Jai Narain Vyas, who was the first popular Chief Minister of Rajasthan and President of the Pradesh Congress Committee. Until his death in 1963 he was the leader of a major factional coalition in the Rajasthan Congress. Secondly, Nagaur District has produced a dominant caste group from among the Jats in the Congress which had a considerable impact on politics at the State level. This Jat group, unlike the political groups from this caste in other areas of Rajasthan, has maintained considerable cohesion in politics and has provided more ministers than any other district level political group in the State. These two elite groups — the Vyas group and the Jat group — though in alliance during the first few years after the consolidation of the party, eventually got crystallised into two factional coalitions which competed for control over positions in the government and party apparatus at all levels of political organisation from the State Ministry and Pradesh Congress Committee down to the Tehsil Congress Committees and Municipal Boards in the districts of Jodhpur Division.

We will attempt to cope with our concerns by focusing on three major aspects of caste and political organisation. First, we analyse the origins of social and political change in Jodhpur prior to independence and relate the elites and political groups which developed during that time to the new political order. Second, we examine in some detail the changing pattern of social representation and political control in the Congress Party between the first and second General Elections and the influence which conflict over positions of power and prestige has had on patterns of participation in the political process. Third, we consider the relationship of the District Congress Party to its political environment, analyse some of the reasons for its continued political supremacy in the Nagaur area, and probe into the rise and continued supremacy of a single dynamic caste group within the party organisation.

I. *The Development and Organisation of Political Groups Prior to 1952*

The pattern of social representation and the organisation of factions in the Congress Party in Jodhpur Division since 1947 has been greatly influenced by the development of political movements in the former Jodhpur State. Since the consolidation of the Congress Party in Jodhpur shortly before the first General Elections, there have emerged two major groups within the Jodhpur Congress, and each of these is a continuation of the two major political movements which developed prior to 1947 — the Marwar Lok Parishad and the Marwar Kisan Sabha. The pattern of political mobilisation and the organisation of power in both of these movements differed considerably. So were the social groups from which the respective members and leaders of the two movements were recruited and the objectives which they pursued. They were further distinguished by the absence of overlap in political elites and structures of political support. These differences have continued in contemporary politics, and have formed the basis of factional conflict within the Congress party in this area.

The Origins of Political Change: The Autonomy of Urban and Rural Traditions

The Marwar Lok Parishad was founded by an urban elite which consisted largely of young men from ritually high castes who had been introduced to Western education and political ideas and who had become enamoured with the nationalist movement in the British Provinces. The primary objectives of the movement did not reflect local grievances but were concerned with the propagation of social and political ideas and with changing the nature of the traditional polity — the creation of representative government under the aegis of the Maharaja, the promotion of civil liberties within the State, the identification with nationalist symbols and the aspirations of the Indian National Congress, and the eventual merger of the State into an independent India.[2]

Although the Lok Parishad was the first, most vocal and most popularised political movement in Jodhpur State, its base of recruitment and its scope of political support were limited, in terms both of social group and geographical spread. The movement originated in Jodhpur City, the capital of the State, and was dominated by a City elite from the time of its founding. Even at the time of independence the majority of activists were from Jodhpur City as were the three major leaders of the movement — Jai Narain Vyas, Mathuradas Mathur and Dwarkadas Purohit.[3] Within the capital city the vast majority of leadership and membership was recruited from the Pushkarna Brahmin, Oswal, Kayasth and Maheshwari castes, while representation from ritually 'low' castes was rather limited, though not by design.

Although the Lok Parishad had been making several efforts to gain support in the rural areas, representatives from peasant castes never became permanently involved in the movement although they cooperated with it at certain junctures.

Though exclusively recruited from urban castes, the movement did not command the support of all sections of these castes; each of the caste represented in the movement had traditional divisions which precluded unified action. Some major families in the Pushkarna Brahmin, Oswal, and Kayasth communities had traditional affiliations with the royal house of Jodhpur, those from the first having served various priestly functions for several centuries while the latter two had a tradition of competition for positions of power in the state ministry. The Pushkarna Brahmin community was also split socially into two groups which did not inter-dine, inter-marry, nor participate in common life-rite ceremonies. One *jati panchayat* of the community publicly opposed the Lok Parishad and called for the outcasting of all members of the caste who participated in it. This basis of caste division, although less intense than was the case previously, has continued in contemporary politics.

That the Lok Parishad was not able to develop active organisations in the rural areas has been one of the crucial factors that has restricted its effectiveness in post-independence politics. In the case of Nagaur, Lok Parishad 'outposts' were established in five of eight district towns between 1942 and 1947 by local leaders who had either been educated in the British provinces or had come into contact with the nationalist movement, either through the Jodhpur City elite or through serving 'political apprenticeship' in the British provinces. These groups had exclusively personal followings and membership was largely restricted to the caste of the local founder-leader. Like the movement in Jodhpur City, the social composition of these 'outposts' was from the higher castes. Three of the five groups were primarily Brahmin, one was Maheshwari, and one was a coalition of Brahmins and Oswals, created and led by a young Oswal advocate. As was true in Jodhpur City, these local units in no case involved the participation nor commanded the support of any of these castes in their entirety.

These local movements were never linked on a district-wide basis but were restricted in leadership and membership to the town in which they originated. The leader and group in each town was more directly and closely associated with the Jodhpur City elite than they were with their counterparts in the other rural towns. The political concerns of these activists were also closer to those of the Jodhpur City elite than to the peculiar problems of the quasi-feudal peasant society in which they lived — problems which were to become of primary importance during the first decade after independence.

There were several factors which militated against the development of a cohesive and integrated movement among the rural towns. One of the most important was the diffusion of power within the traditional political order itself. Most of that area of Jodhpur State which became Nagaur District was sub-divided into *jagirs* which were under the direct rule of *jagirdars* drawn from the Rajput caste. Although these local chiefs owed allegiance to the central *Darbar* and were formally restricted to the powers which they could legitimately exercise within their *jagirs,* they enjoyed considerable autonomy in day-to-day administration which often involved ultimate judgement in both civil and criminal disputes. Since the locus of power in the traditional order was highly fragmented and without any real supra-power in day-to-day control of these local lords, there was not one centre of power and suppression against which a common movement could be mobilised linking the urban movement with the movements in the rural towns in a combined effort and for a common cause.

Furthermore, there was no tradition of intense conflict between the Rajput elite and the dominant urban castes, and the latter were often a part of the structure of power in the traditional polity. The Brahmin castes were often linked to the local chiefs through priestly functions, several of the educated Brahmins from the Nagaur area had been drawn into positions of authority by the State Darbar, and many others had been involved in the administration of some of the larger *jagirs.* The 'Mahajans' — almost exclusively Oswals and Maheshwaris — were associated with the local lords in three very important ways. First, some families had served as money-lenders to the local ruling families and did not want to disrupt these traditional associations which also involved good business. Second, several dominant families from this area and caste fellows from Jodhpur City had served as managers in the major *jagirs* and in several cases had become exceedingly powerful elements in the rural areas from where they could ply their trade of usury with increased effect.[4] Third, and of central importance, these 'Mahajan' castes had been granted almost complete freedom movement between the local *jagir* in which their ancestral homes were located, and the major trading centres of British India, where a considerable number of local Mahajan families had developed reputations of being among India's more shrewd and able businessmen.

Finally, it should be noted that there was no single dominant urban caste which might have served as a basis for an area-wide political movement.

Participation and support for the Lok Parishad were thus segmented in terms of both area and social group. The elite in Jodhpur City became the nexus of the movement and mobilised only a few and on the whole inactive units in the rural towns. Furthermore, even in the capital city the movement did not gather the support of an entire caste or castes. This pattern of mobilisation and organisation of political power greatly influenced the role and effectiveness of urban elites in post-Independence politics. First, the absence of a cohesive political elite from the urban area of Nagaur District inhibited the cohesion of urban castes in politics. Second, the lack of widespread support in rural areas diminished the political potential of the city elite when the elements of political power in the system appreciably changed with the introduction of universal franchise and the ascendancy of electoral politics everywhere.

The origins, organisation and objectives of the Kisan Sabha were quite different from those of the Lok Parishad. The Kisan Sabha did not start as a political organisation but was the outgrowth of a social reform movement within the Jat community which originated in the late 1920s. This reformist movement resulted from increasing contact of the Jats with the outside world and particularly with movements and ideas prevalent in the British Provinces concerning social reform. The vehicles for the communication of these 'modern' concepts were the traditional religious festivals and fairs in both Nagaur and Ajmer-Marwar which the Jats attended in large numbers.[5] The movement was given institutional organisational form in 1938 with the creation of a reform movement called the Jat Krishak Sudharak at the Pushkar Fair in Ajmer. Leadership in this organisation was assumed by old and young, educated and uneducated alike.

The Jat movement was highly innovative from the beginning and involved attempts at achieving social mobility by subscribing to value orientations found outside the traditional order. Emphasis was placed upon change and progress, participation in and adaptation to the wider world of social action, and the development of attitudes, resources, and techniques among the Jats which would stimulate this process. In the initial stages of the movement the primary objectives were internal to the caste itself. It was particularly concerned with such social reforms as the abolition of *nukta* and restraints on the payment of dowry, with the encouragement of western education, and with participation in new occupations such as the administrative and military services.

The second source of change resulted to a large extent from the impetus of the first. This involved increasing involvement of Jats 'in the outside world' through participation in the administrative services of Jodhpur State as well as in the education of the younger members of the caste in increasing numbers. The Jat movement in the late 1930s and the 1940s was to a large extent paced and controlled by Baldev Ram Mirdha, a dominant Jat leader who had risen through the ranks to become the Deputy Inspector General of Police in Jodhpur State. Because of his training and vocation Mirdha promoted participation in government jobs and the pursuit of education with a view to prevent energy being channelised through inter-caste conflict and violence: he has been described by members of his family and close Jat associates as having been a loyalist to the end.[6] It was largely because of Mirdha's position and encouragement that posts were made available for Jats in the State Services, primarily in the Police and Railway Departments.[7] Furthermore, he was successful in acquiring State grants and authorisation for the establishment and support of secondary schools and student hostels. Although these were formally reserved for all peasant castes, the Jats were the primary beneficiaries, not because of any policy of enforced exclusion, but by virtue of initiative from within the Jat community and the absence thereof among the others. The founders and leaders of the Kisan Sabha and the dominant Jat political leaders in post-independence politics had all either held positions in the State Services, had attended these educational institutions, or had lived in these community hostels.

The final phase in the Jat movement started with the creation of the Marwar Kisan Sabha by Baldev Ram Mirdha after his retirement from the State government in 1946 and after the return of a number of young Jats from the British provinces where several had graduated in law and received LL.B. degrees.[8] The objectives of the Kisan Sabha, unlike those of the Lok Parishad, were not primarily concerned with nationalist aspirations and the reconstitution of political authority from traditional to modern lines. The primary aims of the organisation were: (1) the abolition of *jagirdari* and the institution of land reforms; (2) abolition of *begar* and other forms of forced labour and illegal cesses which had traditionally been exacted by the *jagirdars* from the poorer peasantry; and (3) the institution and protection of tenancy rights.[9]

Both the early Jat movement in Marwar and the Kisan Sabha, first started in Nagaur District and enlisted support of the caste from the district to the local level. The Nagaur elite also served as the central leadership of the Jat movement on a Jodhpur-wide basis and was instrumental in mobilising *kisan* movements in the Barmer and Pali areas of the State as well as in some areas around the capital city.

There was minimal opposition within the Jat community to the

objectives of social and political reformers. One of the most important reasons for this was the character of traditional political organisation
in the Jat caste. Unlike many castes, structures of power and prestige
in traditional Jat society were diffuse. The traditional *jati panchayats*
of this caste were *ad hoc* rather than permanent and hereditary, and
'accepted' leaders were called upon at the time of dispute to pass
judgement. Cases have been reported when there were wide participation in these deliberations.[10] Thus when the wind of change blew
there were few traditional leaders within the caste who opposed the
advocates of change. It was seen that this change was designed to
bring to an end traditional disabilities and exploitation. In fact leadership positions in the caste went over to those who had achieved status
in accordance with the 'modernist' aims to which the Jat movement
had aspired, the dominant leaders of the Kisan Sabha and the majority
of Jat leaders in post-independence politics having been either highly
educated or those who held positions of status and gain in the
'outside' world or sometimes both.

Thus there were considerable differences in the Kisan Sabha and
Lok Parishad movements. First there was the difference in ultimate
aims. The former was primarily concerned with changing the basis of
economic power upon which the traditional order rested while the
latter was primarily concerned with changing the basis of political
authority from hereditary rights to representative political institutions.
The Lok Parishad movement did not result from widespread discontent with the traditional order but represented the strivings of a
cultivated elite group which attempted to elicit public support for the
realisation of their ideological and political goals. The Kisan Sabha, on
the other hand, was concerned with grievances which were widely
shared among the Jat peasants. A second difference was the recruitment of leadership and membership. The Lok Parishad was entirely
urban based and drew its leadership and support largely from Brahmin and Mahajan castes although it did not command the support of
any caste in its entirety. The *kisan* movement was entirely rural based
and was restricted to the Jat caste, although there was no explicit
policy of caste exclusiveness. Third, there was a difference in the
organisation of political support. The Lok Parishad's centre of power
was at the State level and was focused on the capital city. The group
also had a few outposts in rural towns but it did not engage in intensive
political activity in these areas. The Lok Parishad movement in the
Nagaur area was fragmented and without any common political
organisation, leadership or structure of support within the area; its
only source of common identification was to be found in the person-

alities and names of its leaders, and the activities of these leaders in the Jodhpur City movement. The Kisan Sabha, on the other hand, was organised primarily in the Nagaur area where its leaders and members were recruited at all levels, through institutional channels of employment, education and professional status, and directed towards, concrete concerns of the caste they came from and the area in which they worked. Finally, the foundations of political cohesion among the Jats were established prior to Independence. First there was participation of the community in a common caste movement and a shared identification with its new dominant values. The new political elite included those, who had achieved success in terms of those new values and who themselves constituted a cohesive group having been reared and educated in common institutions. Furthermore, conflict with a commonly perceived antagonist — the Rajput *jagirdar* — served to solidify this underlying commonality. The myths and stories embodied in the folklore surrounding this confrontation had tended towards the maintenance of a sense of organic cohesion within the caste and in contemporary politics.

The Organisation of Political Groups in the Congress Party

The integration of the Rajputana States and the creation of Rajasthan as a State within the Indian Union entailed major changes in the nature of political conflict and in the organisation of factions and power within the newly formed Rajasthan Congress Party. Prior to independence the primary focus of conflict was against the traditional regimes in the Princely States, redefinition of political authority and legitimacy, and the creation of new institutions which would provide for popular participation in the making of law. Independence brought with it the realisation of these previous demands. A second major change involved the creation of the Rajasthan Congress Party. Prior to 1946 and the formation of a provincial assembly called the Rajputana Prantiya Sabha there had been no common organisational framework which brought together the peoples' movements in the various Rajputana States. Until that time each protest organisation had been directly connected with the nationalist movement through the All-India States' Peoples' Congress (AISPC), the planning and decision-making concerning agitations and political activities in each of the Princely States being taken after direct consultation between leaders in these States with leaders in the Congress High Command. A Regional States' Peoples' Congress had existed from the 1930s but its activities were restricted largely to debates and pronouncements at the annual sessions.

The organisation of political support in the Prantiya Sabha, which subsequently became the Pradesh Congress Committee, included only those organisations which had been a part of the AISPC and was segmented on the basis of the Princely States which formed the units of representation on the State level body.[11] Thus the Lok Parishad automatically became the Congress Party in Jodhpur State. There was no popular leader in the Rajputana States who enjoyed a base of support outside his own State, although a few did have 'wider' reputations than others by virtue of their official positions in the AISPC and their life of political activity and sacrifice in the pre-independence movement.[12] It was around these dominant regional leaders that the first State-level factional coalitions gravitated. The movements in each of the Princely States, however, were not all cohesive units although cohesion was greater in some than in others. These cleavages in local political support had come about in several ways. In some cases division existed as a result of either competition for formal positions within the organisations themselves or from conflict in elections to municipalities. A second source of cleavage resulted from conflict over positions in the popular ministries which were established in some of the Princely States prior to the integration of Rajasthan. After the merger of the States and with the formation of the first Congress Government in Rajasthan in 1950, these regional groups divided and aligned into major factional coalitions at the State level, one in support of the government, and the other in opposition.

The factional coalition which formed the first ministry was headed by Hiralal Shastri, one of the founders of the Praja Mandal in Jaipur State, who had the support of Sardar Patel, the Union Home and States Minister, but who did not have a majority support in the Pradesh Congress Committee.[13] The persons taken into the Shastri Ministry were not the dominant leaders of the pre-independence movements in their respective states and in some cases were the leaders of minority factions. The opposition coalition was headed by Jai Narain Vyas who received the support of most of the principal regional leaders and factions. The Vyas and Shastri coalitions were not organised along caste lines but around strictly political factions, depending upon whether they were or were not included in the first ministry. Those who were not allied in opposition to the Ministry, subsequently gained control of the PCC, and eventually displaced the first Congress Ministry within a few weeks of the death of Sardar Patel. The new Ministry was headed by Vyas and continued until the first General Elections in 1952.

Like the factional coalitions at the State level, regional factions were normally based upon more than one caste, although there were two major and a few minor exceptions to this general rule. The two major exceptions were the Jat factions from Bikaner and the Shekhawati area of former Jaipur State, whose leadership and support rested almost exclusively in the Jat community, and which were allied at the State level with the factional coalition headed by Jai Narain Vyas until after the first General Elections. Vyas was the predominant leader in the Rajasthan Congress and his Marwar Lok Parishad was the dominant faction among the regional factions in this coalition at the State level.

The creation of the Congress Party in Nagaur District was also limited to those groups and activists who had been active in the Lok Parishad. Since there had been no members of the Kisan Sabha active in this organisation, it did not have representation in the Congress at the time of its founding. There was no official party organisation in the district until late in 1949 when the Executive Committee of the PCC directed that an *ad hoc* Congress Committee be formed in each district of the State in order to give the locally based political groups a sense of belonging and in order for the Congress to have a wider base of political support in the rural areas. Prominent members of the PCC were assigned as organisers for the five major administrative divisions of the State and were directed to suggest a list of names of the PCC Executive for appointment to positions on the new DCCs after due consultation with local political leaders as well as with 'prominent' and prestigious persons' in the area.[14] Until after the first General Elections formal positions of leadership in the district level party organisations in Nagaur were by appointment and were limited both in membership and leadership to those who had been affiliated with the Lok Parishad. This included not only the District Congress Committee and its Executive but also the Tehsil Congress Committees which became the political preserves of local urban groups in the Lok Parishad.

The Congress Party in Jodhpur Division remained almost exclusively an urban-based organisation until the eve of the first General Elections when Vyas and his two chief political lieutenants engaged in several efforts to extend the party to the rural areas. Negotiations were held with, on the one hand, the Maharaja and the Kshatriya Mahasabha which represented the dominant Rajput *jagirdars* in the area, and on the other hand, the Kisan Sabha. For a variety of reasons the negotiations with the Kshatriya Mahasabha proved abortive, while the entry of the Kisan Sabha into the Congress Party was arranged, based on an agreement in late 1951 that gave the Kisan Sabha the right to nominate 50 per cent of the Congress candidates for

Jodhpur Division, and ministerial representation in a Congress government.[15]

There was little open conflict in the District Congress between the Lok Parishad groups and the new Jat group prior to the first General Elections in 1952. The Jats had entered the Congress only six months before the elections and the terms governing their entry provided for participation in the elections on the Congress ticket as well as position in the party and the government for major leaders. Moreover, the Jat elite was more concerned at this juncture with winning elections than with capturing control of the party apparatus. Furthermore, when the Nagaur Jat group entered the Congress, it also entered a coalition with the two regionally based Jat groups from Bikaner and Shekhawati which were in the Vyas coalition at the State level. Therefore, although there were two distinct elites and two distinct bases of political support in the District Congress, these did not come into open conflict since participation was granted each group in the elections and because of the amelioratory function played by the organisation of factional coalitions at the State level.

II. *Institutional Conflict and Factional Alignment and Change*

There were several changes which occurred in the factional organisation and pattern of control in the Congress Party at both the State and district levels between 1952 and 1957. The first change involved a split between the Jat and Vyas groups at the State level and the withdrawal of Jat support from the Vyas Ministry in 1954. The second was the development of a corresponding cleavage between these two groups in the Nagaur District Congress and the assumption of control of the Party by the Jat group.

These changes were a part of a larger change in the organisation of political power within the State. The introduction of democratic political institutions and the creation of a mass electorate changed both the aims of political conflict and the basis of power within the system. The ultimate aim of political conflict was control of the Chief Ministership, this being preceded by representation on the Ministry, and the allocation of ministerial portfolios. This in turn involved representation and control of the Congress Legislative Party from which ministers are selected and to whom they nominally owed their support.

The creation of a mass electorate and the institution of popular elections introduced a new criterion of political power. From independence to the first General Elections the Congress Party organisation had been conceived as the embodiment of the 'popular will' and claimed authority to govern by virtue of its having been in the vanguard in the creation of the new political order. Control of the party meant control of the government. After the first General Elections, however, this role of the party diminished and political power passed increasingly into the hands of elected representatives. The importance of controlling the party organisation has continued to exist, but for different reasons. The most important reason has been to gain an *entry* to the electoral process, i.e. to obtain the maximum number of party tickets for one's group as a prerequisite to participation in the government. This in turn has involved attempts to control the party organisation at all levels and attempts to participate appreciably in the selection of persons to positions of power within the party.

The mobilisation of support within the party came about in two general ways. First, there were attempts by the existing elites to attract support from persons and local factions which were already a part of 'the Congress system' and to maintain such support. Second, there were attempts to mobilise new resources for the party and into the support of the particular faction. This involved three different strategies: the attraction of castes and groups which were already politically active but which were not a part of the Congress system; the attraction of other castes which had not become politically active; and the mobilisation of increased support from the same caste as the elite, which was of crucial importance in the Jat rise to predominance in the District Congress.

The 1952 elections were crucial in changing the basis of power in the Congress Party in Jodhpur Division and ultimately at the State level as well. First, the Congress Party was roundly defeated in Jodhpur Division, winning only 4 of 35 seats (11%), and these four were all in Nagaur District. In three of the other four divisions of the State the Congress was returned with a majority, and in the fourth it was not as badly defeated as in Jodhpur. In Jaipur Division the Congress won 43 of 62 seats (69%), in Udaipur Division 19 of 33 seats (58%), in Bikaner 9 of 14 seats (64%), and in Kotah 7 of 16 seats (42%).[16] Second, the majority factions in each of these areas were not considered 'close' associates of the incumbent Chief Minister, Jai Narain Vyas. Third, Vyas was defeated in both of the constituencies in which he contested. In his 'home' constituency he was defeated by the Maharaja of Jodhpur, who received 62.2 per cent of the vote to 17.2 per cent for Vyas. In the second constituency Vyas was defeated by the dominant local *Thakur*, who received 65.7 per cent of the vote to Vyas' 8.9 per cent. The defeat of Vyas in the elections was indicative of the limited base of popular support for the Lok Parishad movement, even in the centre of its most intense activity and for its most popular leader.[17]

At the State level the dominant regional factions continued to support the leadership of Vyas and although an interim Chief Minister was selected in the person of Tika Ram Paliwal, it was with the unanimous understanding in the Congress Legislative Party that Vyas would subsequently be supported in a bye-election and be made Chief Minister.[18] The manoeuvre was successfully carried out in October 1952. Whereas Vyas had a personal base of political support in the Jodhpur group in the PCC prior to 1952, after his election he had to rest his support on a confederation of regionally based factions over which he had little direct control. This absence of a firm base of personal support in the Congress Assembly Party permitted the passing of a no-confidence motion against him in October 1954 and his replacement as Chief Minister by Mohanlal Sukhadia. The Jat group in the Congress Legislative Party, which included four MLAs from Nagaur District, was instrumental in the collapse of the Vyas Ministry.[19] This division at the State level had a permanent effect on the patterning of political support and factional alignments in Jodhpur Division, and in Nagaur District, from that time on.

There were several reasons for the withdrawal of Jat support from the Vyas coalition; the reasons were largely the same for all State level factions although there was difference in detail.[20] First, the minority factional coalition at the State level, which had supported the Shastri Ministry, had been largely excluded from positions of power in the Party organisation as well as in the Legislative Assembly and thus did not offer a threat to the coalition of dominant regional factions. Second, there was considerable resentment against the Chief Minister over the issue of group representation in the Ministry and in the allocation of portfolios. Third, many regional leaders felt that while Vyas was a towering political leader in the pre-independence movement, he was not sensitive to the requirements of political leadership in the new political order. He was not permissive enough in allowing ministers to enter administrative decision-making and in handling administrative appointments in the ministries under their charge. Fourth, Vyas successfully supported the entry of 22 *jagirdar* MLAs into the Congress Legislative Party in 1954, a move which alienated several factions from his support but particularly the Jat group which perceived this as a threat to their own position within the Congress organisation as well as in the Legislative Assembly Party.[21] Finally, there was increased conflict between the Jat and Vyas groups in the District Congress organisations.

The realignment of political support at the State level which caused the defeat of Vyas had several repercussions on the organisation of political support in the Congress Party in Nagaur District and Jodhpur Division. First, the Jat coalition at the State level and particularly the Jat group from Nagaur became exceedingly powerful with respect to ministerial positions which enabled it to maintain the cohesion of its basis of political support in Nagaur District. There were three Jats in the Ministry after the fall of Vyas, two of whom were from Nagaur, and Jat representation in the Ministry has been continuously maintained since. The Vyas group in Jodhpur Division, on the other hand, did not have representation on the Ministry until 1962 and had considerable difficulty in 'getting things done', something which the Jat group from Nagaur had a great facility for doing. Second, the Jat group became the channel of political access for the dominant peasant castes in Jodhpur Division. The Nagaur Jat group consistently nursed these peasant castes and in return secured their political support. The division-wide faction was based almost entirely upon the Jat, Sirvi, and Vishnoi castes from four of the other six districts, and each caste had its own political leadership at the district level that was associated with the Nagaur Jat group.

Political Change and Congress Party Organisation

The period between the first and second General Elections also witnessed several major changes in the structure of political support within the District Congress organisation. These changes, once carried out, set the general pattern of support which has characterised District Congress politics since. This resulted from competition for control of positions of power in the institutions of local government, primarily Municipal Boards, in the Congress Party organisation, and in the allocation of party tickets for the second General Elections. In the case of the district party organisation the axis of conflict was set between the Lok Parishad groups which desired to maintain the positions of power which they had assumed at the time of founding the district committees, and the Jat group which wanted to transfer its base of support from the Jat community and the Kisan Sabha into the Congress system.

This competition within the District Congress was of particular importance. First, the District Congress Committees play a role in the allocation of Congress Party tickets for elections. Second, control of these local party institutions is instrumental in legitimising demands of groups within the party to higher levels. Third, local control and participation is a prerequisite to representation in the Pradesh Con-

gress Committee and its attendant committees. Fourth, such a generation of conflict within the District Congress encouraged competition
for the support of existing tehsil level political units and groups which
had autonomous origins in urban politics after independence and
particularly after the 1952 elections. Finally, it also encouraged extensive efforts on the part of the contesting groups and elites to extend
their support base into the hitherto politically unmobilised sectors of
society. This became particularly true in the politics of ticket allocation
immediately prior to the 1957 elections.

There were two types of political cleavages which developed
between urban groups in the District Congress during the period from
1952 to 1957. The first type involved splits within the Lok Parishad
elite, between those who were closely associated with Vyas and who
had received his support in the allocation of tickets in 1952 and, those
who felt that their aspirations for a political career had not received the
support from Vyas which they deserved. Two of these leaders had
been founder-leaders of Lok Parishad outposts in their respective
towns, but neither received the party ticket in 1952. A third was one
of Vyas' closed and most able political strategists in the Lok Parishad
but who had not been taken into the Vyas Ministry. After 1954 these
three leaders aligned with the Jat faction in district politics.

The Second type of cleavage resulted from the development of
new political groups in four of the five towns in which there had been
a pre-independence movement. In each case the rise of new groups
resulted from conflict in Municipal politics— elections to Municipal
Boards and / or the election of the Chairman of the Municipality. There
were several characteristics which all of these urban factions — old
and new - had in common. Seven of the eight urban Congress groups
were recruited almost entirely from a single caste, although each had
an 'outer circle' of affiliates and supporters from other castes. (The one
exception involved a Brahmin-Oswal coalition which had been
closely affiliated with Vyas and the leader of which had been the lone
MLA from Nagaur who continued to support Vyas after 1954.) Three
of the urban groups were created after the first General Elections and
each of these drew its leadership and major support from a single
caste. In two cases these were Brahmin groups which developed in
opposition to the Lok Parishad groups which were also primarily
Brahmin. (So although most groups were single-caste, there may have
been more than one group from the same caste.) In the third case a
Brahmin faction developed in opposition to a Maheshwari group
which had constituted a Lok Parishad 'Outpost' but which shifted its
loyalty from Vyas to the Jat group after 1954.

In each case the dominant leaders in the new groups had entered politics after Independence and had entered Congress after the first General Elections. These leaders also tended to be more highly educated than those of the older groups against whom they rebelled. In each case the leaders of the new groups were law graduates, whereas the leaders of the old groups had little formal education, or had received education that was more indigenous than 'westernised' — one of them being literate with no formal education and the other two having received degrees from the Hindi Sahitya Sammelan. The 'older' leaders were also more inclined to traditional activities, pursuits, and styles of life than the earnest young lawyers. The rise of new urban groups, therefore, was not so much a result of unrepresented castes demanding a place in the scheme of political things, but of new political elites that wanted to actively participate in Congress politics.

In the Congress Party organisation the conflicts between the urban factions became part of the major conflict between the Jat and Vyas groups in both the tehsil and district organisations. In those tehsils where competing urban factions had developed, the Tehsil Congress Committee Executives were split between the local Vyas group and an opposing coalition which in each case included the Jat faction in the tehsil and the anti-Vyas urban group. In three of four such tehsils, however, the Vyas groups were able to maintain control of the party apparatus, although in two cases the TCC Executive had been replaced by appointed *ad hoc* committees and convenors.[22] In the other four tehsils where the Lok Parishad had been non-existent, the Jat group was able to capture control of the party apparatus without competition.

Although the Jat group was able to establish complete control in only four out of eight Tehsil Congress Committees, and controlled one another through a coalition, by 1956 they had become the predominant caste on the District Congress Committee.

Table I : *Caste Composition of the Nagaur DCC (1956)* *

Consti-tuency	Brahmin	Jat	Kayasth	Mahajan	Muslim	Sched. Caste	Total
1	10	3	—	2	—	3	18
2	2	5	—	5	1	1	14
3	5	5	1	2	—	—	13
4	3	7	—	1	—	—	11
5	—	13	—	—	—	—	13
6	—	8	—	—	—	—	8
7	—	6	—	—	—	—	6
8	—	6	—	—	—	—	6
Total	20	53	1	10	1	4	89

* The caste of two members could not be ascertained.

Representation of the DCC was directly related to the history of political organisation in each of the constituency areas. Jat representation was related to the location and intensity of political activity of pre-independence groups as well as to representation in the Legislative Assembly. Each of those constituency areas where the Jat group did not have dominant representation had been the preserve of major non-Jat leaders all of whom had been associated with the Lok Parishad movement. In those areas where there was only Jat representation, the pre-independence movement had been minimal or non-existent. The first three constituencies, where urban representatives outnumbered Jats, constituted the same areas in which the Vyas groups controlled the Tehsil Congress Committees. Similarly, the constituencies with Jat predominance were precisely the areas from which Jat candidates had contested the 1952 elections, whereas the areas of continued urban representation were where members of the Vyas group had contested in 1952.

The conflicts and resulting factional groupings in the Tehsil Congress Committees were extended to the DCC. The Vyas group had a majority of the representatives from only one constituency area and this was in that tehsil where the local Vyas group had maintained an elected majority in the Tehsil Congress Committee.

The Jat group did not constitute a majority of the representatives on the DCC from constituencies 2 and 3, however, in spite of the fact that they 'controlled' the TCCs in these areas through appointed convenors and *ad hoc* committees. The highest incidence of party activity ad representation on the DCC was located in precisely those areas where factional conflict had been most intense and where the Lok Parishad had developed local units before independence.

The Jat group afforded an alternative channel of access to the larger political process for 'dissident' urban factions. Prior to 1954 the Jat faction and functioned largely as a closed and autonomous unit within the District Congress and was primarily concerned with making of the Congress an organisational weapon for the continuation of its own political aspirations. After that time, however, it started to attract the support of some urban factions which had not been able to achieve positions of power and access through the Vyas group and which desired to have rural support in competition for the Congress tickets and electoral support for the 1957 elections. The Jat group, on the other hand, welcomed urban support not only for the expansion of its own position of power within the District Party organisation, but also for purposes of creating an image of being an aggregate of a number of caste and leadership groups and local interests rather than

Table II : *Composition of the Nagaur DCC (1956)**

Constituency	Brahmin		Jat		Kayasth		Mahajan		Muslim		Sched.Caste		Vyas	Mirdha	Total
	V	M	V	M	V	M	V	M	V	M	V	M			
1	8	2	—	3	—	—	2	—	—	—	3	—	13	5	18
2	3	2	—	5	—	1	1	1	—	—	—	—	4	9	13
3	1	1	—	5	—	—	3	2	1	—	1	—	6	8	14
4	—	3	—	7	—	—	—	1	—	—	—	—	—	11	11
5	—	—	—	13	—	—	—	—	—	—	—	—	—	13	13
6	—	—	—	8	—	—	—	—	—	—	—	—	—	8	8
7	—	—	—	6	—	—	—	—	—	—	—	—	—	6	6
8	—	—	—	6	—	—	—	—	—	—	—	—	—	6	6
Total	12	8	0	53	0	1	6	4	1	0	4	0	23	66	89

*   The caste of two members of the DCC is not known.

**   V = Jai Narain Vyas and M = Nathuram Mirdha. Although the organisation
of persons from the Jat caste in the Nagaur Congress is referred to
locally as the Jat group, the name of the dominant Jat leader is used
here and in subsequent tables to refer to that group.

a narrow caste based faction out of tune with party ideology. This was
particularly important with respect to the political activity of the Jat
group at higher levels in the party hierarchy.

The confrontation between the Jat and Vyas groups, however, was
primarily focused on the Executive Committee of the DCC, the central
decision-making body in the District Congress organisation. The
composition and control of the Executive reflects the pattern of
representation in lower Congress organisational bodies and has been
important not only for its own sake and for the legitimacy it gives the
Jat group in higher levels of the Party organisation, but also because
of the formal role it plays in the process of ticket allocation through the
acceptance of applications and the making of recommendations to
the PCC as to who should be awarded tickets from each constituency.
The major change in the composition of the DCC Executive since 1952
has been the decrease of the urban castes and the concomitant increase
of the rural based Jats. Between 1952 and 1956 representation was
dominated by the urban based Brahmin and Mahajan caste groups but
since 1956 they have continually declined in power while the Jats have
constituted more than 50% of the total members since 1958.

The Jat control of the DCC Executive Committee began with the decline of the Vyas group in State politics and became paramount after the 1957 elections, when the Vyas 'candidates' were badly defeated on a State-wide basis. Vyas subsequently resigned as President of the Pradesh Congress Committee, thus leaving the Vyas coalition without control of any major positions of power at the State level.[23]

The Jat group became the focus of a district level coalition in 1954 which controlled 50 per cent of the members of the Executive, although 3 members of the new coalition were incumbents on the committee and, until then, had been allied with Vyas. After 1956 the Jat group achieved an absolute majority and from 1958 controlled all but one position on the DCC Executive.

There has also been considerable overlap between membership in the Legislative Assembly and membership on the DCC Executive Committee. All but one Congress MLA have been members of the DCC Executive and all but two have been members during their tenure as members of the Legislative Assembly. Furthermore, all Congress party candidates, with the exception of five, were members of the Executive at the time they were granted the Party ticket and of these five, three eventually became members of the Executive after their selection for the Party ticket.

Table III : *Caste Composition of the DCC Executive from 1952 to 1962*

Year	Brahmin	Jat	Kayasth	Mahajan	Muslim	Sched. Caste	Vishnoi	Total
1952*	3	2	1	2	—	—	—	8
1954	7	2	1	4	—	—	—	14
1956	4	4	1	2	1	—	—	12
1958	2	8	1	1	—	1	1	14
1960	1	8	1	1	—	1	—	12
1962	1	8	1	—	1	1	—	12

*The figures for 1952, unlike the others, are not taken from an official party list but have been gleaned from references in party files and materials. It is possible, however, that total representation in 1952 was only 8 since the directive which called for the creation of District Congress Executive Committees in 1949 indicated that they should have between 3 and 9 members.

Table IV :   *Composition of the DCC Executive Committee by Caste and Faction from 1952 to 1962*

Year	Brahmin		Jat		Kayasth		Mahajan		Muslim		Sched. Caste		Vishnoi		Total	
	V	M	V	M	V	M	V	M	V	M	V	M	V	M	V	M
1952	3	—	—	2	1	—	2	—	—	—	—	—	—	—	6	2
1954	5	2	—	2	—	1	2	2	—	—	—	—	—	—	7	7
1956	3	1	—	4	—	1	1	1	—	1	—	—	—	—	4	8
1958	1	1	—	8	—	1	—	1	—	—	—	1	—	1	1	13
1960	1	—	—	8	—	1	—	1	—	—	—	1	—	—	1	11
1962	1	—	—	8	—	1	—	—	—	1	—	1	—	—	1	11

With respect to the Jat group, the major leaders have always been represented on the DCC Executive but the remaining positions have been rotated so that ten Jats who have not been MLAs have, at various times, been members of the Executive Committee since 1958. This has included representation at one time or another for Jat groups from each constituency in the district. Furthermore, positions of leadership on the Committee have been rotated among Jats and non-Jats in order to maintain a sense of participation among all sections of the coalition.

The expansion of Jat participation and the assumption of control in the Party organisation by the Jat group at the local levels has also been reflected in the pattern of representation from the district on the Pradesh Congress Committee.

The composition of the Nagaur section of the PCC reflects changes similar to those which occurred in the DCC and its Executive Committee. While urban castes constituted the major part of representation prior to 1954, after that time the dominant caste was Jat. Secondly, after 1954 the Vyas group at no time had more than one representative in the PCC from Nagaur District. With the exception of three persons, all representatives were the leaders of more or less autonomous factions within the support structure. There has also been considerable overlap between membership on the DCC Executive Committee and the PCC. With the exception of 6 of 35 cases, all representatives were members of the DCC Executive at the same time that they were on the Pradesh Congress Committee and in 12 cases these representatives were sitting MLAs.

Table V :   *Composition of Representation from Nagaur District on the Pradesh Congress Committee : 1952-1963*

	Brahmin		Jat		Mahajan		Sched. Caste		Kayasth		Muslim		Vishnoi		Total
Year	V	M	V	M	V	M	V	M	V	M	V	M	V	M	
1952	3	—	—	2	2	—	—	—	1	—	—	—	—	—	8
1954	1	—	—	4	—	1	—	1	—	1	—	—	—	—	8
1956	1	1	—	2	—	—	—	—	—	1	—	—	—	—	5
1958	1	1	—	4*	—	1	—	1	—	1*	—	—	0	1	10
1960						(no figures)									
1963	—	—	—	3*	—	1	—	1	—	1*	—	1	—	—	7

* In 1958 and 1963 one Jat and the Kayasth member of the PCC were elected from constituencies in Jodhpur District although each had been politically active largely in Nagaur District. Each has been elected to the Legislative Assembly from Nagaur twice and one was elected an MP in 1957. Elections from three constituencies in 1956 were disputed and only five representatives were elected from Nagaur in 1963.

Caste and Political Mobilisation: The Politics of Ticket Allocation

One of the most important aspects of Congress politics has been the competition for the party ticket for the General Elections. It is at this time that the divisions within the structure of political support within the Congress become most evident. This process, as has been true in conflict for control óver the party apparatus,has entailed important efforts on the part of factions to mobilise new political resources in support of their claim for the party ticket. This has involved efforts not only to widen the basis of support within the social group or groups from which a particular faction draws its main support or from other groups represented in the factional coalition, but also from social groups which had not hitherto been mobilised into the representative and political processes of the Congress Party. There have been, therefore, three distinct objects of mobilisation involved in the politics of ticket allocation. First, candidates or factions attempt to extend the base of their support within their own caste. Second, attempts are made to attract and mobilise the support of those castes which may participate in elections but which have not yet developed autonomous organisations and leaders that are involved in politics on a continuing basis. The third object of mobilisation involves those political groups which have been mobilised and have continuity and autonomy in the political process but which have not become a part of the Congress system.[24]

The process of ticket allocation in 1952 was not as elaborate as it became in 1957 and 1962, since an agreement had been arrived at between the Kisan Sabha and the then Congress leadership concerning how candidates would be selected. The choice of constituency then was not a major object of confrontation since the areas of Lok Parishad activity and of Jat predominance happened to be different. In 1952 party tickets were largely assigned and not competed for.

The factional coalitions and structures of political support which had developed between 1954 and 1957 became more crystallised in the competition for the Party ticket prior to the 1957 election and set the pattern of factional alignments in the Congress which has continued since. Each faction put up at least one member for each constituency with the major leaders in each of the factional coalitions applying for a ticket from at least one constituency. However, in no case where more than one member of the same coalition applied for the same ticket did this involve a conflict within the coalition. The negotiations for the ticket, concern not only who the recipient will be but also for what constituency recipients will receive the ticket. Thus in several cases an aspirant has applied for the ticket from more than one constituency so that if there is considerable opposition at higher levels in the Party to his contesting from one constituency he will have an alternative to 'offer'. Conversely, if two representatives from the same faction or factional coalition have applied for the ticket for the same constituency and one is given the ticket for another, then there still remains a second applicant from the group to negotiate for the ticket from the first constituency. Furthermore, several dominant leaders apply from more than one constituency, not only for the purpose of having alternatives, but also to demonstrate the wide base of public support which they enjoy, thus bolstering their claim of being truly popular and mass leaders. A major corollary to this gambit has been to have several members of the same faction apply from the same constituency in an attempt to demonstrate a wide base of support for the group, thus reducing the claim of the opposing faction for the ticket. This is sometimes followed by the withdrawal of some applicants from the competition and the transfer of their support to one aspirant thus giving credence to the latter's claim to widespread support from local influentials and potentates.

Another aspect of strategy has involved the use of caste and community. In the case of the general seats, dominant factions often set up a Scheduled Caste candidate not as a serious contender for the ticket, but to indicate 'support' from the Scheduled Castes in that area for their group. Another facet of this ploy has been to set up a candidate from the same caste as that of the dominant opposition faction thus reducing the implicit claim of the opponent to wide-spread support from his own community. The assumption involved here is that if an applicant does not command considerable support from his own caste in the constituency, he is a political risk. This tactic has been employed most frequently by the Jat coalition, the reverse not being possible since members of the Vyas coalition have never been able to attract a candidate from within the Jat caste.

Table VI: *Composition by Caste and Faction of Applicants for the Congress Party Ticket in Nagaur District for the Second General Elections*

Caste	Vyas Group		Mirdha Group		Total
	Core	Aligned	Core	Aligned	
Brahmin	4	1	—	5	10
Jat	—	—	11	—	11
Kayasth	—	—	—	1	1
Mahajan	1	4	—	2	7
Muslim	—	6	—	1	7
Sched. Caste	—	2	—	4	6
Total	5	13	11	13	42

The caste of applicants for the Congress Party tickets in 1957 was to a large extent reflective of the caste composition of each of the factional coalitions in the District Congress organisation.[25] The pre-dominance of applicants from the Vyas coalition was from the ritually high urban castes, the central core of the faction being primarily Brahmin. All applicants from the core of the Vyas faction had entered politics prior to independence and had been involved in the Lok Parishad movement. Those who were aligned had all entered politics after independence. All 18 applicants from the Vyas group were from urban areas.

The composition of the Jat group was quite different. Jats alone formed the central nexus of those who applied from this group. The 'aligned' groups were affiliated in two different ways. Some were directly linked to the Jat group at the constituency level where mutual support was rendered in political conflicts at that level. In other cases, urban factions were loosely linked with a major non-Jat leader of the coalition who, while he was not a part of the Jat support structure, was a part of the decision-making elite in the Jat group both at the State and district levels. The applicants who were affiliates of the Jat faction were all from urban areas while the Jats were all from rural areas.

The extension of support to applicants in the ticket allocation process followed the organisation of factions. In only one case did members of the Jat group support an affiliate of the Vyas group and in no case did members of the Vyas group support members of the Jat group. Another interesting feature of the process involved attempts on the part of applicants and factions to expand their base of support and this involved extending support to persons and groups which were not officially affiliated with the Congress Party.[26]

Table VII : *Caste Composition by Constituency of Supporters for Applicants for the Congress Party Ticket for the Second General Elections**

Consti-tuency	Brahmin	Jat	Mahajan	Muslim	Rajput	Sched. Caste	Total
1	12	11	9	3	—	17	52
2	11	12	4	7	—	17	51
3	13	21	13	1	4	8	60
4	1	22	—	—	—	—	23
5	6	29	1	2	—	—	39
6	1	9	—	—	—	3	13
7			(arranged)				
8	5	6	3	14	—	2	30
Total	49	110	30	27	4	48	268

* The caste of 11 supporters is not known.

There was considerable unevenness in the extent of participation by constituency and by caste. The highest incidence of participation occurred in those constituencies in which there were competing urban groups and where there had been intense conflict over control of the Tehsil Congress Committees. These were also the same constituencies which had the highest number of representatives on the District Congress Committee. Thus those areas which had had the most intense conflict between groups have also had the highest degree of activity in the Congress Party. This proposition is also substantiated by competition between different caste groups. In those constituencies where participation by caste was highest, there were competing groups from the same caste supporting different applicants for the

Party ticket. In two of the first three constituencies the dominant groups were Brahmin.

The highest degree of Jat participation occurred in the constituency in which the Jat caste was split between the local group, which controlled the Tehsil Panchayat and the Tehsil Congress Committee, and the Jat MLAs group which consisted almost entirely of 'outsiders' but who were primarily Jat. The MLA had not been an integral part of the Kisan Sabha movement and was not widely accepted as a district-wide Jat leader by the Jat community but was supported by the dominant Jat leadership in the district because of his education and political acumen. By 1957 he had also developed a considerable base of support through his position as President of the State Co-operative Bank in the district and as a result of his growing activity in the co-operative movement.[27] This conflict was resolved by the dominant Jat leader in the district when assurances were allegedly given that the local group would continue in positions of power in tehsil level organisations and that punitive action would not be taken against them directly nor in the form of withheld benefits at the disposal of the MLA.

The participation of Scheduled Castes and Muslims was limited to four different constituencies.[28] Muslims concentrated their efforts in Constituency 5 which included the largest percentage of Muslims of any constituency in the district. There were four Muslims who applied for the ticket from this constituency, which again was not indicative of intra-community conflict, but was rather a strategic move to indicate the widespread participation of Muslims in the Congress Party and their extensive support for the party ticket.

Prior to 1957, there had been no serious efforts on the part of factions to coopt Scheduled Castes into the Congress organisation nor had there been any demand from within these castes for more extensive political participation. In 1957, however, a reserved seat was established in Nagaur District by the merger of constituencies 1 and 2 into a double member constituency. Since these two seats — one general, one reserved — involved the same constituency, the competition for the seats was inter-linked. The creation of this reserved seat gave rise to the extension of conflict between the Jat and Vyas elites into the Scheduled Castes. Each faction supported a candidate for both the general and reserved seats. The competition for the reserved seat involved the greatest concentration of effort on the part of members of the Scheduled Castes, none of whom led an autonomous political group, and all of whom drew their power in the Congress from the faction with which they were aligned and which had coopted them into the Congress system.[29] The person who was eventually given the ticket and who was elected had not been active in politics prior to the fall of 1956, when he was coopted into the Jat group, made a member of the Congress Party, and eventually was selected and maintained as the lone Scheduled Caste representative on the DCC Executive Committee.

In the negotiations for the Congress Party ticket in 1957, however, support for particular applicants was not extended exclusively on a caste basis, but rather the majority of support (56 per cent) for the various applicants was received from castes other than their own. Brahmin, Mahajan, Scheduled Caste, and 'other' caste aspirants received respectively 81, 82, 65 and 100 per cent of their support from castes other than their own. Furthermore, with the exception of Jats, the largest share of support 'units' went to aspirants whose caste was different from that of the supporters. 88 per cent of Brahmin support units went to non-Brahmins, 57 per cent of Mahajans supported non-Mahajans, 52 per cent of Muslims supported non-Muslims and 60 per cent of Scheduled Castes extended their support to aspirants whose caste carried 'clean' ritual status. With the exception of Brahmins, however, the largest aggregate of supporters from each caste went to aspirants from the same caste.

The dispersion of caste support was most noticeable in the cases of aspirants from urban castes. Although the central core of urban factions has been restricted largely to a single caste, these groups have continually attempted to widen the support base of their factions by attracting affiliates from other castes. This has been extremely important in the case of the general elections where the area of conflict is considerably wider than in elections to local bodies, which have constituted the primary impetus in the rise of new urban groups.

The highest degree of cohesiveness in the extension and receipt of support occurred in the case of the Jats and Muslims. The majority of support (89%) for Jat aspirants came from the Jat caste while 61 per cent of the total number of Jats in the supportive process extended their support to Jat aspirants and only 39 per cent to non-Jats. This, however, is not so much an indication of purposeful exclusiveness on the part of Jats, as Jats were found to support aspirants from all castes. Nor is it indicative of anti-Jat bias among other castes. The quest for support results from canvassing, the extension of support resting more upon the volition and action of the supported than upon that of the supporters. The concentration of Jat support for Jat applicants is also indicative of the cohesion which has characterised the Jat community in politics.

Table VIII : *Composition of Support by Caste for Applicants for the Congress Party Ticket in Nagaur District for the Second General Elections**

Caste of Applicants	Caste of Supporters							
	Brahmin	*Jat*	*Mahajan*	*Muslim*	*Sched. Caste*	*Rajput*	*Total*	*Total of Own Caste*
Brahmin	6	7	7	3	8	—	31	6
Jat	4	66	—	2	2	—	74	66
Mahajan	21	12	13	6	18	4	74	13
Muslim	—	1	1	13	—	—	15	13
Scheduled Caste	13	11	9	3	19	—	55	19
Other	5	13	—	—	1	—	19	—
Total	49	110	30	27	48	4	268	117

* The caste of 11 supporters could not be ascertained.

The case of Muslim participation in the politics of ticket allocation is somewhat different and has been shaped to a large extent by the peculiar relationship of the Muslim community to politics in general and to the Congress in particular. The Muslims have not played an active role in Congress organisation and factional politics although their political affinities and electoral support have been for the Congress. The Muslims have instead rested their claims for the Congress ticket largely on the standing policy of the Party that Muslims be allotted tickets in areas where their numbers are politically significant. This standing assurance for the allocation of tickets has tended to militate against Muslims actively organising within the Congress to pursue positions of power and the promise of positive gain has been one reason for not becoming a part of the opposition. Another factor militating against the participation of Muslims in politics is the spectre of the communalist image, politically permissible with respect to caste, but much less permissible with respect to religion.

The competition for the Congress ticket, as has been true in the elections, has involved a far more complex set of relationships between castes and political groups than would be suggested by the way groups have been organised in the Congress system. Although most political factions consist at the primary level of members from a single caste. these different political groups have been affiliated in two competing factional coalitions within each of which mutual support is extended in the pursuit of political goals. Each of these factional coalitions has necessarily involved a multi-caste base of political support. In the politics of ticket allocation the pattern of support has not followed strict caste lines; rather the support from particular castes has been dispersed. Furthermore, this multi-caste base of political action and support has involved not only an aggregation of caste and political groups which have previously been mobilised into the political process; political conflict itself has encouraged the search for wider bases of support and has entailed appeals not only to the castes of particular leaders and groups, but to other castes as well. This multi-caste base of support has been most characteristic of urban castes, some of which have been split into competing groups and all of which together constitute a minority of the total electorate — a condition which has been particularly conducive to lateral association with other castes. Finally, there is a direct relationship between the caste basis of political groups and levels of political organisation. The 'lower' the level of politics, the greater the probability that groups will have a restricted base of caste recruitment. Conversely, the 'higher' the level of politics, the greater the probability that membership in political groups will be recruited from a number of castes. This is not to imply that caste becomes less important in political life from the district level on up, but that political conflict has provided a new type of social activity which did not exist in the traditional social order and which is conducive to inter-caste alignment and co-operation.

III.   *Caste, Party and Representation: The Congress and its Political Environment*

The Congress Party has not been separated from its political environment by distinct and clearly discernible 'boundaries'. There is a relatively spacious and fluctuating margin where the Congress system 'meets' its environment and there is considerable entry and exit of certain persons and groups as well as association and alliance between certain Congress groups and their non-Congress counterparts. The Congress, while it has a fairly wide social base, does not include representation from all major castes and those that are represented are not necessarily a part of the Congress system in their entirety. There are also factions within the Congress which have extensions outside the party organisation that become important in elections. Sometimes these extensions take on party labels which often result in charges by competing Congress factions that a certain leader or faction within the party is a representative of an opposition party. Third, and this is most important, factions within the Congress engage in coalitions with non-Congress political groups for election purposes or coopt non-Congressmen to contest against Congress 'opponents', with the express purpose of gravitating a block of caste votes away from those opponents. This form of activity has in all cases involved an extension of the factional conflict within the Congress organisation to the arena of 'public' politics.

The Structure of the Opposition

The opposition to the Congress in Nagaur District has been frag mented and has been confined largely to the Rajput community and to groups associated with them by virtue of traditional loyalties and obligations. The basis of opposition has not been so much against the Congress as such, although some *jagirdars* perceive the Congress as the usurpers of their traditional prerogatives, but has primarily involved the politicisation of social conflict between Rajputs and Jats in the rural areas. Unlike the Jats, however, the Rajput community has been divided in politics on the basis of status and power relationships which governed traditional, social and political organisation before independence. The Rajputs have been segmented to a large extent on the basis of the former *jagirs*, between which there have been long traditions of feuds and mutual suspicion, and like the urban political movements and groups, have had no common focus of political identity within Nagaur District.

Shortly after independence, however, major efforts were made towards the integration of the Rajput community into a common organisational framework. The first series of efforts involved the creation of a common front for negotiations concerning the proposed abolition of *jagirs* and the institution of land reforms, policy objectives which were given the highest priority in the Congress programme. For this purpose the Kshatriya Mahasabha, which had existed as a loosely organised social organisation of Rajputs for several decades, was organised on a statewide basis for the formulation and representation of *jagirdari* demands to the Congress Party and the government.[30]

A second effort resulted from the decision to turn the Kshatriya Mahasabha into a political party for the purpose of contesting the first General Elections. It was ultimately decided that the Rajput community in Rajasthan would contest the elections on a State-wide basis although the actual decisions concerning the candidates, the organisation of elections, the planning of election strategy, and the choice of party symbol would be left to the regional units of the Kshatriya Mahasabha operating from each of the five major Rajput States — Bikaner, Kotah, Jaipur, Jodhpur, and Udaipur. Although it did not actively engage in local political affairs, a central coordinating office was established in Jaipur and was headed by a respected and politically able Jodhpur *thakur* who was to become one of the major political strategists among the Rajputs until his death in 1964.

The organisation of the Rajputs in Jodhpur and in Rajasthan as a whole took on a new impetus with the entry of the dashing young Maharaja of Jodhpur into politics. The Maharaja served as the central organiser and ticket allocator for the entirety of Jodhpur Division where his candidates were immensely successful in the elections, winning 31 of 35 seats in the division. The four seats lost, were in Nagaur District as was the highest incidence of Rajput dissidence over candidates set up by the royal house. There were several cases where major Rajput *jagirdars* in particular constituencies did not support the Maharaja's candidates and in each of these cases those candidates were defeated.

The Maharaja reportedly over-ruled some of his political advisers and granted tickets to representatives of non-Rajput castes who were sympathetic to the interests and problems which the traditional elite faced in the new order.[31] Of the eight candidates supported by the Maharaja in Nagaur, four were Rajput, three were Brahmin and one was Muslim. Three of the four Rajputs, who were major *jagirdars* in their constituencies, were successful, while the fourth, who was from a rather small estate, was defeated. In each of the constituencies where the Maharaja's candidates were unsuccessful, Rajput support was divided. In the case of the Muslim candidate the opposing non-Jat Congress candidate, in one of his frequent strokes of political brilliance, negotiated the support of the three major *thakurs* of the area as well as the support of the Jats. In the case of one of the Maharaja's Brahmin candidates, some of the local *thakurs* set up their own candidate, a Rajput, and are reported to have told His Highness that his *acharya* would lose his security deposit, which he did. The second Brahmin candidate supported by the Maharaja was unable to attract widespread Rajput support and the dominant *jagirdar* of the Nagaur area, although belonging to that constituency, did not actively engage in the campaign on his behalf. Moreover, the third Brahmin candidate, who had also held positions of authority in the Jodhpur court, defeated his Congress opponent in a two-way contest.

The death of the Maharaja in a plane crash on the eve of his election victory removed the one common integrator and symbol of social and political obligation among the Rajputs. Since the first General Elections, the Rajputs in Nagaur District have made no concerted effort at establishing a common political organisation for the purpose of contesting elections.

Although the symbol of the Ram Rajya Parishad, a sort of Hindu party on the rightist fringe, was used in the 1952 elections, it was never given organisational form nor were all of those who used this symbol official members of the party. Since 1952 there has been no party symbol used commonly by Rajput candidates.[32] (See Tabe IX.)

This segmentation among the Rajputs, a result of status differentiation and animosities in the traditional order, was augmented by yet another split with the creation of an association of smaller *jagirdars* known as the Bhoomiswami Sangh and the precipitation of a *Bhoomiswami Andolan*, between 1956 and 1958, which radically divided the small from the large *jagirdars*. This organisation was formed because of dissatisfaction among smaller *jagirdars* with the agreement concerning *jagirdari* abolition, reached between the Congress and the Kshatriya Mahasabha in 1953. The Bhoomiswamis claimed that this organisation was composed only of large *jagirdars* who acted in their own narrow interest although they claimed to speak for the entirety of the Rajput community. The precipitation of the *Andolan* and the considerable social disorder which resulted from it radically disrupted the Rajputs not only in Nagaur, where the movement orginated, but in numerous other parts of Rajasthan as well.

Although the Rajputs have formed a permanent, if unorganised, opposition to the Congress, the Congress Party itself has supplied a large part of its own opposition in the General Elections. We may call this the Congress-opposition as although it orginates within the party, it steps out of the party during elections and thus takes a form different from intra-party contests for power. The large number of Congressmen who have contested the elections against the official Congress candidates has been indicative of this phenomenon. In Nagaur District in 1952, 9 of the 26 opposition candidates were either Congress members at the time of the election or were members of groups which were largely in the Congress Party. In 1957, 10 of the 22 opposition candidates were members of the Congress at the time of elections and in 1962, 12 of the 26 opposition candidates were members of the Congress. The opposition of certain groups within the Congress to the official party candidates is directed ultimately towards maintaining or enhancing their position within the party organisation vis-a-vis other competing but dominant groups. Each of the above cases represented an extension of factional conflict within the Congress Party to the electoral arena, the 'Congress-opposition' candidates in each case being persons and/or representatives of a faction which had not been awarded the Congress ticket.

There is another factor in electoral strategy which has at times been pursued by Congress, 'Congress-opposition', and opposition candidates alike. This has involved the setting up of a candidate who is not expected to win the election but who may enable a dominant candidate to win by virtue of his attracting the votes of his caste away from the opposition candidate. This is directed not only towards splitting the votes of the caste of which the opposing candidate is a member, but also towards the attraction of votes from a particular caste which would be expected to go to the opposing candidate had this alternative choice not been offered and had the latter been the only candidate from that caste. The confusion created by more than one candidate from the caste is aimed at breaking the cohesion of that caste in politics and fragmenting its vote, a section of it also going to the side that initiated the strategy. It is not possible to determine the extent to which this strategy has been successful since data is not available as to the caste composition of votes for particular candidates. What is important, however, is that there is a universally shared belief among political activists that votes are extended largely on the basis of caste and that this strategy works. 'Vote banks' are perceived and pursued on the basis of caste and although a particular caste may be divided the resulting divisions still share a common base in a common caste.

Caste and Political Representation

Participation in the three General Elections has involved candidates from all major castes and communities in Nagaur District. The largest number of candidates in the three General Elections, as well as in each bye-election, have been Jats and Rajputs, the two dominant castes in the district. These have been followed by Mahajans, Brahmins, Scheduled Castes, Muslims and Kayasthas respectively. The number of candidates from the same caste has tended to remain constant with a few notable exceptions. (See Table IX.) In the case of Brahmins, Muslims and Scheduled Castes there has tended to be considerable change. The total number of Brahmin candidates has decreased from 5 in 1952 to 2 in 1962. This is not so much indicative of political alienation of Brahmin elites from the Congress as it is of the change in the basis of political alignment. Most Brahmin political activists have been in the Congress Party and the three non-Congress Brahmin candidates in 1952 subsequently joined the Congress. The other prominent Brahmin groups have remained loyal to the Congress either by virtue of long association with the Congress movement, or as supporters of dominant Mahajan leaders. The two main Brahmin groups in the Congress, however, have functioned in an area that was converted into a reserved constituency for the Scheduled Castes and were thus barred from contesting, although each group was found active in the support of different Scheduled Caste candidates. Scheduled Caste candidates did not contest the elections until the creation of a reserved constituency in the district. In both 1957 and 1962, however, only two candidates contested the reserved seat while the others were aligned with candidates from other castes for their own strategic purposes.

Several important relationships, between caste and party affiliation of candidates, emerge. With the exception of Rajputs, the Congress Party has supported candidates from all major castes and communities in at least two of the three General Elections. This to some extent is the result of a conscious effort on the part of the Congress at the State and national levels to offer a wide enough representation to social groups in the allocation of tickets (although at the same time underplaying caste as a basis of political recruitment). The major assumption on which this policy rests is that the Congress, in claiming to be an 'open' party representing the 'popular will', must be responsive to all sectors of society and give them a sense of participation in the Congress, and through it in the larger political process.

The other two 'major' political parties in the district, the Ram Rajya Parishad and the Jan Sangh, have contested candidates from fewer castes than the Congress. Neither party has established a district-wide organisation. The RRP has been restricted to a few major Rajput *jagirdars* and their affiliates while the Jan Sangh has largely been the preserve of persons from the Mahajan castes and its base has been limited to three towns. In three cases the Jan Sangh candidates have been aligned with a Congress group recruited from the same caste.

Elections have also involved several cases of competition between candidates from the same caste. For one thing, use is being made of 'nonentities' by the principal competing candidates for their own strategic purposes. Second, 'outsiders' who have political aspirations but who have not been previously active in politics are found to enter the field or are persuaded to do so. Such a conflict situation has existed under two conditions: either where the candidate of the dominant party is of the same caste as the opposition, or where neither the dominant party nor the opposition candidate comes from a particular caste.[33]

Table IX : *Caste of Candidates in Nagaur District for the Three General Elections. (By Party Affiliation.)*

Party	Brahmin	Jat	Kayasth	Mahajan	Muslim	Rajput	Sched. Caste	Not known	Total
(1952)									
Cong.	1	4	1	1	1	—	—	—	8
RRP	2	—	—	—	—	5	—	—	7
JS	—	—	—	3	—	—	—	—	3
OP	—	3	—	—	—	—	—	2	5
Inds.	2	2	—	—	4	—	—	3	11
Total	5	9	1	4	5	5	0	5	34
(1957)									
Cong.	1	4	—	2	—	—	1	—	8
RRP	—	—	—	1	—	3	—	—	4
JS	1	—	—	—	—	1	—	—	2
PSP	1	—	—	—	—	—	—	—	1
Inds.	1	5	—	1	1	1	3	3	15
Total	4	9	0	4	1	5	4	3	30
(1962)									
Cong.	—	4	1	1	1	—	1	—	8
RRP	—	—	—	1	—	2	—	—	3
JS	—	—	—	3	—	—	—	—	3
Swt.	—	1	—	—	1	1	1	—	4
Inds.	2	5	—	1	1	3	4	—	16
Total	2	10	1	6	3	6	6	0	34

Legend for Table IX
 Cong. = Congress, RRP = Ram Rajya Parishad, JS = Jan Sangh, OP = Other Parties (Krishikar Lok Party and Kisan Janta Sanyukta Party), PSP = Praja Socialist Party, Swt = Swatantra Party, and Inds. = Independents.

There have been 17 cases of intra-caste competition in the three General Elections — 5 in 1952, 2 in 1957 and 10 in 1962. The most frequent incidence of conflict has occurred among the Jats. In the three cases which involved Jats in 1952, one involved a Jat candidate who contested against the nominee and member of the district-level Congress Jat elite. This constituency was also the single case of conflict between Jats in 1957 and in both elections this electoral conflict involved an extension of a factional division in the Congress organisation (constituency 5). In each of two other constituencies in 1952, two Jats opposed the Congress candidates who had been nominated by the Vyas group. In none of these cases did the combined vote for the Jat 'dissidents' total more than 9.3 per cent of the total valid votes polled, and in no case did they have the political blessings of the district-level Jat elite, although it must be stressed that they were not threatened, discouraged or punished for such action by the dominant Jat elite.[34]

The 1962 elections brought a new kind of Jat dissident into the political process. In these elections there were four constituencies in which intra-caste opposition occurred. Three of these involved opposition to a major Jat political figure in the district. With the exception of one case, these new Jat activists were young political novices who were defeated by their Congress opponents, having received only 2.9, 14.0 and 7.0 per cent of the total valid votes polled in their respective constituencies. In the other case the Jat candidates polled a total of 21.5 per cent of the vote, but in this case the Maheswari Congress candidate lost to a Rajput who had formerly been a large *jagirdar* and who had been elected an MLA in 1952.[35] Although numerous Jat 'dissidents' have contested in the three General Elections, they have received a comparatively small share of the vote and in no case have they 'caused' the defeat of a Congress Jat candidate.

Almost all of the other politically active castes and communities at one time or another have experienced open competition in public elections. Candidates from the Maheswari, Rajput and Muslim communities have contested against one another, one time each while Brahmin and Balai candidates have twice contested against their caste fellows from the same constituency. With the exception of two cases, all of these involved an extension of intra-Congress factional struggles.

The Pursuit and uses of Political Power

Since 1952 the Congress Party has established nearly complete hegemony over Nagaur and Jodhpur politics. Within the Congress, supremacy has increasingly gone to the Jat-led factional coalition and within this coalition to the Jats themselves. In the first General Elections the Congress won four of the eight seats to the Legislative Assembly from Nagaur District and these were evenly divided between the Jat and Vyas groups, although one Vyas MLA subsequently transferred his political loyalties to the Jat group. Congress candidates were also successful in each of the two bye-elections held between the first and second General Elections. In one case the Congress candidate, who defeated his prominent and well-educated Rajput rival, was the son of the founder of the Kisan Sabha. In the other case a Mahajan member of the Vyas group defeated the incumbent Brahmin MLA who had received the support of the royal house in 1952.[36] By 1954, the Congress had claimed six of the eight Assembly seats from the district, four from the Jat coalition and two from the Vyas group.

The 1957 General Elections marked a further decline in power for the Vyas group in both district and State politics. In 1957 all eight Congress candidates were successful in Nagaur, but only one was from the Vyas group while the other seven were all members of the Jat coalition, four of whom were from the central core of the Jat group itself. The distribution of legislative power also changed considerably in Jodhpur as a whole. In the 1957 elections the Congress won 14 of the other 28 seats from Jodhpur Division (not including Nagaur) and nine of these were members of the Jat coalition, only three were supporters of Vyas, and two were supporters of the Chief Minister, Mohanlal Sukhadia. Three of the independent MLAs were also members of the Jat group.[37]

In 1962 all Congress tickets from Nagaur went to members of the Jat coalition, six of whom were successful in the elections. Although the Congress 'officially' won only six seats, it in fact won seven. The one independent MLA was a member of the Jat group who had been refused the ticket in both 1957 and 1962. He contested independently in 1957 but was defeated and suspended from the party. It was somewhat ironic that this Jat MLA was the first member of the opposition to be admitted into the Congress Legislative Party in 1962, giving the latter a precarious but sufficient majority (89-87) and enabling it to form the government of Rajasthan.

In the other districts of Jodhpur Division the Congress increased its majority to 19 of the 28 seats in these districts. Of these 19 MLAs only one was a member of the Vyas group, 11 supported the Nagaur Jat coalition and 6 the Chief Minister. There were also several independents elected who owed their political allegiance to the Jat coalition.

Only the Jat group has been able to maintain major positions of power at the State and district levels since 1952. This has been true in the party organisation, in the ministry and in other so-called 'non-political', but politically important institutions. Since 1957 the Nagaur Jat group has been continuously represented on the PCC Executive Committee and on the Pradesh Election Committee, which screens applicants for Congress Party tickets from the State, and makes final recommendations to the Central Election Committee. Between 1958 and 1962 two members of the State level Jat group, including one from Nagaur, served as the president of the Pradesh Congress Committee, and another from Nagaur was a General Secretary of the PCC during this time.

Table X : *Caste of MLAs Elected from Nagaur District in the Three General Elections.*

| | | | | Caste | | | |
| | | | | | | | Sched. |
Year	Brahmin	Jat	Kayasth	Mahajan	Muslim	Rajput	Caste
1952	1	2	1	1	—	3	—
1957	1	4	—	2	—	—	1
1962	—	5	1	—	—	1	1
Total	2	11	2	3	0	4	2

The Jats have also been well represented in the Congress ministries since 1952 and have continually held important portfolios. Since 1952 at least one member of the State level Jat coalition has been a member of the ministry and, with the exception of a one-year period, the Nagaur Jat group has had at least one minister in the Cabinet. Since 1954 the portfolios of Agriculture, Co-operatives, and Irrigation, all of which are important in a primarily agricultural state, and strategic from the standpoint of increasingly dynamic peasant castes, have been in the hands of the Nagaur Jat leadership. Other portfolios of importance which have been controlled by Jats for considerable periods of time have been Transport, Public Works, and Electricity. Furthermore, the Speaker of the Legislative Assembly since 1957 has been Ram Niwas Mirdha, the son of the founder of the Marwar Kisan Sabha, who has been elected because of the high esteem and respect which he commands not only from the various groups within the Congress Party but from all quarters of the Legislative Assembly. This 'non-caste' prestige, however, has not failed to be reflected in Nagaur District. The Jats have also been predominant in two other types of politically important institutions : (1) the co-operative movement, and

(2) the panchayats. Since its creation in 1957, the Jats have controlled the State Co-operative union and a member of the Nagaur Jat group has continually held the position of General Secretary.[38] This institution serves as a general clearing-house for a number of different co-operatives in the State, offers avenues for employment, and allocates loans to local co-operatives. The State Co-operative Bank in Nagaur District, which has considerable funds at its disposal, has also been controlled by the district Jat group.

The creation of elected panchayats has offered new positions of prestige and power at the local level and has provided channels through which local Jat leaders can participate in the new political order. From 1953 to 1959 these were Tehsil Panchayats which had restricted powers but which nevertheless offered new status resources at the local level. These panchayats were almost exclusively controlled by the Jats. In 1959, new institutions of Panchayati Raj were established creating a three-tiered structure of institutions from the village to the district level.[39] In these institutions the Jats have maintained a small majority. However, the competition between the Rajput and Jat groups has tended to intensify the cohesion of the latter at these local levels.

The continued control over positions of power has distinguished the Jat from other political groups in Nagaur district and Jodhpur Division. The ability to allocate and distribute valued resources at the disposal of government has been important in maintaining the cohesion of the Jat group itself and in the attraction of other local political units. The sensitivity and responsiveness of the Jat elite to the interests and demands of the peasant castes has often resulted in accusations of 'casteism' being levelled against it by opposing groups both within and outside the Congress Party. Other groups are also responsive to the demands of their supporters, but with the exception of a few cases, these supporters are not recruited from one or cognate castes.

The creation of new local institutions has contributed to the cohesion of the Jat group, first by establishing a new situation in which conflict occurs between the Rajputs and Jats, and second by offering a channel of participation in the political process which carries with it considerable prestige and power at the local levels and which has reduced the demands from within the group for positions in 'higher' political bodies.

IV. Notes and Conclusions

The organisation of power in the Congress Party in Nagaur District and Jodhpur Division has been shaped primarily by conflict between the Lok Parishad and Jat elites out of which the party was created.

Although the Lok Parishad group maintained supremacy in the party organisation as well as dominance in positions of power in the State government until 1954, the Jat group ultimately succeeded in establishing permanent control over the party organisation at the district level, as well as over certain 'permanent' positions in the state ministry.

There were several reasons for this changed pattern of control. First, and of considerable importance, was the creation of democratic political institutions and the selection of leadership in the Congress Party itself by elections, which placed a premium on mass political support. The Vyas group did not bring a widespread base of public support into the new political order and the castes from which it recruited its supporters were relatively small and often fragmented. The Jat elite, on the other hand, based its support on a single dominant caste which had formed a cohesive social movement before independence and which was easy to transform into a cohesive political group in the new political order.

Besides the difference in the structure of political support and its influence on effectiveness in the context of the new set of political institutions, there was a second important difference between the Vyas and the Jat groups, and this involved the character of the elites themselves. The Vyas group did not develop cohesive district level elites during the pre-independence period, which might have afforded a minimum of cohesion in post-independence politics. Instead, this elite was a congeries of separate leaders who had not experienced intense and common involvement in political affairs and each of whom had personal aspirations for political positions. The Jat elite, on the other hand, had already before 1952 developed a sense of cohesiveness and common purpose as a result of shared experiences in educational training, political endeavour and social and economic reform; it had also in the course of such an effort developed an 'accepted' hierarchy of roles in its elite structure. All this was prior to the coming of democratic politics. A third significant difference involved competing conceptions between the Vyas group and the Jat elite as to what political leadership in the new order entailed: the former conceived leadership and political action in terms of universal standards and the 'good of the State as a whole' as the proper criterion whereas the latter looked upon their function more in terms of responsiveness to those who had been deprived under the traditional regime. It was not the rightness or wrongness of either of these competing views which determined the outcome of this conflict, but the difference itself was important in influencing the use of power at the disposal of the Jat group vis-a-vis other groups, to shape its outcome.

Conflict over positions of power in public institutions and in the Congress organisation has been a primary vehicle for the mobilisation of new political resources. The first and major object of support has been the caste from which a particular elite or political factor comes. This channel of mobilisation was of particular importance in the rise of the Jats in district politics. Second, existing leaders and elites have vied for the support of groups which are already a part of the Congress system and in a few cases have attracted the support of political groups from outside the party. Third, and this is of crucial importance for the 'system', political groups have attempted to expand their base of support through the mobilisation of 'new' castes into the Congress, by coopting existing caste leaders or by 'creating' new leaders in these castes by the very act of cooptation and the grant of political access. This process has followed not only out of conflict between the two dominant elites at the district level, but also from conflict between local groups in municipal and tehsil level public institutions and party organisations.

Most units in the Nagaur Congress Party have been recruited from a single caste and tend to cluster around a leader or a small group of leaders from that same caste. No caste, however, has maintained complete cohesion in politics, although the Jats have to a greater extent than others, nor has either of the two dominant elites based its support exclusively on one caste. There have been two major factors which have been conducive to caste fragmentation and fission in political action and political organisation. The first concerns the inherent segmentary character of social organisation. One type of segmentation involves status differentiation within the traditional caste elites. This has existed primarily among Rajputs and has tended to inhibit political collaboration among the large *jagirdars* on the one hand and between large and small *jargirdars* on the other. Another type of segmentation has been traditional divisions within castes which have come about as a result of a number of different kinds of disputes and differences, some of which have been extended to the realm of politics. Third, there is considerable segmentation by geo-graphical area. With the exception of the major peasant castes — Jats, Vishnois, and Sirvis — which have their own district level elites and caste-based structures of political support, no castes have been organised politically on a Jodhpur-wide, or even on a district-wide, basis. In Nagaur, Brahmins, Oswals, and Maheshwaris have been limited in political organisation to particular towns. The Scheduled

Castes have been split on the basis of tehsils and have competed on this basis for the Congress ticket for the one reserved seat in the district. The Jat group in Nagaur also includes tehsil-level leaders, some of whom have resented what they consider to be excessive encroachment in their areas on the part of the 'outside' Jats. These traditional divisions within society have become politicised as a result of conflict between different leaders from within the same caste for public and party office.

With the exception of the Jat faction, caste-based political units have existed only at the municipal and tehsil levels. At the district, divisional and State levels, this field of political units has been divided; alignments have taken the form of two opposing factional coalitions each of which has had continuity in the political process and each of which includes a number of units from different castes that are in conflict with similar units from the opposing coalition. This has involved elections to positions on party committees and to official positions on these committees, in the allocation of party tickets for the elections, and in the elections themselves. At the district level the Jat coalition has included Brahmins, Oswals, Maheshwaris, Vishnois, Kayasths and Balais while the Vyas coalition has been composed of Brahmin, Oswal, Muslim and Balai elements. In the General Elections certain prominent Rajputs have supported Congressmen, although inconsistently, against the Jat coalition. At the divisional level the Nagaur Jat group has attracted the suppport of peasant castes from other districts, primarily Vishnois, Sirvis and other Jat groups, while the Vyas coalition has recruited support from urban castes together with a major contingent of Rajputs who entered the Congress in 1954 and after. Thus at each succeedingly higher level of political organisation subordinate units have been organised into mutually exclusive support groups and the higher the level of political organisation, the wider the caste base of political support. Furthermore, political groups at each of these levels is locally perceived as being associated with one of these larger coalitions and new leaders and groups which became a part of the Congress system have been coopted into these larger factional coalitions. It has been this system of mutually exclusive alliances which has afforded connecting links and channels of access between all levels of political organisation.

Finally, there have been several conditions which have been conducive to the cohesion of political groups and this has been particularly relevant with respect to the Jats. First, this interaction between caste and politics has involved a shared identification with a common set of dominant values. The Jats had a common tradition in a caste movement; they were further able to create a political collectivity out of the solidarity of the caste largely because of an absence of rigid ascriptive status differentiation of the antecedent caste structure — a prerequisite which might be considered necessary, but not necessarily sufficient, to a cohesive social and political movement. The urban castes did not inherit this type of traditional social organisation nor a social movement which involved the entirety of a caste. On the contrary, there were divisions between young advocates of change on the one hand and the traditional *jati panchas* and leaders who advocated the conservation of traditional obligations, rules and statuses on the other. The small units which developed within the urban castes, however, have maintained their cohesion, albeit separately, in large part because of common strivings and traditions which they have shared. These traditions, like those of the Jats, have been concerned with the objective of social change and the creation of a totally new political order rather than with the preservation of traditional social and political forms. The difference is that in the case of Jats the objective of social change has coincided with a sense of preservation and strengthening of traditional solidarity as well, whereas in the case of urban castes it has meant change without any feeling of continuity.

Another important condition has been a sense of competition among a given social group against a commonly perceived antagonist and a continued feeling of threat to its interests and aspirations held out by the antagonist. In the case of the Jats this is represented by their conflict with the Rajputs who were not only the primary adversaries in the traditional order but who have continued to be perceived as such by the Jats in modern politics. This tradition of social conflict has been politicised in elections to the Legislative Assembly and to panchayats.

The Rajputs, however, have not taken modern politics as seriously as the Jats. After the first General Elections only two large *jagirdars* have contested for the Legislative Assembly. Politics appears to lack the reasonable degree of predictability which governed conflict resolution in traditional society. Also, it involves compromises, deals, risks and bribes, the 'degrading' necessity of having to appeal for support, and the constant spectre of defeat — and this at the hands of the Jats. The Rajput *thakurs* still maintain considerable status and prestige in their areas by virtue of their social inheritance. The protection of this status does not involve competition; it is ascribed by an organic tradition. The Jats, on the other hand, can achieve and maintain new social status, not by appeals to ascribed status and position in the traditional social hierarchy, but by competing for control of positions of power in the new political order which carry with them a new kind of social status. Since social mobility is achieved largely in terms of caste rather than on the basis of the individual, value is placed on collective action and this has not been lost on the Jat political elite.

In the case of the urban groups, cohesion has been stimulated, for instance among the Vyas groups in various towns, by the rise of competing elites at the local level who are not quite accepted by the old guard as bona fide party men since it is perceived that their 'commitment' to the Congress and its 'mission' is of recent vintage, and that their loyalty to the party is more out of considerations of political power than of moral duty. These new groups are not a result of any fission in the older groups; they have come up autonomously and have maintained a modicum of cohesion, out of competition with the older groups, in their efforts to achieve political mobility.

Given these characteristics, perhaps the central factor in the political cohesion of caste groups has been the cohesion of elites within particular castes. In the case of the Jats, the elite, while it has experienced differences, has not become split politically and has not engaged in public acrimony or public competition. All other castes have been divided by elites which compete for relatively scarce political positions.

Such cohesion, however, would not have lasted long had it not been for the fulfilment of yet another condition. We may call this the 'political pay off' that results from organised activity, the desired returns on one's political investment. This has been a major factor distinguishing the Jats from other castes and the Jat coalition from other coalitions and groups. These returns are of various kinds: (1) employment and patronage; (2) government loans, permits, and local amenities such as schools, electricity, and irrigation facilities; (3) intercession in administrative decision-making and in the posting of local administrative officials. Command over the allocation of these political goods has not only been important in the maintenance of cohesion within the Jat caste and the Jat coalition, but has been instrumental in the ability of the Jats to attract the support of new political groups.

In sum, then the Jat group in politics, although distinguished from other groups by the wide and cohesive base of support it has maintained, is also distinguished by its intense commitment to and involvement in the political process. Politics for the Jat elite has become a vocation and this new vocation has been pursued through command over important and strategic positions in the Congress Party and the government of Rajasthan. The success story of the Jats in Rajasthan has resulted in large part from such internal cohesion and such an open and positive commitment to the political process, and it is through this sustained experience that they have gained their sense of political efficacy.

NOTES

1. Jodhpur Division included the area of former Jodhpur State, which included five districts, and the Princely States of Jaisalmer and Sirohi, each of which became a district after the final integration of the Rajputana States.
2. There had been several protest movements in Jodhpur prior to the establishment of the Lok Parishad. These included the Marwar Sevak Sangh, Marwar Hitkarni Sabha and the Marwar Navyukt Mandal. The primary concerns of these groups were with peculiarly local grievances and included opposition to the standardisation of weights and measures, the export of foodstuffs and milch animals from the State, demands for the enlargement of representation in the State administration for Marwaris, and reduction in the employment of outsiders who, although primarily Indians, were locally termed *videshi*. Some of the activists in these movements were later leaders in the Lok Parishad. Prominent among these were Jai Narain Vyas, Anand Raj Surana and Bhanwarlal Saraf.
3. There were 26 members of the Lok Parishad on the newly created Rajputana Prantiya Sabha (subsequently the Pradesh Congress Committee) in 1946. Seventeen of these 26 members were from Jodhpur City and 9 were from various rural towns in the State. The caste composition was as follows: 13 Brahmins, 6 Oswals, 4 Maheshwaris, 2 Kayasths and 1 Sunar.
4. One important cleavage in the Lok Parishad in Jodhpur City occurred between a group which clustered around a Maheshwari whose family had served as managers in the large *jagirs* and who engaged in private trading for the royal family. This group tended to support cooperation with the royal house and the traditional ruling elite and engineered a split in the Lok Parishad group in the first popularly elected Municipal Council in Jodhpur City that resulted in a minor split within the Lok Parishad movement as well.
5. The Nagaur fairs, particularly the Tejaji Festival in Parbatsar, were also attended by Jats from the Haryana State. In the case of Ajmer-Marwar, the Jats came into contact with protest movements and activities of which Ajmer was a centre and also with religious revivalist and social reform movements, primarily the Arya Samaj, which also sent *pracharaks* through rural areas singing and preaching social reform.
6. Interview. Mirdhas commitment to the responsibilities of his official position is also testified to by a former member of the Jodhpur State Services. Cf. Kishen Puri, *Memoirs of the Marwar Police* (Jodhpur: Jodhpur Government Press, 1938), pp. 139-43.
7. The leader of the Kisan Sabha in the Barmer area of Jodhpur State, Ram Dan Choudhry, and several of his associates held positions in the Railway Department. There were also two Jat companies in the State forces, recruited primarily from Nagaur, which were disbanded during World

War II after they revolted against the replacement of their Jat commanding officer by an unwanted Rajput.

8. The President of the Kisan Sabha was Baldav Ram Mirdha and the
General Secretary was Nathuram Mirdha, who was subsequently to
become one of the dominant Jat leaders in Rajasthan, having served as
the Agriculture Minister in the first popular Ministry in Jodhpur State and
as a member of the Ministry in Rajasthan from 1952 to the date of writing
this paper, with the exception of one year.

9. Interview.

10. A frequent point made by Jat politicians is that their's has traditionally
been a democratic caste and that even today there are no sanctions taken
against Jats who choose to contest against candidates of the Jat group in
Nagaur.

11. Representation on the Prantiya Sabha also varied from State to State. The
breakdown of elected memebers by State, is as follows: Jaipur 30,
Jodhpur 26, Udaipur 19, Bikaner 13, Alwar 9, Kota 8, Bharatpur 6,
Banswara 3, Sirohi 3, Dungarpur 3, Bundi 3, Karauli 2, Shahpura 1 and
Kishangarh 1. Members were also coopted from Tonk, Jaisalmer and
Pratapgarh as well as from functional groups. Cf. Rajputana Prantiya
Sabha, *Bulletin No. 2*, May 7, 1946.

12. Jai Narain Vyas (Jodhpur), Hiralal Shastri (Jaipur), and Gokul Bhai Bhatt
(Sirohi) had all served, on the All-India AISPC Executive Committee and,
as General Secretaries. Shastri and Vyas were the first two Chief Ministers
of Rajasthan. Bhatt and Vyas served as the first two Presidents of the
Pradesh Congress Committtee.

13. Hiralal Shastri had not received majority support in an initial vote in the
PCC prior to the formation of the first ministry. After negotiations with the
major leaders from the various States, who were assured of being
consulted in the formation of the ministry, he was given a vote of
confidence. These major leaders, however, were allegedly not consulted
and approximately two weeks after the formation of the ministry, the
PCC passed a motion of no confidence against it. Cf. Rajasthan Pradesh
Congress Committee (Executive Committee), *Minutes*, June 23, 1949.

14. *Ibid.* October 6-7, 1949.

15. Interview.

16. These figures have been compiled from Government of India (Election
Commission), *Report of the First General Elections in India*, Vol. II, pp.
650-69.

17. Another major Lok Parishad leader, Dwarkadas Purohit, who had been
a Minister in the first popular ministry in Jodhpur State, was defeated in
the other Jodhpur city constituency by an Oswal candidate supported by
the Maharaja. Purohit received 22.7 per cent of the total valid votes polled
while the winner received 54.1 per cent. It shoud also be noted that in the
bye-election in the constituency left vacant by the Maharaja's death, a
Communist candidate, who was a Pushkarna Brahmin like Vyas, was
successful. This constituency included a large number of Pushkarna
Brahmins.

18. *The Hindustan Times*, February 23, 1952.
19. The Jat group was the only caste-based group in the Congress Legislative Party besides the Rajput group. All 15 members of the Jat group opposed Vyas while the Rajputs, although as a group they had decided to support Vyas, split in the voting — 16 voting for Vyas and 7 voting against him. All other groups were organised on the basis of the former Princely States. The Udaipur and Alwar MLAs with the exception of one MLA in each, opposed Vyas while the representatives from all other areas were divided.
20. Interviews.
21. The major regional factions had decided even before the entry of the Rajputs that Vyas would have to go. This merely hastened the process. Interview.
22. These tehsils generally corresponded in area to constituencies 1, 2 and 3 as used in subsequent tables. Cf. Government of Rajasthan, Election Department, *Delimitation of Constituencies for General Elections, 1957* (mimeographed), p. 24.
23. Efforts were made at the State level from the Spring of 1956 to resolve differences between the Vyas and Sukhadia factional coalitions. In August, largely as a result of the 'trouble-shooting' abilities of Lal Bahadur Shastri, a rapprochement came about and Vyas was declared elected President of the Pradesh Congress Committee without contest. *The Hindustan Times*, August 21, 1956. Vyas stepped down as PCC chief and from 1958 to 1962 the Jat group controlled the PCC presidency.
24. Although the elaborate apparatus and rules for allocating tickets were followed, the final decision as to whom the Pradesh Election Committee would recommend for Jodhpur Division was made at an informal meeting between the leaders of the Jat, Vyas and Rajput groups in the Jodhpur area. There was considerable dispute but a final list was agreed upon. After this list was submitted to the Central Election Committee, the Vyas group again attempted to change the list and a few changes were made, but those in Nagaur District remained the same. Our concern, however, is not primarily with how judgements were ultimately made, but with how factions and castes at the local level participated in the process of ticket allocation.
25. Although 42 different persons submitted applications for Congress Party tickets for Nagaur District, several were disqualified and only 31 applications were accepted as official by the PCC and the district observer. For us, however, all applications are relevant since they bring out the total configuration of factions and patterns of political support in the district Party organisation.
26. The district observer and others involved in the allocation of tickets have experienced difficulty in distinguishing between Congressmen and non-Congressmen and, even when distinctions can be made, the support of non-Congressmen is not always ignored, particularly when they are prominent local persons and/or hold positions in *panchayats* and local voluntary groups such as religious and caste associations.

27. One of the major complaints of the local Jat leaders was that this MLA had established a parallel Congress organisation in this constituency in order to develop a more personal base of political support.

28. The highest number of caste and religious associations which participated in the supportive process were from among Scheduled Castes and the Muslim community although there were also some caste associations from among Mahajan and Brahmin castes. In all cases these groups were urban centred and only supported candidates from urban areas. There were 56 different associations that participated, each with different sets of leadership and leadership roles, and claims to different bases of social support. Second, although several organisations were part of larger State-wide organisations, all participated on the basis of local town or tehsil units. The highest incidence of participation of these primordial groups was precisely in those constituencies in which competition between urban groups was most intense, including the double member constituency in which Scheduled Castes were for the first time competing for a ticket, and in Constituency 5.

29. It should be emphasised that while at this juncture Scheduled Caste representatives were dependent upon existing factions who could give them access, the fact of access has enabled them to establish an autonomous base of support which in turn has demanded more responsiveness and sensitivity on the part of the elites from the dominant castes to maintain support. This has been an important pattern of political mobilisation among the various Scheduled Castes in other parts of Rajasthan as well.

30. These demands were almost exclusively concerned with *jagirdari* abolition and land reforms. Agreement was finally reached in 1953 through the mediation of the late Pandit Govind Ballabh Pant, then Chief Minister of Uttar Pradesh, and was made into law later the same year. Cf. Pandit Govind Ballabh Pant, *Report on Rajasthan Jagirdari Abolition*, Jaipur: Government of Rajasthan Press, 1953; Government of Rajasthan, *The Rajasthan Land Acquisition Act*, 1953, Rajasthan Gazette, Part IV-A, December 12, 1953; and Government of Rajasthan, *The Rajasthan Land Reforms and Resumption of Jagirs Rules*, (Jaipur: Government Central Press, 1954).

31. Rajputs formed the bulk of the candidates chosen and supported by the Maharaja. There were 26 Rajputs, 4 Brahmins, 2 Malis, 1 Oswal, 1 Muslim and 1 Jat. The fourth Brahmin candidate contested in Pali District but was opposed by the *jagirdars* of the area who set up a Rajput candidate who defeated the Maharaja's candidate.

32. The segmentary character of Rajput social and political organisation has been conducive to electoral alliance with certain non-Jat groups in the Congress and has served in some cases as the *entree* of urban groups into the rural areas. On the other hand, in rural politics it has been the very fear of Rajput ascendancy that has contributed to the continued cohesion of the Jat group and this has been complemented to some extent, with respect to intra-Congress politics, by real or anticipated alliances be-

tween Rajputs and other groups in opposition to the Jats.

33. In each of the three General Elections the two top candidates have received over 80 per cent of the total valid votes polled, with the exception of one constituency in 1952, one in 1957 and four in 1962. Also in each constituency in the three General Elections, there have been two main candidates that have been commonly accepted as such. In each of these cases, however, the lesser candidates have contested, or have been made to contest, to draw away votes from the caste of one of the main candidates.

34. Interview.

35. The chief contestants in this constituency were a Rajput who had won from this constituency in 1952 but lost in a bye-election in 1954 and in the General Election in 1957, and the Congress candidate, a Maheshwari, who had successfully contested in this constituency in 1957 with the support of the Jat group. The support of this group, however, was less intense in 1962.

36. Cf. Government of India (Election Commission), *Results of Bye-Elections Held since the First General Elections upto the 31st July, 1955*, pp. 86-89.

37. The Vyas group started to become a political anachronism at both the State and district levels after the heavy defeat which it sustained in a no-confidence motion against the Chief Minister in late 1958. After this, with the exception of Jodhpur Division, the sub-groups within the Vyas coalition started to extend their support to other centres of power as the axis of conflict within the party at the State level started to shift towards a division between the Jat group and the Chief Minister.

38. The Executive Committee has also been controlled by the Jat group. From 1957 to 1960, 3 of the 11 members were Jat while 8 of the 11 were considered members of the Jat group. From 1960 to 1963, 8 of 23 members of the Executive were Jats while 15 of the total were considered to be in the Jat group. Currently 10 of the 23 members are Jat and 15 are considered to be in the Jat group. Members of the Jat group have continually held elected positions on the Executive.

39. Cf. Ralph H. Retzlaff, 'Panchayati Raj in Rajasthan: A Case Study', *The Indian Journal of Public Administration*, Vol. VI, No. 2, (April-June, 1960), pp. 141-58 and Iqbal Narain, 'Democratic Decentralization and Rural Leadership in India: The Rajasthan Experiment', *Asian Survey*, Vol. IV, No. 8 (August, 1964), pp. 1013-22.

CHAPTER SEVEN

Caste and Political Recruitment in Bihar

RAMASHRAY ROY

I

The connection between social stratification and the political system is very close.[1] The system of social stratification provides a broad frame of reference for the functioning of the political system both in terms of selection of ends and adoption of means. Moreover, the function of the political system, that is 'the authoritative allocation of values', to borrow David Easton's phrase, could not be deemed to be authoritative unless it is recognised as such by the prevailing value system manifested in social stratification.

This connection, however, is not a one-way traffic. If the functioning of the political system is influenced by the system of social stratification, the system of social stratification itself is influenced by the political system. As David E. Apter observes, "the action of government affects stratification in some significant manner."[2] It is true that in tribal as well as other societies under colonial rule, a great deal of change has occurred in social stratification under the impact of so-called non-political — commercial, colonial and technological — forces. But nationalist movements and the actions of government, particularly in the field of education and social welfare, also create alternative mobility channels, the effect of which is to modify both the existing stratification systems and the valuations of these patterns.

The crucial connecting link, however, between social stratification and the political system is political party, association or movement. A political party consists of "those whose entrepreneurial activities are essentially devoted to the recruitment of followers who attempt to modify the system either by participation in government or by directing their action against it."[3] Moreover, by prescribing rules governing the recruitment of members, selection of leaders, and the intra-party relationships — which emphasise the impersonal, universal, functionally specific and achievement oriented criteria of organisation and distribution of power, the party makes available ᵗᵒ the people norms of behaviour which are usually opposed to those inherent in the traditional social stratification system. This tends, in the long run, to modify the stratification system. The party itself is, in turn, influenced by the stratification system. To quote Apter again:

> The actions of political groups depend ultimately upon the social stratification system in so far as there is a search for basic issues and grievances and in so far as recruitment to political groups is deeply affected by social strata. Depending upon who is recruited, considerable limitations are normally imposed upon political parties...[4]

We explore, in this paper, the relationship between caste and political recruitment in the case of the Bihar Pradesh Congress Party. We first discuss the nature of stratification in Bihar and its implications for the political system. We then examine some of the influences that have created dissatisfaction against the traditional system of social stratification. Thirdly, we analyse the impact of social stratification on recruitment as well as other political processes within the Congress party. Fourthly, we discuss some of the the trends that indicate a shift in the stratification system. Finally, we examine the ways in which political processes themselves have modified the stratification system.

II

Bihar is one of those States where the upper castes,[5] although numerically not large (Table 1), have traditionally enjoyed ritual superiority and social prestige.

The upper castes form only 13.22 per cent of the population of Bihar, but their dominance in Bihar life is much greater than their number would suggest. The numerical weakness of the upper castes is more than compensated by their ritual status, social prestige and economic power. In ritual matters the Brahmins enjoy the first position followed by the Bhumihar Brahmins and the Rajputs. The Kayasthas, although low on scale of the ritual status, have 'rivalled the

Brahmins, in everything connected with the pen'.[6] Likewise the Brahmins, including the Bhumihars, and the Rajputs own a major part of land and thereby dominate the economic field. This is due mainly to historical facts. As Misra observes:

... Before the coming of the British, the influence which dominated village community was that of a particular kind, especially of Brahmins and Rajputs, who owned most villages either as village zamindars in the upper provinces and parts of Bihar or as taluqdars in Bengal, as mirasdars in the south or inamdars in the west. The other occupational groups worked in subservience to the dominant landed interest of a village.[7]

Table 1 : *Percentage Distribution of Castes, by Districts, Bihar, 1961**

Districts	Upper Castes[1]	Lower Castes[2]	Scheduled Castes	Scheduled Tribes	Mus-lims
Saran	22.65	55.02	10.33	—	12.00
Champaran	11.79	57.75	14.56	0.10	15.80
Muzaffarpur	16.84	59.57	14.89	—	8.70
Darbhanga	15.80	56.33	14.67	—	13.20
Saharsa	10.00	66.08	17.18	0.44	6.30
Purnea	5.27	42.38	12.24	3.91	36.20
Shahabad	26.59	49.81	16.01	0.69	6.90
Patna	15.19	59.47	16.09	0.05	9.20
Gaya	16.64	49.10	24.54	0.02	9.70
Monghyr	21.28	53.23	15.81	1.38	8.30
Bhagalpur	10.66	62.59	11.58	3.77	11.40
Santhal Parganas	4.18	40.62	7.56	38.24	9.40
Palamau	9.24	36.09	25.93	19.24	9.50
Hazaribagh	7.03	58.12	12.55	11.30	11.00
Ranchi	2.62	25.92	4.55	61.61	5.30
Dhanbad	20.27	41.09	17.86	11.08	9.70
Singhbhum	2.93	43.59	2.97	47.31	3.20
All Bihar	13.22	52.16	14.07	9.05	11.50

* Source : Figures for Upper Castes projected from 1931 Census Caste figures; figures for Scheduled Castes and Tribes taken from *Census of India 1961*, Vol. VI, Bihar, Part II-A, p. 353 and figures for Muslims, *Census of India, 1951*, Vol. IV, Bihar.

1. 'Upper Castes' include Brahmins, Bhumihar Brahmins, Rajputs and Kayasthas.

2. 'Lower Castes' include all the castes intermediary between the Upper and the Scheduled Castes.

The picture has changed little if we accept the findings of the All-India Agricultural Labour Enquiry, which in 1951 conducted sample surveys over the entire country to discover the caste basis of agricultural occupations. The following table summarises its findings:

Table 2 : *Caste and Agricultural Occupations, Bihar, 1951**

	Brahmin	Rajput	Vaisbya	Backward Classes	Scheduled Castes and Tribes	Tribals and Aboriginals	Others
No. of families	491	429	372	3,639	2,210	207	2,195
% of total No. of families	5.1	4.5	3.9	38.1	23.2	2.2	23.0
Land-owners	81[8] (71.84)	8.2 (6.32)	1.1 (0.72)	1.1 (7.22)	3.5 (13.90)	—	—
Tenants	—	78.6 (14.07)	31.7 (4.92)	44.0 (66.82)	15.4 (14.19)	—	—
Agricultural workers	—	6.3 (0.95)	18.0 (2.35)	35.2 (44.99)	66.6 (51.71)	—	—
Non-Agricultural workers	19.0 (6.96)	6.9 (2.25)	49.2 (13.68)	19.5 (53.10)	14.5 (24.01)	—	—
Total	100.0	100.0	100.0	99.8	100.0	—	—

*Source: All India Agricultural Labour Enquiry, *Rural Manpower and Occupational Structure*, pp. 55-57. (The figures in parenthesis indicate the dispersion of each occupational category over various castes.)

It is evident from the table that 78.16 per cent of land-owners are concentrated in two upper castes. The lower down in the caste hierarchy, the greater the extent to which lower castes depend for their living on farm labour. Only one upper caste, the Rajputs, constitute 0.95 per cent of the total agricultural labour force, as compared to the Backward Classes (44.99 per cent) and the Scheduled Castes and Tribes (51.71 per cent). In other words, the economic position of a particular caste is highly correlated with its ritual status in the caste hierarchy. Moreover, the Backward Classes and Scheduled Castes do not own land to any significant extent, which increases their dependence for means of livelihood on the land-owning Brahmins and Rajputs.

The economic inequality reflected in land-ownership has its repercussions in other fields as well. When new opportunities in various walks of life were created as a result of contact with the outside world, it was usually the upper castes which took advantage of these opportunities. Thus, the existing inequalities were cumulated. Take, for example, the utilisation of newly-created opportunities by different castes. The 1931 census for Bihar and Orissa[9] reveals that of the four upper castes, the Kayasthas have been the most literate caste (372 literates per 1,000), followed by the Brahmins (195 literates per 1,000), the Bhumihars (136 literates per 1,000) and the Rajputs (120 literates per 1,000). Among the lower castes, on the other hand, for the Kurmis and Goalas there were only 40 to 50 literate persons per thousand and the Telis had only 52 literate persons per thousand.

It is evident that the Kayasthas constituted the most literate caste.[10] The 1931 census further shows they excel all other communities in respect of English education. The Kayasthas are followed by Brahmins, Bhumihar Brahmins and the Rajputs. The gap between the upper castes and the lower castes again is very wide. In the case of

Table 3 : *Caste and Education in Bihar: Admissions to B.A. Classes in Patna College, 1936-1963* *

Castes	1936 N=30	1943 N=34	1948 N=41	1953 N=47	1958 N=64	1963 N=67
Upper Castes						
Brahmins	10.00	20.59	26.83	29.79	23.43	11.94
Bhumihar Brahmins	20.00	5.88	17.07	25.53	14.06	25.37
Rajputs	10.00	5.88	9.75	8.51	12.50	7.46
Kayasthas	30.00	35.29	19.51	23.40	15.62	17.91
Sub-total :	70.00	67.64	73.16	87.23	65.61	62.68
Other Castes	6.66	11.76	7.31	6.38	26.56	25.38
Muslims	23.33	20.59	19.51	6.38	7.82	11.94
Total	99.99	99.99	99.98	99.99	99.99	100.00

* Source: Office of the Patna College, Patna. The table is based on a twenty per cent random sample.

higher education, this imbalance is even more noticeable. Modern education forms the gateway to a vast area of new opportunities for status mobility. Recruitment to the fields of politics, public services, business and professions is in some degree dependent on access to and acquisition of higher education. Imbalance in this respect reinforces the relative capacity of various social sectors to take advantage of the available opportunities, particularly since taking advantage of higher education depends on previous resources; one could conveniently invest in highly costly education. Such imbalance is clearly manifest in the field of higher education (Table 3).

A large majority of students come from the four upper castes: 70.00 per cent in 1936, 67.74 per cent in 1943, 73.16 per cent in 1948, 87.23 per cent in 1953, 65.61 per cent in 1958 and 62.68 per cent in 1963. Even among the upper castes, the prominence of the Kayasthas in education is remarkable. Considering the fact that the Kayasthas form less than 2.00 per cent of the population of Bihar, the percentage of Kayastha students — 30.00 per cent in 1936, 35.29 per cent in 1943, 19.51 per cent in 1948, 23.40 per cent in 1953, 15.62 per cent in 1958 and 17.91 per cent in 1963 — indicates that the Kayasthas as a caste utilise the educational facilities much more than others. But the table also shows that the number of Kayastha students has been decreasing over the years, and this is true of the upper castes, in general.

This decline, although not very sharp, in the number of upper caste students is contrasted with the slow but steady rise in the number of students coming from other castes. This gradual rise in the number of students from the 'dispossessed' sections of Bihar society reflects a change taking place in the stratification system, and presumably points to the growing appreciation among underprivileged groups of education as an instrument of status aspirations. Upper castes still dominate the field of education, however, and to this extent maintain the process of cumulative inequality.

Our discussion so far has emphasised the nature of social stratification in Bihar and has indicated the inequalities it has induced. Needless to say, such a stratification system conceals a very great potential for creating tensions potentially disruptive of the equilibrium of the society. "The existence of a social system which perpetuates great inequality in status, worldly goods and opportunities depends among other things not only on the acquiescence by the non-privileged groups but also on the feelings in the higher groups that they have a right to rule."[11] This was provided by the Hindu religious and philosophical system which, through the doctrines of *Karma* and *Dharma* justified the existence of the upper castes and legitimised their superior position. It also, at the same time, made it possible for the lower castes to accept their position in the caste society inasmuch as the doctrine of *Karma* suggested that the status of an individual in this birth is nothing more than the result of his own deeds in his previous birth(s). Similarly, the doctrine of *Dharma* signified that one's own duties were preferable. Moreover, the whole system of Indian philosophy tended to encourage conformism to the existing pattern of social order in so far as the universal laws in operation could not be changed except by adhering to one's own assigned *Karma* and *Dharma* and carrying them out in the best possible manner. Thus the philosophical system provided legitimacy to the structure of society based on caste.

Another point worth considering in this respect is the fact that the magnitude of dissatisfaction with and alienation from the existing system depends on the one hand on the alternatives available and on the other on the capacity of the system itself to absorb or keep within manageable limits the conflicts that arise in the system. Regarding the first, there is no doubt that the caste society had at times to cope with internal influences that were released through external invasion and alien rule. Indeed, these influences posed such serious threats to the whole fabric of Indian society that, broadly speaking, the society withdrew into a defensive shell and was able to neutralise the disruptive tendencies. It is also true that some parts of the society took advantage of the opportunities that were presented by the 'alien' system, but the new groups that emerged were more or less assimilated into the system.[12]

This resilience of the caste system was due to the fact that the caste system was elastic enough to allow each new group, to quote Karve:

> to become a part of the caste society in whichever way it chose or in whichever way historically accommodation became possible. By its very nature the caste society presented a loose structure which could take on new units and in so doing rearrange old units.[13]

This looseness of structure made it possible for the caste society to survive many upheavals in history; some of its parts were lost to it and, in course of time, some others were joined to it. Thus the caste society demonstrated great capability in resolving tension. But one significant consequence that followed from this was that although in the spiritual realm the parts of the caste society could feel a sense of oneness, they never developed a sense of identity in the political realm.

III

So far we have sketched the social structure in Bihar as if the system were static and in perfect equilibrium. We also assumed that the external influences have had little or no impact on the caste society. No society, however, can remain in absolute equilibrium nor can it completely neutralise external influences for long. Bihar society has continuously been disturbed by manifold forces making for change. These forces were released primarily under the impact of contact with the West, particularly the British rule. These forces both initiated changes in many aspects of traditional society, on the one hand, and intensified certain internal forces within the society itself that acted as catalytic agents for change, on the other.

This is not the place to analyse in detail the nature of changes induced by internal and external forces, but it may be indicated here that the benefits created during the British regime offered alternative sets of opportunities for status mobility and induced different social sectors to take advantage of them. The provision of social benefits by the colonial rulers worked in the direction of increasing the flow of information, expanding internal markets, introducing modern technology, expanding the transportation networks, increasing educational facilities and encouraging industrialisation and urbanisation. In other words new channels of social mobility were created.

Perhaps as important was the limited introduction of democratic institutions, and gradual extension of the franchise, although the entire adult population was not included until the Constitution of 1950. The process of democratisation was slow, but it had a marked influence on society. Perhaps the most important effect was the subtle introduction of a different set of culturally-relevant value orientations. The universalistic, achievement oriented and functionally specific criteria typical of Western democracies, coupled with gradually expanding opportunities for status mobility, helped to break the rigidity of the established caste and status structure. One effect of these tendencies was to make the non-privileged castes conscious of their low status and dissatisfied with the existing social order. From this consciousness sprang an urge to improve their status in the social hierarchy by assuming names other than those by which they were commonly known and getting such claims accepted by the government as well as society at large. Caste associations sprang up to make these claims good as well as to give an organisational sustenance to these claims. In most cases, adoption of new names was coupled with adoption of new behaviour patterns usually practised by the upper castes.[14]

One thing worth noting in this connection is the tapping of traditional sources to justify the claim for social mobility. It indicates the preoccupation of the lower castes with traditionally legitimate means of achieving social recognition; it also, at the same time, indicates their unawareness of the potentialities of modern opportunities in improving their status. Their attempt to achieve higher social status utilising traditional symbols was, however, to be channelled through modern means, that is, through organised action bringing together hitherto territorially separated similar caste groups under the auspices of an association which functioned as does any modern organisation. Previous successful but isolated attempts by individuals to acquire higher status through wealth or achievement were not to be emphasised, accent was rather on concerted action for acquiring a new status for the whole group.

Here two distinct varieties of identity were emphasised. In some cases, for example in the case of Rajputs, the traditional concept of *Varna*, so far in abeyance, came to be of crucial importance. In others, particularly in the case of those castes which were traditionally already at the bottom of the *Varna* hierarchy, a new identity transcending sub-caste barriers and emphasising ocupational as well as social affinities was sought to be forged. Such an identity although not coincidental with the *Varna* was instrumental in levelling, or, at least, neutralising traditional barriers erected either between various sub-castes of a single caste or between similar status caste groups. One reason why the *Varna* or a fraction of it was projected as the basis of identity is that, on the one hand, it afforded a wider scope for mobilisation of support for getting social and later political demands fulfilled and, on the other, it served to bring under one fold castes and sub-castes of similar status while at the same time differentiating them from other caste groups. The new identity was emphasised through the activities of the various caste associations. Thus aspirations for achieving higher social status were instrumental for the lower castes to discover identical interest; these interests led them to organise for the realisation of an identity broader than a caste or a sub-caste.

Although the caste associations functioned in the social realm for a cause which was primarily social, they nevertheless prepared the background for transforming social identity into political identity. The fact that aspirations of different caste groups for acquiring a higher social status were resented as well as resisted made newly discovered larger identities firmer and thus hardened the feelings of caste antagonism. Had other avenues of social advancement and status mobility been available to the aspirant caste groups, it is doubtful whether politics would have been so much influenced by caste as it is. Due to the extremely underdeveloped nature of social mobility, politics, when it assumed some importance in allocating power and prestige, increasingly came to be pressed into service both by individuals and social groups to function as a vehicle of their social as well as political aspirations. To lend strength to such aspirations, the broad identity forged on the social plane became available at the political plane and thus the *Varna* (or a fraction of it) referrent of caste identity was lent with political implications. The *Varna* (or a fraction of it) became the basis of a political calculus; the concept which was relevant only for a peculiar rationale of a peculiar social order assumed new importance in the new realm of politics.[15]

Thus under the impact of the colonial rule, which opened up new vistas of upward social mobility and the working of democratic institutions, albeit limited, the legitimacy of traditional system of social stratification came to be challenged. The dissatisfaction against the traditional social order led the underprivileged caste groups to seek the redress of their grievances through organised action. If on the social plane, caste associations succeeded in demolishing, to a great extent, the barriers that divided similar status caste or sub-caste groups, it projected, on the political plane, a new identity, a new consciousness and a new orientation towards organised political action. But, as we have already seen, the utilisation of the opportunities created under the colonial regime was unequal; the privileged caste groups, because of their control over social and economic resources, took unproportionate advantage of the created opportunities and left far behind the underprivileged social sectors.

No doubt, the activities of the caste associations and the impact of modern politics were to activise the underprivileged caste groups, bring to them the realisation of the deprivations they suffered, and spur them on to organised action to mitigate these deprivations. But their meagre hold on social and economic resources hindered them from fully utilising the created channels of upward social mobility. For instance, they lagged far behind the upper caste groups in taking optimum advantage of expanding educational facilities and therefore were unable to develop appropriate skills and resources for getting most out of the changed situation. This had also a decided impact on their entry into politics, the skills that they brought with them, and the resources they could muster. These various underprivileged caste groups entered, as we shall see shortly, into politics at different periods and held leadership positions much later than the privileged caste groups.

IV

The birth of politics in Bihar, in the proper sense of the term, is connected with a cause which, although it was not popular, was sponsored by the intellectuals. This was the issue of separation of Bihar from Bengal. Bihar, till 1911, formed a part of the greater province of Bengal. The government services as well as the professions of law and teaching were dominated by Bengalees.[16] This dominance of Bengalees over the public life of Bihar was a great obstacle for the educationally advanced castes, particularly the Kayasthas. To find the doors of services closed after getting an expensive western education is a painful experience; it is still more painful to compete with those who repay hospitality by creating conditions of imperfect competition in the employment market for their hosts. The Bengalees who dominated the services were often alleged to have resorted to nepotism in taking on their own kin or other fellow Bengalees when vacancies in different sectors of employment happened to occur. This was particularly intolerable to the Kayasthas who depended for their livelihood and advancement upon professional and public services. It is not surprising, therefore, that the separation of Bihar from Bengal movement was spear-headed by Sachchidanand Sinha, a Kayastha.

The separation of Bihar from Bengal in 1911 and the consequent expansion in services were beneficial to the educated classes, the Kayasthas and the Muslims. To make these benefits even more secure the so-called Domicile Rules "were framed at the instance of the Bihar leaders to prevent as far as possible recruitment to the public services of the new province of men from the territorial jurisdiction of Bengal."[17] This security may well have served the interests of the educated Kayasthas, but gradually as education spread, other castes also began making claims for share in the 'divisible benefits'. But recruitment to public offices being a scarce commodity, it irrevocably generated rivalry among the claimants. Once competition for positions has hardened feelings and created animosities, the feelings of antagonism come by easily. It also becomes easier to transfer antagonism from one sphere to another. Thus when the Congress became active in Bihar and as it slowly acquired power first at the municipal and district levels and later on at the state level and was therefore in a position to distribute power and position, rivalry in the sphere of divisible benefits was easily transferred to the political sphere.

Thus, the dominance of the Kayasthas in public services and public affairs was soon challenged by other caste groups who emerged to demand a share in the newly created opportunities. In Bihar, as Walter Hauser aptly observes:

> ... this meant Bhumihars, Rajputs and Brahmins and successive opportunities for their attractions to politics were provided by the non-co-operation movement of 1920 and the civil disobedience movements of 1930 and 1932. As landholders of moderate means, these groups were financially capable of providing an education to a son, and when the time came, of supporting a family member in a political career.[18]

If the consecutive waves of civil disobedience and non-cooperation movements brought into political activity an undifferentiated mass of new political actors, the prospect of office, jobs, favours, contracts and distribution of rewards categorised this mass into different classes — mainly according to the caste one belonged to. It did more. The rising aspirations of the more numerous and economically entrenched castes, particularly the Bhumihars, brought home to the Kayasthas, the prospect of dislodgement from power. In order to safeguard their privileged position, if not their survival in politics, the Kayasthas had necessarily to hitch their political wagon to one or another of the more numerous castes. Alliance led to counter-alliance, and the competing caste groups, by coopting men from politically inarticulate castes to positions of second rank leadership, who in due course emerged as leaders in their own right, brought more and more castes into the vortex of politics.

To sum up, we encounter in Bihar the phenomenon of a gradually enlarging circle of political competition. In the initial stages the political scene was dominated by one or two castes. As political awareness grew and hitherto politically immobile caste groups realised the importance of politics as an instrument of satisfying mobility aspirations, the domination of upper caste groups came to be challenged. This, in turn, led to defensive alliances and counter-alliances bringing more and more castes into the political realm. In short, political competition first made it possible for the political realm to mobilise individuals in the upper castes, and then gradually to activate and assimilate on a broader basis the submerged caste groups. This process was also reflected in recruitment to the Congress party.

V

The patterns of recruitment in the Congress party reflect all basic social divisions in Bihar society. They also reflect what we have already referred to as 'cumulative inequality', namely, the disproportionate access to power positions by members of higher status castes. But there is also noticeable another 'countervailing' trend. This is the tendency of increasing representation of the lower-status caste groups in the party, which may be referred to as a trend towards 'the dispersal of inequality'. In other words, the virtual monopoly of the upper castes over political resources has ended, and the operation of democratic politics has endowed the underprivileged lower castes with two attributes of political influence, number and organisation. The recruitment patterns in the Congress Party, therefore, can be taken to indicate a shift in the distribution of power, notwithstanding the fact that the political scene in Bihar is still dominated by the upper castes.

To illustrate these propositions we will examine the recruitment patterns in the Congress Party by analysing the composition of the Bihar Pradesh Congress Executive Committee (B.P.C.E.C.), and the active members of the Congress Party in a few selected districts of Bihar (for criteria of selection see footnote 21). The first category symbolises the highly competitive area of Congress Party work, inasmuch as membership in the Executive Committee requires, by and large, a long record of public service and a viable support base in order to compete successfully at this level. Active membership, on the other hand, denotes the first step towards a climb on the steep leadership ladder and therefore constitutes a crucial landmark for those Congressmen who aspire to leadership positions. An analysis of the composition of these two categories should yield fruitful results and fairly indicate the trends that are in operation.

The Executive Committee of the Bihar Congress is the most crucial organ at the State level. It is elected by and responsible to the Pradesh Congress Committee. It is responsible for giving effect to the decisions made by the PCC and looking after the day-to-day business of the Congress in the State. But owing to the fact that the general body of the PCC is too large and meets infrequently,[19] the Executive Committee enjoys vastly more power and prestige than its constitutional parent. Historically speaking, the Executive Committee acted as the effective agent of the State Congress during the struggle for national freedom, and was composed, during this period, of the most prominent of the first rank leaders in Bihar. Even after independence the Executive

Table 4: Caste Composition of the Bihar Pradesh Congress Executive Committee, 1934-1962 (in per cent)
1934-1946

Castes	1934	1935	1936	1937	1938	1939	1940	1942	1946
Upper Castes									
Brahmin	—	—	—	—	7.15	—	13.34	14.28	6.66
Bhumihar Brahmin	15.38	35.72	23.07	23.53	7.15	13.34	13.34	21.43	20.00
Rajput	7.70	14.28	23.08	17.63	21.42	26.67	26.67	28.58	26.68
Kayastha	53.84	28.57	29.41	23.53	35.70	26.67	6.66	7.15	20.00
Sub-total	76.92	78.57	75.56	64.69	64.27	66.68	60.01	71.44	73.34
Others									
Lower Castes	—	—	7.70	5.88	—	—	—	—	—
Scheduled Castes	—	—	—	—	—	6.66	6.66	7.15	—
Scheduled Tribes	—	—	—	—	6.66	6.66	—	—	—
Sub-total	—	—	7.70	5.88	6.66	6.66	6.66	7.15	—
Muslims	23.08	14.28	15.38	11.77	14.28	20.00	26.67	21.41	20.00
Not known and others	—	7.15	7.70	11.76	14.30	6.66	6.66	—	6.66
Total	100.00	100.00	100.00	100.00	100.00	100.00	100.00	100.00	100.00
Cases	13	14	13	17	14	15	15	14	15

Table 4 : Caste Composition of the Bihar Pradesh Congress Executive Committee, 1934-1962 (in per cent)

1947-1960   Contd.

Castes	1947	1948	1950	1952	1954	1955	1958	1960
Upper Castes								
Brahmin	7.15	9.52	12.50	21.05	10.53	15.00	14.28	14.29
Bhumihar Brahmin	14.28	14.29	12.50	21.05	21.05	20.00	23.81	28.56
Rajput	35.71	23.82	37.50	26.33	21.05	20.00	19.15	14.29
Kayastha	21.43	14.29	12.50	5.26	5.26	5.00	9.53	4.76
Sub-total	78.59	61.92	75.00	73.69	57.89	60.00	66.67	61.90
Others								
Lower Castes	—	19.04	12.50	10.53	21.05	20.00	14.28	14.29
Scheduled Castes	—	4.76	6.25	5.26	5.26	5.00	4.76	4.76
Scheduled Tribes	7.15	4.76	—	5.26	5.26	—	—	—
Sub-total	7.15	28.56	18.75	21.05	31.57	25.00	19.04	19.05
Muslims	14.28	9.52	6.25	5.26	5.26	5.00	9.53	14.29
Not known and others	—	—	—	—	—	10.00	4.76	4.76
Total	100.00	100.00	100.00	100.00	100.00	100.00	100.00	100.00
Cases	14	21	16	19	19	19	21	21

Committee continued to be composed of first rank leaders of the Bihar Congress, although its importance as a decision-making body came to be reduced vis-a-vis the ministerial wing of the party. Table IV gives the caste composition of the Executive Committee.

Some very interesting facts emerge from Table 4. In the first place, the Kayasthas, who in 1934 occupied about 54 per cent of the seats in the Executive Committee, lost their dominance to other castes. In 1960 they occupied only about 5 per cent of seats. The early political dominance and later dwindling political importance of the Kayasthas tell a very significant political history of Bihar, and particularly of the Bihar Congress. The Kayasthas constituted less than two per cent of the total population of the State and yet they were in the forefront of the political scene of the State. As we have seen, they were the first to take to higher education and to be incorporated into the political scene. But as the circle of political involvement widened and other social groups like the Brahmins and the Rajputs were attracted to the struggle for freedom movement, the Kayasthas had increasingly to be concerned with safeguarding their dominant position. The social group that emerged to challenge the supremacy of the Kayasthas was the Bhumihars. The political rivalry which began in the 1920s continued well beyond independence in which the Kayasthas had to align themselves with the Rajputs. But they could not prevent the emerging social groups from acquiring leadership positions inasmuch as these social groups outnumbered the Kayasthas. It was therefore natural that the proportion of the Kayasthas in the Congress leadership should decline over the years.

In the second place, we find the Brahmins acquiring leadership positions for the first time in 1938. From then on they have been strengthening their position. From 7.15 per cent in 1938 they increased their proportion to 14.29 per cent in 1960. In other words, the Brahmins were late in arriving at leadership positions, but once they emerged as a political force they have steadily enhanced their position. However, considering the fact that they constitute about 5 per cent of the total population of Bihar, their share in leadership positions is still less than that of the Bhumihars.

Third, the waning political importance of the Muslims is also noticeable. If we compare their position before and after independence, it readily becomes apparent that their importance greatly diminished after independence. The reason for this is not far to seek. The growing feeling of Muslim separatism in pre-independence days made it necessary for the Congress leaders to include Muslims in leadership rank in order to counteract the influence of the Muslim League. This necessity was no longer felt after independence.

Finally, and most importantly, the Congress in Bihar still remains a party dominated by the upper castes. The lower castes, including the Scheduled Castes and the Tribes, for example, had very meagre representation before 1947. Only after 1947 are they regularly represented in the Executive Committee. Moreover, they steadily increased their representation after 1947, but their numerical preponderance in the population still is not reflected in the Congress leadership.

The above analysis leads us to conclude that the upper castes do not form a single cohesive and coherent group. On the contrary, each unit of the upper castes is a serious contender for political power. In other words, the political rivalry among the upper castes is the main driving force behind politics in Bihar. It is among the upper castes that a major portion of political rewards, measured in terms of political leadership, is distributed.

This political rivalry among the upper castes in Bihar has, however, a significant impact on the way different social groups have been allowed entry into the political system and assimilated. The fact that the upper castes contended among themselves for political power required that each contending caste group go beyond its own *Varna* and seek support from other caste groups. This necessarily widened the scope of political involvement and the caste groups which stood on the periphery of the political universe were inducted into it. With growing intensity of factional feuds in the Congress party, almost all the social groups were slowly drawn into the political arena. This is evident from the fact that different caste groups entered into leadership rank of the Congress party in Bihar at different time periods. At the time of their entry into politics, most of these caste groups functioned as appendages of the main contenders in the upper castes; leaders from the upper castes coopted men from the lower castes to leadership positions. The latter were for a time satisfied with their role as political apprentices of the former but slowly they succeeded in building their own autonomous support structure and emerged as leaders in their own right. Thus a slow process of induction into politics of the underprivileged caste groups has been in operation in Bihar. This process has, however, led to the emergence of the underprivileged caste groups as crucial political forces to be reckoned with in any political calculation.

It is true that the underprivileged caste groups have, more or less, succeeded in breaking through the social barriers and effecting an entry into the political realm, thus overcoming many difficulties in their path of upward social mobility, but this is attributable, by and large, to the levelling effect of democratic politics and the compulsions that such a politics creates in its wake. Considering the numerical strength that the underprivileged castes command, their representation in the Executive Committee cannot be said to be more than meagre. This indicates that these caste groups have not yet acquired necessary political skill to put their resources to better advantage. In other words, there exists a wide gap between skill and resources in the case of the underprivileged caste groups.

This discrepancy between their potentiality and accomplishment becomes all the more sharp when we analyse the composition of active Congress members (Table 5).[20] Some very interesting facts emerge from this table. First, the overall picture that emerges from this table indicates the dominance of upper castes in the Congress Party in all the four districts. The percentage of Congress members coming from the upper castes in Saharsa, for example, is 55.55 in 1956 and 46.15 in 1961, while they form only 10 per cent of the district population. This is true in the case of other districts also. In Shahabad the upper castes form only 26.53 per cent of the district population but 57.07 per cent of the Congress membership. This indicates that the traditional hold of the upper castes in these districts has not weakened considerably.

Second, although the dominance of the upper castes in the Congress Party is beyond doubt, it should be emphasised here that if we take all the caste groups separately, the lower castes seem to be better represented than other underprivileged caste groups. It indicates the growing political importance of the lower castes which takes on added significance in view of the fact that political rivalry among the upper castes lends strength to the political emergence of the lower castes.

Third, Scheduled Castes and Muslims form a very small part of the Congress membership in these districts. The Scheduled Castes, whom Gandhi rechristened as Harijans (children of God) have been the most depressed castes in Indian society and their lowliest social status is reflected also in their economic conditions and educational achievements. In order to insure their advancement the government has provided for them special privileges in the form of reservation of seats in educational institutions, public services and legislative bodies. Nevertheless, it seems that their backwardness hinders them from fully utilising these opportunities and from this perhaps stems their inability to acquire key positions in the Congress party.

The case of the Muslims is entirely different. The partition of India in 1947 into India and Pakistan must be said to have left a deep scar

Table 5 : *Caste Composition of Population (Projected for 1961) and Active Congress Members in the Districts of Sabarsa, Shababad, Saran and Darbbanga*

Castes*	Sabarsa			Shababad		Saran		Darbbanga	
	Population	Active Members 1956 N = 585	Active Members 1961 N = 78	Population	Active Members 1961 N = 191	Population	Active Members 1961 N = 152	Population	Active Members 1961 N = 244
Upper Castes									
Brahmin	4.80	23.42	15.38	10.00	22.51	7.11	12.50	10.15	27.86
Bhumihar Brahmin	1.00	1.20	2.56	3.07	7.33	3.84	14.47	1.55	6.56
Rajput	3.75	29.73	21.80	11.69	19.37	10.11	19.73	2.82	20.90
Kayastha	0.45	1.20	6.41	1.83	7.86	1.59	2.63	1.28	4.09
Total	10.00	55.55	46.15	26.59	57.07	22.65	49.33	15.80	59.41
Lower Castes	66.08	29.06	23.07	49.87	17.27	55.02	21.71	56.33	14.24
Scheduled Castes	17.18	2.40	17.94	16.01	7.33	10.33	5.27	14.67	13.30
Muslims	6.30	3.99	2.56	6.90	2.62	12.00	6.59	13.20	8.19

* other minor castes and cases not known have been left out

on the minds of those Muslims who remained behind in India. The carving out of Pakistan was at once a victory and defeat for the Muslims. It was a concession to the demand for a separate nation for the Muslims but its fruits could be enjoyed only by those who became the citizens of the new State. Those who were left behind had to live down the stigma of being disloyal to the country. This created a psychological gap between the Muslims and other communities in India and gave birth to a feeling of insecurity in the minds of the Muslims which is reflected in their political posture. They are perhaps afraid of playing a vigorous political role for fear that their motivations might be misunderstood. It is, therefore, very likely that they have drawn themselves into a defensive shell and, as a result, are prone to be politically apathetical.

Our analysis of the composition of the B.P.C.E.C. and active Congress members in four districts of Bihar have shown that the upper castes wield a considerable influence on Bihar politics in spite of their weak numerical strength. But this dominance is by no means absolute; there are trends which indicate that gradually the dominance of the upper castes is declining. The lower castes have succeeded, over a long period of time, to enter the fields of political significance which for long remained an exclusive precinct of the upper castes. They have, moreover, increased their representation, for example, in the Bihar Congress Executive Committee, and to the extent that they succeed in developing appropriate political skills and acquiring secular symbols of status, such as higher education, their growing influence on politics in the state will, if a prediction may be hazarded, be an established fact in not too distant a future.

VI

There are some indications that the underprivileged caste groups do manifest tendencies which point to the fact that there exists among them a consciousness of inequality in the social system and a belief in the feasibility of eradicating the existent differences. It is interesting to find that the Congressmen from lower castes are educationally more advanced than those of the upper castes (Table 6). As will appear from the table, except for Darbhanga, lower castes are more educated than any of the upper castes. Scheduled Castes, on the contrary, have remained educationally backward even though they enjoy special privileges in the field of education. Even the Kayasthas, who were the first to take to Western education and use it as a stepping-stone for upward social mobility, give a poor account in education when

Table 6: *Caste and Education of Active Members in 4 Districts of Bihar, 1961 (in per cent)*

District	Castes*	Literate	Middle	High School	Inter-mediate	Graduate	Post-Graduate	Law	Tradi-tional	Total
1	2	3	4	5	6	7	8	9	10	11
Saharsa	Brahmin	—	3.85	6.41	3.84	1.28	—	—	—	15.38
N = 78	Bhumihar Brahmin	—	1.28	—	—	—	1.28	—	—	2.56
	Rajput	3.85	8.98	3.85	1.28	—	—	2.56	1.28	21.80
	Kayastha	—	2.56	1.29	—	2.56	—	—	—	6.41
	Lower Castes	1.28	1.28	7.69	2.56	3.85	3.85	1.28	1.28	23.07
	Scheduled Castes	1.28	8.98	2.56	2.56	1.28	—	—	1.28	17.94
	Muslims	—	—	1.28	—	—	—	—	1.28	2.56
	Total	6.41	29.93	23.08	10.24	8.97	5.13	3.84	5.12	89.72
Saran	Brahmin	—	3.29	1.31	1.31	0.67	0.67	1.31	3.94	12.50
N = 152	Bhumihar Brahmin	—	3.94	1.97	1.97	1.97	1.32	3.30	—	14.47
	Rajput	0.67	7.23	3.29	1.97	1.97	1.97	1.97	0.67	19.74
	Kayastha	—	—	—	1.31	0.66	0.66	—	—	2.63
	Lower Castes	0.67	5.92	3.94	2.62	3.29	3.29	1.31	0.67	21.71
	Scheduled Castes	—	3.93	0.67	—	—	—	0.67	—	5.27
	Muslims	0.66	0.66	0.66	1.32	—	—	3.29	—	5.27
	Total	2.00	24.97	11.84	10.50	8.56	7.91	11.85	5.28	82.91

Table 6 : *Caste and Education of Active Members in 4 Districts of Bihar, 1961 (in per cent) Contd.*

1	2	3	4	5	6	7	8	9	10	11
Darbhanga	Brahmin	0.82	5.74	4.10	2.87	2.05	2.05	5.74	3.68	27.05
N = 244	Bhumihar Brahmin	—	1.23	0.82	1.23	0.82	0.82	—	1.23	6.15
	Rajput	0.82	5.33	2.87	1.64	1.64	1.23	3.28	2.87	19.68
	Kayastha	0.41	0.41	0.82	0.40	—	0.41	0.41	1.23	4.09
	Lower Castes	—	3.69	3.69	0.82	3.28	0.41	1.63	0.82	14.34
	Scheduled Castes	1.23	4.91	2.06	1.64	0.82	0.41	—	0.41	11.48
	Muslims	—	—	1.23	1.64	2.05	—	1.23	1.23	7.38
	Total	3.38	21.31	15.59	10.24	10.66	5.33	12.29	11.47	90.17
Shahabad	Brahmin	—	5.25	6.28	2.62	2.09	1.04	1.57	2.62	21.47
N = 191	Bhumihar Brahmin	—	2.09	2.09	—	1.04	1.58	—	0.53	7.33
	Rajput	0.53	5.23	3.66	0.53	1.58	2.09	3.13	1.04	17.79
	Kayastha	—	1.57	3.16	0.52	0.52	—	1.04	0.52	7.33
	Lower Castes	1.57	3.65	5.72	1.04	0.53	1.04	2.10	1.04	16.69
	Scheduled Castes	0.53	4.17	1.04	—	—	—	0.53	0.53	6.80
	Muslims	—	0.52	0.52	0.52	0.53	0.53	—	—	2.62
	Total	2.63	22.48	22.47	5.23	6.29	6.28	8.37	6.28	80.03

* Other minor castes and cases not known have been left out.

compared to the other caste groups.

This points to a very interesting aspect of the process of social change going on in Bihar. The Brahmins, Bhumihar Brahmins and Rajputs, as has been shown earlier, enjoy higher social status and constitute the landed gentry of the state although their combined numerical strength is not high. These castes, in other words, enjoyed and still enjoy ritual status, social prestige, economic well-being and political dominance. They control the avenues of social mobility and are, therefore, in a position to distribute social and political benefits. As such, they do not need the additional prop of advanced education to sustain and support them in their advantageous position. They enjoy political power because of their dominance in very crucial areas of social, ritual and economic systems. Their urge for higher education, therefore, is more in answer to individual needs than to a response to their desire to continue to be dominant politically.

The lower castes, on the other hand, have to find new avenues of social mobility. The traditionally sanctioned avenues of social mobility are virtually closed for them and employment and business opportunities are scarce and highly competitive. Moreover, to succeed in business they need capital and in order to gain employment in public or private services, they need higher educational degrees. But to achieve status in non-social fields is not equivalent to achieving social status. Their achievements in non-social fields add to their prestige and earn adulation for them in their own group. Unless they succeed in weakening or completely destroying the social barriers erected in their path of upward social mobility, they cannot hope to succeed in getting themselves socially accepted. This they can achieve only through politics. Politics is a great leveller of social distinctions inasmuch as by evolving new criteria of selection of leaders, it weakens the traditional bases of social structure and thus affords to the lower caste an opportunity to achieve through politics what they cannot through social instrumentalities. But lacking other instrumentalities of achieving power and thus status, they can be effective in politics only by their educational achievement. It is therefore, not surprising that the lower castes are educationally more advanced than other privileged castes. This is also reflected in the Congress members.

But this is not true of the Scheduled Castes. As we have indicated earlier, their sense of security, perhaps, makes them insensitive to the advantages of higher education.

The above analysis leads us to conclude that while upper castes use their traditionally privileged position as a lever to become effective in the political realm, the non-privileged caste groups, without the advantage of any social resources save their numerical strength, have necessarily to seek other avenues of upward social mobility. Politics provide them with such a channel. But to be effective in politics, where achievement and universalistic criteria of selection predominate, they have to prove their competence. This competence they can hope to gain only by higher achievement in education and by organising their own support base.

VII

Thus far we have discussed the nature of inequality of social system in Bihar and its impact on the recruitment patterns of the Congress Party. We also noticed that the Congress Party in Bihar is still dominated by the upper castes, although a trend is in operation which signifies the growing importance of the underprivileged caste groups in political calculus. There is one factor of great significance which has helped this trend to grow in strength over the years. This is the phenomenon of factionalism.

As we indicated earlier, with the spread in education and political consciousness other caste groups emerged to challenge the dominance which the Kayasthas enjoyed in the early periods of freedom struggle in Bihar. The Kayasthas, conscious of their weak numerical strength, had to make an alliance with a larger caste group in order to survive politically. Thus by 1937 two groups had emerged in the state — one composed of the Kayasthas and the Rajputs and the other composed of the Bhumihars. But as competition for political power intensified, the contending groups had necessarily to look beyond their own caste groups. In their bid to capture power and strengthen their power base, they resorted to cooptation of leaders from different caste groups. Until 1952 two factions, composed of different caste groups, functioned in the Bihar Congress. But from then on disaffection with and alienation and defection from one group started after the formation of Congress Ministry in 1946, which gathered momentum after the formation of Ministry in 1952.[21]

The formation of the Congress Ministry in 1946 and 1952 disappointed some of the non-Bhumihar lieutenants of the Chief Minister. One additional factor was the inclusion into the Cabinet of M.P. Sinha, a Bhumihar and a close relative of the Chief Minister. On the one hand, it terrified K.B. Sahay who had his own aspirations to succeed as the Chief Minister; as he found in M.P. Sinha a serious rival with greater advantage at his disposal, and, on the other, it further lisillusioned the non-Bhumihar supporters of the Chief Minister who, hey thought, had further proof of the Chief Minister's intentions to promote his own caste men to positions of power. As a result, there emerged in Bihar a centrist group with an objective to discredit the Bhumihar leadership. This is the beginning of the fragmentation of the tructure of the Congress party. By 1963, there emerged in the party ix or seven groups based, more or less, on exclusive caste groups.

The phenomenon of factionalism gives rise to two contradictory endencies which have a great impact on the recruitment patterns of he Congress party. The first tendency arises out of the necessity felt py the contending groups of widening the political support base in order to forge a winning sub-coalition. This necessity drives the contending groups to seek and win support from different caste groups. This is usually done through the device of cooptation. The lominant group would usually sponsor a promising person from a politically ineffective caste and push him up to junior positions of eadership. This way the dominant group would secure the support of the caste the person belonged to. However inasmuch as all the contending groups could take recourse to such a device, this tended o induct different politically dormant caste groups into the political process and thus widen the circle of participation. This also tended to ntensify political competition inasmuch as the 'junior' leaders, when hey built their own support structure, began clamouring for more power.

Another tendency that arises from the factional nature of politics elates to the endeavour of the leaders of the different caste groups to onsolidate their political support base. The existence of intense ompetition among the leaders and the consequent move on their part to consolidate their political support base, predispose the leaders o prefer their own caste men in positions of power. Referring to the ivalry between M.P. Sinha and K.B. Sahay, Anugraha Narayan Sinha omments:

> After the entry in 1952 of Mahesh Prasad Sinha in the Cabinet, Krishnaballabh Sahay who was aspiring to succeed the Chief Minister became apprehensive that his aspirations might now be eclipsed. M. P. Sinha too was not to sit passive. He was manoeuvring to denigrate K.B. Sahay in the eyes of the Chief Minister. In addition, he was also busy in denigrating the non-Bhumihar favourites of the Chief Minister, ... and to replace those persons by men from his own caste ...[22]

The predisposition of the leaders to prefer their own caste men in positions of power is not by any means a new phenomenon. As early as 1945 a Congressman complained to Dr. Rajendra Prasad that :

> In all its forms and deeds the Indian National Congress is essentially a
> national organisation. But I am pained to say that the composition of the
> higher ranks of the Congress in this province of Bihar is predominantly
> sectional. Among the Congress members of the Provincial Assembly, just
> dissolved, the Bhumihars, the Rajputs, the Kayasthas and the Harijan
> together comprised almost two-thirds of the actual members of the
> Congress MLAs. But actually speaking, it was and it is to this day, that the
> ruling trio of Bhumihars, Kayasthas and Rajputs lays down the policy and
> fills most of the executive posts of the district and provincial Congress
> Committees.

Then he went on to say that:

> It is an open secret that our provincial Congress is split up into two parties
> led by two ex-Congress Ministers ...
> The highly objectionable and the most condemnable result of this
> sectional politics within the Congress has been the constant suppression
> by the trio of those Congress workers who, due to the will of God, do no
> belong to any of the three communities. Such Congress workers, tested
> and capable, have been ousted either in favour of workers of the trio or in
> favour of unimportant workers of other communities who have accepted
> the leadership of any of the trio. This is an exceedingly serious matter
> indeed, specially as it is pursued as a matter of policy.[23]

It is enough to indicate that different caste groups consciously
attempt to eliminate from effective power those elements which could
not be relied upon or posed serious threats to them. This means that
various rivals for political power must adopt the same tactics in order
to survive. The search for support necessarily takes the line of least
resistance, that is, exploitation of the feeling of caste solidarity for
political purposes.

This resulted in the emergence of several groups formed round
several leaders taking more or less, the character of one or more
composite caste groups.

However, these tendencies promote widening of political
participation and thus lead to structural change in the society. The
non-privileged caste groups have benefited from these tendencies
inasmuch as this has helped them to increase their representation in
the Congress Party.

VIII

To conclude, caste is the basic category of social differentiation in Bihar and as such it has deeply impressed the recruitment patterns of the Congress Party. The caste system posited several inequalities and these tended to accumulate on one side. The new opportunities for social advancement created under the impact of the colonial regime were initially exploited by the traditionally privileged caste groups. This in a sense meant cumulation of inequalities. The unequal access to resources benefited the upper castes in the initial stages of political awakening in that they dominated the political scene to the exclusion of other non-privileged caste groups. But then the impact of democratic politics was felt and the competition among the upper castes for political power began to widen the circle of political participation and politically ineffective caste groups began to be inducted into the political process. This meant that a trend of dispersal of inequalities started. But the time is still far away when the numerically stronger underprivileged caste groups will come to dominate the political scene in Bihar.

NOTES

1. I am indebted to Professor Avery Leiserson who read an earlier draft o
    this paper and gave valuable suggestions for improving it. I am alone
    responsible for the shortcomings that still persist in the paper.
2. 'A Comparative Method for the Study of Politics', in Harry Eckstein and
    David E. Apter, eds. *Comparative Politics : A Reader* (Glencoe: The Free
    Press, 1962), p. 83.
3. *Ibid.* p. 86.
4. *loc. cit.*
5. For the purpose of this paper, upper castes include Brahmins, Bhumiha
    Brahmins, Rajputs and Kayasthas.
6. B. B. Misra, *The Indian Middle Classes: Their Growth in Modern Time*
    (London: Oxford University Press, 1961), p. 54.
7. *Ibid.* p. 55.
8. The A.I.A.L.E. does not give figures for different categories of agricultura
    occupation in the case of Brahmins; it lumps together the differen
    categories and simply indicates that the main occupation of about 8
    per cent of Brahmins is cultivation. It does not also give relevant figure
    in the case of 'Tribals and Aboriginals' and 'others'.
9. Bihar and Orissa formed, till 1936, one State.
10. The explanation of the Kayasthas enjoying dominant position in the fiel
    of education is very simple. The Kayastha community, which rose i
    status through royal patronage, "constituted a class of clerks and writers
    and though not highly paid, exerted considerable influence on th
    Moghal government because of their shrewdness and knowledge c
    Persian, as well as their partiality to alcohol which commended them t
    royal favours. They rivalled the Brahmins in everything connected wit
    the pen." Misra *op. cit.* pp. 53-54. As the social status of the Kayasthas di
    not depend on their economic or ritual strength as was the case wit
    Brahmins or Rajputs, and as they had to depend for their livelihood o
    their 'penmanship' they naturally were the first to respond to nev
    opportunities in the educational field.
11. Irawati Karve, *Hindu Society — An Interpretation* (Poona: Decca
    College, 1962), pp. 102-3.
12. The emergence of the Kayasthas as a distinct caste is a case in point.
13. *op. cit.* pp. 102-3.
14. "The formation of caste *sabhas* to advance the social status of the lowe
    castes is not a new phenomenon, but it has become very much mor
    common during the last decade. In most cases the procedure is more c
    less uniform. A new name is selected for the caste, its members are t
    adopt the sacred thread and various resolutions are passed dealing wit
    such questions as food and drink, the abandonment of 'degradin
    occupations, postponement of age of marriage, etc. etc." *Census*
    India, 1931 (Bihar and Orissa), Vol. VII, Part I, p. 267.
15. It is not suggested here that it is only the concept of *Varna* that is relevar

for political considerations. It all depends on what level of politics is being discussed. At the village level, it is not unusual to find two or more groups of the same caste pitched against each other in political struggle. But when we move up to levels above the village the pattern changes. At these levels, political alliance takes place either at the *Varna* level or a fraction of it.

16. Anugraha Narayan Sinha, *Mere Samsmaran* (My Reminiscences), (Patna: Kusum Prakashan, 1961), p. 1.

17. Manindra Narayan Ray, 'Reaping the Whirlwind', (Tenth of the series 'The Bihar I Knew'), *Indian Nation*, December 14, 1964. Later on, it was very easy to equate 'men from Bengal' with every Bengali whether in or out of the province. This gave rise to Bengali-Bihari disputeswhen the Congress formed a ministry in 1937 in Bihar and the matter was referred to the A.I.C.C.

18. *The Bihar Provincial Kisan Sabha, 1929-1942 : A Study of an Indian Peasant Movement* (unpublished Ph.D. dissertation, University of Chicago, 1961), p. 75.

19. It is generally composed of more than two hundred members and meets not more than once a year.

20. Three considerations have influenced the selection of districts for the purpose of this table. First, as the concentration of upper castes is heavier in North and South Bihar, Chhotanagpur regions are excluded. Second, the availability of data restricted the choice of districts. Third, it was felt desirable to select those districts which reflect different patterns of caste composition in their population. Saharsa, for example, is very low on upper caste composition, while Shahabad is very high. Saran and Darbhanga on the other hand, were selected because they represent districts which lie in-between the categories represented by Saharsa and Shahabad.

21. We need not go into details about the circumstances responsible for this. For details, however, see my *A Study of the Bihar Pradesh Congress Committee, Bihar.* (Unpublished Ph.D. dissertation, University of Berkeley, 1965), Chapter 7.

22. *op. cit.* p. 437.

23. *Letter from Shyam Krishna Agarwal to Dr. Rajendra Prasad*, October 2, 1945.

How the leaders of one caste attempt to eliminate potential rivals from other castes is evident by the following communication to Dr. Rajendra Prasad from Thakur Ram Nandan Singh, MLA from Sitamarhi dated March 3, 1946 (original in Hindi).

"... Dr. Ramashish Thakur has complained to you about me in regard to elections. Before that he had got an enquiry committee appointed by the Muzaffarpur District Congress Executive Committee in its meeting of February 20 ... when he saw you he did not mention to you about this; he wanted simply to inform you about my activities. His and his supporters attitude has recently changed. His supporters control the D.C.C. and a few Thana Congress Committees in this sub-division.

Therefore, he is always attempting to bring certain charges against non-Bhumihar workers who are associated with me and take disciplinary action against them so that they may not be in a position to contest the next delegates election. Only yesterday in the meeting of Sitamarhi Thana Congress Committee he recommended to the D.C.C. to take disciplinary action against more than two dozen non-Bhumihar Congress workers. He is contemplating to take similar action in other thanas too."

CHAPTER EIGHT

Caste and Political Group Formation in Tamilnad

ANDRE BETEILLE

I

It is a truism that the nature and content of politics undergo transformation from one territory to another. What is less obvious is that the caste system also evinces several levels of differentiation. These levels require to be specified before a proper understanding can be achieved of the transformations in the relations between caste and politics from one level of organisation to another. Firstly, these relations are more immediate at certain levels than at others. A failure to recognise this is likely to lead to hasty and unsound generalisations. It is also likely to divert attention from the fact that the relations between caste and politics are not static but change continuously over time. Secondly, there are many alignments other than those based on caste which play an important part in the political process. Their role has often been undervalued because of their fluidity, amorphous nature, and less identifiable dimensions. Particularly, recent studies by Nicholas[1] and Brass,[2] show how alliances are often made across caste for the pursuit of political objectives.

II

I shall begin with a consideration of how the problems of distribution and process relate to caste politics.

Problems of distribution: Every society has its typical structures of power. One important feature of contemporary India lies in qualitative and quantitative changes in the traditional structures of power. New types of structures such as parties, *panchayats* and machines have proliferated since Independence and penetrated into the rural areas. The two main factors behind this are the adoption of adult franchise and the institution of Panchayati Raj.

These structures have also become more differentiated. In the past at the local level the dominant caste was often the principal locus of power. Today there are differentiated political structures of various kinds such as parties, *panchayats* and machines. Such differentiated structures are generally more easy to identify since they have often a formal organisation. But it has to be remembered that particularly at the local level real power may be vested in an informal body such as a group of lineage elders rather than in a formal structure such as the statutory *panchayat*.

Each structure of power can be examined for its caste composition and comparisons can be made between structures at different levels of organisation. This will tell us about the distributive aspects of the relationship between caste and politics. It is often found that a particular caste is highly represented in the village *panchayat* or the *panchayat samiti* or the *zilla parishad*. This high representation may at times be due to the fact that the caste in question is numerically preponderant and highly represented in the population as a whole. Also it seems likely that over-representation of castes in structures of power is more characteristic of certain territorial levels than of others. A second kind of distributive problem relates to changes in the caste composition of particular structures of power over a period of time. This problem can be analysed by comparing the caste composition of relatively small units at different points of time.

Two kinds of change seem to be taking place in the relation between caste and politics in Tamilnad, as well as in other parts of the country. In the first kind, power shifts from one dominant caste to another. This happened when Kallas and a few other castes wrested control over village politics from Brahmins in Sripuram.[3] It happened on a wider scale in Tamilnad as a whole when Brahmins were displaced by non-Brahmins in important political bodies.

The second kind of change is perhaps more radical than the first. Here the locus of power shifts from the caste system itself to differentiated structures of power. As indicated earlier, a vast body of new structures of power have emerged in India since Independence. Today traditional bodies such as groups of caste elders (which are functionally diffuse) have to compete increasingly with functionally specific structures of power such as parties and statutory *panchayats*. Often there are mechanisms which bring about the interpenetration of the two sets of bodies.

Problems of process: Structures of power exist within a framework of events and activities. This flow of events and activities creates changes in personnel and, over longer periods of time, changes in the structures themselves.

This implies that it is necessary for incumbents of political office to maintain support, in order both to acquire such office and to act effectively within it. In societies having representative government, such as contemporary India, there are specific institutional arrangements through which support is given, withdrawn or manipulated.

This support may be given in return for material benefits. But material benefits cannot be granted directly or immediately in exchange for every kind of support. For this reason the mobilisation of support requires appeal to loyalties of various kinds which do not always have a tangible material basis.

It is in this sense that 'primordial loyalty' to caste provides powerful bases for political support in India. *Other things being equal,* people are expected to support members of their own caste or kin group. To the extent that traditional values persist, loyalty and obligation to caste and community are considered 'good'. It is natural that they should be carried over to the field of institutional politics.[4]

Even in traditional Indian society there were non-caste allegiances like loyalties of class and of patron-client relationships. The latter in particular often cut across caste and are in conflict with it. Thus, the Palla client of a Vellala patron has one set of loyalties to his fellow Pallas and another to his patron who is of a different caste. Such divided loyalties, which are an inherent feature of the system, give to it a certin indeterminacy and always leave room for some manipulation of support. This is one reason why political events are difficult to predict although it is possible to interpret them.

Caste may enter into the political process in a number of ways. Firstly, appeals may be made to caste loyalties in a general way as when Vanniyas are exhorted to vote for Vanniya candidates. The force of this kind of appeal is made evident in Tamilnad where rival parties often match caste with caste in the selection of candidates for electoral office. Secondly, networks of interpersonal relations are activised both during elections and at other times for mobilising support along caste lines. Since kinship, marriage and commensality often stop short at the boundaries of caste, intra-caste relations are very important. Thirdly, caste associations such as the Vaniyakkula Kshatriya Sangam may seek to articulate caste interests in an organised manner.

III

I now turn to a brief consideration of the nature of caste. The caste system in Tamilnad is both elaborate and deeply segmented. Segments of different orders assume importance at different levels of the political system. It seems that the political process itself plays some part in bringing about changes in the nature of segmentation in the caste system. Organised politics often necessitates the fusion of adjacent segments and this political fusion is likely in the long run to affect other aspects of inter-caste relations, such as commensality or intermarriage.[5]

Again, the caste system is characterised by several levels of differentiations:[6] the larger units are divided into smaller ones and these are subdivided on the basis of fairly enduring cleavages. The divisions and subdivisions either merge with one another or are placed in opposition, depending upon their context. In a given context, a unit of a lower order may lose its identity through merger with an adjacent unit, in another it may reappear as an independent entity. Thus the system as a whole retains a degree of continuity over time.

The segments themselves are differentiated according to styles of life. Each segment — whether sub-caste, caste or caste group — is characterised on the one hand by certain *diacritical* distinctions and on the other by a set of *syncretic* values. The diacritical distinctions "define the unity of the segment in terms of differentiation from other segments", whereas syncretic values "define the unity of the segment in terms of internal solidarity".[7] One caste differs from another in matters of dress, diet and other habits, while within the caste there is a consciousness of community. It is this which facilitates the mobilisation of support on the basis of caste as opposed to other social categories such as class.

These diacritical differences are elaborate in Tamilnad. Further, some of the reinforcements they have had in the past still persist. Food habits, types of habitation, styles of dress and many other customs varied from one caste to another. The higher castes jealously preserved their traditonal styles of life, even to the extent of cooking or serving food in a particular manner. The lower castes could imitate these ways to some extent, but ritual and other sanctions prevented such imitation proceeding beyond a certain point. In Tamilnad such sanctions were employed with considerable force even thirty years ago.[8]

The unity which a caste derives from its diacritical distinctions is more in evidence at higher than at lower levels of segmentation. Members of a broad division such as the Brahmins share only a few diacritical elements in common, whereas those of a subdivision of the Smartha Brahmins, for instance, share many. Similarly, internal solidarity is likely to be more intense within a sub-caste than within a group of related castes. The highest order of segmentation in the caste system is represented by a small endogamous unit whose members are the bearers of a homogeneous cultural tradition and are in fact related to each other by ties of kinship and affinity. At the other extreme are the primary segments (viz. Brahmins, non-Brahmins and Harijans) whose members share a few common customs and are bound together by a broad feeling of community.

We can present here only a very brief account of the caste structure of Tamilnad. The population of Tamilnad can be broadly divided into three groups, the Brahmins, the non-Brahmins and the Harijans (or Adi-Dravidas). In the villages the three groups are generally segregated in different residential areas. The Brahmins live in brick and tile houses in a separate part of the village known as the *agraharam* and are marked off from the others by distinctive patterns of speech, dress and diet; within the *agraharam* there is a fairly intense community life from many areas of which non-Brahmins and Harijans are excluded. The Harijans in their turn live in their own streets known as *cheris* which have a unity no less distinctive than that of the *agraharam*. The non-Brahmins represent a broader spectrum of cultural variations and appear to be on the whole less cohesive than the two other primary segments.

Each primary segment, which appears as a unit in relation to the others, is internally subdivided. The Brahmins in Tamilnad are subdivided into Smartha, Shri Vaishnava, etc. Each of these evinces a greater measure of unity (both diacritical and syncretic) than the Brahmins taken as a whole. The Smartha Brahmins in their turn are similarly sub-divided into Vadama, Brihacharanam, Astasahashram and Vattiman. The Vadama Brahmins are sub-divided into Vadadesha Vadama and Chozhadesha Vadama. Segmentation among the non-Brahmins is more complex and the Harijans as a unit appear to be less segmented than the Brahmins. But everywhere the pattern is broadly similar.[9]

At which level of segmentation does caste enter into the political process? When we seek to analyse the role of caste in politics, which should be our unit of investigation, a broad grouping such as the Brahmins or a small sub-division such as the Vadadesha Vadama or the Pramalai Kalla?

Some have been inclined to argue that castes can successfully enter politics only when they combine into fairly large aggregates; too much segmentation, in their view, tends to reduce the viability of castes in the competition for power. There can be little doubt that organised politics at the State level has tended to bring about a certain aggregation of adjacent segments within the caste system. This phenomenon appears to have an all-India character and has been commented on by many. Srinivas for instance writes, "In order to be able to take advantage of these opportunities, caste groups, as traditionally understood, entered into alliances with each other to form bigger entities."[10] He gives the example of the Okkaligas in Mysore who now include, in the context of State politics, several related but distinct entities. The same can be said of the Vellalas or the Kallas in Tamilnad.

The non-Brahmin movement provided a common platform not only for a wide variety of Hindu castes but also for Christians and Muslims. It also added a new dimension to the unity of the Brahmins, which grew in response to the non-Brahmin challenge. However, it would be a mistake to view this unity as something absolute or as having significance in every context. It is well known how the unity of the non-Brahmins was loosened after they gained ascendancy in Tamilnad because of competition between rival dominant castes among them for power and office. It is hardly surprising that cleavages which are ignored in the interest of a particular objective should reassert themselves once that objective has been achieved.

The unity one encounters in the caste system is in a very real sense relative. Although a minor segment of a caste may be too small to act as an independent unit in State politics, it may be a viable unit in the village. Again, the fact that a group of subcastes unites against a like group over a certain issue does not mean that they cannot be divided over a different issue. Conversely, the fact that two subcastes contend for power in a particular arena does not mean that they cannot unite against a different caste in a wider arena. In fact, such fissions and fusions are an important feature of caste politics in Tamilnad. Further, since caste is a highly structured system, they are inclined to follow clearly-defined patterns.

Many have observed that the unity provided by caste has different degrees of inclusiveness.[11] Srinivas tries to account for this in a way which appears to be characteristic.

> The point which needs to be emphasised here is that for purposes of sociological analysis a distinction has to be made between caste at the political level and caste at the social and ritual level. The latter is a much smaller unit than the former.[12]

The distinction is drawn at the wrong place. What is important here is to distinguish not between political and social levels, but between different levels of organisation in a 'merging series',[13] State, district and village, or caste-group, caste and sub-caste. Srinivas' conclusion derives from his pre-occupation with the role of caste in State politics. But caste may also play a part in village politics and there the effective unit of organisation may be fairly small. Nor is it correct to maintain that larger aggregates have no social or ritual unity. Such broad groupings as the Brahmins and the Harijans (and to a much lesser extent the non-Brahmins) do have a measure of diacritical and syncretic unity and it is this fact which largely accounts for their persistence at every level of political organisation.

Srinivas also appears to suggest that the larger aggregates are somehow new to the Indian scene. Even this position cannot be well sustained. Broader groupings such as Brahmins, Shudras and Panchamas were relevant to a wide variety of contexts even in traditional society.[14]

We conclude that caste may be significant to the political process at every level of segmentation, although organised politics at State and district levels has often led to a quasi-permanent aggregation of segments. Further, there seems to exist some broad relationship between the arena of politics and the level of segmentation at which caste enters into it. At the State (or even district) level, minor segments merge with one another so as to be able to operate as viable units. But this kind of merger easily comes about precisely because a basis for it already existed in the traditional structure. At the village level a major segment may subdivide and its component units be opposed to one another, again because the cleavage was present in the past.

The principle of segmentation operates even *within* the subcaste, viewed as the smallest unit of endogamy. In such cases the units which stand in opposition to each other are generally lineages. (A subcaste which is an *endogamous* unit is often subdivided into lineages which are exogamous.) In certain parts of Tanjore district where the Kallas are decisively dominant, rival candidates for political office often belong to different lineages of the same subcaste. (In other contexts the three related castes, Kalla, Marava and Ahamudiya, may together operate as a single unit.) When a sub-caste is large, culturally homogeneous and decisively dominant, the cleavages within the lineage system often assume great importance.[15] Thus for certain purposes lineage, sub-caste, caste and caste-group may be viewed as constituting a single series.[16]

Although both the territorial system and the caste system show a similar pattern of division and subdivision, it would be wrong to assume a high degree of correspondence between levels of segmentation in the two. Even a broad grouping within the caste system such as the Brahmins may be relevant to village as well as State politics. Much depends upon the caste composition of the village or other territorial unit in question. A village which has a few castes of which one is decisively dominant will show a different kind of alignment from one where there are many castes and none enjoys decisive dominance. Everywhere, however, the caste system provides *one* set of cleavages along which units tend to merge or subdivide. Whether they do merge or subdivide depend upon a variety of other factors, some of which are extraneous to the structure of caste. It cannot be too strongly emphasised that political alliances (at every level) often cut across caste and are frequently based upon affiliations which have little direct connection with caste.

IV

The threefold division of society into Brahmin, non-Brahmin and Harijan provides perhaps the broadest basis for 'communal' politics in Tamilnad. (In the present analysis I ignore altogether the Hindu-Muslim cleavage; on the whole it has been of less importance than the cleavage between Brahmins and non-Brahmins or between non-Brahmins and Harijans.) This division provides the basic framework for the analysis of problems of both distribution and process, and influences of political organisation at all levels. Its importance is given tacit recognition in the composition of a variety of political bodies. The Madras Municipal Corporation, for instance, has long followed the convention of rotating the Mayoralty between 1 Brahmin, 2 non-Brahmins, 1 Harijan and 1 Muslim.

To what extent are we justified in treating such broad divisions as castes? I have shown that a certain measure of unity is associated with each category, and Brahmins and Harijans at least are certainly viewed as castes in a variety of contexts by the Tamil-speaking people. The non-Brahmins admittedly are a more heterogeneous division and sometimes (though not generally) they are so broadly defined as to include even the Harijans. Even so the non-Brahmin movement gave them a certain coherence and unity, which seem to have outlived the movement itself. For that reason it becomes necessary to analyse their role in Tamilnad politics even though they constitute a kind of residual category. (The term non-Brahmin has been criticised by many precisely on this account; however, it has become a part of the political history of Tamilnad and it would be unreal to dispense with it, at least in this context.)

Perhaps the most important consequence of the non-Brahmin movement (of which more later) was the introduction of a 'communal' or caste idiom into South Indian politics. The composition of political bodies was changed by it, sometimes artificially, through reserved seats, and everywhere communal loyalties became important in giving or withdrawing support. It is doubtful whether the movement even attempted to organise politically the entire body of non-Brahmins. But it certainly did succeed in creating a lasting impression that in virtually every political context it was important whether a person was a Brahmin or a non-Brahmin.[17]

We can start our discussion with the Brahmins. As a social stratum they were the first to be politicised and up to the 1920s they enjoyed a dominant position in the former Madras Presidency. Their representation in most of the political bodies was far in excess of their proportion in the population as a whole. The changes in their political fortunes over the last fifty years bring into focus not only the role of caste in politics but certain major shifts in the bases of power in Tamil society. Certainly no section of Tamil society of comparable size[18] has for so long occupied the storm centre of political debate and it is doubtful whether any other section has undergone a more radical change in its relation to the distribution of power.

To what do the Brahmins owe their unique position in Tamil society? I have already commented on the diacritical differences between the Brahmins and the others. These are certainly sharper in Tamilnad (and in South India as a whole) than in North India. Two of them may be considered to begin with: the real difference in linguistic usage and the imputed difference in racial origins. These distinctions, in part real and in part imaginary, have combined to create a popular and widespread belief that the Brahmins represent an 'Aryan' element superimposed on an indigenous 'Dravidian' sub-stratum. This belief has had far-reaching consequences for the development of political attitudes in Tamilnad.

The opposition to Brahmins has been expressed in economic as well as ethnic terms. On the whole Tamil Brahmins enjoyed a favourable position in the traditional economic system. A considerable section of them owned land, though there was a large class of landowners — both big and small — among the non-Brahmins.[19] But Brahmin landowners, whatever be the size of their land holdings and whatever be their location, have been related to the productive organisation in a significantly different way from the non-Brahmins. They are debarred by scriptural injunction from the actual work of tillage and, hence, a Brahmin who owns even a small parcel of land has to depend for labour on non-Brahmins and Harijans. A non-Brahmin landowner, on the other hand, in a comparable situation may not only till his own land but will probably take some additional land on lease and perhaps also work as a part-time agricultural labourer. Again, the majority of non-Brahmin landowners are peasant farmers, tenants or agricultural labourers or some combination of the three. Among Brahmin landowners a large proportion are rentiers and absentee landlords. Thus the contrast between Brahmin and non-Brahmin landowners, arises from difference not so much in size of holding as in styles of life. This has played a most important part in the development of the non-Brahmin movement.

The initial conseqences of British rule were probably to increase the structural distance between Brahmins and the rest of Tamil society. Brahmins were the first to take to Western education and Western-educated Brahmins entered the professions and services in large numbers. Those who entered Government and other services used the ties of kinship and affinity to recruit more Brahmins. It is difficult to form an accurate estimate of their representation in professional, administrative and managerial positions, but there is little doubt that during the first quarter of the present century it was extremely high. This was projected as a major issue by the Justice Party which emerged in 1917 as a champion of non-Brahmin interests and demanded more equitable representation for them in the educational system, in local bodies and in the services.

In this initial phase (which may arbitrarily be considered as ending with the formation of the Justice Party in 1917) the cleavage between Brahmins and non-Brahmins was widened in two important ways. As Brahmins entered the institutions of higher learning, the professions and the services, everywhere they formed cliques from which non-Brahmins were excluded. Between 1892 and 1904, out of 16 successful candidates for the I.C.S. 15 were Brahmins; in 1913, 93 out of 128 permanent district munsifs were Brahmins; in 1914, 452 out of the 650 registered graduates of the University were Brahmins.[20] In a system which was ostensibly competitive but in which the scales must have seemed heavily weighted against non-Brahmins, the latter inevitably developed deep feelings of resentment.

There was another important consequence of westernisation. As its pace mounted, Brahmins began increasingly to look outwards to the towns and cities. They left the *agraharams* in large numbers — at first temporarily but with an increasing measure of permanence — and joined schools, colleges and offices in the urban centres. They had at no time had the same intimate relations with the land as the non-Brahmins and Harijans, and westernisation loosened considerably such bonds as they did have with tenants and labourers in their ancestral villages. But although they began to turn outwards, they did not dispose of their land to any great extent, at least not in the initial period. Rather, they became rentiers and absentee landowners, returning to the village from time to time and even while there keeping one eye on a job as a clerk or school teacher in a neighbouring town. It is evident that even within the village relations between Brahmin landowners and non-Brahmin tenants were weakened as a general consequence of the Brahmins' westernisation. This is certainly true of other districts as well, although the changes in some districts seem to have been far less marked.

This then is the social background out of which the non-Brahmin movement emerged. The Brahmins were politically isolated first because they constituted a separate ethnic entity and then because they occupied privileged positions in the economy, both as landowners and as professionals and administrators. In addition, they formed a very small minority, only about 3 per cent of the total population of the old Madras Presidency. (Their proportion in contemporary Tamilnad cannot be very much higher.)

Once non-Brahmin opposition was organised, it did not take long to dislodge the Brahmins from their privileged positions. In 1921 Madras Presidency came under the control of the Justice Party. Non-Brahmin representation in political bodies increased and they were favoured by a series of legislative and executive actions. The Brahmins suffered on two accounts: they were in a minority and they were largely behind the Congress Party which either boycotted the elections or refused to form ministries. However their decline during this period was only relative, in terms of their dominance prior to the formation of the Justice Party in 1917.

Nevertheless, they were never able quite to regain the dominant position 'which they had once occupied in the Presidency. After a brief revival between 1937 and 1939,[21] their position again declined, this time perhaps irrevocably. The Congress itself came gradually to be dominated by non-Brahmins. The 'forties' saw the emergence of the militant Dravida Kazhagam which preached and at times practised violence against the Brahmins. With the extension of the franchise after Independence and the introduction of *Panchayati Raj* a keen awareness developed among the Brahmins of their weakness and political isolation. In 1916 the non-Brahmin Manifesto had made angry protests against Brahmin domination. In 1962 Brahmin voters in Trichy had to be escorted to the polling booths for fear of violence from the Dravida Kazhagam. Brahmin representation in the Ministry, the Legislature and the Congress Party had dwindled into insignificance. (There is little precise information regarding the representation of Brahmins in political bodies at different levels. That there has been a general decline is beyond question. But it is possible that even today Brahmins are over — rather than under — represented in at least certain types of political organs.)

Political developments over the last fifty years have created among Tamil Brahmins a strong sense of identity as a minority. I have heard Brahmins with a flair for metaphor describe themselves as the Jews of South India. A strong feeling has taken root among them that they were made victims of every kind of discrimination. But they have not sought escape from organised politics. On the contrary, because of their feeling of political isolation and also because of the high rates of literacy and education among them, they are perhaps the most highly politicised section of Tamil society.

There is ample indication that the Brahmins are rapidly growing alive to the fact that if they are to survive politically they must come to terms with the non-Brahmins. In both 1962 and 1967 they supported the D.M.K. in spite of its non-Brahmin background. Many among them see the need to forge new alliances, transcending caste identities. In fact the most bitter critics of 'communal' or caste politics today are the Brahmins. The non-Brahmin movement in its turn seems to have spent itself, having achieved its principal objectives. The D.M.K. renounced its anti-Brahmin bias several years ago and canvassed actively for Brahmin support in the last three General Elections. It seems very likely that in the near future conflicts between Brahmins and non-Brahmins will play a far less important part than have done in the past.

It may now be useful to take a close-up view of the Brahmins at the district and village levels. I shall consider here only one district, Tanjore, and this for two reasons. Firstly, Tanjore is the cultural homeland of Tamil Brahmins and contains the highest proportion of Brahmins in Tamilnad. Secondly it has been studied more intensively by social anthropologists than any other district in the State. In what follows I shall draw on the field materials of Gough, Sivertsen and my own research in and around the village Sripuram.[22] Since these studies were all made in the same culture area but at different points of time (Gough's during the first and mine during the third General Elections), they offer useful material for an assessment of change.

Tanjore district has been the classic stronghold of Brahmin *mirasdars*. Gough estimates that the Brahmins "number about 2,00,000 in this district" and "own land and have administrative rights in about 900 out of a total of 2,611 villages."[23] The Tanjore Brahmins are also highly educated and show a high degree of political consciousness. For all this, they are not very highly represented either in the organs of local government or in the local organisation of the ruling party.[24]

When Gough made her study in the early fifties the Tanjore Brahmins were under attack from two quarters, the Communist Party and the Dravida Kazhagam, both of which were then quite strong. Further, the two parties were united in their opposition against them, the first on the ground that they were *mirasdars* and the second because they were Brahmins. At about this time peasant riots were organised in Mannargudi *taluka*, a stronghold of Brahmin *mirasdars*. The alliance with the staunchly anti-Brahmin Dravida Kazhagam seems to have made the Communists a little wary of antagonising the non-Brahmin landowners. And there can be little doubt that in Tanjore district the Communists drew much of their strength from the Dravida Kazhagam. In 1952, when the D.K. supported the Communists, the latter held 6 Assembly seats out of a total of 19 from the district.[25] When in 1962 the D.K. supported the Congress, the Communists were not able to win a single seat.

Till the mid-fifties the Tanjore Brahmins appear to have been solidly behind the Congress. This support was based as much on their traditional association with the Congress as on their opposition to the Communists and the D.K. who were then the two principal antagonists of the Congress. Things began to change rapidly after the mid-fifties. The veteran Brahmin leader, C. Rajagopalachari, was replaced by the non-Brahmin Kamaraj as Chief Minister and the Dravida Kazhagam, known and feared for its militant anti-Brahminism, switched its support to the Congress. The Congress enacted a series of laws curtailing the rights of landowners and many of the Brahmin *mirasdars* in Tanjore viewed these as being specifically directed against themselves. Finally in 1959 the Swatantra Party was formed under the leadership of Rajagopalachari and many of the Brahmins of Tanjore turned avidly towards the new party. In each of the half-a-dozen Brahmin villages I visited in 1961-62, the Swatantra Party had a solid core of supporters in the *agraharam*. In Tanjore district the Swatantra Party soon came to be known as the Brahmin Party, although many of its members are in fact non-Brahmins.

The 1962 elections found the Brahmins largely opposed to the Congress and, if anything, the mood was intensified in 1967. Since the late fifties their political attitudes appear to have been defined primarily in terms of opposition to the party then in power. In 1962 they supported D.M.K. candidates where the Swatantra Party did not put up candidates and the electoral alliance between the two parties in 1967 appears to have made their choice even simpler. In 1962 the Brahmins generally supported the Congress in only those rare constituencies where the Congress itself put up Brahmin candidates.

As indicated earlier, the Brahmins in Tanjore have developed a strong sense of unity in response to their political decline. Formerly there was active rivalry between the Smartha Brahmins and the Shri Vaishnavas and between the two sections of the Shri Vaishnava Brahmins. These are now largely forgotten. There is a conscious effort on their part today to foster a sense of oneness. The Brahmins today define their identity in terms of their distinctions from the non-Brahmins and not on the basis of sub-castes. In this regard they differ somewhat from the non-Brahmins.

Although the Brahmins constitute a very small minority in the district, their position is different in each of the three villages studied in detail. This is because these are all *agraharam* villages, i.e. villages with large concentrations of Brahmins, unlike the majority of Tanjore villages where there are no *agraharams* and at best only a few families of priestly Brahmins. Both Gough and Sivertsen report a decline in the traditional authority of the Brahmins in the villages studied by them. In both cases political parties and associations have played a leading part in organising support against the Brahmin *mirasdars*. In Thyagasamudram the Brahmins organised themselves into a Landlords' Association while the non-Brahmins and the Harijans rallied round the Cultivators' Union. Some of the bigger non-Brahmin landlords at first supported the Brahmins, but they seem to have been pressurised at a later stage into joining the Cultivators' Union.[26]

The case of Sripuram merits discussion at greater length because changes there seem to have been more decisive in character. At the beginning of the present century Sripuram was a flourishing *agraharam*-village, well known throughout Tanjore district for its large and prosperous community of Brahmins. The *agraharam* at Sripuram is rather unusual in the sense that it contains Brahmins, belonging to a number of different castes and sub-castes. Fifty years ago the Brahmins of Sripuram enjoyed decisive dominance. However, the internal cleavages between the Smarthas and the Shri Vaishnavas, and among the latter between the Thengalai and Vadagalai sections, were reflected in the competition for power relating to the control of the village temple and other local institutions. Today the power of the Brahmins has declined considerably, the old disputes between the Smarthas and the Shri Vaishnavas have been largely (though not entirely) forgotten and the Brahmins try to face the challenge of the emerging non-Brahmin leadership with a measure of unity.

Sripuram is, in Dahl's terminology, being transformed from a 'system of cumulative inequalities' to one of 'dispersed inequalities'.[27] In the past the Brahmins enjoyed the highest positions in the hierarchies of status, class and power. Today they continue to enjoy ritual and economic dominance but political power has shifted to the non-Brahmins. The shift in political power has been hastened by the introduction of *Panchayati Raj.*

Till the mid-forties the Brahmins dominated the village *panchayat*. The *panchayat* head was always a Brahmin and the *panchayat* room was situated in the *agraharam*. Non-Brahmin members of the *panchayat* had more or less the status of second-class citizens. Everything changed after Independence. Now the *panchayat* is completely dominated by the non-Brahmins; there are six non-Brahmin members as against three Brahmins. Both the President and the Vice President are non-Brahmins and have been non-Brahmins ever since Independence. Symbolic of the transfer of power from the Brahmins to the non-Brahmins has been the shift in the location of the *panchayat*-hall from the *agraharam* to the non-Brahmin streets. In fact this shift is of more than symbolic significance. In an *agraharam*-village Brahmins and non-Brahmins live more or less segregated in their different residential areas and Brahmins do not formally go to the non-Brahmin streets unless specifically invited. Now that the *panchayat*-hall is the venue of important political gatherings in the village, many of the Brahmin residents find themselves automatically excluded from such gatherings. For instance, when the Minister for Co-operation came to the village in 1962, he was entertained in the *panchayat*-hall; few of the Brahmins attended the gathering and many of them came to know of it only after the event.

These changes in Sripuram reflect changes in the bases of power in the wider system. In the traditional system power was derived largely from landownership and high ritual status. The introduction of new political structures and specialised political organs have helped non-Brahmin leaders of Sripuram (who command the support of numerically preponderant groups and have access to leaders and party bosses outside the village) to edge out of the *panchayat* the Brahmin landowners.

In the 1957-62 period the Brahmins' isolation from structures of power in Sripuram (and to some extent in Tanjore district as a whole) was partly a consequence of their alienation from the ruling Congress Party. In 1962 the Brahmins in Sripuram supported the D.M.K. candidate for the Assembly seat. The influential non-Brahmins, including the *panchayat* President, had then supported the Congress. This time the D.M.K. has been returned to power, partly on Brahmin support. This may have some effect on the political situation of the Brahmins although it is difficult to say how permanent or far-reaching this effect will be. In any event it seems more than likely that the levers of power will for sometime to come be wielded largely by non-Brahmins.

V

The non-Brahmin ascendancy in Sripuram can be made fully intelligible only in relation to wider structures of power and changes in the distribution of power over the last half a century. The non-Brahmin movement was formally launched with the issue of a Manifesto in December 1916. It presented detailed figures showing an extremely high concentration of Brahmins in the public services, in public bodies and in the educational system and contrasting this with the 3 per cent they formed of the total population of the Presidency.[28]

The movement gathered strength within a very short time. The Manifesto was followed by the starting of three daily papers, in English, Telugu and Tamil, the English paper being called the *Justice* which became the mouthpiece of the movement, and supplied the name also to the party itself.[29] The Party held its first Conference at Coimbatore in August 1917. Thereafter a series of Conferences were held in the Tamil and Telugu districts of the Presidency. The Conferences were evidently organised with expense and care and attended by a large number of notables.[30]

The Justice Party sent a powerful delegation to England in 1919 to present the non-Brahmin case before the Joint Parliamentary Committee set up in connection with the Government of India Bill. The Memorandum presented by K. V. Reddi Naidu on behalf of the non-Brahmins was one of the longest and was once again armed with facts and figures showing the domination of the Brahmins in every field. It argued that the interest of Brahmins and non-Brahmins were incompatible, that they claimed different racial origins and that if power were transferred without communal representation,

> that power will be utilized for the aggrandisement of the Brahmins and to the detriment of the non-Brahmins; that a Brahmin oligarchy will be substituted for a British bureaucracy; ... and that the Brahmin oligarchy will never be responsible to the masses and the middle classes, the poor and the proletariat...[31]

In retrospect, the non-Brahmin movement appears to have achieved singular success within a remarkably short period of time. Although the full demands for communal representation were not met, 28 out of the 98 elected seats in the newly constituted Madras Council were reserved for non-Brahmins.[32] The Justice Party captured the polls in the elections of 1920, no doubt partly because of the withdrawal of the Congress. The three Indian Ministers placed in charge of 'transferred subjects' were all non-Brahmins and Justicites. The same pattern was repeated in the succeeding Legislature constituted in 1923. In 1926 the Justice Party was defeated by the Swarajists, but the latter refused to form a Ministry and an independent ministry was formed under the non-Brahmin leader, P. Subbaroyan. The Justice Party rode into power again in 1930 and, though defeated in the elections of 1934, was not finally dislodged till 1937 when the Congress formed a Ministry under the leadership of C. Rajagopalachari.

After their success in the 1920 elections the leaders of the Justice Party settled down to the task of improving the position of non-Brahmins through legislative and executive action. The debates in the newly-constituted Council were replete with questions and counter-questions regarding the representation of Brahmins and non-Brahmins in the services and public bodies.

Forming a vast majority, the (Justice) party concerned itself with little more than communal questions, including the problem of communal representation in various areas of government service, and within one year the Council had become a forum of anti-Brahmin propaganda.[33]

One of the first movements of the Council was to recommend the appointment in every district of a Protector of non-Brahmin Subordinates in Public Services (G.O. No.114, dated 3-3-1921). Reservations for non-Brahmins were introduced in increasing proportion in the services, in local bodies and in the institutions of higher learning. With the Justice Party acting as the watchdog of non-Brahmin interests, changes began to come about in the distribution of power between castes.

Why did the non-Brahmins need a separate party and how far did the Justice Party represent their interests? The need for a separate party was made clear in the non-Brahmin Manifesto. The Brahmins had virtually monopolised some of the crucial advantages offered by British rule and the threat of a 'Brahmin oligarchy' must have appeared very real to many non-Brahmins. The latter, in spite of their enormous strength of numbers and their wealth (for most big *zamindars* were non-Brahmins), lacked organisation. The only existing party, the Congress, was virtually controlled by Brahmins. As the Manifesto pointed out,

... of the fifteen gentlemen elected from the Presidency to represent it on the All-India Congress Committee, with the exception of one solitary non-Brahmin Indian, all are practically Brahmins.[34]

It is small wonder then that the Justice Party met with such immediate response when it was formed.

However, although the Justice Party opposed the Brahmins and claimed to speak on behalf of the 40 million non-Brahmins of Madras Presidency, it would be a mistake to identify it with the interests of the non-Brahmins as a whole. First of all, the 40 million non-Brahmins on whose behalf the Party claimed to speak included Muslims as well as Harijans, and people belonging to three language groups, Tamil, Telugu and Malayalam. While it is true that in its broadest definition the non-Brahmins included all who were not Brahmins, in practice the Depressed Classes and the Muslims were generally considered separate. Even without these two communities, non-Brahmins were a very heterogeneous group. Moreover, those who led and organisationally controlled the non-Brahmin movement in its first phase were drawn from a very narrow social base. The Justice Party actually was an elite party dominated by urban, western-educated, landowning and professional people. It contained a formidable array of Rajas, *zamindars,* industrialists, lawyers and doctors. It was by no means a mass party and it is doubtful whether any serious effort was made to draw peasants and workers into its organisation.

I cannot do better here than to quote K. B. Krishna, himself a non-Brahmin:

This movement represents the emergence of the educated middle classes who are not Brahmins ... The non-Brahmin professional classes are no more champions of social justice than the Brahmin professional classes ... The non-Brahmin movement of Madras Presidency is no other than the movement of the later educated middle classes who happen to be non-Brahmins against the earlier educated middle classes who happened to be Brahmins.[35]

A more recent student has made a similar point:

The leadership, financially well endowed, was drawn almost exclusively from a socially stable element of the urban population. While Chetty, Nair, Mudaliar and the early leaders of the movement spoke of the illiterate non-Brahmin masses of Madras they in no way represented them ... With the franchise limited to but a few hundred thousand, the party made little attempt to aggregate support at any wider level. Its demands were formulated, not so much to attract a following, as to influence the official policy of the British in Madras Presidency.[36]

Though markedly elitist in character, the leadership of the Justice Party was heterogeneous in some ways. It was not a 'middle class' party for, besides professional people, there were in it landed and capitalist elements. It also included a fairly wide range of castes although most of the prominent people belonged to the upper crust of non-Brahmin castes such as Mudaliyars, Chettiyars and Vellalas among the Tamils, Rajus, Reddis and Naidus among the Telugus and Nairs among the Malayalis. In the Tamil districts some large non-Brahmin castes such as the Padayachis and the Kallas and particularly the artisan and servicing castes do not seem to have been very strongly represented.[37]

Two broad conclusions emerge from a consideration of the non-Brahmin movement. Firstly, it created alliances which cut across linguistic and cultural divisions. The significance of this in a society in which 'linguism' and 'regionalism' played such an important part only a short while later can hardly be over-emphasised. Secondly, the political arena in which Brahmins and non-Brahmins stood poised against each other was a very restricted one: the participants were drawn almost wholly from the urban, western-educated, landowning, business and professional classes.

It seems that little change took place in the distribution of power in the districts except in the towns. Non-Brahmin dominance in the organs of State and Municipal government began with the success of the Justice Party in the elections of 1920. Yet in the villages things appear to have remained unchanged for many more years. Brahmin dominated villages did not witness a transformation comparable to that taking place in the Provincial Legislature and Municipal bodies. In Sripuram (and presumably also in Kumbapettai and Thyagasamudram), the Brahmins continued to enjoy decisive dominance and to control the *panchayat* well into the forties. It was only after the introduction of adult franchise and particularly of *Panchayati Raj* that the tables were turned on the Brahmins. By this time the Justice Party had been almost forgotten and the non-Brahmin movement had acquired an entirely different character.

Yet it would be a mistake to minimise the role of the Justice Party and the non-Brahmin movement of the twenties. The Party not only prepared the ground for the induction of a new social strata into the political system but also created a distinctive idiom for South Indian politics. This idiom remained as a crucial element in the political process long after the Justice Party itself disintegrated. It permeated every kind of political organisation including the Congress Party.

The Justice Party was routed in the elections of 1936 and there after it was almost completely eclipsed. But this did not completely reverse the non-Brahmin ascendancy. It is true that the helm of Madras politics was taken over for some time by the two Brahmin Congressmen, C. Rajagopalachari and S. Satyamurti. But the non-Brahmins began increasingly to infiltrate the Congress and to acquire key positions within it. Several prominent Justicites joined the Congress after the defeat of their party. But the non-Brahmins had to wait for the First General Elections in Independent India for their control over the Congress to become complete.

The Non-Brahmin Movement was not merely narrowly political. From the late twenties onwards the Self-Respect Movement began to make concerted efforts to undermine the supremacy of the Brahmins in the ritual and social spheres. The movement was welcomed by the Justice Party although its immediate objectives were not political. It sought rather to create in non-Brahmins self-confidence and to liberate them from the ritual tyranny of the Brahmins. In the late twenties and early thirties it gained a measure of popular appeal under the leadership of the non-Brahmin ex-Congressman, E.V. Ramaswami Naicker. In 1944 Naicker created the Dravida Kazhagam and this association became the spearhead of militant anti-Brahminism in the South. Idols were desecrated, sacred books were burnt and some violence was practised against Brahmins. We have seen how during the mid-fifties the D.K. switched its support to the Congress which had by then come largely under non-Brahmin control.

The non-Brahmin ascendancy reached its peak in the mid-fifties. In recent years, with the consolidation of non-Brahmin power, internal cleavages have developed within it. These, an inherent feature of the caste structure, were partly overshadowed by a wider unity during the initial phase of the non-Brahmin movement. With the introduction of *Panchayati Raj* rifts amongst sub-castes have probably widened, particularly at the village and Block levels.

Today the category of non-Brahmins has therefore become too broad to remain analytically useful and it is now necessary to employ the concept of dominant caste. This concept was first used systematically by Srinivas. He has defined it in the following way:

> A caste may be said to be 'dominant' when it preponderates numerically over other castes, and when it also wields preponderant economic and political power. A large and powerful caste group can be more easily dominant if its position in the local caste hierarchy is not too low.[38]

Dominant castes have come to play an important part in every sphere of Tamil politics and today every dominant caste of any significance is non-Brahmin. Each of these castes enjoys a greater measure of unity than the non-Brahmins as a whole although most of the major ones are themselves subdivided.[39]

The major peasant castes are not evenly distributed throughout the State but have areas of concentration within it. Although there is no exact correspondence between these areas of concentration and the division of the state into districts, certain castes can be said to be dominant only in certain districts. Again, there are certain districts in which more than one caste is dominant and certain castes which are dominant in more than one district. Thus the Mudaliyars are dominant in Chingleput district, the Padayachis in North and South Arcot districts, the Thevars in Ramnad district, the Gaundas in Coimbatore district, the Vellalas in Tinnevelli district and the Nadars in parts of Madura district. In Tanjore district dominance is shared between the Kallas and the Vellalas.

Srinivas has enumerated a number of criteria on which dominance is said to be based.[40] In addition to the ones enumerated, geographical concentration may itself be seen as a criterion of dominance. Artisan castes are almost never dominant because they are territorially dispersed. A Peasant caste may be dominant, although small in size, provided it is concentrated within a limited area. A caste tends to enjoy a higher position in a village within the area of its dominance than outside. Thus the Kallas of Sripuram, although outnumbered by the Vellalas, enjoy great power in the villages in Kalla-dominated areas.

It is also probable that every State has its pattern of dominant castes. Tamilnad has a number of dominant castes, each concentrated in a particular area. (In this it appears to be different from Maharashtra where a single caste, the Maratha, enjoys dominance, or Mysore where dominance is shared between two castes, the Lingayat and the Okkaliga.)

The relationships between non-Brahmin dominant castes are important at every level of contemporary Tamil politics but particularly in villages. Where the non-Brahmins operate as a single unit, they do so generally in opposition to the Brahmins (and today, increasingly, to the Harijans). In the vast majority of Tamil villages there are either no Brahmins or only a few families of priestly Brahmins who are politically insignificant.[41] In non-*agraharam* villages (which constitute the overwhelming majority of villages in Tamilnad), the primary cleavages are often between two non-Brahmin castes or between two sub-castes of a single non-Brahmin caste. (The relationship between non-Brahmins and Harijans in such villages will be considered later.)

Fairly powerful associations began to emerge among certain non-Brahmin castes from the end of the last century. These associations addressed themselves to social reform within the caste and sought to secure a better position for the caste in the wider society. A good example is the Nadar Sangam in the southern districts which agitated successfully for the rights of temple entry for the Nadars. Such associations have occasionally provided useful bases for the mobilisation of political support. How this could be done was demonstrated effectively by the Vanniyakkula Kshatriya Sangam (a caste association), whose two principal branches transformed themselves into political parties (Tamilnad Toilers' Party and Commonweal Party), fought the 1952 elections and bargained with the Congress for positions in the State Cabinet.[42]

The Vanniyakkula Kshatriya Sangam appears to have remained politically inactive for a long time but was again revived on the eve of the 1967 elections. The southern district of Ramnad has been a stronghold of the Forward Bloc which is dominated by the Thevar caste and is generally referred to as the Thevar Party. This kind of association between a particular caste and a political party appears, however, to be exceptional rather than general. Caste interests — whatever their nature — are articulated more commonly through informal networks of interpersonal relations than through formally organised caste associations. A caste which is dominant in particular districts or *talukas* is likely to find strong representation in local bodies as well as in local units of the major political parties. This is so for two reasons. The dominant caste in a district or *taluka* is almost always a caste which enjoys numerical preponderance. Hence even if recruitment were made on a purely random basis, its representation would be high. But political recruitment is not made on a random basis. Ties of kinship and affinity and other personal ties play a very important part in this process at the local level where the syncretic unity of a caste or sub-caste is fairly strong. This unity tends to give additional weight to the representation of the dominant caste in local politics.

Thus *panchayats*, Panchayat Union Councils and local units of the Congress and D.M.K. parties are likely to be dominated in South Arcot district by Padayachis, in Coimbatore district by Gaundas and in large areas of Tanjore district by Kallas.

The dominant caste operates in the political process not only through networks of interpersonal relations but also through an idiom which has come to be accepted by almost every section of Tamil society. A feeling has grown among people that members of non-dominant castes cannot compete successfully with those of the dominant caste. Political parties act on the basis of this feeling and are often unprepared to take the risk of setting up candidates from the non-dominant castes. Out of this has emerged the familiar electoral pattern of matching caste with caste. Even in the absence of statistical data, there is little doubt that the feature is a very general one. Later I shall discuss in some detail the manner in which it has worked in a particular Assembly constituency.

In what way is caste utilised for the mobilisation of political support? At the village level, leaders of the dominant caste have direct ties of kinship and affinity with their caste-fellows. Such ties may also play an important part at the level of the Assembly constituency. But electioneering at that level also involves a more general appeal to caste sentiments. A typical example is the election slogan quoted earlier: the Vanniya vote is for Vanniyas alone.

The Vanniyas provide only an extreme example of what was a general pattern in the 1962 (and other) elections. Consistently, the chances of candidates were assessed in term of their caste affiliation. To take the example of the key constituency of Sattur where two dominant castes, the Nadars and the Thevars, rallied round the two principal candidates:

> The intensity of communal feelings is evident from the fact that people irrespective of political affiliation are openly discussing the polling of votes on a communal basis. In Sattur, an enthusiastic Nadar worker confessed that he was a D.M.K. follower, but because he belonged to the Nadar community he would vote for Mr. Kamaraj (a Nadar). Not a single Nadar vote, he added, would go to a non-Nadar.[43]

The Thiruvaiyar Assembly constituency in Tanjore district which I observed during the 1962 General Elections, is a Kalla area, with Kallas accounting for about 30 per cent of the total population. They have a strong feeling of identity in relation to outsiders and their local leaders have close contacts with influential Kallas in every village. In the 1962 elections three parties put up candidates for the Assembly seat, the Congress, the D.M.K. and the P.S.P. All three candidates were Kallas. Since 1952, when the First General Elections were held, only Kalla candidates have been successful at the polls. In 1952 the Congress put up an influential Muslim candidate but he was defeated by a Kalla. In 1957 the Congress changed its tactics, put up a Kalla candidate and won the seat. In 1962 the Congress again won the seat but with a different Kalla candidate. In 1967 the sitting member was defeated by a Kalla candidate put up by the D.M.K.

My first insight into Kalla politics was gained from a Kalla lawyer who had earlier contested the Thiruvaiyar seat. He began by saying that the much publicised unity of the Kallas was largely an illusion. This unity manifested itself only on certain occasions: in fact in relation to other non-Brahmins, the three closely related castes, Kalla, Marava and Ahamudiya, often acted as if they were one. But in the heart of the Kalla area there were deep rivalries between villages in which different groups of Kallas were dominant. Even a single village, he said, may be sharply divided between different lineages of the same Kalla sub-caste. Thus here again we see the operation of the segmentary principle.

VI

So far I have not considered the Harijans as an entity distinct from the non-Brahmins. As indicated earlier, a good deal of ambiguity attaches to the term 'non-Brahmin'. A more precise term would no doubt be preferable to it but for its historical association with important political movements and parties of South India.

The Manifesto of 1916 used the term non-Brahmin in its most inclusive sense, to cover not only Muslims and Christians but also the Depressed Classes. In his address to the Non-Brahmin Conference in July 1921, K.V. Reddi Naidu said,

> The great non-Brahmin movement transcended over caste, over religion and over the language .... It really transcended caste and religion, and there were assembled Mohammedans, Christians, Hindus and Panchamas.[44]

Other non-Brahmin leaders also made occasional references to the Depressed Classes and the need for ameliorating their conditions of life.

For all this, the separateness of the Depressed Classes remained a persistent feature of social and political life in Madras. They had hardly any representation in the leadership of the Justice Party — not very surprising in view of the limited social base of the Party. In the Memorandum presented to the Joint Parliamentary Committee in 1919 by the non-Brahmin delegation, the Depressed Classes were listed separately from the non-Brahmins in the Table showing the population analysis of Madras Presidency. Further, the separateness of the Depressed Classes was given implicit recognition in the Constitution of 1919 in which 5 seats were reserved for them, to be filled through nomination by the Governor.

It is difficult to say how far the policy of separate representation for the Depressed Classes adopted by the British fostered a sense of isolation among them as Gandhi had feared it would. But it seems clear that in the cleavage-ridden Tamil society and in the atmosphere of 'communal' politics, the Harijans could hardly fail to emphasise the special character of their social and political needs. But their political demands were to remain unorganised for a long time. During the first three decades of the present century organised politics was largely the prerogative of the Western-educated urban middle class and the representation of the Harijans in this class was negligible.

In Maharashtra the Harijans had found in Ambedkar a leader who within a short time could inculcate in them a degree of political consciousness. In Tamilnad this was on the whole absent. Though the British gave some protection to Harijan interests for a variety of reasons and in Madras there were also a few western-educated Harijan leaders,[45] the group had to await the extension of the franchise after Independence before their impact as a significant political force in Tamilnad, could be felt.

The issue of civic rights has played a major part in the politicisation of the Harijans in Tamilnad. Among the non-Brahmins politicisation was spearheaded by a western-educated urban middle class. Such a class did not exist among the Harijans in Tamilnad and perhaps does not exist even today. In their case it was more the ferment caused by the introduction (largely from outside) of liberal social values which contradicted the traditional interests of the dominant castes, thus creating the basis for organised political action. Traditionally Harijans had accepted their disabilities as a matter of course. As these disabilities came to be removed by law and as the Harijans sought to translate the new laws into practice, they came increasingly into conflict with the organised opposition of the dominant castes.

The disabilities which the Depressed Classes suffered with regard to the use of amenities such as wells, roads and temples or status symbols such as dress and ornaments, were generally more severe in Madras Presidency than elsewhere. Under the liberating influences of British rule and Gandhism the Harijans made attempts to do away with some of these disabilities. These attempts often met with reprisal from the dominant castes. In Tamilnad, Ramnad district has been a major arena of such conflict, and conflict has particularly been a pervasive feature of the relations between non-Brahmins and Harijans throughout the State during the last three decades.

Hutton provides a graphic account of conflicts between Kallas and Adi-Dravida (i.e. Harijans) in the 1930s:

In December 1930 the Kallas in Ramnad propounded eight prohibitions, the disregard of which led to the use of violence by the Kallas against the exterior castes, whose huts were fired, whose granary and property was destroyed and whose livestock was looted.[46]

Again,

> In June 1931, the eight prohibitions not having been satisfactorily observed by the exterior castes in question, the Kallas met together and framed eleven prohibitions, which went still further than the original eight, and an attempt to enforce these led to more violence.[47]

For all the stubborn opposition of the Kallas (and other non-Brahmin castes), the Harijans have forged rapidly ahead in their bid for civil equality. But their journey has not been easy; the price of every significant advance has been some violence. Today one can perceive everywhere a change of mood among them, particularly among those of the younger generation. In Tanjore district and elsewhere young Harijans acquired a taste for organised politics in the fifties when their support was mobilised by the Communists and the D.K. against the Brahmin landowners. Independence, and subsequently four General Elections have now made them sensitive to their political rights and today they are no longer in a mood to have their houses burnt or their property destroyed without retaliation.

Adult franchise has changed their political situation more radically then in the case of any other comparable section of Tamil society. Although fewer in number than the non-Brahmins, they account for no less than 18 per cent of the population of Tamilnad. Their situation in relation to the non-Brahmins is, therefore, rather different from that of the Brahmins who constitute only about 3 per cent of the total population. There are *talukas* in Tamilnad where Harijans are matched fairly evenly with non-Brahmins and not a few villages in which they outnumber them.

The Harijans also evince a high degree of unity. There are still many diacritical differences between them and the non-Brahmins and their internal solidarity in relation to the latter is often very strong. This internal solidarity derives from many factors of which I shall here consider only one. In the Tanjore-Trichy area (and elsewhere too, though perhaps less noticeably) their unique position in rural society is made clearly visible in the settlement pattern of the village. They live in separate streets (known by a separate term, *cheri*) which are generally at some distance from the main village; frequently they are situated in the midst of paddy fields at a distance of 3 to 4 furlongs from the village centre. Further, the layout of these *cheris* differs significantly from that of the main village, so that two *cheris* which are physically contiguous and form a single social unit may be attached to two revenue villages which are quite distinct from each other. These *cheris* are linked by social and political ties which often cut across the boundaries of the 'village' as this is perceived by non-Brahmins or Brahmins.[48]

Perhaps because of the physical isolation of the Harijans, traditional caste organisations seem to have survived to a greater extent among them than among other castes. At least in those areas of Tanjore district which I came to know directly, the traditional *kuttam* of the Pallas and their leaders, the *nattanmaikkarans,* still exercise a measure of authority, whereas similar institutions which once existed among some of the non-Brahmins are now no longer to be found. The existence of these traditional institutions often facilitates the mobilisation of support by Harijan leaders on a caste basis.

Along with numerical strength and organisation, the Harijans are also able to carry a certain measure of violence into political life. The role of organised violence in politics, particularly local politics, has not been sufficiently stressed in studies made in India so far. Yet the support of people with a reputation for violence is an important factor in village politics in contemporary India. In Tamilnad the Brahmins find the odds heavily against them in this regard. Nothing is more repugnant to the western-educated Brahmin than to be engaged in a village brawl with members of the lower castes. Such considerations of self-esteem do not deter the Harijan from confronting the non-Brahmins.

However, although the Harijans constitute important reservoirs of political power, there are many factors which stand in the way of this power being actualised. Their economic position is in general very weak and this weakness is frequently used against them by the non-Brahmins. A long tradition of servility often prevents them from asserting their rights, although young Harijans are rapidly developing a spirit of challenge. Finally, lack of education and contact with the outside world stands in the way of their developing some of the skills which are essential for organised politics.

When this spirit of challenge confronts the entrenched interests of the dominant castes, the result is often a measure of violence. In my research area, the Kallas constitute the dominant caste and they are widely feared for their violent ways. Their relations with the Harijans have been strained for some time. In the village *panchayat* of Sripuram, the Harijans have 5 members against 6 non-Brahmins and they generally have a submissive attitude towards the Kalla President of the *panchayat*; in fact, meetings of the *panchayat* are often held without the Harijan members being informed, and the latter are too weak to protest against this kind of irregularity. In the adjacent village of Ponavasal, however, things are very different: the Harijans are in a majority in the *panchayat* and the *panchayat* President is himself a Harijan.

In another neighbouring village also the *panchayat* President is a Harijan. In this village, known as Maharajapuram, hostilities between Harijans and Kallas led to the murder of a Kalla landowner, allegedly by or through the collusion of the Harijan President of the *panchayat*. Some of the Harijan residents of the village were arrested and the Kallas tried to storm the court room at Tanjore in order to assault them.[49]

Certain sections of the non-Brahmins are becoming resentful of the militant attitudes of the Harijans which, in their view, are fostered by the ruling party and the Government. For the poor and the landless non-Brahmins, the concessions to which the Harijans are entitled by law are a thorn in the flesh. For the landowners of the dominant caste, the rising demands of Harijan tenants and labourers are threats to their social and economic position. Clearly the dominant castes in the villages are not reconciled to the ideals of equality and social justice set by State and Central legislatures. These conflicts are likely to persist irrespective of changes in the party in power. And the party leaders in their turn cannot afford to ignore the demands of the Harijans who constitute such an important reservoir of votes.

Old conflicts between the Harijans and the non-Brahmins are sometimes expressed in the new idiom of party politics. Ramnad district became the centre of turmoil in 1957 when riots broke out between the Harijans and the Thevars (who are closely related to the Kallas discussed above). This time the issue was a bye-election in which the Harijans supported the Congress candidate against a Forward Bloc candidate set up by the Thevars. A young Harijan leader called Immanuel was murdered because he is said to have insulted the much-respected Thevar Forward Bloc leader, U. Muthuramalinga Thevar. The Thevars were put down with a heavy hand by the Government, allegedly because they had consistently opposed the Congress Party then in power.[50]

The politicisation of the Harijans has, in a sense, helped to sharpen their identity in relation to the upper castes. But it has also drawn them into new relationships which cut across the barriers of caste. Harijan and non-Brahmin leaders have learned to depend upon each other for support and patronage. New forms of association such as parties and *panchayats* are developing which are based on other loyalties than those of caste. It is true that such associations often mirror the cleavages of the wider society, but this is by no means always the case.

VII

I have described above the part played by social entities such as sub-castes, castes or caste-groups in Tamilnad politics. Although there are enormous differences between a sub-caste such as the Vadama Smarthas and a broad aggregate such as the non-Brahmins, they are similar in one important respect: they are both based on particularistic criteria and as such are to be distinguished from universalistic groupings of the kind which democratic parties and governments are in principle supposed to be. In a traditional system, it would be unreal to expect the democratic process to operate without taking any account of them. But are such particularistic identities the only ones which are relevant to politics in India today? And does not the political process itself create new identities which cut across those of sub-caste, caste or caste-group?

Although most scholars would agree that caste and politics are closely related in certain parts of contemporary India, their assessment of the significance of this is likely to vary. Some like Srinivas argue that the political process tends to strengthen the loyalties of caste at least in the short run: "One of the short-term effects of universal adult franchise is to strengthen caste."[51] Others like Gough believe that politics in the modern sense tends to be disruptive of caste.[52]

Before turning to these questions it is well to remember that there are everywhere in India today forces external to the political system which tend to erode the loyalties of caste. I shall consider briefly some of the factors which, on the one hand, weaken the diacritical and syncretic unity of caste, and, on the other, create interests based on income, occupation, education, etc. which tend increasingly to become dissociated from the structure of caste.

As status groups, castes are differentiated from one another by their tradition of distinctive styles of life.[53] Over the last hundred years new criteria of social differentiation have been introduced — western education, occupation in non-traditional sectors and so on. To the extent that the new forms of differentiation run along traditional grooves, caste loyalties tend to be reinforced. We saw how the introduction of western education at first served to increase the social differentiation between Brahmins and non-Brahmins, leading to political conflict between them. However, when these differentiations cut across traditional ones, castes become more heterogeneous in terms of income, occupation and education and new status groups based on these criteria are likely to compete with caste for people's loyalties.

It appears that caste is less crucial to one's status identification in urban as compared with rural areas. In the cities, Brahmins frequently work with non-Brahmins in the same profession, live in the same neighbourhoods and send their children to the same schools. The life styles of such people are likely to have more in common with one another than with their caste fellows in the rural areas, although it must at once be pointed out that traditional patterns of behaviour tend to show remarkable persistence in Tamilnad. Even though urban, western-educated professional Brahmins and non-Brahmins do share many common patterns of behaviour, they are mutually differentiated with regard to many others.

It is also probable that caste plays a less important part in urban than in rural politics. A recent study of trade union politics in Coimbatore tends to confirm the view that caste enters into the political process there in only a marginal way.[54] Among textile workers in Coimbatore, income, occupation and personal loyalties tend to play a far more important part in the determination of political attitudes than caste. The factory system tends to break down the homogeneity of caste and to replace it by unities of a different kind.

The political process seems to have a dual effect on caste. To the extent that the loyalties of caste or sub-caste are consistently exploited, the traditional structure tends to become frozen. Thus there can be little doubt that the non-Brahmin movement arrested to some extent the attenuation of caste identities. But the political process does not operate by mobilising only the loyalties of caste. To the extent that it leads to new associations and alliances cutting across caste, it loosens the traditional structure.

There are some who have gone even further and argued that the political process destroys irrevocably the very nature of caste. Leach raises the question, "If a caste group turns itself into a political faction does it then cease to be a caste?"[55] His clear affirmative answer to this is based on a peculiarly personal view:

People of different castes are, as it were, of different species — as cat
and dog ... But with members of different grades of the same caste, the
exact opposite is the case.[56]

Enough has been said earlier about the manner in which castes are
divided and subdivided to expose the futility of trying to impose a
radical opposition between 'different castes' and 'different grades
of the same caste'.

In Leach's view, competition for power is antithetical to the
very nature of caste and consequently wherever castes act "in
competition against like groups of different castes ... they are acting
in defiance of caste principles."[57] In a democratic system virtually
any kind of social identity may be used as a basis for mobilising
political support and it is difficult to deny that caste continues to
play a major part in this regard in Tamilnad today. It is equally
difficult to see how a particular mode of social grouping becomes
its very antithesis by the sole fact of engaging in competition with
groupings of a like order. To quote an earlier statement,

> The continuity of the politically organised castes of today with their
> forebears is not simply one of habits and tradition, but also one of
> personnel. Shall we say that as soon as people start talking about the
> 'Padayachi vote', the Padayachis cease to be a caste, and become its
> antithesis? What shall we call them then?[58]

Some others have drawn attention to the part played by caste in
political factions. Brass has characterised Indian politics as a politics
of factional bargains.[59] In many ways factional politics may be
contrasted with caste politics. A faction is generally mixed in its
caste composition and factional loyalties cut across caste. It happens
very rarely that groups which contend for power are homogeneous
in their caste composition. A political unit, if it is to be viable, has
generally to draw its support from a number of castes and not just
one. Conversely, a caste whose members enjoy social prominence
is likely to be divided by rival contenders for power. But even
when a caste is divided by factions, support within the faction may
still be partially drawn on the basis of caste. Faction leaders often
choose their inner circle from among persons who enjoy some
support in their respective castes. When two rival groups are similar
in their caste composition it does not follow that their leaders cease
to appeal to caste in their efforts to undercut each other's support.

There are various ways in which participation in organised
politics tends to alter the structure of caste. The processes by which
this comes about are now beginning to be investigated. Rudolph

and Rudolph have drawn attention to an important change which accompanies the emergence of caste associations. A caste association is no longer a birth status group in which membership is automatically ascribed at birth: membership in a caste association has to be acquired, although the base of recruitment may be restricted to a single caste or a group of castes.[60] Party programmes also may (and increasingly do) lead to splits within a caste and to alliances across castes.

Political alliances between castes and between castes and political parties tend to be rather unstable. Traditional groups which are in the same camp today may find themselves in opposite camps tomorrow. It is perhaps becoming less and less common for the same caste or sub-caste to identify itself persistently with a particular political party or movement over any significant length of time. And to the extent that a caste does not identify itself persistently with any particular party but tends to divide and subdivide and to enter into multifarious alliances across its boundaries, its very contours ultimately become blurred.

Politicians in Tamilnad have learned to manipulate caste in the furtherance of their interests. But politics is a dynamic phenomenon and the politician whose only skill is caste politics is likely to become obsolete. In this context what Dahl says of ethnic politics in the U.S.A. is particularly relevant. "In order to retain their positions, politicians are forced to search for new issues, new strategies, new coalitions."[61] This is in many ways as true of caste politics in India as of ethnic politics in the U.S.A.

The disruptive effects on caste of flexible and changing political arrangements must not be exaggerated. It is true that political parties tend to cut across caste but so do factions and, as Brass has rightly pointed out, factions are a feature of the traditional order.[62] Caste loyalties have persisted in spite of decades of factional politics and it is unlikely that party politics by itself will lead to their immediate dissolution. They are relatively persistent elements in the cultural idiom of Indian society in general and Tamil society in particular.

Parties, to the extent that they are responsible for the aggregation of interests, increasingly cut through the organisation of caste. Everywhere leaders of the dominant caste try to capture the major political parties and this is rarely if ever done on a basis of planned, mutual understanding. Parties in their turn try to create an appeal for every major group and not merely a single group. As Lipset has argued, "stable democracy requires a situation in which all the major political parties include supporters from many segments of the population".[63]

The relevance of Lipset's argument to Tamilnad politics can be illustrated with a brief consideration of the changing relations between the Brahmins and the D.M.K. When the D.M.K. started its career as a separate political party in 1949, its leaders were closely associated in the popular mind with anti-Brahminism. The party decided to start with a clean slate, declared itself against discrimination and even offered to accept Brahmins as members. The Brahmins remained for a long time suspicious of the new party and were not in any case much in sympathy with either its style or its policies. However, in 1962 the D.M.K. emerged as one of the strongest opposition parties in any State, and this it did only *after* it had come to terms with the Brahmins and shown itself prepared to treat them with consideration. In fact, in more than one constituency the D.M.K. owed its success to Brahmin support. In 1967 Brahmin support for the D.M.K. was, if anything, even more enthusiastic. Today the Brahmins' attitude towards the D.M.K. is very different from what it was in 1957 although even now not all of them are its ardent supporters. Even the Congress, which has in recent years alienated itself so much from the Brahmins, set up Brahmin candidates in certain constituencies and gathered Brahmin votes.

Today the political system is not unrelated to caste and class nor will it be so in the near future. But as it becomes more and more differentiated, new loci of power are developing and these are acquiring a weight of their own. In the past — at least at the local level — dominant caste and faction were probably the only significant loci of power, and the faction itself was largely structured by caste. This is no longer the case. Now it is possible for a man to acquire a certain measure of power by virtue of his position in the party hierarchy, irrespective of his caste or class. No doubt membership of the dominant caste helps a great deal, but other factors are also becoming important. A fuller understanding of politics in Tamilnad can be achieved only by considering the changing relations among the major sources of power, traditional and modern.

NOTES

1. Ralph W. Nicholas, 'Factions: Comparative Analysis', *Political Systems and the Distribution of Power*, A.S.A. Monographs 2, (London: Tavistock Publications; New York: Fredrick A. Praeger, 1965).
2. Paul R. Brass, *Factional Politics in an Indian State: The Congress Party in Uttar Pradesh*, (Berkeley and Los Angeles: University of California Press, 1965).
3. See Andre Beteille, *Caste, Class and Power: Changing Patterns of Stratification in a Tanjore Village*, (Berkeley and Los Angeles: University of California Press, 1965).
4. A slogan used by candidates of the Meena caste during the elections in Rajasthan illustrates the manner in which loyalties from one field are carried over into another: 'Do not give your daughter or your vote to anyone but a Meena'. Similar slogans have been widely used during elections in Tamilnad: *vanniyar vottu anniyirkku illai* (the Vanniya vote is not for anyone else).
5. Cf. M. N. Srinivas, *Caste in Modern India and Other Essays*, (Bombay, 1962), p. 5.
6. Andre Beteille, 'A Note on the Referents of Caste', *European Journal of Sociology*, V (1964), pp. 130-134.
7. S. F. Nadel, 'Dual Descent in the Nuba Hills', *African Systems of Kinship and Marriage*, ed. Radcliffe, Brown and Forde, (London, 1950), p. 337.
8. J. H. Hutton, *Caste in India*, Third Edition, Bombay, 1961, pp. 205-206.
9. See Andre Beteille, *Caste, Class and Power, op. cit.* especially Chapter 3.
10. Srinivas, *op. cit.* p. 5.
11. Beteille, *op. cit.*
12. Srinivas, *op. cit.* p. 5.
13. For the concept of merging series, see Jack Goody (ed.), *The Developmental Cycle in Domestic Groups*, Cambridge, 1958, p. 60.
14. Andre Beteille, *Caste, Class and Power, op. cit.* Chapter 3.
15. A very good example of this is provided by the Jats of Northern India.
16. See Andre Beteille, 'Race and Descent as Social Categories in India'. *Daedalus*, Spring 1967. We must recognise that a lineage itself is often internally segmented.
17. It is this which gives the politics of South India (including Maharashtra, but probably excluding Kerala) its distinctive character when compared with the politics of the north. The special position of the Harijans in the political system is acknowledged everywhere in India and is in fact sanctioned by Constitution.
18. The Brahmins in Tamilnad constitute between 3 and 4 per cent of the total population.
19. The non-Brahmin castes we have in mind are the Poondi Wandiyars,

the Kapisthalam Muppanars and the Ukkadai Thevars.

In Tanjore district, for example, which has the highest concentration of Brahmin landowners, the three biggest landowners prior to the fixation of ceilings were non-Brahmins. But the *proportion* of landowners among the Brahmins was much higher in Tanjore than among any non-Brahmin caste or caste group of comparable size (with the possible exception of the Mudaliyars). It is however probable that large or moderately large Brahmin landowners were concentrated primarily in the Tanjore-Trichy area and that few were to be found elsewhere.

20. Quoted in G. V. Subba Rao, *Life and Times of K. V. Reddi Naidu*, Rajahmundry, 1957, pp. 17-19. I am grateful to Miss G. Uma for having drawn my attention to this book and for having provided me with other interesting material on the non-Brahmin movement.

21. In 1937 when the Congress staged a come-back, C. Rajagopalachari, the veteran Brahmin leader, became Chief Minister of Madras and other Brahmins were appointed to the Ministry.

22. E. K. Gough, 'The Social Structure of a Tanjore Village' in *Village India* (ed. Marriott), Chicago, 1955; 'Caste in a Tanjore Village' in *Aspects of Caste in South India, Ceylon and North-West Pakistan* (ed. Leach), Cambridge, 1960; Dagfin Sivertsen, *When Caste Barriers Fall*, New York, 1963; Andre Beteille, *Caste, Class and Power, op. cit.*

23. Gough, 1955, p. 38.

24. This was written when the Congress was in power; it applies even more to the present situation.

25. Selig Harrison shows the tie-up between the Communists and the D.K. in his book, *India: The Most Dangerous Decade*, Oxford University Press, 1960, pp. 182-90.

26. Sivertsen, *op. cit.* p. 126.

27. Robert A. Dahl, *Who Governs?* New Haven, 1961.

28. Quoted in Subba Rao, *op. cit.* pp. 17-23.

29. *Ibid.* p. 30.

30. *Ibid.* pp. 30-39.

31. *Ibid.* p. 53.

32. Robert L. Hardgrave (Jr.), *The Dravidian Movement*, (Bombay: Popular Prakashan, 1965), p. 19.

33. *Ibid.* p. 21.

34. *Ibid.* P. 19.

35. K. B. Krishna, *The Problem of Minorities*, London, 1939, pp. 154-55.

36. Hardgrave, *op. cit.* p. 16.

37. A word about the territorial framework of the Justice Party and the non-Brahmin movement in South India. Boundaries between States have changed considerably over the last half a century and the Madras State of today is very different from the Madras Presidency of the twenties and thirties. The older unit was not only larger but culturally much more heterogeneous. It is difficult now to isolate the exact contribution of the Tamil-speaking people to the non-Brahmin

movement. But one must remember that a large number of the leaders of this movement were Telugu-speaking people who combined with their Tamil and Malayalam-speaking counterparts against the Brahmin elite which appears to have been predominantly, though not wholly, Tamilian.

38. M. N. Srinivas, 'The Social System of a Mysore Village' in *Village India* (ed. Marriott), Chicago, 1955, p. 18. See also M. N. Srinivas, 'The Dominant Caste in Rampura', *American Anthropologist*, Vol. 61, No. 1, 1959.

39. It has been said earlier that the non-Brahmins in Tamilnad constitute a congeries of castes. They include landowning and cultivating castes such as Vellala, Gaunda and Padayachi; trading castes such as Chetti; artisan castes such as Tachchan (Carpenter), Kollan (Blacksmith) and Tattan (Goldsmith); servicing castes such as Ambattan (Barber) and Vannan (Washerman); and a whole host of other specialist castes.

40. Srinivas, 1959; 1955.

41. In this sense, Kumbapettai, Thyagasamudram and Sripuram are exceptional rather than general.

42. Lloyd I. Rudolph and Susanne Hoeber Rudolph, 'The Political Role of India's Caste Associations', *Pacific Affairs*, Vol. XXXIII, No. 1, 1960, pp. 5-22.

43. *The Mail*, 13 Feb. 1962.

44. Subba Rao, *op. cit.* p. 107.

45. Notably M. C. Raja and Dewan Bahadur Srinivasan; the latter was chosen to represent his community at the Round Table Conference in 1930-32 along with Ambedkar.

46. Hutton, *op. cit.* p. 205.

47. *Ibid.* p. 205.

48. Beteille, *Caste, Class and Power, op. cit.*

49. *The Mail*, 9 June 1961.

50. This case was reported in detail in the September and October 1957 issues of *The Hindu*; see, in particular, the issues of September 15,16, and 22, 1957.

51. Srinivas, 1962, p. 75.

52. Gough, 1960, pp. 58-9.

53. Castes can best be viewed as status groups and as such they should be distinguished from classes. Max Weber, *The Religion of India*, Glencoe, 1958.

54. I am grateful to Mr. E. A. Ramaswami for the information on Coimbatore where he is making an intensive study of textile workers' unions.

55. E. R. Leach (ed.), *Aspects of Caste in South India, Ceylon and North-West Pakistan*, Cambridge,1960, p. 6.

56. *Ibid.* p. 7.

57. *Ibid.* p. 7.

58. Beteille, 1964, p. 133.

59. Brass, *op. cit.*

60. Rudolph and Rudolph, *op. cit.*
61. Dahl, *op. cit.* p. 34.
62. Brass, *op. cit.*
63. S. M. Lipset, *Political Man*, London, 1963, p. 31.

CHAPTER NINE

Caste and Political Mobilisation in a Gujarat District

ANIL BHATT

I

Forms of political mobilisation differ. They are shaped in particular by the perception of the actors, in a given situation, of the problems and values confronting them and the range and variance of the larger social reality within which the confrontation takes place. The case study we present here seeks to underline the factors that shaped the organisation and mobilisation of a local community in pre-Independence Gujarat and to show the extent to which support for the Independence Movement entailed not simply commitment to modern goals but also the involvement of antecedent social institutions in new problems and power conflicts, as well as the transformation of motivational and institutional bases of the local social structure. The study deals with little known background history of the national movement. It is the story of the role played by the Patidar Mandal, an association of the Patidar caste, in an important phase of the national movement that took place in Surat district.

The data for this research was collected during a larger study on 'Emerging Leadership at the District Level', sponsored by the Gandhian Institute of Studies, Varanasi.

The research was carried out under the close guidance of Rajni Kothari. I am also grateful to Ramashray Roy and D. L. Sheth for carefully going through the manuscript and making valuable suggestions. Special thanks are due to Shri Kunvarji Mehta, Shri Khushalbhai Patel and other leaders of the Patidar Yuvak Mandal but for whose frank and active cooperation the study would not have been possible.

In the late nineteenth century and early twentieth century men of public affairs in India were faced with a dilemma. The issues they faced related to basic social and political change. Some rejected the caste system altogether, whereas others wanted to revive the old system of the four *varnas* in place of a rigid hierarchy of multiple caste groups. There were a large number of social reformers who thought for their own different reasons that social reform should precede nationalist activity. They believed that without the enlightenment of the masses their organisation for political activity was not possible. If you really want self-government, they argued, you must show that you are fit for such responsibility. On the other side of the argument there were the ardent nationalists under the influence of Tilak, who believed that if political power came, social reform would either automatically follow or become easier to pursue. All efforts should be directed towards overthrowing the British rule. They said that it was impossible to carry out social reform activities under British rule because at every stage they would have to face officials who would never allow them to work freely. Secondly they argued that mere pursuance of social reform and criticism of the Hindu or Muslim social system would only strengthen the position of the alien government. Tilak thought that the English - educated reformers thought themselves to be learned and began to look contemptuously at past traditions. They lacked real self-knowledge and were playing into the hands of the Christian missionaries. Above all, the Tilak group feared that if they started social reform activities in any radical fashion, they would alienate large sections of the Hindu population whose support was necessary for the movement.

All these leaders were operating at the national level, and while they were trying to set the framework for the activities they had not brought themselves face to face with the realities obtaining at the base nor were they faced with the tasks of actual execution and day-to-day problem solving. Consequently their attempts to spread enlightenment percolated only to the already enlightened.

What follows here is a study of how local level leaders through a caste association organised support for the national movement in their district by combining various approaches and without alienating any section of the society. While these leaders took their inspiration from the national leaders, they addressed themselves to the actual tasks of execution by their own methods. They could demonstrate, by making their approach realistic and adaptable to the demands of the situation that there was no contradiction between social mobilisation and political mobilisation. On the contrary, with a proper approach, they may be complementary to each other. The leaders of the Patidar Mandal found quite early in their movement the need for taking along various groups with them in their effort to mobilise mass opinion, instilling awareness of the utility of political means for serving divergent needs, and developing wider categories of social organisation for effective political action. As this realisation grew, the perceptions of the leaders directing the activity took on a complex character and this shaped the Mandal's organisation and ideology.

In their task of organising public support for the national movement at the local level, the leaders confronted several problems. First of all they had to prepare the traditional leaders to relate their roles to the political movement, by supporting their caste reforms while at the same time driving home to them the utility of political means in achieving their goals. Secondly, they had to seek the approval of higher level leaders whose style and idiom were dominated by universalistic and secular symbols. They had also to gain recognition from the urbanised, high-caste sections of society. Since political activity in this period was confined to a small section of the English - educated urban elite, the efforts of these rural leaders towards a mass movement were often looked down upon or even ridiculed, by the former. It was therefore important, in the beginning, to win their recognition, and by a slow process to incorporate some of them into the new leadership and to make them see the utility of traditional society and loyalties for a broad-based political movement.

Working through their caste association, these rural-based leaders played the role of mediators between the universalistic values of the national leadership and the parochial orientations of the masses with whom they had to work, always addressing themselves to the task of solving concrete problems. In doing so, they developed a political style that was applicable to the existing structure of society, thereby making the structure responsive and adaptable to the demands of the national movement. Let us examine the case in some detail.

II

The Patidar Yuvak Mandal was formed in 1908 at the village Vanz of Surat district. Its main purpose was declared to be education and social reform among the peasant caste of Patidar in Surat district.

The Yuvak Mandal has been formed for spreading education among the Patidars, for social reforms, for abolishing harmful customs and traditions in the caste, for *mobilising and cultivating public opinion* and for protecting the interests of the farmers.[1]

The main founder of the Mandal was a young man in his early twenties, Kunvarjibhai V. Mehta, who belonged to the Leva sub-caste of the Patidars. His father Vithalbhai Mehta was a primary school teacher, a businessman and an agriculturist who was a recognised leader of his caste and also of his village. He was police patel from 1913 to 1920 and resigned from this position in response to the call of Gandhi during the 1921 movement. Thus Kunvarji Mehta had been socialised into public life from early childhood. He had been educated upto the 7th grade of the primary school. Even as a student he had displayed political leanings. The biography of Garibaldi had influenced him and the Russo-Japanese war had caught his imagination. In his leisure hours he used to play out the Russo-Japanese war with other children, he being always on the side of the Japanese.

His political activity distinctly started with the movement against the partition of Bengal in 1905-6 — known as the Bang-Bhang movement. During Bang-Bhang, activities like the boycott of British goods, nationalist education and revolutionary propaganda, bomb-making and the like influenced Kunvarji and he, in his individual capacity, started participating in them in his village.

In 1907, the All India Congress Committee held its session in Surat city. Kunvarji's political heroes at the time were the trio of Lala Lajpat Rai, Tilak and B. C. Pal. Kunvarji, who idealised them, was very eager to attend the session and see his idols. He collected six of his friends including his younger brother Kalyanjibhai Mehta, and went to Surat on foot from his village because of the group's shortage of funds. As is well known, at Surat the differences among Congressmen, between the 'extremists' and the 'moderates', sharply came out into the open. Tilak was the leader of the extremist group while the moderates were led by Pherozeshah Mehta. Kunvarji's hero was Tilak. The differences took a violent form, there was pandemonium at the session, and the extremist leaders had to be escorted out of the pandal. Kunvarji immediately assumed the position of a volunteer, escorted Tilak and other extremist leaders and attended their group meetings.

The whole incident stirred Kunvarji and motivated him into action. He started the Patidar Yuvak Mandal with seven young men of his village; two others from another part of the district were added later on. The Mandal was a caste organisation and its declared goal was the all-round development of the Patidars through reformist activities. The aim, as evident from the declared objective quoted above, was essentially political organisation.

Working in his individual capacity in the nationalist movement in 1905-6, Kunvarji had realised that such activity was not yielding any substantial gains as it tended to be fragmented and the colonial regime could easily crush it. (A Patidar nationalist had been arrested for such activities, condemned to life imprisonment, and deported to the Andaman Islands.) Kunvarji saw the need to mobilise a more organised front. This, however, could not be done openly through a formal political organisation. On the other hand, it was quite safe to engage in social activities in caste and other social organisations.

This was a period of social and religious reform in Gujarat. Various caste organisations had sprung up, mainly to promote education. Alongside this, the reformist movement of Arya Samaj was also gaining momentum in Surat district and Kunvarji and other public workers of the district were influenced by it. Being a man of considerable insight, Kunvarji could also see that a caste organisation was at once the most effective and the safest way of mobilising support for the national cause.

> Before 60 years from today, many young men were coloured by the nationalist ideas ... To kill or to get killed was their motto. Their activities were secret; one such rebel youth was Kunvarjibhai. But he soon realised that such activities would not yield results as they could not be done on a mass scale. So in order to create mass contact he, under the name of social reform activities, started mixing with the masses. He disguised himself in the form of a social reformer and started social reform activities.[2]

The Mandal's scope of activities covered all sub-castes of Patidars in all regions of Gujarat. In practice, however, for some time its activities were carried out mainly through the Leva sub-caste in two *talukas* — Choryasi and Bardoli — of Surat district.

From 1906 Kunvarji had joined the primary school at the village Vanz as a teacher. A little later his brother Kalyanjibhai Mehta also joined the school as a teacher. 1906 was the year when Tilak was given six years' term of imprisonment; Kunvarji called a meeting of the residents of surrounding villages. This was the first meeting that he had ever called and at which he strongly advocated the cause of 'Swadeshi'.

The Education Department came to know of Kunvarji's activities. There was an inquiry by the Deputy Education Inspector and he was transferred to village Varad of Bardoli *taluka* in Surat district. This is how he came into contact with Bardoli *taluka* which at a later stage became the main centre of his activity. Even before he joined his duties in Varad, he was already known as a rebel teacher. The headmaster of the school did not allow him to take his classes and the leader of the village, who was a leading Patidar of the area, a village headman and a strong and powerful person, asked him to quit Varad in twenty-four hours. Kunvarji put up a strong resistance to this and ultimately forced both the headmaster and the village leader to yield.

In the school he made students vow that they would not use foreign textile and would not eat foreign sugar. He would read nationalist papers before them and while giving his lessons in history draw an uncomplimentary image of England and Englishmen. He was a popular teacher.

> His hold on the children was immense. He put them in simple uniforms. He introduced among them community singing of the national songs, and photographs of national leaders decorated the school's walls.[3]

III

The period 1908 to 1915 formed the first phase of the activities of the Patidar Yuvak Mandal. During this phase three main activities were carried out: publication of caste journals, holding of caste conferences and establishment of a hostel for caste students. Although the participants in the movement shared a common perspective, their activities at this time lacked political articulation and remained sporadic. Also, because of the confusion in the nationalist movement, they were unable to establish close links with leaders at the higher level. Whatever they did was on their own and their efforts were primarily directed towards getting recognition and support from their own caste fellows.

In 1908, soon after the Patidar Yuvak Mandal was founded, Kunvarji started its mouthpiece, a caste journal called *Patidar*

Hitechhu. The journal, as we shall see, proved a useful and effective instrument for spreading his views and establishing communication with people. In the same year, Kunvarji came to know about Gandhi's activities in South Africa. Through Gandhi's weekly, *Indian Opinion*, Kunvarji, for the first time, came to know about 'satyagraha' His uncle, who was associated with Gandhi's activities and who had returned from South Africa, took a sympathetic view of Kunvarji's work and helped him in many ways. He acquainted Kunvarji with the ideas of satyagraha and non-violence. It is at this time that Kunvarji slowly came under the influence of Gandhian views. He collected a small sum of money for Gandhi's satyagraha fund and sent it to South Africa.

Along with political activities, he and his colleagues in the Mandal were trying for caste reform. Their exhortations, aimed at the removal of evil customs and traditions of their caste, were interspersed with nationalist ideas and appeals to boycott foreign goods. Kunvarji made it his daily routine to make rounds of nearby villages in the evening after the school was closed, call the people, and address them on the necessity of caste reforms and boycott of foreign goods. In case people did not attend his meetings, he would go round the houses, beating a metal plate as a gong, and persuade people to come to his meetings. At times of marriages in the caste, he would speak about the harm done by child marriage. Similarly he would attack the customary after-death dinner and characterise *ladus* (sweet balls) served there as *ladus* of blood. He also called for the removal of the custom of crying and breast-beating by women whenever there was a death. However, while he insisted that evil traditions be done away with, he at the same time used traditional arguments and evoked traditional sentiments among the people. He would, for example, say: "Do not eat sugar imported from other countries, because it is made of bones. Do not pollute your body by eating such sugar. You sin when you offer sweets to Gods prepared with such sugar."

Through the journal, *Patidar Hitechhu,* he was slowly building contacts with young and educated Patidars of other regions also. Some of them contributed articles to his journal and came to know about the activities of the Mandal. By 1909, Kunvarji had to resign as a teacher because of his transfer from Varad to another village for his anti-government activities. Probably he also had realised the impossiblity of pursuing his goals while he continued to be a government employee. He thereafter came to Baroda to edit a new journal which came into being through the merger of *Patidar*

Hitechhu and *Patel Bandhu,* the latter also a caste journal started by one Gordhanbhai Amin in 1908. For some time the new journal retained both the names, but later became simply *Patel Bandhu* — an instance of Kunvarji's accommodative style.

Although *Patel Bandhu* was a caste journal, its scope was wide and even non-Patidars contributed to it.

The objective of this monthly is not partisan, and subjects useful to all will be discussed here. It is also its objective that the Patidar class which is the integral part of the people in general may also benefit from it. Its focus is human life. With this purpose in view, social, religious, political, ethical and educational subjects will be discussed here. Occasionally literature will find place in it. Above all these, service of the country will be the principal subject.[4]

In 1910 the Patidar Yuvak Mandal called the first conference of Gujarat Patidars. Sardar P.V.Desai of Kaira district, a British title-holder, was invited to preside. The conference was to be held at Vanz, the headquarters of the P.Y.M. The venue of the conference was announced only towards the end out of fear that the village elders might create difficulties thinking it to be a naive attempt of young boys. When the elders came to know of it at the last moment they had to cooperate, willingly or unwillingly, since the success of the conference had become a matter of prestige for the village. Even those caste leaders who saw in the conference an attempt to challenge their leadership, attended it as the name of P.V.Desai had brought to it respectability. The tact and cautiousness of young Mandal workers had apparently paid dividends.

Once the caste leaders came to the conference, the Mandal leaders were anxious to get their backing and see that they did not have any cause to oppose their activities. They went all out to convince them that the conference did not seek to challenge their leadership. They also recognised the importance of caste leaders by coopting them on the reception committee. As a result the Mandal members succeeded in receiving and holding the support of traditional caste leaders.

The conference passed various resolutions. The first resolution declared allegiance of the Patidars to British rule. Referring to the murder of the British collector of Nasik by a Hindu, it criticised anarchist tendencies.[5] The expression of allegiance to British rule may seem anomalous inasmuch as the motivating force of Patidar movement was nationalism. But there were various factors at work. First, the Mandal leaders had to keep up a pro-British posture in an open gathering like the Patidar Parishad because they were not, at this stage, prepared to offer organised opposition to the government. The government officials at Surat were already suspicious of their activities, and the conference received wide press coverage. The President himself was a British title-holder. Secondly, it was the first conference and was organised by young workers. They were interested mainly in popularising their activities in other parts of Gujarat, bringing together the Patidars of Gujarat, and recruiting prospective workers for their cause. It is noteworthy that the conference requested the government to give representation to farmers in the legislative body; it also urged people to use Indian goods more and more.

Other resolutions underlined the necessity of abolishing certain harmful conventions, such as child marriage, the practice of taking dowry in marriage, after-death dinner and so on. In another resolution, the conference resolved to *integrate various segments and divisions of the Patidar caste*. Other resolutions emphasised the need to educate Patidar children, requested the government to make education compulsory, pleaded for an agricultural college in Gujarat, and resolved to start a Patidar boarding house.[6]

Three subsequent conferences were held, in 1913 at Mota in Surat, in 1914 at Surat city and in 1917 at Junagarh in Saurashtra. These conferences, like the first, discussed educational, economic, agricultural and political problems and reiterated the need for social reform. As in the first instance, a resolution expressing allegiance to British rule was coupled with an expressed interest in the activities of the Congress and *Swadeshi*. The leaders of P.Y.M. never missed a chance to invoke nationalist spirit and patriotic ideas. The 1917 conference, attended by about 8,000 persons, is significant in this respect. A committee under the chairmanship of Chandulal Behecharlal Patel, who was attracted to the Mandal through *Patel Bandhu* and had become one of its most active members, was appointed to enquire into the conditions of the farmers of Saurashtra. This committee, as far back as in 1916, when there was hardly any nationalist movement in Saurashtra, visited many princely states and published reports on the condition of farmers in various newspapers. Commenting on the role of the conference, one observer says:

This conference is a good example of the new spirit that has started flowing in Gujarat. Unlike other caste conferences it is not only a social institution but an institution encompassing social, political, economic and ethical activities. This is not merely a communal activity but embraces the whole of Gujarat .... In the public life of Gujarat the one thing that always pains us is that there is no way of bringing out the grievances of the people of the princely states. Neither there is any such institution nor even a newspaper. But we are glad to note that the Patidar Parishad is making some efforts in this direction.[7]

These conferences proved to be a very effective medium of communication between the Mandal and the people at large. Through them the Mandal leaders could increase their contacts and spread their ideas. Secondly, they provided a meeting ground to both the advanced and educated sections of the Patidar caste and the traditional caste leaders. Thirdly, they attempted to raise the status of the Patidars by emphasising adoption of modern practices in all spheres of life. Lastly, for the first time the symbol of *khedut* (peasant) to indicate the occupational identity of the Patidars was used in the 1917 conference. It was argued that all Patidars were peasants by occupation and the well-being of the peasants was therefore the well-being of the Patidars.

Simulataneously *Patel Bandhu* became very useful as a channel of communication. The articles and poems that appeared in the journal during this period were of a mixed quality: some praised the British government; others expressed nationalist ideas. In 1911, for example, a poem on the coronation of George V by Kunvarji's brother Kalyanji Mehta, prayed for the king's long life.[8] Another by Govindbhai Diwakar praised British rule and expressed the hope that Patidars would prosper under the British.[9] In 1913 again, the annual report of the journal declared that "each and every line of this magazine is meant to strengthen relations between the government and the people".[10]

At the same time articles emphasising past national glory, criticising British Raj, and describing the activities of nationalist leaders, also appeared in the journal. In its news sections, the activities of the Congress, Gandhi's work in South Africa and such other items were reported prominently and with a nationalist bias. When Gandhi came to India in 1915 his activities were closely followed and his views were explained and discussed. Poems depicting the cunning and cruelty of the Britishers, urging people to attend Congress sessions and imploring them to use Indian goods appeared in almost very issue. A section called 'Disha Darshan' (showing the direction), was started in which purely nationalist views were presented.[11]

This vacillation between pro-government and pro-nationalist postures was perhaps necessary. The conditions then obtaining in the society forced the leaders to move cautiously and build a viable support structure in order to give effect to their political ideas. This was so for two reasons. First, they did not want the authorities to come down upon them because of their outright opposition to the government. Secondly, the traditional caste leaders held effective power and it was necessary to win them away from British allegiance. Outspoken anti-British posture might, it was feared, antagonise the traditional caste leaders.

However, after the Kaira Satyagraha in 1917 the *Patel Bandhu* openly turned anti-British. Gandhi's photographs and complete accounts of the first Rajkiya Parishad (political conference) of Gujarat appeared in it. Speeches of Gandhi were given priority and prominence. Kunvarji wrote an editorial about the Kaira Satyagraha and openly criticised some Patidar landlords of Kaira who had sided with the British Government.[12] Till 1925 when the publication of *Patel Bandhu* stopped, it remained predominantly nationalist. Meanwhile the journal continued to be devoted to the task of educating Patidars. Articles about the importance of the Patidars in the society, the need for improving their status and prestige, for forging unity among not only the Patidars but all the farmers everywhere, continuously appeared in the journal. Information about social and political activities in India and abroad, stories and articles imparting patriotic, religious and ethical education, were published. Biographies of caste leaders, social reformers, patriots, saints and political leaders were also featured.

After 1911 the range of activities of the Patidar Yuvak Mandal and the Patidar Parishad, which primarily catered to the Patidar caste, had widened. In 1913 Kunvarji attended the All India Kurmi Parishad, which he considered to be a body of Patidars all over the country. The Mandal became a member of this all - India body. Its activities catered mainly to northern India and the Patidar Yuvak Mandal was the only association from western India to join it. Kunvarji arranged its 1914 session to be held at Ahmedabad. On being requested to preside over it he declined because he feared that his doing so might antagonise many educated and advanced Patidars of Gujarat. He was adamant and refused to hold any formal office; he wanted to work silently and promote others. On his suggestion Professor Swami Narayan presided over the conference. Many of the Mandal workers became secretaries of the Kurmi Kshatriya Sabha and its various committees. Apparently the Patidars were trying to identify themselves with other similar castes elsewhere in India and to forge unity on a broader plane. This desire was neatly expressed by Kalyanji Mehta who, writing in *Patel Bandhu*, asserted that all agricultural communities of India were Patidars and so there should be some organisation to bring them together. "Marathas of Maharashtra, Vokalingas of Mysore, Reddis of Andhra, Naidus of Madras, are all Patidars."[13]

It thus becomes clear that the activities of the Patidar Parishad gradually widened. Starting with the objective of bringing solidarity among Patidars and their various territorial segments in the Surat district, the Parishad slowly widened its scope so as to include the Patidars of Gujarat region, then the Patidars of Saurashtra, and eventually to include all agriculturists of India. The emphasis as can be seen had clearly shifted; from organising the Patidars as a caste group the Mandal sought to organise farmers as an occupational group. The parochial basis of organisation began to broaden out into a more secular identity.

We have noted earlier that the members of the Mandal were trying to start a hostel for Patidar students. They had realised that education could bring to their caste both enlightenment and status in society. They also believed that only under the impact of education their caste would be able to change obsolete social customs and imbibe the spirit of nationalism. In order to persuade their caste fellows to help in building a boarding house, they employed various tactics. Articles comparing the poor educational attainments of Surat Patidars with that of Patidars elsewhere in Gujarat and with that of other castes appeared in *Patel Bandhu*. It was also pointed out that the Brahmins' disrespect for Patidars was due mainly to the latter's educational backwardness.

Kunvarji in one of his articles entitled 'Religious Education and Need for a Boarding House' attempted to harness Patidars' religious sentiments to the cause of the boarding house. He wrote,

> In the government public high schools religious education is not imparted because students of different religions are studying there. There is a Muslim college in Aligarh and a Hindu college in Benares. There they impart religious education very successfully. We are not in a position to start a college; therefore we should start a boarding house in which religious and ethical education can be imparted. Such a boarding house has been started by our caste fellow Motibhai Amin in Kaira district.[14]

Nothing, however, came of these efforts till 1911. Meanwhile in Surat where Kunvarji had now opened a shop, he was keeping four Patidar students in his house and was running a miniature boarding house. In 1911 a boarding house, run by the Kadva Patidar

Association at Rander (near Surat) and open only to Kadva Patidar students, had to close down because of factional rivalries in the association. Seizing upon the opportunity, Kunvarji discussed with his partner the possibility of starting a students' hostel. Getting favourable response from the latter and an assurance of possible help from the Patidars of South Africa, Kunvarji collected necessary resources on credit and started at Surat, on November 13, 1911, a boarding house of the Patidar Yuvak Mandal with nine students. Kalyanji Mehta, then a teacher in the Surat High School, was made an honorary superintendent.

In starting this boarding house Kunvarji's ultimate objective was to educate students and prepare them for the nationalist struggle. From his experience as a teacher he had seen that it was easy to infuse young students with nationalist and reformist ideas. Also, he felt that if he had young students with him, it would be easier to get the support of their parents through them. Again he knew that if the Mandal could work through students, it would ensure non-interference by govenment officials who would be reluctant to arrest or do any harm to young students.

As an old student of the Ashram observes:

> The founders of this Ashram Kunvarji and Kalyanji were both primary school teachers, without English education and villagers; even then they saw dreams of social reform and national independence and relentlessly fought for them their whole life. To realise those dreams they started this Ashram and prepared the background for the national movement before Gandhi came to India.[15]

Within 15 days the strength of the Ashram[16] went up from 9 to 22. Kunvarji felt that the time had come when his other caste fellows should support his work. He prepared the first budget of the Ashram and called a meeting of the Patidars of Surat in November 1911. 12 workers of the Mandal and 28 caste leaders from 14 different villages attended the meeting. The first budget of Rs. 625 was passed and the caste leaders and other workers resolved to collect that amount from their respective villages. In addition, responding to an appeal for help the Patidars of the district living in South Africa formed, 'The Transvaal United Patidar Society' and donated about Rs. 3,000 to the Ashram fund.

The management of the Ashram, consisting of three members, Kunvarji, Kalyanji and Chandubhai Patel, took special care to create interest in the Ashram among the learned people of their caste.

They consulted Motibhai Narsinhbhai Amin, an educationist and social worker, and the organiser of a similar boarding house at Petlad in Kaira district. They also consulted two Brahmins, one a Sub-Registrar and the other a teacher with nationalist inclinations. Many Patidars, well placed in government service or pursuing other professions, together with traditional caste leaders were invited to visit the Ashram. In the very first year 18 such persons visited the place and Vithalbhai Patel, elder brother of Sardar Vallabhbhai Patel, was one of them. Vithalbhai later pleaded before Gandhi, Kunvarji's case for selecting Bardoli for Satyagraha. Through all this the Mandal was trying to get recognition from the advanced sections as well as the traditional leaders of their caste on the one hand and from the nationalist leaders on the other.

For the last forty years the Patidar Vidyarthi Ashram is open to students of all castes, but in the beginning only Patidar students were admitted. Unlike other caste hostels which admitted students from particular sub-castes of Patidars, such as the Kadva Boarding House at Rander, this Ashram admitted students from all sub-castes of the Patidars. It also abolished restrictions on inter-sub-caste dining. For instance, the Bhakta Patidars who would eat food cooked only by Bhakta[17] and the Matia Patidars with whom no other Patidar would dine[18] were made to eat together. This practice aroused great opposition against Kunvarji in the Bhakta and Leva Charotaria castes because they felt that he was polluting their children. Consequently there was a move to ostracise and out-caste Kunvarji.

In order to out-caste Kunvarji a meeting of the caste Panch was called. Kunvarji realised that in the event of his being out-casted, his effectiveness as a social reformer would come to an end. He had before him the examples of several social reformers who were ineffective because they had no foothold in society. In the caste meeting Kunvarji argued that by out-casting him they would be out-casting his father and the whole family which would not be fair inasmuch as they were not the offenders. Further he had already polluted certain sections of his caste. There were people in the meeting whose children had as inmates of the Ashram dined with the Matia students and who wanted to support Kunvarji because they were also fearful of the same treatment. Then there were people who had returned from South Africa and were not so orthodox. Thus in the meeting itself Kunvarji had certain sympathisers. These sympathisers convinced the other more adamant leaders of the unfairness of out-casting Kunvarji's father. Their suggestion was to out-caste Kunvarji alone. But Kunvarji did

Table Giving the Caste-Composition of the Students Studying in Patidar Vidyarthi Ashram (1911— 1960)

Year	Patidars				Non-Patidars				Total
	Matia	Bhakta	Other Patidars	Total Patidars	Scheduled Tribes	Scheduled Castes	Other Non-Patidars	Total Non-Patidars	
1911	15	—	8	23	—	—	—	—	23
1912	13	—	21	34	—	—	—	—	34
1913	16	—	44	60	—	—	2	2	62
1914	13	—	30	43	—	—	1	1	44
1915	8	—	24	32	—	—	2	2	34
*1916-1935	NA	NA	NA	NA	NA	NA	NA	NA	NA
1935	9	6	16	31	—	—	21	21	52
1936	12	7	29	48	—	—	22	22	70
1937	15	11	35	61	—	—	28	28	89
1938	17	12	51	80	—	—	21	21	101
1939	18	8	47	73	1	—	24	25	98
1940	28	3	51	87	1	—	32	33	120
1941	36	4	51	68	1	—	36	37	105
1942	42	8	40	90	1	—	29	30	120
*1943	—	—	—	—	—	1	—	1	—
1944	46	6	40	92	—	2	30	32	124
1945	47	12	32	91	—	2	30	33	124
1946	48	15	31	94	1	—	44	45	139
1947	23	9	36	68	1	—	36	38	106
1948	17	11	37	65	1	—	36	38	103
1949	27	8	42	77	1	1	31	35	112
1950	21	6	33	60	—	—	23	24	84

In 1932 the Patidar Vidyarthi Ashram was raided and sealed by the government for its nationalist activities. Its charge was not handed back to the management till 1935. All its documents were seized and destroyed. The documents containing figures from 1916 to 1935 have also been destroyed and the figures from 1916 to 1935 are not available here.

not want to get formally out-casted because even his sympathisers
then would hesitate to mix with him, and his coming back into the
caste-fold would become difficult as it would require another formal
decision in the caste meeting.[19] He, therefore, argued that his out-
casting would in reality be inconsequential as all the dealings with
the caste were carried out under his father's name. How are they
going to write off his, Kunvarji's, name from the books of the caste
records when it did not exist there? Instead, he suggested that he
himself would not attend their social functions if they so desired.
To this the caste leaders agreed. After that he would go to attend
the social functions but would sit and dine separately in the outer
portions of the house and would clean his dish himself after dining.
However, he went on helping them in their personal and social
problems and thus created sympathy for him among his caste
people. Some of them felt that it was not fair to treat such a helpful
person as an untouchable. The bolder among them accepted
Kunvarji as their caste fellow which was not difficult since he was
not formally expelled. Once he was accepted by some, others also
followed suit and Kunvarji not only staged a come-back, but in
doing so avoided tension, thus safeguarding the solidarity of the
caste.

Starting initially as an exclusively Patidar caste hostel, the Ashram
opened its door to students from other castes in 1913 (see Table).
The management changed the rules, admitted first ten per cent
non-Patidar students, and subsequently increased this to 15 per
cent and then to 20 percent. From 1921 onwards even this limit
was abolished. As the table shows, even Scheduled Tribe and
Scheduled Caste students were permitted to join the Ashram. Thus,
the management, without antagonising the caste leaders, tactfully
and gradually gave it a secular character. In the beginning the
management took care in admitting only those students whose
parents did not have objection to their social and political activities.
For instance, students whose parents were in South Africa and who
were helping Gandhi in his satyagraha were admitted because they
were less orthodox. Also, it will be noted that throughout the number
of Leva and Matia students, with whose families these leaders had
greater contact, was greater. Again, the table shows that for the first
few years Charotaria and Bhakta students did not join the institution.
However, the management was anxious to get the support of these
castes and gradually they and the Patidar leaders won over the
more conservative parents and pro-British caste leaders.

The management utilised every opportunity to induce caste

people to take active interest in the Ashram's affairs. To this end
they took advantage of the ceremonial, religious and other similar
occasions. In the process they changed some old customs and
traditions and started a few new ones. Also, the Mandal workers
while campaigning in villages for funds for the Ashram, contacted
caste leaders and persuaded them by various methods to contribute
to the Ashram. In one village in Mahuva *taluka,* for instance, the
following resolutions were passed to help build up the fund:

1. Every farmer should give 4 annas per bale of cotton at the time of
   the harvest, 10 seers of jawar at the time of the harvest of jawar, 10
   seers of rice at the time of the harvest of paddy.
2. At the time of marriage ceremony unnecessary expenses should be
   avoided and instead the bride's family should contribute 8 annas
   and the bridegroom's family should give 1 rupee.
3. After-death dinner should be abolished and instead Rs. 2 should be
   contributed towards the Ashram Fund.[20]

Life at the Ashram was well organised. Classes of various types
were held and speakers from Surat city were invited to speak to the
students. Stress was placed on physical training and ethical
education, and religious and mythological stories were narrated to
make the students aware of India's glorious past. They were also
kept informed about contemporary nationalist activities and
biographies of great Indians of the past and the present were read
out to them. Along with these curricular activities students were
given training in social welfare activities and public service. From
the beginning, an attempt was made to build up a tradition of
working among the poor, the needy and the sick and render
concrete help to them. For instance it was resolved by the students
that they would not take milk once a month and would donate the
savings to the institution for the welfare of the poor. Some of them
contributed towards the expenses of poor students in the Ashram.
In 1912 the students formed a Seva Samaj in which each of its
members was supposed to contribute half an anna every month.
The collection provided poor students with books.

The students were also given some training in organisation and
were sent outside to help in caste conferences. In the last three
Patidar Parishads the students worked as volunteers and presented
cultural programmes. In 1913 when the All India Kurmi Parishad
was held at Ahmedabad, 30 students from the Ashram were sent as
volunteers. In the second Patidar Parishad at Mota in Bardoli *taluka,*
the students impressed the people with their work. So much so

that the Baleshri Panch[21] and the Patidars of Mota village contributed money to poor students' fund of the Ashram.

The Mandal also tried to involve other non-Patidars in their activities and sought their help and guidance. For instance they sent their workers to broader secular organisations. In 1913, Bhikshu Akhandanand, a saint and social worker, started publishing religious and ethical literature in simple language for mass consumption through his organisation Sastu Sahitya Vardhak Karyalaya at Ahmedabad. In 1914 he visited the Ashram and came to know that Kalyanji Mehta had a working knowledge of Bengali, Hindi and Marathi. The Bhikshu sought his help in translation. The P.Y.M. immediately agreed and Kalyanji was released from his responsibility as the Ashram Superintendent. Amritlal V. Thakkar, the first member of the Servants of India Society from Gujarat and an eminent social worker, observed:

> Patidar Yuvak Mandal deserves congratulations for sending workers to the wider sector of public service from the narrow sector of the caste activity. It was my belief that those who are involved in doing service for their caste cannot go to the wider field of public service. The Patidar Yuvak Mandal has corrected my mistake.[22]

In the realm of social reforms the Mandal continued to be active. The members would not miss a single opportunity of urging people to give up traditional practices. They would attend, and propagate their ideas in every caste meeting, marriage ceremony and after-death dinner. They appointed a paid worker known as 'Updeshak' to go from village to village and give lectures on social reforms.

The organisational work was also continued and many caste associations were formed. During 1911-1916, the members of the Mandal helped in starting eight Patidar youth organisations in different parts of the district. They also encouraged other sub-castes among the Patidars to start district-wide organisations. Keshavji Patel, a Kadva Patidar primary school teacher, who from 1917 onwards became Kunvarji's closest colleague, started a Kadva Patidar Seva Mandal with the help and guidance of Kunvarji. The Surat Patidar Samaj was similarly inspired by Kunvarji and the Patel Bandhu Sorath Samaj at Saurashtra by Kalyanji. By 1915 there were five such organisations of Patidars in Gujarat out of which three were in Surat alone.

In their reformist activities the Mandal proceeded slowly and step by step in order to avoid reaction from the orthodox caste fellows. For instance, if they wanted to abolish dinner after death, they would persuade the family concerned to reduce the number of dinners from three to two. They would request some other family to hold only one caste dinner. After some time they could almost abolish the practice of after-death dinner. Kunvarji especially was most tactful and careful. He would go to attend child marriages, help the family concerned in various ways, but would not participate in the marriage feast and go on preaching against child marriage. Unlike radical social reformers, he took great care not to hurt the feelings of the caste leaders. He would give them all due respect and would never pose as a social reformer. For example, the original name of the Kadva Seva Samaj, was 'Kadva Samaj Sudharak Mandal'. Kunvarji asked its members to change the name saying that they should not pose as reformers. Who were they, he asked, to reform the society? They could only serve it. If they used such a name, traditional leaders would be startled and might not give their support. So the name was changed to Kadva Seva Mandal.

While engaged in these activities, workers of the Mandal would also emphasise the past glory of Patidars, of farmers, of Hindus, of India, and generally of oriental countries. In addition they also engaged in critical self-appraisal. In their articles in *Patel Bandhu* and in their lectures they compared Patidars with Brahmins, Jains and Parsis, Indians with British and so on. They would say, "how patriotic the British people are. They search for British goods and use them even when they are in India"; or "how backward the Patidars are in education, in comparison to Brahmins?" Thirdly, they attempted to sanskritise Patidars in order to raise their social status, using as their frame of reference Brahminic practices. For instance, the leaders urged the Patidar women to observe four days' pollution period during menstruation like Brahmins; they argued that Brahmins considered the Patidars 'Shudras' because of the absence of this ritual.[23]

The Mandal advocated Vedic rituals for marriage ceremonies as prevalent in higher castes. They encountered opposition from the Brahmins in this. One Brahmin protested on the ground that Patidars were Shudras. Kunvarji, challenging this contention, asserted that it could be proved that Patidars were Kshatriyas and not Shudras.[24] He even performed thread ceremony in the Ashram and students were made to wear the Brahma Sutra — a privilege of Brahmins only. Like Brahmins, students were made to recite Sanskrit *slokas*.

Early in the twentieth century, the Patidars in Gujarat were popularly known as 'Kunbis' and 'Bhabhas', names indicating the rural and backward character of the caste. The word Patidar was hardly used in Surat district. Even in the school register their caste was entered as 'Kunbis'. It was mainly the Mandal which popularised the word Patidar in the district.

Thus the first phase of the activities of the P.Y.M. laid the ground for the recruitment of parochial elements into the national movement. During this period forces which later led to active political mobilisation were being slowly shaped and strengthened through social reform. Caste practices and rituals in the process acquired new orientations, thus making traditional social structure more receptive to new patterns of behaviour. Through the *Patel Bandhu* and through lectures and tours, some awareness, enlightenment and degree of secular identity with the nation was also spread. The caste conferences helped to build up contacts, solidarity and recruitment, and involved more and more people in the activities of the Mandal. The proliferation of caste associations provided an organisational network. They employed generally acceptable methods to meet quite new situations which on the face of it seemed anomalous, but which later on helped the nationalist ideology to take root, and mobilised the resurgence of traditional values in favour of new ideas and practices. If they emphasised the great past of India to create confidence in the people, they also urged the people to follow good British practices and imbibe their dynamism. Again, the ideas of inter-caste integration as well as inter-caste competition were introduced simultaneously. Lastly, adoption of Brahminic practices and the higher status of Patidars in the *varna* scheme were preached along with modern education and modern politics.

IV

The appearance of Gandhi on the Indian political scene marked the beginning of the second phase of the Mandal. Till then the Mandal leaders were on their own and were unable to establish links with higher-level leadership. Tilak was their hero, but the Tilak group had no organisational contact with the lower levels, least of all in Gujarat. Because of its typical approach towards the traditional social institutions, the Mandal's efforts to get recognition from the urban leadership through the Home Rule League also failed. And yet, by themselves, they were unable to launch a well organised movement in the absence of a national programme. When Gandhi returned to India, and began to give to the national movement an altogether new orientation, the Mandal leaders found the Gandhian approach congenial.

They realised that Gandhiji was the only militant leader at the time, and that he offered a healthy contrast to the earlier no-action national leadership.[25]

Very soon after his entry into Indian politics, Gandhi succeeded in creating an organisational network which percolated to the lower tiers of society. Through his intermediaries like Sardar Patel the activities of organisations like the Mandal also received recognition and legitimacy at the higher level. Gandhi gave them a well articulated programme which they could implement. Most of all, in Gandhi's leadership they found a strong link at the top which they did not have previously.

Kunvarji had come under the Gandhian influence in 1910. He continuously kept himself informed about Gandhi's activities in South Africa, and wrote letters to Gandhi informing him about the activities of the Mandal. He had also requested him to visit the Ashram. The Mandal collected funds for Gandhi's satyagraha in South Africa and the students of the Ashram had observed fasts and donated savings to the fund. In 1915 when Gandhi came to India, Kunvarji went to Bombay to receive him and reminded him of his invitation. In 1916 Gandhi came to visit the Ashram. Before that Kunvarji persuaded some caste leaders and the Mandal to pass a resolution expressing their happiness in receiving him in the Ashram. Kunvarji tried to associate as many caste leaders as possible in the reception for Gandhi. He thought that once they were involved in nationalist activities, there would be no turning back. He therefore asked one caste leader of Bardoli *taluka* to garland Gandhi when he came. Gandhi was very much impressed by the Ashram and the activities of the Mandal. He said:

> I had respect for Patidar Yuvak Mandal while I was in Africa. Many people told me there that when I would come to India the Mandal would surely give me support in my work even if others did not. In South Africa Patidars helped me much. I shall see how they help me here when time comes.[26]

From 1917 onwards the activities of the Mandal took a distinct political turn. Caste reform was thrown into the background for a while and politics came to the fore. In 1917, a satyagraha in Kaira district against the government's refusal to postpone the collection of land revenue took place. Kalyanji Mehta was asked to be a member of the Inquiry Committee appointed by Gandhi to examine the case of the farmers before starting the satyagraha; later he joined the satyagraha. Now the Mandal openly took an anti-British and nationalist stand. *Patel Bandhu* also became openly nationalist, giving unreserved support to the Kaira satyagraha. In the Ashram too propagation of nationalist ideas and training in public service were given more importance now. Political leaders were invited to address and meet students whenever they came to Surat. Local Home Rule Leaguers were also invited to the Ashram.

Social service, of course, was not altogether dropped. In 1918, for example, the Patidar Yuvak Mandal formed a 'Mitra Mandal' for distributing free medicines to the people during an influenza epidemic. Kalyanji Mehta became its secretary and many other members of the Mandal joined it as members. The students of the Ashram also volunteered to go to various villages in the district and distribute medicine. The Mitra Mandal faced a difficult task because, for lack of resources, it had to distribute indigenous Ayurvedic medicine. 'Backward' social groups and the tribals in the district refused to take the medicine because they believed the epidemic to be God's punishment for their sins, while the educated ones had no trust in Ayurvedic medicine. Through his patient and pragmatic approach, however, Kalyanji Mehta succeeded in persuading the tribals to take the medicine. The problem was also partly solved with help from the Social Service League of Bombay which gave free medicines worth Rs. 8,000. More than 150 centres were opened for distribution of medicines in 13 *talukas* of the district. Medicines were distributed to more than 10,000 people. A few centres were also started in Baroda and Broach districts and in Saurashtra. The financial help also came from certain businessmen and other individuals of Bombay. The members of the Mandal, the alumni and students of the Ashram carried out their work on a large scale and with great drive, especially in Choryasi, Bardoli and Mandvi *talukas* where they started 9, 41 and 66 centres respectively.[27]

The work done during this epidemic proved to be very beneficial to the Mandal. They could effectively reply to the critics by showing that their work was not limited to the narrow field of caste only, that caste activity and secular social welfare activity were not incompatible. Further, this work enabled them to penetrate into the as yet secluded population of the tribals. The respect which they won from the tribals enabled them to mobilise the tribals during later satyagrahas. Finally, it brought to them the admiration of the urban people living in Surat, Ahmedabad and Bombay.

In 1919, Gandhi advocated satyagraha against the Rowlatt Committee's recommendations which were made into law in February 1919.[28] Dayalji Desai — an Anavil nationalist leader of the district — took up the challenge in Surat district. He had founded in 1906 a caste boarding house called 'Anavil Vidyarthi Ashram'. Like the Patidar Vidyarthi Ashram, it admitted all caste students. Both these Ashrams were considered sister institutions and Dayalji Desai, the Superintendent of the Anavil Vidyarthi Ashram, and Kalyanji Mehta worked in close collaboration: the pair were popularly known as 'Dalu-Kalu'. The broader national cause gave these two organisations — one a Brahmin high caste organisation and the other a lower middle caste organisation — a common platform and brought them close together.

The first to join Dayalji Desai was Kalyanji. They formed a 'Satyagraha Sabha'. Dayalji, Kalyanji and two others took an oath to start satyagraha against the Rowlatt Act. The urban elements in the Home Rule League were reluctant to join the satyagraha and it was only after a good deal of persuasion that Dayalji could convince its president to join the movement. These five leaders, adorned by a special satyagraha uniform, led a big procession in which students of both the Ashrams joined. Meetings were held and strong speeches were made by Kalyanji Mehta and by Dayalji whose loud and commanding voice, with which he was able to address a crowd of 10,000 without a microphone, became famous in the city and came to be known as a 'lion's roar'. During all such meetings a couple of students of the Patidar Ashram used to sing patriotic songs written by Kalyanji. In a very short time the students of the two ashrams and their superintendents became a legend in the town.

While Kalyanji was busy with the satyagraha, two senior students of the Ashram looked after the affairs of the Ashram. In 1918 an article describing children's self-management in an American village appeared in *Patel Bandhu*. This inspired the management of the Ashram in 1918 to start similar experiments in the Ashram. The idea was to train the students in self-government which might prove useful in the future. The system, called 'Vidyarthi Swarajya' still continues.

This experiment in self-government deserves a brief description. The concepts of parliamentary government were imitated in many of their essentials. 'Vidyarthi Swarajya' had two bodies, a legislature and a cabinet. The legislature consisted of 13 members elected through secret ballot by all the students of the Ashram studying in and above the third division of the secondary school and above the age of fifteen. Two members of the legislature were nominated by the cabinet. The cabinet elected by the legislature consisted of five ministers out of which one Prime Minister was to be elected every month. There were five ministries — Finance, Education, Health and Sanitation, Agriculture, and Order and Discipline. Each Ministry had an administrative staff. Sessions of the Legislature, which also had a Speaker and Deputy Speaker, were held once a month. Each resolution, before it could become an Act, had to pass through two readings, and if supported by less than a two-thirds majority, had to go through a third reading. Questions were asked with previous notice and supplementaries were allowed. There were neat and clear divisions of power between the cabinet, the secretariat and a one-man judiciary. The functions and powers of the legislature and each Ministry were well defined.[29]

All this was very carefully and studiously worked out. It was not simply a mock performance but was put into practice. Vidyarthi Swarajya not only managed the internal affairs of the Ashram, but introduced the students to democratic norms and to the procedures of a parliamentary system of government.

By 1919, Gandhi decided to launch a non-cooperation movement. In 1920, at the Calcutta session of the Congress, he moved his famous resolution of non-cooperation aiming a 'four point programme' to the nation — wearing of khadi, abstinence in regard to intoxicating drinks, boycott of government schools and colleges and boycott of law courts — he affirmed that if the country followed his programme, independence could be achieved in a year.

Kunvarji attended the Calcutta session of the Congress. Gordhanbhai Patel has graphically described Kunvarji's presence at the session:

> Among thousands that flocked to the session, there was a silent spectator among delegates, lured thither all the way from Gujarat by a patriotic impulse. He knew no English and English was then the language of the Congress. But he heard Gandhi say something which was received with tumultuous applause by those who understood it. He asked his neighbour Dayalji Desai what it was that they applauded and learnt that Gandhiji had said that if his programme was sincerely carried out, Swaraj would be realised within a year. Well, if nobody else took the speaker at his word, he did. This man is Kunvarji Mehta, the real maker of Bardoli. Kunvarji wrote in his diary that he would give up his business and whether or not the country followed Gandhiji's programme, he would implement the resolution in Bardoli *taluka*. He resolved to hoist the flag of independence in Bardoli on Gandhi's birth date next year.[30]

After coming back from the session, Kunvarji convened a meeting of the Mandal in September 1920, and suggested that it should officially declare its intention to participate in the non-cooperation movement. Following his advice, the working committee of the Mandal adopted the following resolution:

The special session of the Congress at Calcutta has decided not to co-operate with the government, till India becomes independent. For the prestige and interest of the country, it is a clear duty of the Patidar caste as a part of the Indian nation to respond to the call. So this meeting resolves that the members of the Mandal should:

(1) persuade voters not to elect any representatives to the Provincial and Central legislatures ;
(2) persuade people not to take help of the law courts for solving their internal quarrels;
(3) request Patidar lawyers to close their practices;
(4) request students, parents and teachers to boycott the government schools or schools taking any help from the government;
(5) urge people to wear hand woven clothes, make efforts to increase the production of such cloth and persuade people to take oath to use only Indian goods;
(6) persuade the Patidars to reject the titles given to them by the British government and resign from their membership in the local bodies to which they have been nominated;
(7) persuade people not to attend any meetings and functions held by the government or its officials;
(8) provide ashram accommodation only to those students who were not studying in government schools or schools receiving government aid or under government supervision;
(9) allow the Rashtriya Kelavani Mandal to utilise the Ashram building for running the national school to be started in Surat;
(10) abolish the previous rule which admitted 20 per cent of non-Patidar students in the Ashram and admit students of all castes without any limit and restriction.[31]

Although its members were engaged in nationalist activities individually, hitherto the Mandal had refrained from directly participating in nationalist and political activities. The above resolution opened the way for it to take part in the national movement formally.

Kunvarji and his whole family now plunged into the movement. His father resigned his post as a police patel of his village and started moving in Bardoli *taluka* to mobilise support of other caste people of Bardoli. Kunvarji's brother, Kalyanji, along with Dayalji

Desai, the Anavil leader, and others started campaigning for municipal elections for Surat city. At the same time Kunvarji along with his colleagues of the Mandal started implementing Gandhi's four point programme in Bardoli *taluka*. The students of the Patidar Vidyarthi Ashram and the neighbouring Anavil Vidyarthi Ashram left government schools and joined the schools run by the Rashtriya Kelavani Mandal.[32]

A Taluka Samiti under the presidentship of Kunvarji was established at Bardoli. Kunvarji collected around him a band of about 40 active workers. The group included 20 old students who, while they were in the Ashram, had been trained and prepared for these activities, and had by then become leading and influential persons in their villages. There was an equal number of caste leaders and colleagues of the Mandal. Besides, Kunvarji enlisted the support of other caste leaders and many other Patidars who had returned from South Africa and were acquainted with Gandhi's activities there. Thus by 1921 he had already established a network of contacts through the Ashram, Patidar Conferences, *Patel Bandhu* and his other activities. The band of these workers, all from rural areas and most of them Patidars, moved from village to village, opened schools, persuaded government teachers to resign from government jobs and join their schools, propagated use of 'khadi' and abstinence, appealed to the people of Bardoli to withdraw their court suits and settle their disputes by compromise and arbitration. The cumulative effect of all this was profound. Hundreds of people resolved to wear khadi and not to touch liquor. All government primary schools and many wine shops had to be closed down.

The group was not idealistic in any dogmatic sense and its appeal was based on concrete programmes. For instance they opened schools in villages where there was none before. They would go to a village and ask one of their colleagues to sing religious songs. As people gathered, they switched over to patriotic songs and then to lectures. After the meeting, some people of the village, whom they had already coached came forward and declared their support in favour of a nationalist school. Others then followed suit. The workers always kept a teacher ready at hand and immediately started a school. People who were reluctant were requested to put one of their children in the school while continuing to send others to schools run by the District Local Board.

While they were busy in the village, in Surat city Kalyanji Mehta and Dayalji Desai were canvassing for the election of nationalist leaders to the municipality. Students of both the Ashrams worked very hard during the campaign. Every day in the morning Kalyanji Mehta, Dayalji Desai and the students of the Ashrams took out processions singing patriotic songs and shouting nationalist slogans. In 1921, the District Congress Committee was established in Surat to contest municipal elections, Dayalji was chosen its first President and Kalyanji its Secretary. The unity of the leaders discouraged others from contesting these positions in most of the cases. Congress won 38 out of 40 seats in municipal elections and the leaders of the Mandal, Kunvarji, Kalyanji and Vice-President Sakarlal Parekh became the members of the municipality.

The Mandal leaders went to see Gandhi and requested him to select Bardoli as the field of battle against the government. Gandhi had originally thought of selecting Kaira but Vithalbhai Patel who had earlier visited Bardoli *taluka* was so impressed by its preparation that he pressed Gandhi for selecting Bardoli. Thereupon Gandhi himself came to visit Bardoli and accepted the request of the Mandal.

On January 31, 1922, the Congress Working Committee met in the Patidar Vidyarthi Ashram and approved the selection of Bardoli for launching a satyagraha in the form of non-payment of land revenue. An 'ultimatum' to the government was sent. Everybody appeared ready and organised themselves for the historic event. Then came the setback. In Chauri-Chaura a crowd burnt several policemen to death. Gandhi, much against the wishes of everybody, withdrew the satyagraha. He called a meeting of the people of Bardoli and asked them to pay the land revenue. Only one day was left for the payment and many of the people did not have the money as they had earlier decided not to pay the revenue. But the leaders persuaded them to pay up their dues and arranged for financial help for the impecunious farmers. This self-imposed discipline not only reveals the quality of the leadership provided by the main actors of the drama but also the feeling of trust and devotion vested in them by the people.

There were other setbacks too. Gandhi was arrested and imprisoned for six years. As a result, a lull came in the country's political activities. Dayalji, under whose leadership a no-tax campaign was carried on by the Surat Municipal Committee, was arrested. In 1923, Kalyanji too was jailed. Kunvarji, because of his exclusive preoccupation with the national movement, found himself in a difficult financial situation and started a commercial dairy.

But the Mandal workers were a hopeful lot. They continued both their social and political activities. After the withdrawal of the movement in 1921, Gandhi, aiming to mobilise the Scheduled Tribes asked them to work among the tribals. "Without their support", he argued, "half of your body is paralysed".

Kunvarji aslo realised that the support of the backward castes and tribes was essential. In 1923, therefore, he, his co-workers, and some Gandhian workers from other parts of Gujarat then staying at Surat, launched an organisation of these tribes called 'Raniparej Sabha'. The main focus of their work was social welfare such as the conduct of adult literacy classes, selling khadi and campaign against alcoholic drinks.

The Mandal workers were mainly Patidars who had little previous contact with non-Patidars. From 1919 onwards, as they were drawn more and more into politics, their contact with non-Patidar political and social workers increased and they realised the necessity of expanding their field of activity. Although they retained their identity as Patidars, they had to function in a universe enlarged by the induction of workers from various social categories.

A Swarajya Ashram was established near the Patidar Ashram in Surat. This provided a base to trained and enthusiastic young workers for implementing Gandhi's four point programme under the leadership of the workers from the Mandal and the Ashram. In fact a network of six Ashrams was established in Bardoli *taluka* itself. All of these were secular in orientation and undertook constructive activities. An association of the six, known as the 'Swaraj Ashram Sangh', was also established with a view to coordinating their activities. Sardar Vallabhbhai Patel, recognised as a disciple of Gandhi and accepted as leader by the Mandal since Vithalbhai's withdrawal from the Congress, became the President of the Sangh with Kalyanji and Khushalbai Patel of the Mandal as Vice-President and Secretary respectively. Many others from the Mandal joined one or the other of the several Ashrams. Those of the Mandal who could not adjust themselves to the highly idealistic methods of work of the Gandhians, helped the work in their own way in the villages. Meanwhile, the caste services of the Mandal continued, though the emphasis had clearly shifted to more secular and political objectives.

V

The year 1928, when the famous Bardoli Satyagraha took place, initiated the third phase in the activities of the Mandal.

In the beginning of 1925, the government undertook to revise land revenue rates in Bardoli *taluka*. The official in charge recommended a 30 per cent increase in land revenue. The people of Bardoli under the guidance of the leaders of the Mandal sent delegations to represent their case to the government.[33]

Responding to these representations, the government reduced the increase to 22 per cent, whereupon the four main leaders of the Mandal, Kunvarji, Kalyanji, Khushalbhai and Keshavji Patel went to Sardar Patel and requested him to launch and personally guide a satyagraha.

The Mandal found in Sardar Patel a leader whose approach was similar to their own. Sardar Patel, like them, was highly pragmatic and had a thorough understanding of the traditional social structure. He came from the Patidar caste and, although a barrister, always called himself a farmer and a son of the soil. Unlike many other urban leaders, he was not isolated from the rural society. In him the Mandal leaders found a hero and a link with the larger society. He also provided a very useful link between them and Gandhi.

On being approached by these leaders, Sardar wanted them to confirm whether the people of the *taluka* were prepared to launch a satyagraha. The leaders therefore undertook a tour of the whole *taluka*. When they went to the Sardar again, they took with them some Gandhian social workers to plead their case before Gandhi. Patel took them to Gandhi. An interview was arranged and the latter, after questioning these leaders thoroughly, was satisfied and permitted them to launch the satyagraha. Sardar Patel agreed to lead the movement. (Leaders from Choryasi *taluka* which was also affected by increase in land revenue urged Patel to include it in the movement. But the Sardar declined to do so.)

Bardoli was selected because of special circumstances prevailing there. It was surrounded on three sides by the native state of Baroda where the British government had no jurisdiction and leaders could cross over to it to escape imprisonment. The total population of the *taluka* was 87,000 in 1927, out of which 50 per cent were Scheduled Tribes; Patidars formed half of the remaining population while other castes formed the other half. Because of the organisational and welfare activities of the Mandal the Patidars of Bardoli were politically more conscious among the rural population of Surat. Some of the Patidars who were associated with Gandhi's movement in South Africa had now come back and settled in Bardoli. The various Patidar sub-castes were well organised and had reached a stage where they could be easily mobilised for political purposes.

Further, the Patidars were affected most by the increased land revenue inasmuch as all of them were owner-cultivators.

The Scheduled Tribes population in Bardoli was also politically the most advanced in Gujarat. Social workers from the *taluka* as well as from elsewhere had, between 1922 and 1927, carried out intensive welfare activities among the backward peoples. In several Ashrams, schools, industrial training centres and khadi production centres they had trained influential youths belonging to the Scheduled Tribes.

The people of Bardoli *taluka* were probably more disciplined, integrated and cohesive. The incidence of crime was very low. The number of civil suits in Bardoli was the lowest of all *talukas* in the area. The people were considered peaceful, law-abiding and religious. Faith in god and in the leaders characterised the culture and the attitude of the Patidars. As Kunvarji wrote to one of his colleagues, "It is fortunate that there is no intellectualism in the people of Bardoli, as they do most of the work on faith, otherwise they would not have followed us without questioning".

On February 12, 1928, a meeting of the people of Bardoli *taluka* was called, which passed a resolution calling for the launching of peaceful satyagraha against the government and stoppage of payment of the land revenue. As in 1921, the Mandal plunged into the movement and assumed its leadership. Many old students of the Ashram, caste leaders and other sympathisers were drafted into service for the purpose of the satyagraha. Leaders and workers from outside were also called to take leadership positions in the movement. Many satyagraha camps were started.

The main workers, however, were all from the Mandal: Kunvarji, Kalyanji, Khushalbhai and Keshavji, known later as the 'four K's' of Bardoli. While Kalyanji, Keshavji and Khushalbhai were given the responsibility of running the various camps, Kunvarji, with some of his chosen colleagues, preferred to work 'behind the scene'. Kunvarji's work through the Mandal for the last two decades, his principle of not antagonising the caste leaders, his method of proceeding slowly and by stages, his attempts to avoid estrangement from the traditional society, his attempts to integrate Patidar subcastes and his self-effacement, detachment and tendency to help even his opponents all now began to pay dividends. And it was as part of this approach that he cast his role in the satyagraha.

Support for the satyagraha was organised on the basis of caste affiliations. Different castes and communities passed resolutions which called for the stoppage of land revenue payments. It was further resolved to out-caste those who paid the land revenue. Religious and caste leaders were called from outside to persuade their respective communities not to pay taxes. Police patels and village accountants totalling about a hundred were pressed by their caste councils, to resign their jobs. Signatures supporting the movement were collected through caste leaders. In meetings held in various villages of the taluka, caste leaders were specifically invited and political leaders while addressing the meeting appealed to them for support. Sardar Patel, for example, while addressing the special caste meetings of Patidars, Kolis, Anavils, Banias and the Scheduled Tribes in Bardoli appealed to their caste feelings and allegiances.

Appeals to caste sentiments were made in different ways. The satyagraha was made out to be an issue which involved the prestige of each of the castes in Bardoli. Support of each caste was sought on the basis that if it did not support the satyagraha its prestige would be lowered. The Anavils, for example, did not have any well-knit caste organisation. Dayalji Desai, the leader of this caste, had tried several times since 1910 to build a caste organisation but the Anavils, proved highly individualistic and Dayalji's attempts did not go very far. As a result, initially there was very little Anavil support to the movement. However, once the atmosphere of the satyagraha was under way, Dayalji successfully provoked his caste members to come forward and support the movement by reproaching them through his caste magazine *Anavil Sevak* for their loyalty to the government. He put them to shame by showing that lower castes like Patidars and even the Scheduled Tribes had fearlessly joined the movement. Upon this Anavils were also mobilised into the movement.

The conduct of the satyagraha on the basis of caste does not mean that other secular organisations were not involved. The satyagraha brought together kinship and caste groups, territorial groups and other secular organisations to realise a common purpose. Even while caste remained the basic unit of support mobilisation, other wider territorial and professional organisations played a complementary role. For instance, one Bania businessman in village Afta, when he paid up his tax, was disowned not only by his relatives and excommunicated by his castemen (notice the role of traditional sanctions) but also excluded from all interactions with his business associates, with the result that he had to migrate from Bardoli to another *taluka*. However, the solidarity was particularly marked among the middle and lower castes. It was a popular expression during the movement that the 'four Ks' under the leadership of Sardar Patel organised three other 'Ks', namely the 'Kubbis' (Patidars), 'Kolis' (a lower caste) and the 'Kaliparaj' (Scheduled Tribes).

Kunvarji did not miss the opportunity, given by the movement, to modernise his own caste. He persuaded the Patidar leaders to make contributions to the satyagraha fund out of funds collected for caste purposes. For instance, fines collected within the caste went to the satyagraha fund. He also encouraged the use and production of khadi. Patidar Khadi Mandals were started. In 1929, by the end of the Bardoli satyagraha, 682 Patidar families in Bardoli were engaged in these Mandals and more than 1,200 spinning wheels were in operation.[34] Kunvarji also called a meeting of two sections of Charotaria Patidars, the Choryasi and the Baleshwari Panchas, and requested Sardar Patel to persuade them to remove restrictions and differences between the two. Since then these segments have remained integrated. Inter-caste cooperation achieved during the satyagraha movement still continues. Harmony between the Muslims and the Hindus was also achieved. In the words of an important observer:

> An excellent outcome of the Bardoli movement is the remarkable unity among the people of the *taluka*. Today Hindus, Mohammedans and Parsis have forgotten all their differences and have accepted the leadership of the Sardar of Bardoli. When I see Hindu, Muslim and Parsi leaders working together, in the same Swarajya Ashram my heart rejoices.[35]

Thus if caste was useful in the mobilisation of support for the satyagraha, the satyagraha in turn integrated and secularised caste.

The battle of Bardoli was ultimately won. This is not the place to describe the impact it had on life in Bardoli or elsewhere, and how and why the satyagraha became a landmark in the history of national movement. The end of the satyagraha marked the beginning of the fourth phase in the nationalist role of the Mandal. It was after the victory at Bardoli that the Mandal leaders drew high caste urban leaders to the movement. Their work continued through various caste associations they organised after 1928 and the Mandal leaders devoted themselves more actively to political organisation. The District Congress Committee which was established in 1921 had become more active by now. As the Congress fought various elections, its importance also increased. Within the Congress, the D.C.C. became a centre of power. Through the Mandal leaders a link between the District Congress Committee and the caste organisations at the district level and below was established. Linkages also developed among caste organisations which were engaged in the task of social and political mobilisation and the D.C.C. as a secular political organisation. And finally it was in this period that complete secularisation of the Mandal was brought about. In fact, by 1960 it no more remained an association of the Patidar caste.

After the victory of 1928, the leaders required a new programme. Kunvarji under the leadership of Sardar Patel formed an organisation for the youth of various castes in Bardoli. Kunvarji and his colleagues also strengthened their campaign against drinking by appealing to these caste organisations. Many educated members of the Mandal settled down in several Ashrams which were engaged in social welfare in Bardoli. Kunvarji was now anxious to involve in his work the urban moderate leaders who till then kept themselves aloof from radical political movements. After Bardoli, their attitudes had undergone a perceptible change. Some of them were fascinated by it. Kunvarji also had noticed that there was a feeling among the urban leaders of being bypassed by the rural leaders controlling district politics. Personally, Kunvarji was on friendly terms with some of the former and he knew that to involve them they should be given some importance so that they did not feel the humiliation of working under rural and less educated leaders.

One such educated high caste individual influenced by Kunvarji was Kanhaiyalal Desai, popularly known as Kanjibhai. Kanjibhai had been engaged for a long time in a campaign against drinking in his *taluka*. He also used to publish a journal for that purpose. Kunvarji and Kanjibhai were good friends and the former always induced the latter to join the movement. Simultaneously, he used to speak to Sardar Patel about Kanjibhai's usefulness. One day, Kunvarji managed to arrange a meeting between the Sardar and Kanjibhai which resulted in Kanjibhai's joining the nationalist cause. In 1930, Dayalji Desai because of his ill-health gave up presidentship of the District Congress Committee. Kalyanji of course was a natural choice of people like Patel. But Kunvarji and Kalyanji himself convinced Patel that in order to attract more urbanised and educated people, this responsibility should be entrusted to Kanjibhai. Subsequently, Kanjibhai emerged as a dominant leader of the district and later became one of the most powerful leaders of the Gujarat Congress. (Notice the reverse ordering of the usually known pattern: here the rural leadership mobilised urban leadership into organised politics.) Mr. Morarji Desai also worked with this group after he resigned as deputy collector and joined the Congress.

The Mandal and its leaders continued to paticipate in subsequent national movements between 1930 and 1942. The idea that obsessed them most was that the Britishers first entered India through Surat and they should go back from Surat. Kunvarji and many of his colleagues went underground to work ·for later movements while others like Kalyanji, Morarjibhai and Khushalbhai worked openly and courted jail. There were warrants of arrest for all of them. The property of many of them was confiscated by the government. Kunvarji's house was confiscated in 1932. A reward of Rs. 5,000 was declared for the arrest of one of his colleagues, Makanji Patel, in 1942. Meanwhile there was increasing pressure on caste members who held government positions like police patels to help the cause of the movement, if necessary by resigning their posts.

There were some who did not like Kunvarji and his colleagues using caste symbols and other shorthand methods in the movement. They complained to Gandhi that Kunvarji was not very scrupulous about his methods. One satyagrahi, during the 1928 Bardoli movement, wrote:

> One can easily see that but for the organisation of the sub-castes and castes we would have never won the battle of Bardoli. But it is immoral and improper. When philosophers of the world consider even nationalism as narrow, has not the Sardar of Bardoli given new life to communalism? Have we not committed immorality in defeating the enemy by throwing at them the mud of casteism? [36]

Kunvarji, who was aware of these critics, dismissed them rather cynically. Writing to Mahadev Desai, private secretary of Gandhi, that many *bhagatdas* (a word used in sarcasm for ideologues) did not approve of his methods, to which Mahadev Desai had replied "What if they do not agree?" But it seems that Kunvarji's methods had aroused strong opposition, because Mahadev Desai in a letter to Kalyanji wrote: "Give secret instructions to Kunvarji that he should not force police patels or bring pressure on them to resign."

In course of these movements, the Ashram had remained the most active centre of nationalist activites in the district. The Vidyarthi Swarajya had resolved in its parliamentary session to support the Bardoli movement and had sent volunteers. In 1930, when the Congress opted for complete independence, students of the Ashram went to the city and announced the beginning of a non-violent anti-British agitation. When the leaders of the Mandal persuaded

Gandhi to extend his protest march against salt tax to Dandi — a village in Surat — they relied on the help of the local students. Before Gandhi reached Dandi, about 20 students of the Ashram went there to prepare the background. During those days, the Ashram functioned, for all practical purposes, as an office of the Indian National Congress. Leaders from all over the nation coming to Surat stayed in it and as a result it hummed with political activity. It was no longer just a students' boarding house.

Right till 1947, when independence was finally achieved, these students went on working for various satyagrahas and movements. In spite of the great risk involved they helped in the printing and publication of the proscribed *Satyagraha Patrika*. The nationalist orientation of the Ashram had become so pronounced that the government in 1932 raided it and forced it to close down. All the inmates were driven out without any prior notice and some of them were not even allowed to take their belongings. The Ashram was kept in government custody for three years and the charge of its empty building — all its belongings were either burnt or destroyed during the government raid — was handed over to the management in 1935. In 1937 the students campaigned vigorously for the candidates put up by the Congress for election to the provincial legislature and during 1942-43 all of them left their schools and colleges and the Ashram remained closed for another year during 1942-43. Many senior students of the institution courted arrest and went to jail. All of this resulted in considerable political involvement of this region in the nationalist cause. In the words of a recent biographer :

> Ever since Gandhi appeared on the horizon of Indian politics a certain region of Gujarat, inhabited mainly by Patidars, held the political stage of India. First it was Kaira, then Bardoli, then Borsad, then again Bardoli and then the territory covered by the famous Dandi march of salt satyagraha of Bardoli. This region received, as it were, continuous training in non-violence and non-cooperation from 1918 to 1930. The two Patidars who gave this region its peculiar distinction were the two brothers — Vithalbhai and Vallabhbhai. There was, of course, one other pair of Patidars, who must be mentioned along with them, who worked with them and for them, but whose names appear to have been forgotten by those who ought to have remembered them .... for they were the real makers of Bardoli — Kunvarji and Kalyanji — Kunvarji, perhaps more than Kalyanji — but for whose initial and pervasive work neither Vithalbhai nor Vallabhbhai nor Gandhiji himself could have achieved the results they achieved in this region .... As their work, along with that of many of their co-workers, was definitely confined to the region and

as the work itself was in the nature of a hundred and one odd jobs that had to be done on the spot, their names have not travelled beyond their own homeland.[37]

Its major work being done, after independence the Mandal as a body has withdrawn from active politics, though many of its members are still active politicians. As mentioned earlier, the Ashram has been admitting students from all castes since 1915. In fact, since 1947, it has no longer even a communal name. It is now called Vallabh Vidyarthi Ashram. Similarly the name of the Patidar Yuvak Mandal, which was changed to Patidar Seva Mandal in 1936 to show that it was not only an organisation of youth but of all Patidars, was again changed in 1962 to Vallabh Seva Mandal. It now admits even non-Patidars as its members.

VI

When the Patidar Yuvak Mandal was started, Gujarat was politically inactive. There was no political organisation nor was there any ongoing political movement. In fact, the general impression about Gujaratis was that they were apolitical. The national level leaders from whom they took their inspiration were themselves divided between social reformers on the one hand and the more politically inclined nationalists on the other. The latter again were divided into the extremists and the moderates. The highly urbanised western educated social reformers in the metropolitan areas hardly knew the masses. Many of them at the time wanted to do away with the caste system. The Mandal leaders had to encounter opposition from such idealists who rejected their methods and who believed that the group was doing a disservice to the country by indulging in caste activities.

In terms of political strategy, the metropolitan social reformers wanted to reject traditional institutions and values and start on a clean slate. They could not see that such an attitude would meet with stubborn opposition from the leaders of society as well as create dislocation and disruption in the society without creating a new order. As against this highly westernised elite Kunvarji and his co-workers showed great realism and displayed remarkable insight into the prevailing state of Indian society. They knew that impatience and doctrinaire idealism could not bring results, that the caste system could not be so easily wished away. To quote one of them:

The presence of innumerable castes and sub-castes is the major weakness of the Hindu society. It is the rule of social development that castes should merge their identity in larger social groupings. But caste is not something external to our human society. It is not a tree or a log of wood which can be cut off by a stroke of axe. What is required is the abolition of the harmful customs and traditions of Hindu society and changes in the caste system, so that it becomes more flexible and easy social intercourse becomes possible. It is my firm belief that this sort of casteism is not opposed to nationalism.[38]

In the early years of the twentieth century when the Mandal started its work, the distance between the national elite and the rural masses was very great. The distance implied a gap between ways of life as well as the 'idioms' of politics. Consequently there was hardly any communication between the two. Moreover the involvement of traditional society was made more difficult by the lack of mass media, illiteracy, deep-rooted ways of the masses and the radical methods of the national elite.

In this situation, the leaders of the Mandal provided a crucial communication link between the 'centre' and the 'periphery'. Working as 'link men' between the traditional masses and the modernised political elite, they acted as integrators of traditional and modern values. The political mobilisation they worked for became social mobilisation too. The Patidars, while consolidating themselves for the nationalist movement, changed some of their traditions and customs and also developed new patterns of social interaction.

When forces of modernisation enter a traditional society it may weaken and destroy the antecedent structure of that society but may not so easily reconstitute a new order. Each aspect of the latter encounters opposition and results in friction. The Patidar Yuvak Mandal provided an example of how a mature and perceptive leadership could help to minimise the disruptive consequences of social and political modernisation.

The history of the Mandal indicates that where politics becomes the major force working for modernisation, involvement in politics secularises caste, because caste then becomes too narrow a group for all practical purposes and is forced to find a wider identity. In order to strengthen support and integrate various levels a forging of coalitions and a federation of structures became necessary. Such support and integration were brought about gradually and stage by stage, first involving the sub-castes, then the same caste in different areas, and finally different castes.

Despite increasing awareness of the role of caste in politics at the lower level, there is still a feeling that at higher levels caste is less potent. Throughout its history the Mandal leaders maintained a continuity between caste activity and wider political activity, and enabled a caste organisation to act as a link between local society and national politics. Also, by being the decision-makers in the organisations which made the Bardoli satyagraha a success, they showed that, given proper leadership, caste symbols and sanctions can sometimes become complementary to secular appeals for many. All in all, the Mandal acted as an agent of modernisation, brought about a meaningful reconciliation between traditional and modern elements in the national movement and contributed to a mobilisation of traditional values and institutions in the cause of political awakening.

NOTES

1. *Patel Bandhu,* Vol. 8, Nos. 11, 12 (September-October, 1916) (Emphasis mine).
2. Keshavji Ganeshji Patel: Memoirs Section, p. 52; *Suvarna Jayanti Ank* (in Gujarati), published by Kalyanji Mehta for Vallabh Vidyarthi Ashram, Surat. To be referred as *G.J.C. Vol.* hereafter.
3. Gordhanbhai Patel, *Vithalbhai Patel* (Bombay: R. A. Marankar, 1950), p. 458.
4. Translated from *G.J.C. Vol. op. cit.* Section V, p. 1.
5. See *Patel Bandhu,* Vol. II, No. 3, (Jan-Feb 1910).
6. *G.J.C. Vol. op. cit.* p. 70.
7. Ranjit Ram Vavabhai Navjivan, 1917, as quoted in *G.J.C. Vol. op. cit.* Section V. p. 72.
8. *Patel Bandhu,* Vol. III, No. 8, (April 1911).
9. *Ibid.* Vol. III, No. 11, (November 1910).
10. *Patel Bandhu,* Vol. V, No. 6, (June 1913).
11. For such articles, news items and poems see *Ibid.* Vol. I, Nos. 2, 4, 6 (1909); Vol. II, Nos. 1, 4, 5 (1910); Vol. III, No. 3 (1911); Vol. IV, Nos. 3, 4, 5 (1912).
12. See especially Vol. X, No. 1, 1917. Kaira Satyagraha was organised against the government's refusal to postpone collection of land revenue during the year 1917 when there was a near-famine condition because of inadequate rains.
13. *Patel Bandhu,* Vol. V, No. 3, 1913. Here is an interesting forerunner of the idea of 'caste federations'.
14. *Patel Bandhu,* Vol. III, No. 1 (1910).
15. I. I. Desai, *G.J.C. Vol. op. cit.* Section II, p. 50.
16. The Patidar Vidyarthi Boarding House, after 1915, came to be popularly known as 'Ashram'. It will hereafter be referred to as Ashram.
17. The Bhakta Patidars follow the Kabir Panth — a religious sect started after the name of Saint Kabir. They are very religious and do not eat food cooked even by Brahmins. The Bhakta Patidars originally belonged to Surat and neighbouring Broach districts.
18. The Matia Patidars used to follow some of the rituals of the Muslims. They buried the dead person instead of cremating him. At the time of marriage they called Brahmin priests as well as Muslim priests to perform marriage ceremony. The other Patidars did not keep any marriage or dining relations with them. On the other hand, the Matia Patidars were the most modernised and educated among the Patidars of Surat in the beginning of the century. Many of them had gone to African countries. During the national movement, Kunvarji got great help and support from Matia Patidars.

The Matia Patidars are to be found in Surat district only. Now they have given up their Muslim practices.

19. The procedure of formal out-casting required wide publicity within the caste. Any social intercourse with the expelled person was prohibited. A defaulter was threatened with out-casting.

20. *G.J.C. Vol. 'Ashram na Pachas Varsh'*, p. 23.

21. There were two territorial factions among the Leva Patidars in the district, the Baleshri Panch mainly covered the area of the Bardoli *taluka* and the Choryasi Panch which covered the area of the Choryasi *taluka*. These factions had arisen because of some differences between the caste leaders of the two areas. There were no marriage relations between the members of the two factions.

22. As quoted in *G.J.C. Vol. op. cit.* section I, p. 14.

23. Kalidas Patel, *Patel Bandhu*, Vol. II, No. 2 (1910).

24. *Ibid.* Vol. 5 (March 1913).

25. Gordhanbhai Patel, *op. cit.* p. 459.

26. Quoted in *G.J.C. Vol. op. cit.* Section I, p. 13. Translated from Gujarati.

27. *G.J.C. Vol. op. cit.* Section I, pp. 34-5.

28. The Rowlatt Committee had recommended the control of the press, trial of political offenders without juries, and imprisonment of persons suspected of subversive aims.

29. See Constitution of Vidyarthi Swarajya, *Patel Bandhu*, Vol. XII, Nos. 4-5, 1920.

30. *Op. cit.* p. 457.

31. *G.J.C. Vol. op. cit.* Section I, pp. 39-40.

32. An organisation established by the nationalists to run schools. It was started to provide the facility of education to those students who had left government schools and colleges in response to Gandhi's call. The schools run under its auspices were known as 'Rashtriya Shala'.

33. For details see Mahadev Desai, *Bardoli Satyagraha* (Gujarati), Navjivan Mudranalaya, 1928, pp. 3-27.

34. *Satyagraha Patrika* (Gujarati), 30 August, 1931.

35. Translated from Khushwadji Nariman's lecture as published in *Satyagraha Patrika*, 1st July, 1928.

36. As translated from *Pratap*, Special Number, October 1928.

37. Gordhanbhai Patel, *op. cit.* p. 521.

38. Kikubhai Desai, *Patel Bandhu* (September, 1923).

CHAPTER TEN

Caste and Political Participation in Two Cities

DONALD B. ROSENTHAL

Local political life in India traditionally reflected the hiearchical structure of Indian Society. The village or town constituted a social system grounded in an *authoritarian consensus*. Domination was not simply imposed from above, but flowed from values which were internalised by all strata of the local population and the stability of this arrangement depended upon the low pressure for major alterations within the structure. Where attempts were made to challenge authority directly, the use of sanctions to bring deviants into line was legitimised by Brahminic teachings.[1] In general, then, local political systems were based on what Durkheim termed as 'mechanical solidarity' and on the compulsions of tradition.[2] Furthermore, the village was not fully integrated politically; it consisted of distinct solidarity units — the castes — which bore major responsibility for adjudicating and resolving their own internal disputes and controlling interactions between members and outsiders.

Social and political changes during the past century, including urbanisation and the propagation of nationalistic and democratic values, have helped to transform social relations towards Durkheim's state of 'organic solidarity'. For our purpose, this describes a system marked by a high order of social and economic differentiation of a kind which weakens solidarity ties within a social group. At the same time, it underwrites a larger social order in which interdependence is more a function of individual action than of group traditions. Under conditions of organic solidarity, restraint is placed on the use of repressive force by sacrally-legitimate holders of power; instead, modern legal codes and secularised political relationships are developed.[3]

Even the more *developed* of modern politics would not be as radically 'organic' as Durkheim's 'ideal type' suggests.[4] At a minimum, however, 'political modernisation' is reflected in the existence of a division of social labour based on the *attenuation* of solidarity group exclusiveness in many areas: disputes are referred to formal political agencies; bars to interactions with non-members are significantly reduced; and, socialisation of the young becomes a function of secondary institutions.[5]

Thus, the resignation of some elements of authority, by a group based on primordial ties (caste, religion, tribe, ethnicity), to the greater social order does not imply its disintegration as a meaningful unit of social and political life. In India, these ascriptive ties are likely to remain salient during the first phase of democratic politics.[6] Collectivities such as castes continue to function because of their ability to adapt their traditional functions to the 'system rules' of the new social order. At the same time, however, the traditional hold of a primordial group on its members appears to loosen under the pressures of general social change; the political and social relevance of the group, therefore, may come increasingly to depend on individual self-identifications rather than on societally-enforced distinctions. In that sense, identifications with caste groups in politics involve some of the same choices as membership in other secondary associations.

The Indian decision to permit freedom of *democratic* participation, when the terms of participation are based on a group's own understanding of its own needs, rather than on the imposition of expectations by ritually-dominant elements, has laid down the basis for a polity which is very different from the traditional order. This is not to argue that the traditional order was necessarily harsher. Political authority in the village carried some obligation to provide for the weak in cases of emergency or disaster. Today, while some of the differences among geographically and hierarchically adjacent *jatis* have been softened,[7] the new politicisation of caste has brought into the open inter-caste conflicts with state-wide ramifications. In the process, some of the complementarity of the traditional social hierarchy has been replaced by open conflict in the political arena.[8]

Despite the frictions in these new inter-group relations, the castes have some freedom in their choice of goals and this gives them a 'stake' in the new system. In fact, though fears have been expressed about the disintegrative consequences of the politicisation of castes this may be a force working in the opposite direction. One of the more interesting subjects for further inquiry may be the kinds of responses which formerly *dominant* castes have made to their changed influence. These castes did not have to continuously struggle in the previous system to maintain their political ascendancy; it was largely a reflection of their high social status. Democratic politics has tended to weaken the linkages between social standing and political influence. If the caste system, in its political setting, is operating on a different basis because of the activities of the formerly 'subject' elements in society, it also has altered sharply for previously dominant groups.

In order to describe a local political system with reference to the local caste structure, it is necessary to clarify how the castes differ in the ways they are organised for political action and the ends which they try to achieve through political participation. In the present paper we shall consider only two aspects of this: the goals which the members of the group seek; the extent of internal cohesion shown by persons born into the caste. These two aspects point, respectively, to the demands which castes put into politics and the likelihood that a particular demand can be identified as the outgrowth of caste sentiment rather than the preference of specific individuals of a particular caste.

To illustrate some of the patterns which emerge from the differential demands and cohesion of caste groups, we will look at the part caste plays in the political life of two cities; Agra in Uttar Pradesh (462,000) and Poona in Maharashtra (598,000). Data for this analysis was drawn from interviews conducted during 1963-64 with the members of two popularly-elected municipal councils and other local political actors. It is significant, to begin with, that nearly every council member in the two cities (125 in all) was able and willing to identify the caste or community of each of the contestant, in his particular ward in the previous municipal elections and to suggest the relative proportions of primordial groups in his constituency. Few high-caste persons, however, clearly identified themselves as 'caste men', specifically pursuing caste interests through politics. Those who did identify themselves as such were invariably persons from groups low in the traditional hierarchy or outside of it. Thus, in Agra, the Jatavs (Chamars) dominated the local unit of the Republican Party of India (RPI) and seemed to treat it as an extension of the caste. Similarly, in Poona, the RPI was dominated by the Mahars, another Scheduled Caste group. Aside from members of the RPI, only two persons in Poona indicated that their candidacies were the result of specific caste actions, although many spoke of their victories as results of substantial caste support. In one case, a low-caste Bhoi (Fisherman) was selected as the nominee of his caste after he won a pre-election primary, held within his caste to determine the caste candidate. In the other case, a Maratha butcher was put up as a candidate against an incumbent Maratha Council member because of an intra-caste dispute. Despite the conflict, both contestants won.

Before we turn to specific examples of caste activity in politics, however, a word should be said about the manner in which the term 'caste' is employed in the present essay. Anthropologists have devoted considerable effort to the task of refining this and other related concepts. While such refinements are useful in describing social structure, in political analysis a different frame of reference is necessary. In fact, in politics, definition of caste solely in terms of intermarriage and inter-dining may be misleading. In order to control political resources, it is necessary to have an adequate supply of votes and this is often done by blurring some of the finer distinctions among groups. Thus, ritually distinct *jatis* may work together through caste associations or federations, or persons of similar *jatis* may co-operate on an individual basis in political organisations denying caste affiliations altogether.[9] Moreover, castes may be highly organised for some functions and not for others. It was frequently found that respondents were active in a set of caste-related educational or social organisations and that their castes operated collectively in matters like dowries, without simultaneously taking part in politics. Since candidates belonging to the same caste but to different parties frequently ran against each other, the aloofness of the caste association from endorsements can readily be understood.

To give some examples, in Poona, respondents spoke of conflicts between the Brahmins and the non-Brahmins and the dominance of the Marathas in the Congress Party, but neither the Brahmins nor the non-Brahmins attributed significant political differences to the Brahmin sub-castes. Similarly, in Agra, it was recognised that there was a major gulf between the Jatavs and the twice-born castes, with the latter being led by members of the Vaisya *varna*; at the same time, conflicts among Vaisya *jatis* did not seem significant. Only in some cases such differences were salient and it became necessary to explore them. The implications of such an approach will become clearer as the analysis proceeds.[10]

Caste Goals and Group Cohesion

The terms on which a caste is absorbed into the political system may themselves affect the internal organisation of the caste. Several studies have noted, for example, that with political activity new men assume positions of leadership displacing the traditional authority figures in the group. The latter apparently find it increasingly difficult to operate in the style demanded by democratic politics.[11]

Aside from the major threshold problem of producing a leadership with skills appropriate for modern political action, any political group must have other basic resources which can be turned to political advantage. These include: economic stability (if possible an economic surplus) and sufficient numbers to make its weight felt. Given these skills and resources, the group may readily be politicised. Once it has entered politics, however, there are a variety of goals which a caste might pursue. Three such major ends are: (1) material benefits; (2) status improvement or status defense ('status ends'); and (3) social reconstruction ('purposive' or 'ideological' goals).[12]

Material benefits are tangible rewards which have direct or indirect economic value; status ends are basically intangible and may vary widely, but they grow out of a sense of group membership and identification; purposive ends involve a "demand for the enactment of certain laws or the adoption of certain practices" which may not benefit "the members in any direct or tangible way", but imply the overall reorganisation of social and economic relations in society.[13]

While the first two ends may fulfil the specific needs of a particular political group, they may also serve the latent function of supporting the existing political institutions, particularly in the context of an expanding economy. Groups pursuing such goals merely demand a larger share of the economic or status pie. On the other hand, purposive goals involve a demand for major changes in the system itself, either through a return to the past or by advancing to some radically different future.

Every real situation involving change, of course, combines elements of all of these ends, but for the purposes of analysis it is possible to make qualitative distinctions among specific caste groups in terms of the relative significance to them, of these goals in general and as perceived objects of political action.

The attainment of these goals, however, depends on the ability and willingness of caste members to work together. Caste cohesion requires that persons must act as part of a collectivity rather than as political individuals with a given caste background. After all, there is a difference between being a politician of Brahmin birth and being a Brahmin 'caste man'. The difference is vital in distinguishing situations in which 'caste goals' are operative from cases in which other factors are at work.

It is in this sense that one can conceive of 'types' of caste cohesion as lying along a continuum. At one end of the continuum is the situation where within group ties are very strong and there is no association with outsiders. At the other end of the continuum, is the situation where so many differences exist within a caste that it cannot function as a meaningful collectivity (evidently, at this point, individuals share many ties with persons belonging to different primodial groups, that caste affiliations become marginal in politics). This continuum must not be viewed as suggesting a series of neat historical stages. There is little evidence to support the existence of such a linear progress. While it is true that some *traditional* caste ties may gradually weaken, in case of full caste participation in politics some of the newer functions of caste may not.

In the American context, Robert Dahl has written of the three stages of assimilation of ethnic groups into the political life of the city of New Haven. Dahl's model emphasises the changes which an ethnic group undergoes while becoming part of the political system.[14]

At first, according to Dahl, members of a low-status ethnic group are largely proletarian and must depend upon persons belonging to previously assimilated groups for political leadership. Few offices are available to group members, except those which depend directly upon the voting strength of the group. The ethnic group, like the caste, can be organised for political action because it is marked by a high degree of political homogeneity resulting from common identifications, social ties and similar economic position.

A second stage is attained when the limited success of the group in organised politics begins to benefit from educational and occupational mobility of certain individuals within it. At this point, the primordial group becomes more heterogeneous socially and economically. Its own leadership emerges and this element aspires to higher positions in government and in party organisations. But the group is still handicapped politically in winning the highest offices until it can unite with voters outside the immediate grouping. During this phase, responsiveness to ethnic origins persists, but socio-economic issues begin to differentiate the membership. Cross-cutting non-ethnic affiliations appear. As long as divisive socio-economic issues are not made salient to the group as a whole, voters are likely to support an ethnic comrade for political advancement over an outsider.

At the third stage, the group becomes highly differentiated and large segments may be guided in their attitudes towards political life by non-primordial considerations. For some of those persons who have advanced socially, ethnic politics may itself become embarrassing, if not actually demeaning. The resort to issues with ideological overtones is likely to fragment ascriptive ties; multiple cleavages develop within the group.[15]

While applying this model to the Indian situation, we must bear in mind three considerations. Firstly, though the model might be applied broadly to cases with mobility aspirations in India, it is not so helpful in analysing the activities of caste which have achieved their major status goals. Secondly, while there is some relationship between the degree of cohesion of a group and the kind of demand which the group is most likely to put forward, this relationship is not strictly one-to-one. Groups which have 'arrived' socially and economically and are highly differentiated may still have some status demands around which members can unite. Similarly, groups which have not begun to make a real impact on politics may make modern demands simultaneously with the most 'primitive' kinds of status demands.

Thirdly, we are dealing with the process of integration into democratic political life and not with social integration. The latter involves the presence of a definite model for the potentially mobile group; such a model has existed, for example, in the style of life connected with the twice-born castes and its effects may be seen in the attempts of low-status castes to raise themselves through emulation of the high castes. Political integration, on the other hand, involves no definite model for action. In a democratic polity, the group determines its own needs and presses its demands through institutionalised mechanisms. In a strict sense, then, there would be no 'Sanskritisation' or 'Americanisation' model in political life comparable to those which have existed in the social system.[16]

Caste Politics in Agra

Many of the lower castes of Agra have not entered politics. The Congress Party maintains an organisation which is supposed to promote the advancement of the Backward Classes, but its meetings are rare and the few politically active Congressmen attached to it do not provide leadership or political education to these groups. Some castes, like the Ahirs, have the necessary political resources, but have been only marginally participative: sometimes castes are either too small or too impoverished (e.g. the Bhangis) to have immediate political effect.

The Jatavs: The outstanding example of a political low-status caste in the city is that of the Jatavs, a Scheduled Caste group. Originally agricultural serfs and leather workers in villages, they have moved to relatively independent economic activity — shoe-manufacturing — and are presently highly active in politics. In the course of this change, Jatavs tried to advance socially by making claims to a *Kshatriya* status. This effort was not very successful. Nevertheless, the promotion of education and the modification of social behaviour which accompanied the effort probably helped them in the long run. Even before national independence, the Jatavs turned to politics as a technique of reaching group goals and effecting status change. The political leadership of the caste was also won over by new men from traditional figures. (Many of the new leadership now hold elective offices in the city or administrative positions in the government.)[17]

Though the Jatavs had their own political organisation in Agra in the 1930s and dominated the Scheduled Castes Federation in the city during the 1940s, their voting strength did not become effective till 1952, when an unrestricted suffrage allowed them to exercise their numerical strength in the city.[18] Their real impact has been felt only since 1957 when the caste was the major force behind the formation of the Agra RPI.

Acting as a relatively cohesive group, Jatavs have used political channels primarily for status improvement. The search for status improvement has been *symbolic*, as well as *substantive*. The Jatavs have tried not only to legitimise their claims to full participation in the system and sought the insignia of self-esteem as political actors, but also the more concrete rewards of the political process like posts and promises of services from government.

The concern for symbolic recognition is apparent in recent efforts of the RPI (including the Jatavs of Agra and the Mahars of Poona) to erect statues and hang pictures in prominent places of B.R. Ambedkar, the late leader of the untouchables. Also, the first on the party's list of ten demands, submitted to Prime Minister Shastri in 1965, was a demand that a picture of Ambedkar be hung in the Parliament building.[19] Such symbolic demands have their analogue in the demands put forward by ethnic groups in the United States.[20] The Jatavs have gone beyond a simple concern with status ends.[21] They constantly try to expand educational and occupational opportunities for the Scheduled Castes through governmental guarantee or grants. Locally, in the municipal body, they keep account of the number of Scheduled Caste persons actually employed by each department and by the public schools and attempt to hold the government to its promise that a certain percentage of positions will be reserved for ex-untouchables. Jatav leaders try to intervene whenever they feel an economic or social injustice has been done to a Scheduled Caste civic employee or citizen. Furthermore, their election manifestoes and public statements have taken on a socialist tone. The national demands of the RPI cited above, for example, include one calling for 'land to the tiller'. For Jatavs and other low-caste groups which include many landless labourers, this indicates an increasing concern with economic self-interest.

However, if the Jatavs in Agra were merely interested in status and material well-being they might have found some means of striking a favourable bargain with elements of the faction-ridden Congress Party in the city. Although there is no evidence that either side ever considered the matter seriously, long-term association of the Jatavs with Congress might have given them additional benefits. Yet, the Republicans have worked hard to keep away from the Congress by emphasising just those class and caste differences which distinguish them from the middle-class and upper-caste Congress Party activists and by public reiterations of their distrust of the Congress Party which Ambedkar first nurtured. The distance between the two groups is heightened by the fact that many of the leaders of the Congress in Agra are orthodox Hindus, while many Jatavs are now Buddhists.[22]

It seems therefore that, for the Jatavs, the purposive ends not only point to the actual needs of the caste which social reconstruction might meet, but also help to forestall the disintegration of caste loyalties which might take place if the party were simply interested in promoting status and material ends. Several Jatavs, elected to the municipal corporation with RPI support, have splintered off from the main body to work elsewhere for their own political advantage. These defectors have attempted to bring caste support over to other political groups, but thus far the strategy has not worked in the city. The strong animus against the Congress remains intact for the present. The caste members, as a result, have continued to pursue political ends containing elements of the three types outlined earlier. Their commitment to political activity as a 'caste party' appears secure unless present internal dissensions within the RPI further fragments the party as in the case of the Mahars in Maharashtra.[23]

The Vaish: Agra is largely a mercantile city and *jatis* belonging to the Vaish (Vaisya) *varna,* appropriately enough play a major part in its business and political life. They have been associated with other high castes, particularly the Brahmins in the Congress organisation since before 1930 and they are also a major force in the local unit of the Jan Sangh, which is the only party representing upper-caste challenge to the Congress in Agra City. These are the influential castes in the city, even though they number only about a fourth of the population. There are several major *jatis* among the Vaish, but the outstanding one in Agra is the Agarwal Banias. The social difference among the Vaish *jatis* does not appear to have any differential impact on political life. In fact, the Agarwal Banias are themselves found in both factions of the Congress Party, in the Jan Sangh and among the Independents in the municipal body.[24]

While the political conflict between the Congress and the Jan Sangh has an ideological aspect, the social distance between members of these two parties, as we have suggested, is small. Many of the Agra Congressmen have conservative attitudes towards political and social questions. Socialism, as defined by the few Congressmen who mentioned it, was essentially Gandhian in character. The existence of a generally conservative set of values in the city does not rule out strong competition among personalities and political factions, but except for the Jatavs such conflicts have not generally taken on explicit primordial undertones. Indeed, the only persistent conflict which follows caste lines has been between the Jatavs and the Vaish-led political organisations.[25] In this the Jatavs have been able to benefit from factionalism within the political groups dominated by the members of the high castes.

Caste Conflicts in Agra: The Agra Congress is a gathering place for a number of castes and a distribution point for those material benefits which are available through its ties to the ruling party. Vaish politicians and their twice-born allies dominate the 'command posts' of the party. Those leading workers of the party drawn from outside of the Vaish castes tend to come from among the Brahmins, Kayasthas, Khatris and Thakurs. Of these groups, only the Brahmins are numerically significant in the city; they constitute about six per cent of the city's population. Prior to 1948, the leading figure in the

Agra Congress was a Brahmin, S.K.D. Paliwal, who held major post in the State Government until he quit the party at the time that the Kisan Mazdoor Praja Party was formed in the State.[26] Since that time, the City Congress has been characterised by two major factions, but they do not seem to reflect caste differences. Leaders of both factions are Vaish and neither appeals to feelings of caste solidarity among the Vaish. The conflict is one for personal authority and control of the party machinery.

Some sense of the relative balance of forces in the Congress and in the Jan Sangh is provided by the figures in Table 1. The data relates to the elections of 1959 to the municipal council, which was the last municipal election held in Agra City. Only the Congress, Jan Sangh and Republican parties ran more than 15 candidates each; the Praja Socialists and Communists each ran less than a handful. All the rest were Independents. The table reveals the relatively high competitiveness and 'openness' of the local political system: there was an average of 4.2 contestants for each of the 54 seats directly filled by public votes in 27 wards;[27] and the low-status groups were fairly represented.

The Vaish and Brahmins in the Congress may actually be under-represented, because the Congress supported Jatavs for reserved seats in the municipality. All of the nine Jatavs running on Congress tickets were defeated; the Jan Sangh did not even try to contest seats in areas where the Scheduled Caste population was concentrated. All 14 Jatavs who won seats in the council were either supported by the RPI or ran as Independents.

While the Agra Congress has received some support from the Muslim community in the past, non of the four Congress Muslims won in 1959; the five Muslims elected included two who ran as Independents, two who received the endorsement of the RPI and one who ran as a Praja Socialist.

Thus, the core of Congress and Jan Sangh support comes from the twice-born castes. In terms of our three-dimensional set of caste ends, it appears that the specific status demands of these castes have largely been satisfied. Some do seek ideological ends through the Jan Sangh, but most partisan activists in Agra have remained with the Congress Party. As a result of factionalism within both the Congress and the Jan Sangh, however, a large number of persons of high caste are currently active in local politics as Independents.

Table 1 : Contestants in Municipal Elections of 1959 by Caste*

Caste	All Candidates		Congress		Jan Sangh	
	N	%	N	%	N	%
Vaish	59	26	20	39	16	47
Brahmins	33	15	6	12	5	15
Thakurs	5	2	3	6	1	3
Kayasthas	10	4	3	6	1	3
Khatris	7	3	2	4	1	3
Kolis	5	2	0	0	1	3
Jatavs	44	19	9	18	3	9
Sindhis	5	2	0	0	2	6
Muslims	29	13	4	8	0	0
Others	31	14	4**	8	4***	12
Total:	228	100	51	101	34	101

*   Only groups with more than five candidates are listed separately.
**   Includes one candidate from each of the following groups: Gujar (Potter),
     Sonar, Sikh and Ahir.
***   Includes one candidate from each of the following groups: Kurmi, Kumhar,
     Kahar and Purovia.

Political factionalism and partisan fluidity of Agra led to the
election in 1962 of a Vaish Independent to the UP Legislative
Assembly from one of the two general seats in the city. He replaced
a Vaish Congressman, who remains the leader of one of the Congress
factions. The victor had been an organiser for the RSS and, later,
leader of the local Jan Sangh. State leaders of the party, however,
refused to back him for a seat in the municipal council and he left
the party in 1959 to enter the council as an Independent. He used
his place there as a vehicle for building a personal organisation
which resembled the Jan Sangh and Congress in its caste
composition, except for the presence of three of the five Muslims
in the corporation. This group of sixteen Independents, calling
themselves the Swatantra Dal (no relation to the national Swatantra
Party), played a significant part in the political life of the municipality
and smoothened the leader's way to his seat in the legislature. That
a Vaish would be elected in 1962 for that particular seat was a
foregone conclusion, since all of the contestants were from that
caste.

In contrast to this high degree of political differentiation among
the members of the Vaish castes, Jatavs have made some impact on
Agra politics because of their cohesion as a caste group. While

Republicans in other parts of Uttar Pradesh have been broadening their appeals in order to attract persons from the Backward Classes into the RPI, the organisation in Agra remains essentially a one-caste party. Except for two upper-caste leaders, few non-Jatavs take an active part in the Agra City RPI. The two men who have played roles in the RPI include a Brahmin. He has been a Jatav-sympathiser for many years but has lost much of his influence as the result of a fall from power of the Jatav leader with whom he was associated. The other, a Vaish doctor, became prominent in the local and State party after joining it in 1959 in order to gain RPI endorsement for the municipal council.

The doctor has been the subject of much controversy in the party. Because by birth he belongs to the dominant community in the city, he has been able to act as a bridge to prospective coalition-partners in the city. The latter might otherwise be reluctant to work with a Scheduled Caste party. The doctor himself was elected Deputy Mayor of Agra with the help of a coalition consisting of Republicans, the Jan Sangh and the Swatantra Dal. A reputation for self-seeking, however, has brought him under increasing attack from within his own party. This is not primarily based on his caste, but on doubts about his real interest in   serving the 'downtrodden' and using their support.

Aside from the doctor, conflicts for power among the Jatavs have recently created factions within the caste. The Jatavs themselves are becoming politically differentiated. They have reached the limits of self-sufficient status politics in Agra and are momentarily at a dead end as far as caste goals are concerned. Further advances depend upon their ability to make coalitions with other elements in society. If they do not, their own strength is likely to be dissipated. Furthermore, should other political groups seriously endeavour to gain Jatav support this would represent a major challenge to their cohesion as both caste and party.[28]

In summary, then, the Vaish of Agra display a high level of political and social differentiation. This is reflected in a weakening of caste as a political force among the higher strata of the community. The Jatavs, on the other hand, are still not highly differentiated internally, but they have exhausted the possibilities which result from acting alone. They are not unaware of the advantages of forming coalitions with other groups. The elections of 1962 suggest the promises of such an alliance with non-Jatav elements and the dilemmas involved in a possible change of goals for the Republican Party.[29] In many areas in western U.P. particularly around Agra and

Aligarh, the Republicans were part of an electoral understanding with the Muslims. Leaders of the Muslim community were dissatisfied with their political position in the Congress and their inferior status in India generally. The result of the Jatav-Muslim coalition was the election of two Jatav members to the State Legislative Assembly from Agra district including one Jatav elected from Agra City. The coalitions' Muslim candidate for Parliament from the City constituency finished a close second to the Congress incumbent.[30]

The last Jatav-Muslim alliance was short-lived. It is however possible that a similar alliance might be formed for the 1967 general elections, but Muslims were reluctant to forsee such a likelihood in interviews held in 1964. Cooperation with the Jatavs threatened their own precarious standing in Agra politics.

Expedient RPI coalitions with the Jan Sangh and the Swatantra Dal in the Agra corporation have made possible the election of a Deputy Mayor and the election and re-election of a Mayor. But these alliances are unstable.[31] Both the Jan Sangh and RPI were unhappy about the ideological difficulties which their alliance might produce.

As part of the agreement by which the Vaish doctor was chosen as Deputy Mayor, he was to resign before the next municipal elections to allow a Jan Sangh candidate to take his place. But he refused to resign when the time came. Some Jatav leaders insisted that the party must live up to its promises, but others felt that they should profit from the fact that the five-man Jan Sangh really had no option unless they were willing to risk bringing the Congress Party into local power. The latter view won out and the coalition remained in office until early in 1966, when all of the five municipal corporations in U.P. (Kanpur, Lucknow, Allahabad, Banaras and Agra) were superseded. The Congress Party was fairing badly in a majority of these bodies and the fact that preparations were already underway for the general elections may have had something to do with a decision to postpone new municipal elections at least until after the general elections of 1967.

Caste Politics in Poona

Poona was the centre of the empire of Shivaji, a Maratha, but was ruled most effectively by Brahmin Peshwas during the eighteenth century. Once British rule was firmly established in the area in 1818, Brahmins shifted, very successfully, to the service of the new rulers.[32] They dominated positions in the administrative services available to Indians and gained training in the westernised professions, especially law, with important consequences for the nationalist movement. The Marathas, on the other hand, were mainly agriculturists. They were socially inferior to the Brahmins, in the traditional status hierarchy, although they enjoyed a higher status than the Mahars or other untouchable castes. During the last thirty years, however, democratic politics has significantly altered the relationship between the Brahmins and Marathas.

The Marathas: One reaction of the Marathas to the social and political superiority of the Brahmins in the Bombay Province was an anti-Brahmin movement organised around 1880. This movement for status improvement was dominated by the Marathas, although they worked with other subordinate castes, like the Malis, to weaken the position of the Brahmins. In fact, one of the pivotal figures during the early part of the movement was a Poona Mali — Jyotiba Phule. A network of educational societies and social organisations were started to stimulate self-advancement among the non-Brahmins; agitations for places in the government services and for other forms of status recognition took place.

Anti-Brahmin feeling assumed various guises. Because the Brahmins played a major role in founding and supporting the nationalist movement, leading Marathas were ambivalent towards the Indian National Congress. Like the Scheduled Castes under Ambedkar, some Marathas sought caste advancement even through cooperation with the British; others, however, advocated the achievement of independence as a preliminary step to the pursuit of caste advancement. During the latter period of the nationalist movement, however, most of the major Maratha figures opted for the second course.

After 1947, the Brahmins continued to dominate the politics of the State of Bombay. Non-Brahmin anti-Congress sentiments were again evident. Congress leaders were by no means exclusionary and prominent Marathas were active in the party, but they rarely controlled the organisational machinery. One reaction was the formation of the Peasants and Workers Party (PWP) which advocated major economic reforms in a socialist vein and performed much the same kind of militant expressive function for the Marathas that the Republican Party has been playing for certain Scheduled Castes recently.[33]

Although remnants of the PWP continue to exist in Poona, the party was weakened by the gradual de-Brahminisation of the Poona City Congress. Leading Marathas, including the recently deceased MP for Poona, S.S. More, returned to the Congress from the PWP and Brahmin dominance slipped. The relatively cohesive Marathas benefited, in part, from ideological differences within the Congress and from the turn of events in Poona, but even more important were the effects of the politics of numbers and the policy of States reorganisation.

In the present State of Maharashtra, the Marathas are the largest single caste; their political strength is greatest in the rural areas where they form the backbone of the agricultural class. The Brahmins are a relatively small caste in the State and more urbanised. In Poona, they hold many of the white-collar and professional positions, while Marathas have come to urban occupations rather late and fill more of the working-class and menial roles. As a result of differential urbanisation rates, however, the Brahmins and Marathas are almost equal in size in the city of Poona. Each constitutes about twenty percent of the city's population.[34]

The Marathas control most of the major elective offices in the State Government of Maharashtra and in the Maharashtra Congress Party. Because of the closer balance between Marathas and Brahmins in Poona, the process of change has been slower there. It was only in the wake of the demand for a separate Marathi-speaking State of Maharashtra in the mid-1950s that the pressure was increased on the Poona City Congress to shift its electoral base clearly in favour of the non-Brahmins. By 1964, Congress was being mentioned by several interviewees (mainly Brahmins) as a Maratha party. Unlike the relationship between the Jatavs and the Republican Party in Agra, however, the Poona Congress is not the *only* party in which Marathas are substantially represented.

Despite the attainment of many of their status goals through politics and their economic advancement, there are a few areas in which Poona Marathas still feel inferior to the Brahmins. Two of these are community education and high positions in the civil service. These perceived shortcomings, of course, reflect belated Maratha internalisation of occupational and educational values. Thus the Poona Marathas are conscious that while they dominate the State Cabinet, the number of Brahmins in the higher rungs of State administrative services is disproportionately high.

This outlook has had one minor effect on city politics: Marathas have remained caste-conscious in matters of administrative appointments. For example, a Maratha appointed to the position of manager of the municipal transport system (with the help of a prominent figure in the Maratha community — a man who subsequently became the President of the City Congress) remained in office for over a decade despite regular attacks on him for mismanagement and favouritism in employment. Congressmen consistently shielded him from such criticism and he was removed only when the Central Government raised formal charges about his alleged misuse of import quotas.

This was an instance of how a caste group, which has otherwise become differentiated internally and has had many of its status demands met, can still be mobilised when group status is threatened.[35]

For the most part, however, the Marathas have stabilized their position at a high level in the politics of the State and locality by assuming a political role much like the one performed by the Irish in American urban politics earlier in this century. The Marathas run the Congress as a 'machine' manifestly for the distribution of material and status benefits and, latently, to integrate middle and low-status groups into Poona politics. They cannot maintain the Congress as an effective one-caste organisation simply because they constitute less than a quarter of the urban population. Instead, 'payoffs' from the operations of the party must be shared with other caste elements in a Maratha-led coalition, much as the old Irish-dominated machines in the United States parcelled out material benefits and status recognition to a variety of smaller and organisationally weaker ethnic groups. Of course, the fact that the Marathas are numerically and politically dominant in the State gives the caste special leverage in the Congress organisation in Poona City.

While the analogy with American ethnic politics is useful, one basic difference should be noted here. It has been suggested that some second-generation Americans turned to politics because their chances of mobility in the status order were blocked and they could capitalise on ethnic group numbers and face-to-face communications in political life.[36] Politics is less of a 'substitutive' activity in contemporary India. The critical role played by the government in an underdeveloped nation and the benefits which it can distribute, relative to other spheres of activity, make control of the major instruments of government an activity which justifies political participation as an end in itself. Loss of political influence, in turn, involves greater psychic costs for the groups which are displaced in India than was the case in the United States.[37]

The Brahmins: To a great extent, the Brahmins were politicised before Independence. While many remained highly orthodox in their personal behaviour, others actively adopted and reformulated Western 'values' for the Indian setting. Some, like Ranade and Karve, led reform movements; others, like Tilak, were militantly nationalistic. Poona Brahmins were active in the founding of the nationalist movement. Indeed, the first session of the Indian National Congress was originally scheduled for Poona, but an outbreak of cholera moved it to Bombay.

By 1920, the Brahmins in Poona had reached an advanced stage of political differentiation. Though differing patterns of political participation in Brahmin sub-groups (for example, the Chitpavans were politically much more active than others) may suggest so, general Brahmin status required no confirmation through politics. Some of the activists possibly participated in politics for the material benefits which it could bring: demands for places in the Indian Civil Service figured prominently among the early goals of the Congress. But these concerns became increasingly marginal as the nationalist movement expanded. Many others were motivated by ideological considerations, although they did not have any single prescription for the social reconstruction they so widely held to be necessary. This may explain the sense of betrayal which some of these ideologues experienced after Independence, when it became apparent that the Congress Party organisation was falling into the hands of men like Sardar Patel.

One such group of Brahmin activists from Poona helped to form the Congress Socialist Party (CSP) within the Congress movement in 1934. When conservative elements in the party demanded the dissolution of the CSP after 1947, the group withdrew. Poona Brahmins led by S.M. Joshi and N.G. Gore helped to form the Socialist Party and, then, the Praja Socialist Party (PSP). Recently, they participated in the creation and splintering of the latest socialist organisation, the Samyukta Socialist Party (SSP). Gore now leads the revived PSP; Joshi is national chairman of the SSP.

In addition to their participation in socialist parties, Poona Brahmins have been active in parties of the right. Purposive parties with strongly traditional and nationalistic biases, like the Hindu Mahasabha and Jan Sangh, have received considerable support from the Brahmins.[38]

As already suggested, disunity in the area of policy need not affect the unity which is forged when a group's status is in jeopardy. In Poona, there may have been some reawakening of Brahmin self-consciousness in response to non-Brahmin mobility. Particularly, the Brahmin community was politically shaken and their status sensitivity revitalised by the assassination of Gandhi by a Poona Brahmin who had been linked to right-wing groups. Anti-Brahmin riots took place in the city at that time. Even today, local Brahmins claim that the Marathas organised the riots to take political advantage of the situation. Extreme disorder was prevented, but the political leadership of the Brahmins became more precarious.[39] A few Brahmins, including N.V. Gadgil, continued to hold positions of prominence in the City Congress until 1957, but their authority in the party gradually declined.

Caste Accommodations in Poona: In 1952 the first post-Independence municipal election were held in Poona, at a time when Brahmins controlled the City Congress Committee. The PSP and other groups in which non-Congress Brahmins were represented collaborated with non-Brahmin elements to form a fusion party at the local level (the Nagri Sanghatna) which defeated the Congress. The Sanghatna, however, could not be sustained after its victory. It represented an expedient alliance between Brahmins trying to maintain their status in politics and a group of dissident Congress Marathas seeking to advance their personal and caste interests through strategic bargaining. The party split midway through the life of the corporation as the Maratha members struck a more favourable bargain with the Congress and returned to that party.

By 1956, however, the regional demand for a Marathi-speaking State united various purposive elements among the Brahmins and gave them a 'cause' in common with non-Brahmins. The Samyukta Maharashtra movement had the desirable effect, from the viewpoint of the Brahmins, of attracting widespread non-Brahmin support to a political agitation in which Brahmins played a leading part. The movement had another 'payoff'; it embarrassed the National Congress in the general elections of 1957. The unity of opposition parties on the issue and the defection of Congress support resulted in electoral defeat for the Congress in State and national seats from the Poona area. After this setback, Congress morale was so low that the local party did not even endorse candidates formally for the municipal elections which were held later the same year.

The achievement of some unity among Brahmins and non-Brahmins outside of the Congress may have been a Pyrrhic victory for the Brahmins. It gave the Marathas an opportunity to become thoroughly entrenched in the Congress organisation. Indeed, the same man who had led the dissident Maratha wing of the anti-Congress fusion party in 1952 was made President of the City Congress in 1957. He is still one of the leaders of the party and in 1962 was elected to a seat in the Maharashtra Legislative Assembly. It is also significant that the party ticket for MP from Poona in 1962 went to a Maratha (S.S. More) for the first time. The choice of candidates was particularly interesting since More had a long history of anti-Brahmin activity behind him.

More represented an older generation of Maratha leadership. During his period of activity in the PWP, he was responsible for ideologising party work and his own ideological commitment made him highly critical of the way the local Congress was run. In turn, many of the local Congressmen treated him with respect but were not ready to follow his leadership. They preferred to run the Congress as a political machine and an arena for inter-group conciliation.

Y.B. Chavan, leader of the State Congress, represents this younger generation of Marathas. He made considerable effort in 1962 to reduce caste frictions in the State and dissociate Congress from its image of being a Maratha party in distributing tickets to non-Marathas. It is alleged that he was prepared to run no candidate against S.M. Joshi for the State Assembly until Poona Congress leaders insisted that such a policy would weaken the party generally. Chavan did encourage S.G. Barve, a former Indian Administrative Service Officer and former Municipal Commissioner of Poona, to run for a State Legislative seat from a Poona constituency. Barve, a Brahmin, was highly respected in the city for his management of civic administration during his tenure around 1952 and for his efficiency as principal relief officer at the time of a major flood in Poona in 1961.[40]

During the campaign of 1962, More characteristically made some anti-Brahmin remarks, even though Barve was on the same ticket. The esteem which Brahmins and other voters may have felt for Barve did not carry over to his party. There was a notable difference between the votes for More and Barve in Barve's Brahmin constituency.[41] Unlike the effective political machine in the United States, which is able to mute conflict by delivering votes across-the-board for all ethnic groups, caste differences still played a part in the general election results. However, it is likely that a Maratha with less of a history of Brahmin-baiting would have done considerably better for Congress in a Brahmin area.

In the general elections of 1962, the ideological parties in Poona could not agree on a common set of candidates and the Congress was able to win back all of the State and national seats elected from the Poona City area which it had lost in 1957. As a partial response to the new vigour of the Congress, several opposition groups re-established the Nagri Sanghatna to contest the municipal elections of 1962 on a 'non-partisan' basis. The Jan Sangh, however, ran a separate slate of candidates. The new fusion party consisted of the PSP, Hindu Mahasabha, the PWP, elements of the divided Republican Party and a good number of non-affiliated 'notables' and non-Brahmins including a few former Congressmen. Running under a common label, the party captured the largest single bloc of seats in the corporation and with the help of the Jan Sangh fashioned a workable corporation majority.

As Table 2 indicates, there were 289 candidates for the 65 seats in the corporation or an average of 4.4 candidates per seat. This is almost the same ratio which existed in Agra for the corporation elections of 1959. The caste structure in Poona is somewhat more heterogeneous because of the presence of a large number of non-Maharashtrians (Gujaratis, Tamils, Telugus, Marwaris) and non-Hindus (Muslims, Christians). Still, if we consider only the relationship between Marathas and Brahmins, we find that the Congress clearly reflects a Maratha bias. Twenty-five of the Congress nominees were Marathas (39 per cent) as against only ten Brahmins (16 per cent). Furthermore, only two of these Brahmins were actually elected as against eleven of the Marathas.

Table 2: *Contestants in Municipal Elections of 1962 By Caste*＊

Caste	All Candidates		Congress		Nagri Sangbatna	
	N	%	N	%	N	%
Brahmins	58	20	10	16	18	28
Marathas	81	28	25	39	18	28
Marwaris	6	2	1	2	0	0
Gujaratis	7	2	4	6	0	0
Muslims	16	6	3	5	4	6
Malis	18	6	5	8	5	8
Christians	5	2	0	0	1	2
Weavers	9	3	1	2	3	5
Shimpi	6	2	1	2	1	2
Pardeshi	6	2	2	3	1	2
Mahar	26	9	0	0	6	9
Chambhar	6	2	3	5	0	0
Mang	7	2	2	3	0	0
Others	38	13	7	11	7	11
Total:	289	99	64	102	64	101

＊ Only groups with more than five candidates each are listed separately.

The Jan Sangh, in contrast, weighted its candidatures in favour of the Brahmins. It supported 23 candidates in the municipal elections; 13 of these were Brahmins (57 per cent) and 4 were Marathas (17 per cent).

The 'image' of the Nagri Sanghatna which emerges from Table 2 is one of almost studious even-handedness. Nominations to Marathas and Brahmins were equal at eighteen each and, in fact, more Marathas were elected on the Nagri Sanghatna ticket than Brahmins: nine to seven.

The organisation of caste conflict in partisan terms not only dilutes the conflict for the main contestants, but helps the management of conflict among other castes. Thus, there exists some tension between Mahars and other Scheduled Caste groups in Poona. The Mahars form the core of the Republican Party, while other ex-untouchable castes have remained loyal to the Congress. The Mahars venerate Ambedkar, who was a Mahar, and many have embraced Buddhism; groups like the Chambhars, Mangs and Bhangis have remained within the Hindu fold and accepted the leadership of Gandhian reformers. It is noteworthy that in the 1962 municipal elections, the Nagri Sanghatna nominated six Mahars to the six reserved seats in the corporation, while the Congress nominated no Mahars but selected three Chambhars, two Mangs and a Bhangi. Evidently, a competitive party system may take advantage of primordial differences, but in the process it can also help to strengthen the political consciousness of low-status groups. The Mangs, for example, were recently encouraged by leaders of the SSP to organise a temple satyagraha; such attempts by opposition party leaders, to create greater political awareness among groups presently loyal to the Congress, may accelerate the process of political mobilisation among previously 'subject' castes. At a minimum, it may cause the Congress to pay greater attention to the felt needs of the Mangs.

Non-Caste Factors

Our analysis should not obscure other factors which operate in the local political systems of the two cities. For example, the social distance which separates the Jatavs from the Vaish in Agra and the Brahmins from the Marathas in Poona has class as well as caste dimensions. The Jatavs are one instance of institutionalised lower-class protest against the dominance of the Vaish and their middle-class allies. Vaish respondents were quick to make slighting references to the educational and occupational shortcomings of the Jatavs, as well as to their traditional status.

Such sentiments are not as readily expressed in Poona by the Brahmins in regard to the Marathas. As we have suggested, the Brahmins are an educated and middle-class group with political elements who represent almost the entire political spectrum, while the Marathas are largely working-class and tend to concentrate on non-intellectual occupations. Still, the very ascendancy of the non-Brahmins in political life has raised a threat to the class values as well as to the caste position of the Brahmins. This probably accounts for part of the success the Nagri Sanghatna had among non-Brahmins. It was able to appeal to middle-class distaste for the kind of political machine and status politics that the Congress represented. Indeed, one of the most prominent figures in the Nagri Sanghatna organisation in 1962 was an elderly Maratha educator, who had done much to develop educational institutions among the Marathas. He ran on the Sanghatna ticket and was chosen *unanimously* as the first mayor of the new body.

It was the non-partisan appeal of the Sanghatna that attracted the support of this educator. Like local fusion parties in the United States, which are frequently upper middle-class in character, the Sanghatna sought votes along 'good government' lines. Its manifesto was built around a demand that State and national political parties had no proper function to perform in local government. Such an argument has great appeal for an Indian public nurtured on Gandhi and Jayaprakash Narayan.

In any case, the Sanghatna is neither a one-class nor a one-caste party. It received support from all groups in the city and its mayoral choices during its four years in power have included two Marathas, a Kirad and a Pardeshi. Two belonged to political parties (PSP, PWP) and two were non-affiliated local notables. Non-Brahmins, of course, are a majority in the Sanghatna in the Corporation. Furthermore, non-communal Brahmins like S.M. Joshi and N.G. Gore helped to form the Sanghatna and are sitting members of the corporation. In no direct sense do they 'speak for' their caste and their political ends do not grow out of their caste backgrounds.

Finally, we would argue that parties themselves weaken caste identifications by seeking material benefits and ideological ends. The Congress organisations in Agra and Poona represent many different social groups with varying goals; that they presently do not meaningfully represent specific caste groups does not make them 'caste parties'.

Conclusion: Caste and Democratic Participation

We have been describing the manner in which caste persists, gets eroded, and changes in the politics of two major Indian cities. We have suggested that the process of caste conflict is influenced by factors internal to the caste (the degree of internal differentiation; the kinds of goals which a caste pursues), as well as by inter-caste conflict and cooperation in the Indian political system.

In our analysis, we have sought to pose some of the difficulties which caste groups face at different stages of political differentiation. In Agra, we indicated some of the problems facing the Jatavs in making a transition from a 'caste party' to a political organisation with some broader potential. The Republican Party in Agra is experiencing factional difficulties similar to those which afflicted the party unit in Maharashtra, where the Mahars were socially in advance of the Jatavs. Part of the factional argument within the RPI in Maharashtra, although by no means the major part, revolved around the kind of association which the party was willing to establish with other parties including the Communists. The problem for such a party, which adopts ideological ends to maintain itself, is that it must strive to hold on to its old adherents while trying to attract new support from outside the group. Thus far, the Agra RPI has held on to its caste support but has failed, in the process, to gain new converts.

While the Jatavs have not completely entered into the integrative pattern which we have described, the Brahmins of Poona represent a theoretical challenge of a different kind. Those Brahmins supporting leftist ideology might be conceived of as belonging to the final stage of caste activity in politics, where there is no correlation between 'caste interest' and partisan affiliation. The case of Jan Sangh and Hindu Mahasabha members is of course different. Like the radical right in the United States, the traditionalism of the Jan Sangh possibly represents the defensive attitudes of previously upper status groups. They fear the prevailing political relationships and react to that fear by opposing the values of the system itself. It is suggestive, for example, that many Jan Sangh members place a high value on the acquisition of technical skills and Western education, while rejecting social change. From this perspective, the real future challenge to the integrity of the Indian political system may eventually come not from those groups which are lowest in the developmental model outlined, but those which have gone 'beyond' integration.

NOTES

* My research into Indian urban politics was made possible by a grant from the American Institute of Indian Studies. I also wish to acknowledge the support of the Research Foundation of the State University of New York in writing up my materials. The present paper was given in a different version at the Upstate New York meetings of the Association for Asian Studies at Rochester, New York in November, 1965.

1 Among the functions of the traditional ruler, one was to maintain the caste system. As Basham notes, "He protected the purity of class and caste by ensuring that those who broke caste custom were excommunicated." A.L. Basham, *The Wonder That Was India* (New York: Grove Press, 1959), pp. 88-89.

2 "What justifies this term is that the link which thus unites the individual to society is wholly analogous to that which attaches a thing to a person. The individual conscience, considered in this light, is a simple dependent upon the collective type and follows all of its movements, as the possessed object follows those of its owner. In societies where this type of solidarity is highly developed, the individual does not appear ... Individuality is something which the society possesses." Emile Durkheim, *The Division of Labour in Society* (New York: Free Press Paperbacks, 1964), p. 130.

3 Durkheim speaks of the replacement of repressive law by restitutive law. Organic solidarity depends upon the recognition of individual differences. Societal cohesion is just as strong, but, as Durkheim writes, "the yoke that we submit to is much less heavy than when society completely controls us, and it leaves much more place open for the free play of our initiative." *Ibid.* p. 131.

4 Recent studies of urban politics in the United States indicate the continued importance of ethnic identifications for political life even at a high level of intra-group economic and status differentiation. A recent revival of interest in this subject was stimulated by Nathan Glazer and Daniel P. Moynihan, *Beyond the Melting Pot* (Cambridge: MIT and Harvard University Press, 1963).

5 One recent definition of 'modernisation' suggests, "The share of activities controlled by spontaneous responses is reduced by increasing efficiency or productivity of activities, by increasing emphasis on calculated social relations (formal organisations), by increasing instrumental view of human relations (universalism, performance orientation, etc.), by increasing specialisation in the scholarly development of theories or doctrines (science, legal scholarship, etc.) and by increasing control over socialisation by such scholars (formal education)." Arthur Stinchcombe, 'Review Symposium', in *American Sociological Review,* XXXI (April 1966), p. 266.

The persistence of a large number of sectarian schools in many 'modern' nations, however, indicates the fragmentary nature of these changes. Certain functions have been absorbed into the central value pattern of the larger society more readily than others. For a discussion of the differential rates of functional assimilation of ethnic groups in the United States, see Milton M. Gordon, *Assimilation in American Life* (New York: Oxford University Press, 1964), esp. pp. 34-51.

6   The present article is part of a growing literature dealing with the performance of castes in democratic politics. The most relevant items include: Lloyd I. Rudolph and Susanne Hoeber Rudolph, 'The Political Role of India's Caste Associations', *Pacific Affairs,* XXXIII (March 1960), pp. 5-22; Lloyd I. Rudolph, 'The modernity of Tradition: The Democratic Incarnation of Caste in India', *American Political Science Review,* LIX (December 1965), pp. 975-89; Rajni Kothari and Rushikesh Maru, 'Caste and Secularism in India', *Journal of Asian Studies,* XXV (November 1965), pp. 33-50; F. G. Bailey, *Politics and Social Change* (Berkeley: University of California Press, 1963), esp. pp. 122-35.

7   In his recent article, Lloyd Rudolph discusses the formation of a caste organisation among three castes in Madras: the Kallan, Maravar and Agamudiar castes. Kothari and Maru describe the organisation of the Gujarat Kshatriya Sabha by several different castes.

8   The case of Kerala, of course, has received special attention. See, for example, Robert Hardgrave, Jr. 'Caste and the Kerala Elections', *The Economic Weekly* (April 17, 1965), pp. 669-72. Selig Harrison's discussion of Andhra politics in terms of the conflict between the Kammas and the Reddis set off much of the current discussion about the threat which caste might represent to the political order. Selig Harrison, *India: The Most Dangerous Decades* (Princeton: Princeton University Press, 1960).

9   Bailey uses the term 'federation' to describe the units of a caste association. These he distinguishes from the 'old caste assemblies'. Bailey, *op.cit.* pp. 130-31. Kothari and Maru, on the other hand, describe the Gujarat Kshatriya Sabha as a caste federation. For present purposes, however, these distinctions are not directly applicable. In neither city were major traditional groups organised for *direct* political purposes, except for the ex-untouchable Jatavs in Agra and the Mahars in Poona, who dominated their respective units of the Republican Party in India.

10   There is a major difference of opinion among anthropologists about the proper definition and delimitation of caste. My usage follows that of Andre Beteille, who suggests that caste has different referents in different contexts. He writes, "The fact that caste is a segmentary system means (and has always meant) that people view themselves as belonging to units of different contexts. A Smartha sees himself as a Smartha in relation to a Shri Vaishnava and as a Brahmin in relation to a non-Brahmin." Andre Beteille, 'A Note on the Referents of Caste', *European Journal of Sociology,* V (1964), p. 133.

11   Bailey, *op. cit.* p. 131; Ashkant Nimbark, 'Status Conflicts Within a

Hindu Caste', *Social Forces*, XLIII (October 1964), pp. 50-57.

12 The typology is drawn, with considerable modification, from Peter B. Clark and James Q Wilson, 'Incentive Systems: A Theory of Organisation', *Administrative Science Quarterly*, VI (September 1961), pp. 129-66.

13 *Ibid.* p. 135.

14 Robert A. Dahl, *Who Governs?* (New Haven: Yale University Press, 1961), pp. 34-36.

15 The full implications of this final stage have not been explored by Dahl and the model has itself been subjected to some criticism by one of his closest followers. Raymond Wolfinger, 'The Development and Persistence of Ethnic Voting', *American Political Science Review*, LIX (December 1965), pp. 896-908.

16 M.N. Srinivas, 'A Note on Sanskritisation and Westernisation'. *Far Eastern Quarterly*, XV (August 1956), pp. 481-96; Gordon, *op. cit.* pp.84-114. The Jatavs in Agra and the Mahars and Marathas (separately) in Poona have claimed Kshatriya status in their efforts at social mobility. As the Mahars and Jatavs became more directly involved in political life, however, such claims were not pressed. Indeed, large segments of both groups have openly rejected the Hindu social order by espousing Buddhism.

17 For a discussion of the history and social organisation of the Jatavs, see Owen M. Lynch. 'The Politics of Untouchability', (unpublished Ph.D. dissertation, Department of Anthropology, Columbia University), 1966. The present study was carried out in Agra at the same time that Mr. Lynch's work on the Jatavs was in progress. Part of my understanding of the Jatavs, therefore, depends upon his work, although interpretations are entirely my own.

18 Reliable figures on caste are not available for Agra City. Estimates made by interviewees and general electoral behaviour indicate that the Vaish constitute about twenty-three per cent of the population, while the Jatavs make up about sixteen per cent. Muslims are about twelve per cent. I have included the Jains among the Vaish *jatis*. As Hazlehurst suggests in his study of a Punjabi market-town, the Jains "fall into the category of an Aggarwal *gotra*, as they provide eligible marriage partners for other ... Banias". Leighton W. Hazlehurst, 'Caste and Merchant Communities', paper for a Conference on 'Social Structure and Social Change in India', University of Chicago, June 3-5, 1965, p. 4.

19 The ten demands were: (1) Ambedkar's portrait in the Central Hall of Parliament; (2) "Let the land of the Nation go to the actual tiller of the land"; (3) Idle and waste land should go to the landless labourers; (4) "Adequate distribution of food-grains and control over rising prices"; (5) slum improvement; (6) implementation of the Minimum Wages Act of 1948; (7) extension of constitutional privileges involving the Scheduled Castes to those persons who have embraced Buddhism; (8) cessation of the harassment of the 'Depressed Classes'; (9) enforcement

of the Untouchability (Offences) Act; (10) promises involving the reservation of places in the government services for the Scheduled Castes and Scheduled Tribes be kept "as soon as possible (and) not later than 1970". These demands were printed in a pamphlet called "The Charter of Demand" put out by the Republican Party of India in New Delhi in 1964.

20 The Italians, for example, were very much concerned that statues of Columbus and Mazzini be erected in New York at the time they were becoming active in politics. The significance of the particular symbols chosen may vary with the particular culture. In the Hindu case, given Hindu polytheism, erecting statues and hanging pictures of one's culture heroes seems in keeping with traditional culture patterns. The readiness with which Dr. Ambedkar is associated with the Buddha in pictures hung in many Jatav and Mahar homes bears out the relationship between 'political religion' and sacred religion discussed by David E. Apter in his 'Political Religion in the New Nations', in Clifford Geertz (ed.) *Old Societies and New States* (New York: Free Press, 1963), pp. 45-104.

21 There is a kind of 'anti-status' demand put forward by some RPI leaders. The practice of reserving seats for the Scheduled Castes in legislative bodies is increasingly opposed by those leaders who feel they are strong enough to win without this concession. They have also found that the general public is likely to vote for Congress-backed reserved-seat candidates, rather than voting for the RPI. By being included in the general seats, particularly at the local level, they would be able to capitalise on caste cohesion. In fact, in 1959 the Jatavs were able to secure all of the reserved seats through the Republican Party. A few of the reserved-seat winners did not run with Republican support, but none of the winners were affiliated with the Congress. Because of the system, however, the reserved seat for the State Assembly from a rural constituency (including a small section of Agra City) was won by a Congressman by a narrow margin.

22 Many Jatavs openly rejected Hinduism by following Ambedkar into Buddhism in 1956. One of the reasons for 'demand' number seven (fn.19) was that Buddhists have not been allowed to run for reserved seats in States like UP and they lose their claim to other privileges. As a result, some political activists among the Republicans are now Buddhists, but still publicly claim Scheduled Caste status.

23 The Mahars have split into two wings in Maharashtra with the result that the Republican Party has been bifurcated.

24 Typically, the six Jains in the municipal corporation are divided among three political groups: one belongs to the Jan Sangh; two are in the Congress; and, three are Independents.

25 For a discussion of other aspects of political conflict and cooperation in Agra and Poona, see my 'Factions and Alliances in Indian City Politics', *Midwest Journal of Political Science.*

26 Paliwal returned to the Congress Party in 1963. In elections for the UP

Legislative Council early in 1966, he was prominently mentioned as a possible Tripathi-faction candidate for the 'local bodies' seat from the Agra region against S.P. Gupta, the incumbent, who was backed by the Gupta faction of the State party. As Paul Brass suggests, in his *Factional Politics in an Indian State* (Berkeley: University of California Press, 1965), caste is not clearly a dimension in UP Congress factionalism. Still the choice of Paliwal may have involved some primordial considerations.

27 In addition, six 'aldermen' were selected by the members of the corporation on the basis of proportional representation. The Congress chose a Jain and a Kayastha; the Jan Sangh picked a Brahmin; the Republicans added a Jatav; and, the Independents agreed upon an Agarwal and a Jain.

28 In fact, the Jatav Congressman who holds the reserved seat for the Assembly does have some following in the caste. However, he has not challenged the leadership of the Republican Party and most of his votes in 1962 seem to have come from non-Jatavs. Thus, the Republican candidate came very close to defeating him on the basis of Jatav and Muslim votes.

29 For a consideration of the problems attendant on changing organisational goals, see Peter M. Blau, *The Dynamics of Bureaucracy* (Chicago: University of Chicago Press, 1955), p. 195 ff.

30 The twice-born castes reacted against the Jatav-Muslim agreement on this candidate by organising a campaign for the Congress candidate which included private appeals for Hindu unity. Rumours were apparently widespread in the last few days of the campaign that the Jan Sangh candidate had withdrawn in favour of the Congress incumbent in order to head off possible Muslim victory. The Jan Sangh candidate, however, denied such an action on his part.

31 Under the terms of the Corporation Act, mayors are elected annually in Agra, while a Deputy Mayor may serve during the life of a Corporation. In Poona, each serves a one-year term.

32 For example, Maharashtrian Brahmins were employed in ruling Guntur district in Madras. Robert E. Frykenberg, 'Elite Groups in a South Indian District: 1788-1858', *Journal of Asian Studies*, XXIV, (February 1965), esp. pp. 264-68.

33 The formation of a political party is not peculiar to India when a primordial group feels that it is not getting its due share of the benefits of government. The Poles of Buffalo, for example, formed a short-lived "EcPole" (Erie County Polish) party in 1937, which expressed the demands of the Polish community in the city. They did well enough at the polls to force the traditional parties to seek greater Polish support through additional 'payoffs'.

34 Richard D. Lambert, *Workers, Factories and Social Change in India* (Princeton: Princeton University Press, 1963), pp. 233-35, provides a breakdown of Poona's population by caste based on an earlier sample survey of the city. By major groups, the figures are: Brahmins — 19.7

per cent; Marathas — 22.1 per cent; Intermediate — 7.6 per cent; Village Artisans — 6.6 per cent; Village Servants — 3.3 per cent; Backward (Scheduled) Castes — 12.5 per cent; Other Regions — 7.0 per cent; Other Religions — 15.5 per cent.

35   The role of caste in administrative relations in Agra and Poona is considered in my 'Administrative Politics in Two Indian Cities', *Asian Survey*, VI (April 1966), esp. pp. 210-13.

36   For a useful statement of the relationship between ethnicity and politics in American cities, see Edward C. Banfield and James Q. Wilson, *City Politics* (Cambridge: Harvard and MIT Presses, 1963), esp. pp. 38-44 and 51-53.

37   Holden suggests that the Anglo-Protestant elite in the United States may have "gravitated to industry *prior to any sense of* 'challenge' by the newcomers", thereby preventing extreme conflict in the political arena and encouraging accommodation between the two. Mathew Holden, 'Ethnic Accommodation in a Historical Case', *Comparative Studies in Society and History*, VIII (January 1966), pp. 168-80. The quotation is from page 178.

38   Poona Brahmins, it should be mentioned, were active in the wave of anti-British violence that hit India at the turn of the century; many followed Tilak's 'extremism' and never fully accepted Gandhian ideas or leadership.

39   The decline of the Brahmins politically and the rise of the Marathas are discussed in Maureen Patterson, 'Caste and Political Leadership in Maharashtra', *Economic Weekly*, (September 25, 1954), pp. 1065-68.

40   A survey of the impact of the flood on the residents of Poona and their responses to it has been undertaken by Dr. Allen M. Grimshaw, Department of Sociology, University of Indiana.

41   The candidate supported by the PSP for Parliament was N.G. Gore the sitting MP from Poona. His notability may have affected the result. A systematic study of the general elections of 1962 in Poona is available in V.M. Sirsikar, *Political Behaviour in India* (Bombay, P.C. Manaktala, 1965). Sirsikar's analysis does not *directly* examine this issue, but he does stress the importance of caste as a variable in electoral behaviour. A recent study of voting in an American City indicates that politics was organised in ethnic terms in a non-partisan election, but that ethnicity was less significant when partisan elections were held. Gerald Pomper, 'Ethnic and Group Voting in Non-partisan Elections', *Public Opinion Quarterly*, XXX (Spring 1966), pp. 79-97. Also, Wolfinger, *op. cit.* At the level of the political activist, caste affiliations may be partially weakened by partisan ties and personal qualities of political associates. Such relationships are considered for the two municipal bodies in Agra and Poona in my 'Deference and Friendship Patterns in Two Indian Municipal Councils', *Social Forces*.

INDEX